When Baseball
Was Still Topps

When Baseball Was Still Topps

Portraits of the Game in 1959, Card by Card

Phil Coffin

McFarland & Company, Inc., Publishers
Jefferson, North Carolina

Topps trading cards used courtesy of The Topps Company, Inc.

Library of Congress Cataloguing-in-Publication Data

Names: Coffin, Phil, 1953– author.
Title: When baseball was still Topps : portraits of the game in 1959, card by card / Phil Coffin.
Description: Jefferson, North Carolina : McFarland & Company, Inc., Publishers, 2024. |
Includes bibliographical references and index.
Identifiers: LCCN 2023051743 | ISBN 9781476693941 (print) ∞
ISBN 9781476651736 (ebook)
Subjects: LCSH: Baseball cards—Collectors and collecting—United States. |
Baseball cards—United States—History. | Topps Company. | BISAC: SPORTS &
RECREATION / Baseball / History
Classification: LCC GV875.3 .C64 2024 | DDC 796.357092/273—dc23/eng/20231107
LC record available at https://lccn.loc.gov/2023051743

British Library cataloguing data are available

**ISBN (print) 978-1-4766-9394-1
ISBN (ebook) 978-1-4766-5173-6**

© 2024 Phil Coffin. All rights reserved

*No part of this book may be reproduced or transmitted in any form
or by any means, electronic or mechanical, including photocopying
or recording, or by any information storage and retrieval system,
without permission in writing from the publisher.*

Front cover illustration © 2023 CSA-Printstock

Printed in the United States of America

*McFarland & Company, Inc., Publishers
Box 611, Jefferson, North Carolina 28640
www.mcfarlandpub.com*

To Mom, even though you threw out my baseball cards,
and to Laura, for always believing in me.

Table of Contents

Acknowledgments ix

Introduction 1

Glossary 3

The 1959 Cards and Their Stories 5

Extra Innings 217

Bibliography 219

Index 221

Acknowledgments

When I began work on *When Baseball Was Still Topps*, it was not with the idea of writing a book. The writeups on each of the 1959 Topps cards were simply going to be the latest in a series of baseball essays I wrote to amuse myself and share with baseball buddies. But as I kept researching and writing—disappearing for hours at a time—my wife, Laura Messina, told me, "You know, this is a book." I shrugged off that notion for months even as I told Laura almost daily that I was heading to my office "to go down the rabbit holes again." It became such a running joke that she began calling the project "Bunnyball." And eventually, I began calling it a book. She had been right, of course, so, like her favorite player, Stu Miller, she earned the save. Without her support and encouragement, *When Baseball Was Still Topps* would not be in your hands right now. And without her, my life would be far less rewarding.

My brothers, Dave and Don Coffin, introduced me to the '59 Topps cards, and even more valuably, they shared their love of baseball with me. Dave provided quite tangible assistance by allowing me to use his cards—carefully preserved all these decades—for the images you see in this book.

My sister, Marjorie Marks, grew up to be an Astros fan, but she has also been a lifelong support system and sounding board. In that way of close siblings, she has helped me flourish without being foolhardy.

My friend and *New York Times* colleague Sean Alfano provided clear-eyed and keen-eyed editing help that saved me from embarrassing errors of fact, grammar and literary excess. Joe Campbell, who has been teaching me about journalism and writing since our days as interns together at the *Plain Dealer* in Cleveland, also provided encouragement and valuable insight into shaping a manuscript and the unknowns of the publishing world.

Rick Bozich is perhaps the world's most ardent White Sox fan. He is also the best friend you could have, and he has shared countless baseball moments with me over the decades. This book would be less rich without his passion and insight. That is also true for other baseball buddies, including Frank Coffin, Jim Luttrell, Ron Wolfson, Doug Lehman and Robb Todd.

Gary Mitchem of McFarland showed faith in this project, trusting an unknown with no publishing track record. His efforts have made a professional author out of me.

This book leans on dozens of sources, but two were indispensable: Baseball Reference and the Society for American Baseball Research (SABR) BioProject. The wealth of reliable statistical information available at baseball-reference.com was invaluable; statistics used here are from B-R, and any mistakes are mine, not theirs. SABR's BioProject is a remarkable online library of biographies of hundreds of ballplayers from throughout the game's history. The bios were a source of inspiration and information (happily credited), and they can enhance any baseball fan's knowledge and appreciation of the game.

The book also would not have been possible without the 1959 Topps cards, and the images of those cards add flavor to *When Baseball Was Still Topps*; thanks to the Topps Company and its parent, Fanatics Inc., for allowing me to use the images. As for the cards themselves, I spent untold nickels, as did my brothers, in an effort to accumulate the entire set. I finally did so—got you at last, Milt Graff!—but you can guess the end of the story: My mother threw them away.

Introduction

In October of 1959, I spent a succession of afternoons sandwiched between my two brothers as we watched the World Series in our TV room in Indianapolis—a pint-size demilitarized zone between a White Sox fan and a Dodgers fan. This was the culmination of the season in which I fell in love with baseball, aided by my efforts to collect the entire set of Topps baseball cards.

The 1959 baseball season itself was sandwiched among momentous events that changed the game. That year, the last of the 16 major league teams at the time finally integrated. It came 12 years after the Dodgers and Jackie Robinson had kickstarted the effort (and three-quarters of a century after Major League Baseball's segregation had begun). In 1958, Major League Baseball had, for the first time, become a transcontinental enterprise when the Dodgers and the Giants fled New York and began play in California, which foretold other franchise changes.

In 1959, Major League Baseball faced a credible threat of competition for the first time since the demise of the Federal League nearly half a century earlier. Branch Rickey, a driving force behind the creation of farm systems and of integration, was putting together a third major league, the Continental League. He had lined up investors/owners for franchises, including in New York, which had just been abandoned by two of its three major league teams. Major League Baseball fended off the competition by agreeing to expand its two leagues to 10 teams each in 1961 (the American League) and 1962 (the National League); it also allowed the Washington Senators to move to Minneapolis, one of the proposed Continental League sites. That shift and the expansion—including to Houston, another Continental League site—were enough to thwart Rickey and his backers. The Continental League never played a game.

Labor issues figured into the era, too. In 1957, baseball had ended its ignoble experiment to depress signing bonuses to amateur players, eliminating the "bonus baby" rules that punished anyone signing for more than $4,000 (and their teams) with a mandatory two years in the major leagues. Those restraints savaged the development, through much of the '50s, of dozens of the top young players that scouts had identified. The rules change renewed the unfettered signing of amateurs to big bonuses—Rick Reichardt, a college star, received a $200,000 bonus from the Angels in 1964—and the owners eventually lashed back. In 1965, they instituted the amateur draft, hoping that would keep spending on amateur players in check. (It did, for a decade, until free agency arrived.)

Introduction

That half-decade surrounding 1959 resulted in more change to professional baseball than perhaps any other similar period since the American League had elbowed its way into major league status in 1901. And it came as the greatest dynasty in baseball history was beginning to show cracks: in 1959, the New York Yankees struggled to finish above .500 and slid to third place in the American League after winning nine of the previous 10 pennants (and seven World Series). Their great run was hardly over—the Yankees, although aging, won the next five pennants and two World Series—but the changes in the game that arose in the '50s were a foundation for the Yankees' mid–'60s collapse.

The game on the field was changing, too. Some teams found an alternative to the walk-and-wait-for-a-home run approach on offense that typified the '50s (sound familiar?), especially in the American League. The Go-Go Sox of 1959, with Luis Aparicio's sprints unsettling the AL, stole more bases than they hit home runs and brought a pennant to Chicago built on pitching and defense. Maury Wills was a Dodgers rookie that year, enabling a surge that won the National League pennant in the team's second season in Los Angeles, and three years later he would make history with 104 stolen bases.

That style of play was reminiscent of the Negro leagues, which had faded quickly after Jackie Robinson's ascension to the majors but continued to fuel major league rosters. At least 17 players in Topps's 1959 set, for example, had played in the Negro leagues.

But beyond the conflicts and changes off the field, the game was flush with personalities. And story after story. The slugger who had a date with Marilyn Monroe (no, not Joe DiMaggio). The catcher who was the first player to wear contact lenses on the field. Two players from the same small town in Georgia who had never heard of each other. The pitcher from Mayberry. The "Rookie Star" who never played in the major leagues and the "'59 All-Star Selection" who was never an All-Star. All-time great hitters and all-time worst hitters. Good-field, no-hit players; good-hit, no-field players. Strikeout kings and wild throwers. Religious stalwarts and hell-raisers. The nephew of a Black Sox player and a pitcher who reported a bribery attempt. The second most famous person from Piqua, Kansas. Pugilists, headhunters and motormouths.

When Baseball Was Still Topps tells these stories, with essays based on each card in the 1959 Topps set, from 1 to 572. The essays reveal history, profiles, tall tales, player comparisons, statistical analyses and oddities of the game, reaching back through the '50s and forward into the '60s and beyond. The book is not about a set of baseball cards; it is a kaleidoscopic story of the era, and the game, one card at a time.

Glossary

Baseball Reference: An online source for baseball statistics of all kinds and the game's history. An invaluable resource for any fan that is the modern-day equivalent of the *Baseball Encyclopedia*—only more complete and updated daily.

Bill James: A longtime and influential baseball analyst and historian (and, later, front-office employee) who was a pioneer in using data in different and often eye-opening ways to view the game. His approach came to be known as sabermetrics (see SABR below).

ERA+: A pitcher's earned run average normalized across the entire league (and accounting for other factors like ballparks). The league average is 100, so a pitcher with an ERA+ of 125 is 25 percent above league average; one at 88 is 12 percent below average. One of my favorite ways to compare pitchers, including across eras.

Fielding Runs: An estimate of a player's Fielding Wins, or the number of games a team won compared with what it would have won with an average fielder—zero Fielding Runs—at that position.

OPS: The sum of a player's on-base percentage and slugging percentage. It is a good way to look at the two prime elements of batting success, getting on base and hitting for power.

OPS+: A batter's OPS, normalized across the entire league (and accounting for factors like ballparks). The league average is 100, so a player with an OPS+ of 135 is 35 percent above league average; one at 80 is 20 percent below average. One of my favorite ways to compare hitters, especially across eras.

SABR (Society for American Baseball Research): An organization dedicated to research of the history of the game, often with a reliance on statistics. If you love the history of the game, SABR is worth checking out.

SABR Bio Project: SABR's effort to write comprehensive biographies of all major league players, plus profiles of managers, front office executives and others. The bios are well researched and rich with detail. Warning: It's a rabbit hole waiting to ensnare you.

Slash line: Batting average/on-base percentage/slugging percentage. For example: .280/.330/485.

Total Zone Fielding Runs: An estimate of the number of runs a defensive player was worth based on the number of plays made.

WAR (Wins Above Replacement): A figure that includes multiple phases of the game to determine how many wins a player is worth compared with a replacement-level player at his position. A handy if not precise way to compare players' all-around value, including across eras. There are two versions: bWAR (from Baseball Reference) and fWAR (from Fangraphs); bWAR is used here.

WHIP: Walks and hits per inning. How efficient a pitcher is in allowing base runners.

The 1959 Cards and Their Stories

1. Ford Frick, Commissioner of Baseball.
   If this were the first card in the first pack that you bought, you might never have bought a second pack. Perhaps Topps bought goodwill by making Ford Frick the No. 1 card in the set. He was a longtime National League president, had a hand in establishing the National Baseball Hall of Fame, was commissioner for 14 years and had one impressive set of eyebrows. He is remembered for saying in 1961 that to break Babe Ruth's single-season record of 60 home runs, a player would have to do so in his team's first 154 games—the length of a regular season when Ruth played, but not when Roger Maris hit 61. (Widespread belief notwithstanding, there never was an actual asterisk in the record book for Maris.) Coincidentally, Frick, who had been a New York newspaper reporter, was a ghost writer for Ruth. And curiously, Ruth's Yankees played 155 games in 1927 because of a 9–9 tie; Ruth did not homer in that game, though.

2. Eddie Yost, Third Baseman, Detroit Tigers.
   Eddie Yost, who hit .254 with 1,863 hits in an 18-year career, had a .397 on-base percentage. Pete Rose, who hit .303 with 4,256 hits in a 24-year career, had a .375 on-base percentage. Yost scored almost as many runs per game (.576) as Rose did (.607) despite playing in sad sack offenses with the Washington Senators (in the worst hitter's park in the American League), the Detroit Tigers and the Los Angeles Angels. He also showed notable power away from Griffith Stadium in Washington (he had 95 career homers on the road, 44 at home; his pop became noticeable when he moved to Detroit and hit 21 homers at age 32 and 14 at age 33, while still leading the league in walks). Yost's lifetime OPS+ was 109; Rose's, 119. Not to say Yost was nearly as good a player as Rose, but his 1,614 career walks and disguised power added a lot more value than was recognized at the time.

3. Don McMahon, Pitcher, Milwaukee Braves.
   Talk about a career bottoming out. Don McMahon had played a substantial role out of the bullpen for the Braves' 1957 and 1958 pennant winners, and he was an All-Star in 1958. But in early 1962, the 32-year-old McMahon was exposed to the National League expansion draft—the league was growing to 10 teams—yet he was

not selected by either the player-needy New York Mets or the Houston Colt .45s and remained with Milwaukee. He had had an abysmal season in 1960—a 5.94 earned run average—but his numbers were pretty good in 1961: 6–4, 10 saves, 2.84 ERA, 130 ERA+. He had faded in August and September, however, and after he went unclaimed in the expansion draft, the Braves were happy to sell him to Houston in May 1962 for $30,000. Money well spent by Houston: McMahon went 5–5, with eight saves and a 1.53 ERA in 76⅔ innings. And he kept pitching productively, lasting another 12 years. He was then a pitching coach for a decade. Working for the Dodgers, he suffered a heart attack while throwing batting practice and died at the age of 57.

4. Albie Pearson, Outfielder, Washington Senators.

In a 1963 profile of Albie Pearson, *Sports Illustrated* wrote: "'He doesn't give an inch,' notes one observer, 'but then he doesn't have too many to give.'" That was the story of Pearson's life as a 5-foot-5-inch ballplayer. He developed into a pretty good offensive player in his final seasons, with the Angels: lots of walks (90-plus three years in a row) and enough pop to hit 20 doubles a season and 28 home runs for his career. I remember one of them: a leadoff home run one Saturday afternoon on TV's *Game of the Week*, when it was the only national baseball you could see.

5. Dick Donovan, Pitcher, Chicago White Sox.

Timing may not be everything, but it sure is something. Dick Donovan came up in the Braves' organization but was traded away before they became an established power. He wound up in Chicago in 1955 and put together five solid seasons in a row for the White Sox (he was second in the Cy Young voting to Warren Spahn in 1957 when one award was given covering both leagues). But in 1959, when the White Sox won their first pennant in 40 years, Donovan was ordinary: 9–10, 3.66 ERA. He was little used the next year, perhaps because of a sore arm, and was exposed to the American League expansion draft. Hello, Washington Senators, dregs of the league. Yet he led the AL in ERA (2.40). The Senators, however, dealt him to Cleveland, where he had a 20-win season but aged out as the team brought up a raft of young fireballers.

6. Alex Grammas, Shortstop-Third Baseman, St. Louis Cardinals.

You look at his photo and can just imagine Alex Grammas would be a coach someday. He was. He coached third base

Card 6: Alex Grammas had the look of a coach, and he was for years. He won two World Series as a coach but got a pink slip as a manager.

for World Series champions in Cincinnati (1975) and Detroit (1984) under Sparky Anderson, part of a two-decade run as a major league coach. He also had a disastrous two-year run as a major league manager—he was Hank Aaron's final skipper, with the 1976 Milwaukee Brewers—but his Brewers went 66–95 and 67–95. The '75 Brewers had many players with mustaches, but Grammas instituted the Reds' no-facial-hair policy in 1976, to expectable derision. One Brewer, Mike Hegan, said that "Alex Grammas is a nice guy, but as a manager he makes a good third-base coach." The Brewers released Hegan that week. They fired Grammas after the season.

7. Al Pilarcik, Outfielder, Baltimore Orioles.

What was up with the 1949 Joplin Miners? With Al Pilarcik stealing 33 bases, second best on the team, the Miners had seven players in double figures in steals and 189 total in an era when no one was stealing bases. The next year some kid named Mantle hit 26 home runs for the Miners, who doubled their home run total over the 1949 team's. That exemplified Pilarcik's problem: He was in the Yankees' organization and did not hit for power. In the majors, with the Athletics, the Orioles and the White Sox, he did not hit for average either. Or steal bases.

8. Philadelphia Phillies Team Card.

Eddie Sawyer was the manager of the Phillies' 1950 Whiz Kids NL champions. In 1959, he was brought back to manage a Philadelphia team that had finished last at 69–85 in 1958. Things didn't get any better: The Phillies went 64–90–1. (Yes, games sometimes ended in ties. That became increasingly rare and has not happened since 2016.) Sawyer returned for another try in 1960 but quit after one game. The Phillies lost it, of course.

9. Paul Giel, Pitcher, San Francisco Giants.

Paul Giel was a two-time All-American in football and baseball at the University of Minnesota, where he was the Big Ten's two-time Most Valuable Player in football. He was drafted by the NFL and the CFL (which offered him $75,000 over three years to play in Canada), but he chose a big bonus from the baseball Giants. His career foundered, and he became a football announcer for the University of Minnesota, then its athletic director for 18 years. From there he became an executive of the Minnesota Heart Institute Foundation. According to his Society for American Baseball Research Bio Project biography, he had already had a quadruple bypass and an angioplasty; he died of a heart attack at 69.

10. Mickey Mantle, Outfielder, New York Yankees.

Mickey Mantle and Derek Jeter came to the Yankees' organization as teenage shortstops, and there were questions about whether they would stay shortstops. In his first season, as a 17-year-old, Mantle made 47 errors in 89 games and had an .889 fielding percentage. The next year, playing for Joplin in Class C (these days Class A), an organizational scouting report said: "Is not now a good shortstop. ... Don't believe he is capable of playing short at AAA." In Jeter's first season, as an 18-year-old, he made 21 errors in 57 games in rookie league and low Class A and followed up by committing an astounding 56 errors in 126 games at Class A Greensboro, also for an .889 fielding percentage. A *Baseball America* scouting report said: "Like Travis Fryman, he has the actions, hands and instincts to make great plays but can't make routine plays consistently. He needs thousands of grounders to refine those skills." The Yankees ended Mantle's shortstop trial at Joplin but kept their faith in Jeter, and were obviously rewarded with both players' Hall of Fame offense.

11. Billy Hunter, Shortstop, Cleveland Indians.

Billy Hunter was the St. Louis Browns' last All-Star, in 1953, when, as a 25-year-old rookie shortstop, he hit .219/.253/.259 with an OPS+ of 37 (not a typo). To be fair, he wasn't .219/.253/.259 bad at the All-Star break; no, he was .245/.283/.281 bad. But that was not the most interesting part of his career in baseball. Hunter became the manager of the Texas Rangers in the 1977 season—their *fourth* manager of the season—and led the team to a 60–33 record (.645) down the stretch. Before one game the next season, Rangers pitcher Rogelio Moret stripped naked in the clubhouse and stood motionless for more than an hour, with a shower shoe extended in his right hand. Hunter, called from his office, took in the scene and said, "What I need is a good left-handed starter, not some damn statue," according to *Seasons in Hell*. Still, Hunter guided those Rangers to an 86–75 record, good enough that the owner, Brad Corbett, offered him a three-year extension and then a five-year extension as manager. Hunter, according to a 2013 interview with *The Baltimore Business Journal*, conferred with his wife, who did not want to leave Maryland permanently for Texas. So Hunter said he wanted only a one-year deal. Corbett, rich but eccentric in his own right, offered to buy the Hunters a house, but still Billy said no. So Corbett fired Hunter with a game left in the season.

12. Vern Law, Pitcher, Pittsburgh Pirates.

Vernon Law, a pitcher, is really wearing a batting helmet on his baseball card. This was not unusual for a Pittsburgh Pirate (check out a whole host of '50s Pirates cards), as their general manager, Branch Rickey, had mandated in 1953 that the players wear helmets both at the plate (unusual for the time in itself) *and* in the field. "Even manager Fred Haney joined the helmet-wearing brigade, apparently to protect himself from banging his head against the top of the dugout when making visits to the mound," wrote Bruce Markusen, a researcher at the Baseball Hall of Fame, and that may not have been hyperbole—the '53 Pirates finished 50–104. The move to all-game helmets was said to be for safety reasons, but Rickey apparently owned stock in the company that made the helmets. The mandate did not last long, but Law's noggin was worth protecting: He was 20–9, 3.08, for the Pirates' 1960 World Series champions.

13. Dick Gernert, First Baseman, Boston Red Sox.

First came Walt Dropo: He hit .322 with 34 home runs and 144 runs batted in for the Red Sox in 1950. He was Rookie of the Year but finished his career 11 years later with an OPS+ of 100—a league-average hitter. Then came Dick Gernert, who hit 19 home runs as a Red Sox rookie in 1952 and 21 more the next year. He finished his career in 1962 with the expansion Houston Colt .45s. Then came Norm Zauchin, who bashed 27 home runs with 93 RBIs as a Red Sox rookie in 1955. He wrapped up his career in 1959 with the last-place Washington Senators. These big, slow, white, right-handed-hitting first basemen never lasted and never took the Red Sox anywhere.

14. Pete Whisenant, Outfielder, Cincinnati Redlegs.

In 1979, Pete Whisenant, a former Reds outfielder and coach, and Pete Rose signed a business deal. They had history; Whisenant ran a youth baseball clinic that Rose co-sponsored. According to Whisenant's Associated Press obituary, their deal concerned the marketing of Pete Rose merchandise with a Little Charlie Hustle caricature. Six years later—in the year Rose broke Ty Cobb's hit record—Rose sued Whisenant over the deal, under which they were supposed to split profits. In 1987, Whisenant countersued for $10 million, *The Chicago Tribune* reported, and the suit claimed Rose's company had not paid Whisenant. The suit was eventually settled, its terms not disclosed. But it was one more unusual chapter in Whisenant's post-baseball life. He started a vending machine company in Evansville, Indiana, which Jim Brosnan contended in *We Played the Game* had mob ties—though he noted that Whisenant vehemently denied it. Brosnan also said that Whisenant sold "adult" clothes, like see-through bras.

15. Dick Drott, Pitcher, Chicago Cubs.

Baseball has its own language. It was about Dick Drott that I first heard the term "flash in the pan" (although the term was appropriated from one that goes back centuries to old firearms). In spring training before his rookie season, *The Sporting News* called Drott the Cubs' "Kid with Greatest Potential." As a 20-year-old in 1957, Drott finished 15–11 with a 3.68 ERA in 229 innings. He was third in the Rookie of the Year voting and got some MVP votes. That was the flash. Over the rest of his career, he was 12–35, 5.38. Wonder why? The back of this card has a hint: "Dick is troubled with lapses of control and in '57 was Bases on Balls King in the N.L." Yep, he led the league with 129 walks. And that was his *good* year.

16. Joe Pignatano, Catcher, Los Angeles Dodgers.

In his final major league at-bat, Joe Pignatano lined into a triple play. Of course, he was a '62 Met. He was also a longtime Mets bullpen coach, best known for the garden he grew in the bullpen. He began his farming at Shea Stadium in 1969, the year the Mets won

Card 16: What says 1962 Met more than hitting into a triple play in your final major-league at-bat? That was Joe Pignatano's fate.

the World Series. His *New York Times* obituary said: "Up came cherry tomatoes, then beefsteak tomatoes. Eventually he grew pumpkins, cucumbers, eggplants, squash, zucchini, radishes and lettuce in a 30-foot long plot, with help from the pitchers who watered the plants." In 1974, when the Yankees were also playing at Shea while Yankee Stadium was being renovated, Pignatano noticed bare spots in his garden when the Mets returned from road trips, *The Times* said. The Yankees—especially Bobby Murcer—were helping themselves. I guess it was the Yankees' farm system.

17. Danny's All-Stars: Frank Thomas-Danny Murtaugh-Ted Kluszewski.

Strictly speaking, this was not true in 1959. Danny Murtaugh *was* the manager of the Pittsburgh Pirates, and Frank Thomas and Ted Kluszewski were Pirates sluggers. And Thomas had been an All-Star in '58 when he hit 35 home runs. But Klu, although still a productive player, had not been an All-Star since 1956. This picture also does not show Klu at his finest: in a Reds uniform with the sleeves cut off. The man had biceps.

18. Jack Urban, Pitcher, Kansas City Athletics.

He graduated from Omaha's Technical High School, but let's say he was not an urban legend, not compared to some other Tech alums. Bob Gibson, eight years younger, went to Tech. So did Johnny Rodgers, who went on to win the Heisman Trophy at Oklahoma. So did Bob Boozer, a longtime NBA player who was part of the magnificent 1960 Olympic basketball team (Oscar Robertson, Jerry West, Jerry Lucas, Walt Bellamy), and Ron Boone, who had a consecutive games streak of 1,041 in the ABA and the NBA. And so did Captain Alfonza Davis, a Tuskegee airman, and Brigadier General Kenneth Walker, who earned a Medal of Honor in World War II. Makes Jack Urban's 15–15, 4.83 career pale in comparison.

19. Eddie Bressoud, Shortstop, San Francisco Giants.

An early lesson in ballpark effects. Eddie Bressoud spent his first six seasons with the Giants, playing in the Polo Grounds, Seals Stadium and Candlestick Park. Not only did he not have home run power (26 homers in 1,380 plate appearances), he also did not really have doubles power (53). His value was so low that he was exposed to the 1962 expansion draft, where the Houston Colt .45s took him with their first pick and traded him immediately to Boston for Don Buddin (basically Eddie Bressoud with less power). But the trade made Bressoud's career—he would now play his home games in Fenway Park. In his first three years in Boston, beginning at age 30 when his numbers should have been slipping, he hit 40 doubles and 14 home runs, then 23 and 20, and then 41 and 15. His career Red Sox numbers versus his Giants numbers: .270/.337/.435 versus .239/.299/.369. His OPS+? 109 versus 81. After the 1962 season, *The Sporting News* wrote, "Bressoud was as valuable as any player on the team, as much as anyone the reason why the 1962 Sox finished eighth instead of tenth."

20. Duke Snider, Outfielder, Los Angeles Dodgers.

At the peak of his career, Duke Snider told Roger Kahn, as reported in *The Boys of Summer*, about his disillusionment with baseball. "If it wasn't for the money,"

Snider, then 26, told Kahn, "I'd be just as happy if I never played a game of ball again." Ah, the money. Snider never made more than $44,000 in a season, far less than the contemporaries to whom he was often compared, Mickey Mantle ($100,000) and Willie Mays ($165,000). Snider told Kahn he had a dream of owning an avocado farm, and he did, but financial reversals forced him to sell it. Then in 1995, he pleaded guilty to not reporting more than $100,000 in income from sports memorabilia shows and was fined $5,000 in addition to having to pay nearly $30,000 in back taxes and more than $27,000 in interest and penalties, according to *The New York Times*. He pleaded guilty in Brooklyn, where he had earned his fame. "Because of who you are, you have been publicly disgraced and humiliated," the judge said. "And it has taken place here in Brooklyn, where you were idolized by a generation of which I was a part." (Darryl Strawberry and Willie McCovey pleaded guilty to similar charges. Sluggers beware.)

21. Connie Johnson, Pitcher, Baltimore Orioles.

Clifford (Connie) Johnson was a teammate of Satchel Paige for years with the Kansas City Monarchs. According to his SABR Bio Project biography, Johnson would often relieve Paige in their team's barnstorming days. "He would come in and relieve Satchel, and when they put Johnson out there, we thought we'd have it easy then," Newark Eagles pitcher Warren Peace said. "And he would come in and throw harder than Satchel did! Just like jumpin' from the frying pan into the fire." When at age 30 Johnson finally got his chance to play in the major leagues with the Chicago White Sox, after one year in the low minors, he must have wondered how "major" the leagues were: The crowd for that White Sox game on April 17, 1953, against the St. Louis Browns was announced at 972. Johnson came on in relief, and in a "you can't make this stuff up" coincidence, the first batter he faced was Paige. Paul Richards was his manager in Chicago, and when Richards moved on to Baltimore, he acquired Johnson as he tried to build a contender out of the lowly ex–Browns. In 1957, Johnson, then 34, went 14–11, 3.20 ERA with the best strikeout-to-walk ratio in the league. Richards called him the "best right-hander in the American League," according to *Crossing the Line: Black Major Leaguers, 1947–1959*. Attitudes died hard, however. *Crossing the Line* recounts a story from Whitey Ford, who said that a Yankees scout, Rudy York, told the team's hitters they could read Johnson's pitches by how he held his hands—because the palms of Blacks (not the word York used, according to Ford) were lighter than the backs of their hands. How'd that scouting report work? Johnson had a 3.45 ERA against those world-beater Yankees in 120 innings.

22. Al Smith, Outfielder, Chicago White Sox.

History can be unkind. Al Smith, an outfielder and third baseman for 15 years, was a two-time All-Star who in four seasons received MVP votes. He was traded along with Early Wynn by the Cleveland Indians to the Chicago White Sox for Minnie Miñoso, cementing the White Sox's ascent in the American League. But what's he remembered for? A beer that was inadvertently spilled on him in the 1959 World Series as a home run sailed over his head. Smith did keep a blow-up of the photo in his Chicago home, and everyone else remembered the play, too. "I've signed that photo 200,000 times," his *New York Times* obituary quoted him as saying.

23. Murry Dickson, Pitcher, New York Yankees.

Murry Dickson was the starting pitcher in one of the most famous World Series games, the Cardinals against the Red Sox in Game 7 in 1946. He was pulled in the eighth inning with a 3–1 lead and the tying runs on base, and a reliever let them in. In the ninth, the Cardinals famously won when Enos Slaughter scored from first on a double and shortstop Johnny Pesky either did or did not freeze on the relay throw home. Dickson did not see the play. Upset at being lifted from the game, he had left the ballpark and was driving around St. Louis and heard it on the radio.

24. Red Wilson, Catcher, Detroit Tigers.

Robert (Red) Wilson is the only University of Wisconsin football player to be named the team's MVP three years. He did it as a center and linebacker from 1947 to 1949, and he was the Big Ten MVP in '49. He was the catcher in Detroit for Frank Lary, known as the Yankee Killer. In their 21 games together against the Yankees, Lary went 16–3 and Wilson hit .354. He was a lifetime .258 hitter. Wilson also was an Athletics Killer: He knocked out 11 of his 24 career home runs against the A's.

25. Don Hoak, Third Baseman, Cincinnati Redlegs.

In 1957, Reds fans, aided and abetted by a Cincinnati newspaper, stuffed the ballot boxes, such as they were, with votes for the homeboys for the All-Star Game. (The paper printed up ballots with Reds players marked.) Seven of the eight position players selected were Reds, based on the fan voting. The commissioner stepped in and benched two Reds so Willie Mays and Hank Aaron would start. Don Hoak was one of those Reds who remained in the lineup, and he really did earn it based on the first half of the season: .292 with 14 homers and 55 RBIs.

26. Chuck Stobbs, Pitcher, St. Louis Cardinals.

On April 17, 1953, Washington Senators left-hander Chuck Stobbs had the misfortune of throwing a fastball to Mickey Mantle at Griffith Stadium. The ballpark was one where home runs were

Card 26: Chuck Stobbs set the standard for long home runs with a blast he gave up to Mickey Mantle. And he didn't want to hear about it.

scarce (it was 366 feet to just right of the left-field foul pole, 391 feet to left-center field, 421 to center, according to Ballparks.com). But the wind was blowing out, at 20 miles an hour with gusts to 40, and this was the 21-year-old Mantle. The ball went out of the stadium, and through the machinations of a public relations director, it was estimated that the ball traveled 562 feet before it came to rest *behind* a two-story building. Or 565 feet. On the fly. Or on a bounce. Years later, a University of Illinois emeritus professor of physics, Alan Nathan, determined that "a physically plausible scenario has been found for the trajectory that is consistent with all the available information and the laws of physics. The minimum distance is found to be at least 538 feet." Stobbs grew tired of hearing about that one home run of the 184 he allowed. "So the guy hit a home run, so what?" he said in 1993, according to *The Washington Post*. "Somebody just sent me a blank piece of paper and asked me to fill out my recollections of that homer. I sent it back blank."

27. Andy Pafko, Outfielder, Milwaukee Braves.
In 1950, Andy Pafko hit .304/.391/.591 with a 157 OPS+ while playing center field for the seventh-place Chicago Cubs. He was an All-Star for the fourth year in a row and the fifth time in six years, and he was 12th in the MVP voting. Warren Giles, the Reds' president, was impressed. "If I could choose any player to help the Reds," Giles said after the season, "I'd choose Andy Pafko." Little wonder: Pafko hit .359/.419/.923 with five home runs and 10 extra-base hits and 14 RBIs in 10 games that year at Cincinnati's Crosley Field. Giles did not pull off a trade for Pafko, but he should have: The Reds' three primary outfielders in 1951 hit .271/.330/.379 with an OPS+ of 91.

28. Al Worthington, Pitcher, San Francisco Giants.
Al Worthington became a born-again Christian after attending a Billy Graham crusade in 1958, and a year later his values led to a conflict with his team, the Giants. Worthington learned that the Giants were using binoculars to steal signs, and late in the season he went to his manager, Bill Rigney, to tell him he thought it was cheating, according to *The Cheater's Guide to Baseball*. "I told Bill that I had been talking to church groups, telling people you don't have to lie or cheat in this world if you trust Jesus Christ," Worthington said in a 1964 interview with *The Saturday Evening Post*. "How could I go on saying those things if I was winning games because my team was cheating?" According to *The Cheater's Guide*, Rigney said, "Naturally, I thought what we were doing was legitimate, but I told him we'd quit it right away if it upset him." Coincidence or not, the Giants lost seven of their last eight games, plunging from first place and a two-game lead over the Dodgers and the Braves to third place. Coincidence or not, he was traded before the next season and finished the year with the Chicago White Sox. Again, his team was stealing signs, this time using a flashing light in the scoreboard to alert White Sox batters what pitch was coming. Worthington complained to manager Al López and general manager Hank Greenberg. They did not end the practice, so Worthington left the team with a month to go in the season. (Chicago wound up 51–26 at home, 36–41 on the road.) Coincidence or not, although he returned to baseball in 1961, Worthington was in Class AAA. And yet he went on to become a top-notch reliever in the majors at age 35, with double-digit

29. Jim Bolger, Outfielder, Chicago Cubs.

What do you do with a young outfielder who has hit .207 with a .287 slugging percentage in his first 177 plate appearances? In the 1950s, you made him a pinch-hitter. That's Jim Bolger, who over his final 239 games was a pinch-hitter 144 times. The ploy worked in 1957, when Bolger led the National League with 17 pinch hits and batted .354 off the bench. He had used up the magic, though, and went 10 for 50 as a pinch-hitter in 1958 and 4 for 31 in '59, a cumulative .173 batting average with a .239 on-base percentage.

30. Nellie Fox, Second Baseman, Chicago White Sox.

Don't tell Joey Gallo, but Nellie Fox averaged a strikeout every 48 at-bats in his 19-year career. He never struck out more than 18 times in a season. He once went 98 consecutive games without striking out. Don't kid yourself; he was not a great hitter. (Career OPS+ of 94, 35 homers. "I was hitting the same ball as the rest of the players, but when the big guys cracked one, it went out of the park. Mine went out of the infield.") But Fox played every day (literally—he played at least 154 games for seven consecutive seasons), led the league in hits four times and scored 100 runs four times (something his speedy teammate Luis Aparicio never did once). He also played very good defense. People noticed. He was an All-Star 12 times, was the American League MVP in 1959 and earned MVP votes 10 times.

31. Ken Lehman, Pitcher, Philadelphia Phillies.

In 1948, the left-hander Ken Lehman was 17–7 for his Brooklyn Dodgers farm team, the Idaho Falls Russets—the Russets! They owned that name from 1939 to 1962, when the Yankees took over and peeled away Russets to call the team the Idaho Falls … Yankees. Idaho Falls eventually lost its affiliated minor league team but gained an independent team, which called itself the Idaho Falls Chukars, after a local game bird. But in 2019, the Idaho Potato Commission sponsored a throwback Russets night, with jerseys resembling the '39 team's. Spuddy Buddy, the commission's mascot, threw out the ceremonial first potato. Donn Clendenon was once a Russet. Then again, so was Cuno Barragan.

32. Don Buddin, Shortstop, Boston Red Sox.

In 1952, the Red Sox paid a reported $50,000 bonus to an 18-year-old shortstop, Don Buddin. The Red Sox's owner, Tom Yawkey, said, "Don Buddin—if nothing ill befalls him—could become one of the top players of his time," noted the book *It Was Never About the Babe*. It was about spending neither wisely nor well. The year before, Boston had shelled out $60,000 for another shortstop, Ted Lepcio. In 1952, the Red Sox also signed outfielder Marty Keough for $100,000, pitcher Frank Baumann for $86,000, catcher Jerry Zimmerman for $80,000 and another catcher, Haywood Sullivan, for $75,000. The next year, the Red Sox spent a reported $65,000 on another teenage shortstop, Billy Consolo. Two years later, they paid out $85,000 to a teenage catcher, Jim Pagliaroni. That was more than $600,000 for eight players in half a decade, and the players earned the nickname "the Gold Sox." The payoff was a decade of mediocrity in the '50s. Start with Buddin. He made the majors at age 22 and committed 18 errors in his first 40 games. In 1958 and '59, he led the league in errors (31 and 35), although he also led the league in double plays. His defense was so indefensible that Bob Ryan of *The Boston Globe* said he should have the license plate E-6. (Which brings to mind the joke years later about José Offerman: How do you spell Offerman? With two f's and 35 e's.) Buddin had his best offensive season in 1961, but the Red Sox still were happy to send Buddin to the expansion Houston Colt .45s. Dan Daniel, writing in *The Sporting News*, quoted an unnamed Boston columnist as saying: "Mike Higgins [the Boston manager] would not have dared to open the 1962 season with Buddin still on his club. The fans hooted Don all last summer." The newspapers were chronically on Buddin's case in Boston, but in retirement he did some writing for his hometown paper in Lake City, South Carolina.

33. Ed Fitz Gerald, Catcher, Washington Senators.

Bing Crosby bought a 25 percent stake in the Pittsburgh Pirates before the 1947 season. The Pirates had just gone 63–91, 34 games out of first place, so the team, aided by Crosby's cash, went on a spending spree, dropping a reported $235,000 on players from the Pacific Coast League. One major addition was Ed Fitz Gerald, whom *The Sporting News* said was acquired for $65,000 and three players. He had just hit .338/.441/.585 with 13 homers in half a season in Class B before moving up to the PCL. Unfortunate investment: Fitz Gerald was a major league backup, even a third-stringer in those days when teams employed three catchers.

34. Pitchers Beware: Al Kaline–Charlie Maxwell.

Yes, pitchers had to beware of Al Kaline. He's a Hall of Famer. And Charlie Maxwell averaged 24 home runs for the Tigers from 1956 to 1960. (Kaline averaged 22.) In 1959, Maxwell hit 35 homers and Kaline 27. But the missing third Tigers outfielder was Harvey Kuenn. He did not earn a warning, but he did a lot of damage that season despite hitting only seven homers, batting .353/.402/.501.

35. Ted Kluszewski, First Baseman, Pittsburgh Pirates.

Over four seasons in the mid-'50s, Ted Kluszewski averaged .315 with 43 home runs and 116 RBIs. He also averaged only 34 strikeouts. He hit only 34 more homers over the final five seasons of his career because of back injuries, but he got to play in the 1959 World Series and hit three homers for the White Sox. Kluszewski (6 foot 2, 225, obviously an early-career weight) became the Reds' hitting coach, and another ex–Reds first baseman, Gordy Coleman (6 foot 3, 215, ditto), was in the front office. They could have been a heck of an office softball team.

36. Hank Aguirre, Pitcher, Detroit Tigers.

Let's acknowledge that Hank Aguirre was a pretty good pitcher. He led the American League in earned run average once and lasted 16 seasons in the majors. But let's also acknowledge that he was a terrible hitter. Perhaps not historically bad—Aguirre *juuuust* missed a list of the 20 worst-hitting pitchers with at least 200 plate appearances put together by the sportswriter Doug Mead—but by .0002. Non-Hammerin' Hank batted .085 (33 for 388). His on-base percentage was .117 and his slugging percentage .108 (he never hit a home run). He struck out in 56 percent of his plate appearances. He had seasons of 2 for 75 (.027), 1 for 28 (.036) and 3 for 53 (.057). He was so desperate that he took up switch-hitting in mid-1962, *Sports Illustrated* reported, and singled. It was his first hit in nearly two years. "I'm 2 for 3," Aguirre said. "That is, 2 for 3 years." But according to Baseball Reference, he went 1 for 57 to end the season (.018). Aguirre knew he was bad. In *The Cubbies, Quotations on the Chicago Cubs*, he said, "I thought hitting .333 was getting one hit in three years." And Hank Aguirre was always a bad hitter—he batted .086 in the minors.

37. Gene Green, Catcher-Outfielder, St. Louis Cardinals.

Gene Green should have been a Yankee. He was a catcher and outfielder, and the Yankees had catcher-outfielders forever in the '50s and into the '60s. Yogi Berra. Elston Howard. Later, Johnny Blanchard. (Even later, Thurman Munson played 27 games in the outfield.) But Green came up a Cardinal. As a catcher, he threw like an outfielder, nailing only 23 percent of potential base stealers (compared with a league average of 37 percent). Pitcher Tom Cheney recalled in Danny Peary's *We Played the Game* that Green, trying to nail a base stealer at second, hit him in the ribs with his throw, sidelining Cheney for six weeks with a rib injury. Green must have run like a catcher—he never had 500 plate appearances in a season but twice led the league in grounding into double plays.

38. Morrie Martin, Pitcher, Cleveland Indians.

His was about as ordinary a career as you could have: a record a little over .500 (38–34), a 4.29 ERA (96 OPS+), almost exactly as many walks as strikeouts (249–245). But Morrie Martin had already had an extraordinary time in World War II. He was a combat engineer at Omaha Beach on D-Day. At the Battle of the Bulge, he was wounded in the thigh, developed gangrene and was saved from amputation by 150 penicillin shots. He also served at Remagen. His SABR Bio Project biography says he received two Purple Hearts, four battle stars and an Oak Leaf cluster.

39. Ed Bouchee, First Baseman, Philadelphia Phillies.

Ed Bouchee, it seemed, could do it all. He was all-state in football, basketball and baseball in Spokane, Washington, then played all three sports at Washington State. In 1957, he was second in the National League Rookie of the Year voting. When he died in 2013, a high school teammate and fellow major leaguer, Jack Spring, said in an obituary in *The Spokane Spokesman-Review* that Bouchee ranked with Ryne Sandberg and the NFL quarterback Mark Rypien as among the best athletes ever from Spokane. But four months after his rookie season ended, Bouchee had pleaded guilty to indecent exposure involving girls ages six and 10 in Spokane. According to *The New York Times*, he continued to receive psychiatric treatment at a Connecticut facility through May, and on July 1 Commissioner Ford Frick allowed him to return to baseball, saying that "the problem here is more mental than legal." Frick added,

"This is not a case of calling for vengeance of society upon a depraved character." He eventually was an original Met but hit .161.

40. Warren Spahn, Pitcher, Milwaukee Braves.

In 1942, when Warren Spahn first pitched for the Boston Braves, Lefty Grove had just finished his career across town with the Red Sox. Spahn kept pitching until 1965, the first year of Steve Carlton's major league career. When Carlton retired in 1988, Tom Glavine had finished his second season in the majors and Randy Johnson was just beginning his career. That's an 83-year passing of the torch among five great left-handers who combined for 1,585 major league victories. (The torch is still burning; Clayton Kershaw reached the majors in Glavine's last season and hit 200 wins early in the 2023 season.) Bill James notes in his *Historical Baseball Abstract* that Spahn's record, 363–245, is almost the same as the records of Sandy Koufax (165–87) and Don Drysdale (209–166)—combined (374–253). Heck, those two Hall of Famers combined to pitch only 500 more innings than Spahn.

41. Bob Martyn, Outfielder, Kansas City Athletics.

Bernard Martyn set the bar high for his son Bob, and not just because he was a high jumper. Bernard was a star at Linfield College in Oregon in the 1920s in football, basketball, baseball and track and field. He earned 14 letters, something no Linfield athlete has done since, according to the Linfield Athletic Hall of Fame. When both the baseball and track teams were at home, the baseball game would be paused so Bernard could hurry over to the track for an event. All Bob did was make it to the major leagues as an outfielder who reminded his college coach defensively of Joe DiMaggio. Martyn was the first Linfield player to reach the majors. (Scott Brosius was the second.) Appropriate company: Bob Martyn was once traded with Billy Martin, and two others, by the Yankees to the Athletics. Funny, he never played with Morrie Martin.

42. Murray Wall, Pitcher, Boston Red Sox.

Baseball Almanac has compiled a list of 91 major leaguers who died by suicide, through the 2023 season. Murray Wall was one of them. He was 45 years old when he was found in his pickup truck in Lone Oak, Texas, with a gunshot wound to the head and a handgun by his side. Nothing in pro baseball ever went quite right for Wall. He was a star at the University of Texas who was signed by the Boston Braves and put immediately on the major league roster. He pitched in only one game, though, and did not make it back to the majors for seven years, sticking for just three seasons. He then returned to the minors and kept hoping he would be acquired by his hometown team in Dallas, even offering to pay $5,000, or half the purchase price, to make it happen. It didn't happen then, but it did a year later. The homecoming lasted only three unsuccessful innings.

43. Steve Bilko, First Baseman, Los Angeles Dodgers.

By the mid–1950s, Steve Bilko's future as a slugging first baseman was dimming. He had spent parts of six seasons never fulfilling his promise with the Cardinals. In 878 plate appearances for St. Louis, he had hit 24 home runs. Then he was purchased by the Chicago Cubs and sent to play in their Class AAA ballpark in Los Angeles, also called Wrigley Field. The ballpark, which would later be used for the TV show *Home Run Derby*, was cozy, with the fences only 345 feet away in the power alleys. There, Bilko put together three magnificent seasons from 1955 to 1957, averaging .330 with 49 home runs, 143 RBIs and 96 walks. He was a local sensation. Gaylon White wrote *The Bilko Athletic Club*, a book about the '56 Angels team that finished 107–61, that focused on the slugger. "There was Bilko-mania long before Beatlemania," White told *The Times Leader* in Bilko's hometown, Nanticoke, Pennsylvania. "More people in L.A. knew who Bilko was than Marilyn Monroe." Maybe an exaggeration, but Bilko's name *was* appropriated for a hit TV show that began in 1955, *Sgt. Bilko*. His play in L.A. earned him another shot at the majors, but sadly for Bilko, he was no longer hitting in Los Angeles's Wrigley Field and struck out (often literally). Until 1961.

Card 43: Steve Bilko's impact as a minor leaguer in Los Angeles was far greater than his impact in the major leagues. "There was Bilko-mania before there was Beatlemania."

The expansion Los Angeles Angels, who would play their first season in Wrigley, took a chance, and Bilko had unequivocally his best major league season: .279/.395/.544 with 20 home runs in 354 plate appearances. He hit 11 homers at Wrigley, including the final one hit there—a pinch-hit shot with two out in the ninth. Alas, the Angels played the next season in Dodger Stadium. He hit only two homers in Chavez Ravine.

44. Vito Valentinetti, Pitcher, Washington Senators.

When he was 23 years old, Vito Valentinetti was called up by the Chicago White Sox. He finally got to make his major league debut on June 20, with the Sox trailing, 10–6, in the ninth inning after, he was quoted as saying in an obituary, "I had spent 40 straight days throwing batting practice." He was about to throw more BP. Valentinetti retired the first batter—the opposing pitcher—but then suffered this sequence: walk, double, walk, triple, single, homer. He managed to get the final two outs, but his ERA stood at 54.00, and as Valentinetti joked, "The next day I was back in Memphis," pitching for the Class AA Chickasaws.

45. Andy Carey, Third Baseman, New York Yankees.

If you spent nine years with the Yankees in the '50s, you saw some World Series moments. Andy Carey *had* Series moments, two of them, on defense, in the same game: Don Larsen's perfect game in 1956. From his *New York Times* obituary in 2012: "In the second inning, the Dodgers' Jackie Robinson smacked a shot between third and short that Carey knocked down, allowing Yankees shortstop Gil McDougald to pick up the ball and nip Robinson at first. In the eighth, he robbed Gil Hodges by snaring a low line drive that seemed headed for left field."

46. Bill Henry, Pitcher, Chicago Cubs.

Imagine Bill Henry's surprise when he learned in 2007 that he had died. Yes, Bill Henry, the longtime reliever, had died in Florida at the age of 83. One big problem: Bill Henry, the longtime reliever, was 79, alive and well and living in Texas. The other Bill Henry had spent years passing himself off as the former major leaguer, according to *The Ledger*, a Lakeland, Florida, newspaper, which ran a paid obituary from the family, leading to an Associated Press obit distributed nationwide. He even told his third wife he was the former ballplayer. His friends at the 19th Hole Lounge at a local golf course said their Henry knew the appropriate highlights of the pitcher's career—the 1960 All-Star appearance, the 1961 World Series. Faux Henry even looked enough like the Henry on baseball cards to fool people. "It's creepy striking—the nose, the face, the squinty eyes," said Jeanine Hill-Cole, the wife of the impostor Henry's stepson David Cole. "I mean, I'm still here looking at the picture we put in for his obituary, and you'd swear that it was the same man." The real Bill Henry died in 2014. We're pretty sure.

47. Jim Finigan, Infielder, Baltimore Orioles.

What happened to Jim Finigan? He excelled for a season and a half and then, suddenly, could not hit. As a 25-year-old third baseman for the Philadelphia Athletics, he hit .302, was second in the Rookie of the Year voting and was the Athletics' last All-Star in Philadelphia. With the A's in Kansas City in 1955, he again made the All-Star team, hitting .286 at the break. At that point he was a .297 career hitter with 15 home runs in 811 at-bats. A 15-for-95 slump after the break started him on a .214 second half, with a single home run. He never recovered, batting .232 with four homers over his final 789 career ABs. Speculation varied, but his SABR Bio Project biography indicates that a sudden onset of astigmatism may have been the culprit.

48. Baltimore Orioles Team Card.

Paul Richards, the Orioles' manager, was sort of the Buck Showalter of his era—a team builder who never won it all. He led the Chicago White Sox to four winning seasons, but could never get past the Yankees; Al López came in and did. Richards moved on to Baltimore in 1955, taking over the erstwhile St. Louis Browns, and slowly built a contender. The Browns/Orioles went 14 years without a winning season before Richards's 1960 team pushed the Yankees to the end. Baltimore was 78–57 in 1961, but Richards, tired of chasing the Yankees, left behind some good young players to become the general manager of the expansion Houston Colt .45s. (Baltimore won the pennant in 1966.) He didn't win in Houston, either, but once again left behind a core of good, young players like Joe Morgan, Jimmy Wynn and Larry Dierker.

49. Bill Hall, Catcher, Pittsburgh Pirates.

This was the 1950s. Bill Hall was a slight catcher who spent his first 11 years in professional baseball with 10 major league at-bats to his credit (and no hits). It was 1955, and he met a hulking young first baseman in the Pirates' spring training camp whom he had never heard of. Then he learned where the kid, R C Stevens, was from—Moultrie, Georgia. *Hall* was from Moultrie, Georgia. As Stevens told *The Moultrie Observer* in 2005: "There's no way we would have" crossed paths, even in a town of fewer than 15,000. "I was from the other side of town." What that meant was Hall, who was white, went to Moultrie High School, and Stevens, who was Black, went to the Moultrie High School for Negro Youth. They wound up as teammates with Hollywood in the Pacific Coast League. Hall finally got his break in 1958 and hit .284 in 51 games with the Pirates. But that off-season the Pirates acquired Smoky Burgess to catch (and hit), and Hall never played in the majors again.

50. Willie Mays, Outfielder, San Francisco Giants.

Eleven months after he signed with the Giants directly out of high school, Willie Mays was in the major leagues. Transcendent players do move fast. Alex Rodriguez was a little faster after signing—he made his debut with the Mariners ten and a half months after turning pro (and about 13 months after his high school graduation)—but he needed some more minor league seasoning before sticking for good. Robin Yount was even faster, becoming a major leaguer 10 months after he was drafted, although, unlike Mays, he was not particularly productive for several years. Mickey Mantle made it to the Yankees 22 months after signing, and Mike Trout needed a hair over two years. When you stand out in that company, as Mays does, you really stand out.

51. Rip Coleman, Pitcher, Kansas City Athletics.

Rip Coleman thought he never got a fair shake with the Yankees—he was so upset at being relieved in one game that instead of handing the ball to manager Casey Stengel, he heaved it into center field. His punishment: a trade the next winter to Kansas City. He had made $17,000 in salary and World Series winnings with the Yankees, but, according to his SABR Bio Project biography, he said that "if I made $77,000 I couldn't have been more miserable." He couldn't have been *too* happy in Kansas City: He was 0–7 and 2–10 before ringing up a record of 0–2 in his final season, with the Baltimore Orioles. Career record: 7–25.

52. Coot Veal, Shortstop, Detroit Tigers.

His real name was Orville Inman Veal, but he was apparently called Inman. Until he was called Kook by his high school baseball coach. And then Coot when his college teammates heard the name wrong. According to one obituary, Mel Ott, the Tigers' broadcaster, made jokes about his *last* name in his newspaper column—when Veal would hit down on the ball, it was a Veal Chop, for example. If Veal were to play against the Braves in a World Series and he snagged a line drive by Frank Torre, it would be Veal Catchatorre. A sportswriter for *The Lansing State Journal* wrote of Veal's promotion to Detroit that "the only thing certain about it is Veal will not hit big league pitching." He didn't: He had a .231/.298/.288 career line. He had one home run in 702 plate appearances, off the excellent White Sox left-hander Billy Pierce. Wouldn't his ideal roommate have been Cot Deal?

53. Stan Williams, Pitcher, Los Angeles Dodgers.

Jason Turbow, author of *The Baseball Codes*, wrote that Stan Williams, a 6-foot-4 right-hander, kept a list with "the name of anyone who had ever offended Williams's baseball sensibilities during the course of a game, either through action or ability." If you were on The List, you were due to be hit by a pitch. Williams enlisted Dodgers first baseman Ron Fairly to get the word around. When a runner reached first against Williams, Turbow wrote, Fairly would say, "Watch out, you're on The List." Presumably this was for intimidation's sake, as Williams hit only 27 batters in his five years with the Dodgers.

54. Mel Roach, Second Baseman, Milwaukee Braves.

Look at Mel Roach's career and it seems impossible. After signing out of the University of Virginia for $40,000, he spent his first two seasons with Milwaukee, as mandated by the "bonus baby" rules. In 1953, he batted twice and played two innings in the field, sitting on the bench every other inning of the season. In 1954, he batted *four* times and played five innings in the field. The next two years were spent in military service. Finally, in 1957, he got to play in the minors, hit .309 and was called up in July … and did not play a game until August. He wound up playing seven games, with 15 innings in the field. So to recap: In two and a half seasons on a major league team, Mel Roach had batted 13 times and played 22 innings in the field. How did anyone think he would ever be able to succeed?

Card 54: Mel Roach, one of the "bonus babies," spent his first two years in pro ball on a major league bench, batting six times and playing seven innings in the field.

55. Tom Brewer, Pitcher, Boston Red Sox.

Tom Brewer won at least 10 games in each of his first seven seasons in the big leagues. It may not sound like much of a feat, but here's a semi-random list of some great pitchers who didn't do that: Whitey Ford, Jim Palmer, Bob Gibson, Randy Johnson, Curt Schilling, Tom Glavine, Greg Maddux, Steve Carlton, Max Scherzer, Justin Verlander, and Pedro Martinez. Granted, Brewer won 10 games three times, 11 once and 12 once (and was never great), and there were good reasons some of those greats didn't make this list. But manager Al López once said Brewer reminded him of Bob Lemon because he could pitch, field and hit. And in 1956 he did just that: He was 19–9 with a 3.50 ERA (132 ERA+), batted .298 with 13 RBIs in 101 plate appearances and led AL pitchers in putouts and assists (which he did again in 1957).

56. Carl Sawatski, Catcher, Philadelphia Phillies.
Carl Sawatski was a left-handed power hitter who played catcher, often not well because he was chronically overweight until, more than a decade into his professional career, he found a weight-loss technique that worked: He officiated high school football and basketball games in the off-season. At that point a .208 career hitter, he hit .264 with 44 home runs in 878 at-bats in his final five seasons. He had a lengthy career off the field, as general manager of the Class AA Arkansas Travelers for eight years and president of the Texas League for 16. He was credited with bringing financial and franchise stability to the league.

57. Al Cicotte, Pitcher, Cleveland Indians.
The question is inevitable: Was Al Cicotte related to Eddie Cicotte, the banned Black Sox pitcher? He was—Eddie was his great-uncle. In a 1953 *Sporting News* article, Great-Uncle Eddie had this advice for Al: "Watch yourself, but watch your companions more. Stay away from gamblers. Stay away from wrong people." Eddie also said, "Work on your control, boy." Al never could follow that last piece of advice, as walks plagued him while playing for six teams in five years. He came up with the World Series champion Yankees and went out with the expansion Colt .45s—a team he was not good enough to stick with.

58. Eddie Miksis, Infielder-Outfielder, Cincinnati Redlegs.
When Eddie Miksis became eligible for the Hall of Fame in 1964, he got a vote. The Eddie Miksis who had a career OPS+ of 62 (the well-below-freezing mark of on-base-plus slugging percentage normalized for home ballpark and the league) and a Wins Above Replacement total of -4.8 (meaning he graded out below a replacement-level player). Arthur Daley, columnist for *The New York Times*, wrote: "Expert observers among the press-box tenants are left aghast by votes for such as Eddie Miksis, Steve Gromek and Bob Kuzava for elevation to a shrine that has such exalted figures as Ty Cobb, Babe Ruth, Christy Mathewson, Walter Johnson and Honus Wagner. How could anyone have so warped a sense of values?"

59. Irv Noren, Outfielder, St. Louis Cardinals.
After playing his first minor league season as a Brooklyn Dodgers farmhand in 1946, Irv Noren, a former Pasadena Junior College baseball and basketball star, took a part-time job that winter playing for an independent pro basketball team, the Los Angeles Red Devils. One of his teammates was another former Pasadena JC basketball star and current Dodgers farmhand: Jackie Robinson. Other teammates, according to *The Post-Herald*, a newspaper in Jamestown, New York, where Noren spent his early years, were George Crowe, a Black athlete who would play 11 seasons in the majors

and had been a Mr. Basketball as a high schooler in Indiana, and Everett (Zigg) Marcell, a Negro leagues veteran who also played for the Harlem Globetrotters. The Red Devils were pretty good—13–3, according to *The Post-Herald*, including two wins against George Mikan's National Basketball League champion Chicago American Gears. Noren jumped to the American Gears in December 1946, but he played in only three games, scoring one point, before deciding baseball was his future. Robinson made a similar decision, leaving the Red Devils in January 1947, three months before he broke the major leagues' color barrier.

Card 59: Irv Noren was a teammate of Jackie Robinson's—on an independent pro basketball team.

60. Bob Turley, Pitcher, New York Yankees.

It was 1958, and the Yankees' dynasty was on the verge of crumbling. They had lost the 1957 World Series to the Milwaukee Braves, and now, in the '58 Series, they trailed the Braves, three games to one. Only one team had recovered from a 3–1 deficit to win a seven-game Series. Bob Turley stepped up in Game 5 to pitch a five-hit shutout while striking out 10. Two days later, he came on in relief in the 10th inning to induce Frank Torre to line out to second base to save a victory that tied the Series at 3–3. And the next day, Turley relieved again, pitching the final six and two-thirds innings, allowing a single run, as the Yankees rallied to capture the Series. It capped the best season of his life: 21–7, 2.97 ERA, 19 complete games, six shutouts. That was not his only World Series highlight. In Game 6 in 1956, Turley had struck out the Dodgers' Hall of Fame catcher, Roy Campanella, three times in a row (and 11 batters in all). "Man!" Campanella said of the player they called Bullet Bob. "When you see me take three swings at three fastballs and not even foul tip one, the fellow throwing 'em must have something. Maybe he was using a little gun to fire that ball up there." Footnote to a different era: Turley lost that game, 1–0, in the 10th inning. Turley was famously upstanding off the field, which manager Casey Stengel noted in 1959 after Turley slipped to 8–11, 4.32, according to *Stengel: His Life and Times*. "He don't smoke, he don't drink and he don't chase around none. But he can't win as good as that drunk I got." That "drunk" was Don Larsen.

61. Dick Brown, Catcher, Cleveland Indians.

Dick Brown was Herb Score's high school catcher in Florida, and, according to biographical information on Baseball Reference, he was dating Score's sister, Helen, when Herb signed with the Cleveland Indians in 1952. Brown planned to attend dental school, but Helen told the Indians they should sign Brown, too. And they did. In 1966, Brown had a brain tumor diagnosed, and another was diagnosed soon after, ending his career. He died in 1970 at age 35.

62. Tony Taylor, Second Baseman, Chicago Cubs.

Tony Taylor came to the United States from Cuba as a 19-year-old in 1954 to play ball (against his parents' wishes) and wound up in the Evangeline League in Louisiana. As recounted in an obituary at RIPBaseball.com, he knew one English word—"OK"—and ordered at restaurants by pointing at the menu. "I was so homesick," he recalled. "The fare to Havana was $72. I looked in my pocket. I had only $62. So I stayed." He was a Cubs regular at 22 and Ernie Banks's roommate. Banks joked that Taylor snored in Spanish. "When I was with the Cubs, I was so lonesome Ernie Banks tried to talk Spanish with me," Taylor said. "Good guy, Ernie Banks. Bad Spanish, but good guy." Taylor was popular wherever he played, and he played for 19 seasons.

63. Jim Hearn, Pitcher, Philadelphia Phillies.

After a successful rookie season with the Cardinals, Jim Hearn spent two increasingly poor seasons in St. Louis. It got so bad that in midseason 1950, the Cardinals' manager and owner were publicly questioning his competitiveness. The Giants, needing pitching, gambled the $10,000 waiver price to acquire him, but even they had doubts, according to *The New York World-Telegram*. Manager Leo Durocher was said to have confronted his new pitcher, saying: "Jim, they tell me you want to be a golf pro. If you are interested more in golf than pitching, let's have it right now so we don't lose any time and effort on you." Whatever his motivation, Hearn went 11–3, 1.94 ERA in 16 starts for the Giants and, despite injuries, lasted through the decade in the majors. But he *was* interested in golf: Upon retirement, according to an Associated Press obituary, Hearn opened the 17-acre Jim Hearn Golf Center, a driving range in the Atlanta area, and ran it for a quarter-century.

64. Joe DeMaestri, Shortstop, Kansas City Athletics.

In 1957, Joe DeMaestri was an American League All-Star, and if you look at the back of this baseball card, you can't imagine why. That year he hit .245/.280/.360 with a 74 OPS+—and that was one of his *best* years. The A's had better players (catcher Hal Smith, infielder Héctor López). Ah, but DeMaestri had the good fortune to begin the season on fire. He was hitting .380 a month into the season. He was still hitting .304 on June 10, about the time All-Star voting would have been in full swing. By the All-Star Game he was still at .288. And that's why Joe DeMaestri was an All-Star. He hit .204 in his 235 at-bats after being an All-Star. Two years later he was surrounded by All-Stars after being traded to the Yankees with Roger Maris.

65. Frank Torre, First Baseman, Milwaukee Braves.

Similarity Scores are a method created by the analyst Bill James to compare players using various statistics and their primary position. On each of its pages for a player, Baseball Reference uses the formula to create a list of the 10 most similar players to that player. Frank Torre was a first baseman in the '50s and early '60s, a time when most first basemen were sluggers. (There were exceptions—Ferris Fain and Bob Boyd come to mind, but they were better hitters.) Torre was not a slugger, hitting 13 home runs in 1,704 plate appearances. His top Similarity Scores are Al Orth, who played from 1895 to 1909 and was mostly a pitcher, although he had a few more times at bat than Torre; Max McQuery, a first baseman from 1884 to 1891; Johnny McCarthy, a slap-hitting first baseman from 1934 to 1943; Bud Clancy, a first baseman from 1924 to 1933 who played most of his home games at cavernous Comiskey Park; and Del Gainer, a Deadball Era first baseman from 1909 to 1922. You really didn't see many first basemen who hit like Torre in the 1950s. He was a player out of time.

66. Joe Ginsberg, Catcher, Baltimore Orioles.

Joe Ginsberg was a backup catcher who made Frank Torre look like a power hitter; Ginsberg's slugging percentage was 52 points lower, at .320. Ginsberg went 11 years between Opening Day starts, his last one coming with the original New York Mets. He caught only one more game and was released on May 1; yes, he couldn't stick with a Mets team that lost 120 games. When I was first learning baseball history, I would confuse Joe Ginsberg and Moe Berg, a backup catcher from an earlier era who may well have been a spy.

67. Brooks Lawrence, Pitcher, Cincinnati Redlegs.

Brooks Lawrence was the only Black student at his school in Springfield, Ohio. He became his high school's first Black quarterback, in the early 1940s, but the baseball team remained segregated, according to his SABR Bio Project biography. After World War II he used the GI Bill to go to college, at Miami University in southwestern Ohio. He pitched for parts of two seasons there before turning pro. He liked to read, especially Hemingway, according to *Crossing the Line*. He broke the color barrier for his Class AAA team in Columbus, Ohio. He had seasons of 15–6, 19–10 and 16–13 in the majors, where his career was curtailed by ulcers. Yet when I attended Miami, which was proud of its athletic heritage, a quarter-century later, I never ever heard anyone mention that Brooks Lawrence, major league stalwart and athletic pioneer, had played there.

68. Dick Schofield, Infielder, Pittsburgh Pirates.

We long ago came to understand that RBIs are a contextual statistic—how many opportunities a batter has to drive in a run is out of his hands. Still. Dick Schofield did not drive in runs. He came to bat 3,545 times and drove in 211 runs. (He had an OPS+ of 73 over a 19-year career.) If you figure 500 plate appearances in a season for a weak-hitting regular shortstop, Schofield had about seven full seasons at bat—thus the equivalent of 30 RBIs a year. Compare Schofield's RBIs to some of the weakest hitters of that era, and he still doesn't measure up. Bobby Wine? OPS+ of 55 3,467 plate appearances, 268 RBIs. Gene Michael? 67 OPS+, 3,095 ABs, 226 RBIs. Frank Duffy? 69, 2,924, 240. A little later in time: Johnnie LeMaster? 60, 3,515, 229. Even

Mario Mendoza—hello, Mendoza Line—drove in more runs per plate appearance than Dick Schofield (0.069 to 0.060). Dick Schofield must have flashed a lot of leather.

69. San Francisco Giants Team Card.
The Giants won the 1962 pennant, although they needed a three-game playoff with the Dodgers to do so. It was a team full of future Hall of Famers: Willie Mays, Willie McCovey, Juan Marichal, Orlando Cepeda, a young Gaylord Perry. But they were no dynasty in the making: They followed up their pennant by finishing third, fourth, second, second, second, second, second, and third before winning a division (but no pennant). San Francisco wouldn't win another pennant until 1989. And what happened? An earthquake.

70. Harvey Kuenn, Outfielder, Detroit Tigers.
Harvey Kuenn led the American League in hitting in 1958 at .353. But just before the next season he was sent to Cleveland in the infamous trade for Rocky Colavito. The Indians' ensuing problems were not his fault; Kuenn hit .308 despite nagging injuries. Still, he was dealt after one season to San Francisco. After a career as a .303 hitter, he became a coach and hoped he was in line then to become manager of his hometown Milwaukee Brewers. He wasn't. In 1976, he had quadruple bypass surgery. In 1977, he developed Crohn's disease. In 1980, circulatory problems resulted in the amputation of one leg below the knee. But Kuenn was resilient—Bob Uecker, the team's radio announcer, said Kuenn was back playing golf a month later and coaching six months later. Then in midseason 1982, Kuenn took over as Brewers manager when Buck Rodgers was fired, and he led the team—Harvey's Wallbangers—to the World Series. He was the toast of the town (and he hoisted a few), but the magic ran out in 1983, the team faded out of first place that August and the Brewers let him go. He was understanding. "If you don't win," he said, according to Shepherd Express, a Milwaukee news source, "you leave." He died in 1988. In his eulogy, Uecker said: "Over the last several years, Harvey was kind of working with a 3-2 count. Each time they tried to slip one past Harvey on the outside corner, he fouled it off. To get one [past] Harvey looking, He must have wanted him pretty bad."

71. Don Bessent, Pitcher, Los Angeles Dodgers.
The life of Don Bessent came to a distressing end in a Wendy's parking lot in Jacksonville, Florida, in 1990. According to *The Los Angeles Times*, restaurant employees found Bessent slumped in his car one afternoon. He declined their assistance, then later asked for it—but, the employees said, their assistant manager threatened to fire them if they did help. Two employees called the police anyway, but Bessent was declared dead at the scene. He died of alcohol poisoning, with a blood alcohol level of 0.35 percent.

72. Bill Renna, Outfielder, Boston Red Sox.
Major league teams have always worked dodges to keep players under their control. Bill Renna revealed how the Yankees played games with his contract. The Yankees did not actually sign Renna; a minor league team they owned in Beaumont,

Texas, signed him. Had Renna been an official Yankees farmhand, he told *Sports Collectors Digest*, the team would have had only three-year options on him. Instead, the clock on his options would not start ticking until the Yankees actually signed him—presumably after he had proved himself with a team like Beaumont. The Yankees' system was stacked with talent, and this end run allowed them to defer making decisions on players while preventing them from going to another organization. Renna finally made it to the Yankees after four years as a minor league slugger and hit .314 as a part-timer for the 1953 pennant winners but was sent packing to the Athletics in an 11-player trade.

73. Ron Jackson, First Baseman, Chicago White Sox.

Ron Jackson was a stud in Indianapolis. In 1957, he hit .310/.382/.519 with 21 home runs (and 11 triples) and 102 RBIs. Two years later, he hit .286/.360/.537 with 30 homers and 99 RBIs in only 130 games. But he couldn't hit in Chicago. The 6-foot-7 Jackson had been a basketball star, winning three consecutive state high school championships in Kalamazoo, Michigan, before starring at Western Michigan, where as a junior he averaged 15.5 points and a school-record 12.3 rebounds a game.

74. Cookie Lavagetto, Directing the Power: Jim Lemon-Cookie Lavagetto-Roy Sievers.

Card 75: Sam Jones was said to always have a toothpick in his mouth. Except in his baseball cards.

There is some irony in a card celebrating the Senators' power, as Washington's Griffith Stadium was for decades one of the hardest parks in which to homer. In every season from 1933 to 1953, Griffith Stadium allowed the fewest home runs of any ballpark. In 1945, the Senators hit one homer at home—an inside-the-park shot—and opponents hit only six. The Senators slugger Goose Goslin hit 17 home runs in 1926—all on the road. Center field was about 420 feet from home plate. The left-field line was 405 feet in 1952, 388 in 1954 and 350 in 1957, a change that was a major boon to right-handed sluggers like Jim Lemon and Roy Sievers; the right-field line was a mere 320 feet but had a 30-foot fence that stretched to center field.

75. Sam Jones, Pitcher, St. Louis Cardinals.

Every profile I have ever read of Sam Jones refers to the toothpick that he was said to always have in his mouth. One of his nicknames was Toothpick Sam Jones. *Sports Illustrated* reported that his wife said he slept with a toothpick in his mouth. So why doesn't his baseball card ever have a photo of him with a toothpick? Not his card in 1952 (his rookie year). Nor in 1953, '55, '56, '57, '58, '59, '60, '61, '62 or '63. (He apparently did not have Topps cards in 1954 or 1964.) His other nickname was Sad Sam Jones (presumably because there was an earlier Sad Sam Jones who pitched from 1914 to 1935). Jones really did look sad on most of his cards.

76. Bobby Richardson, Second Baseman, New York Yankees.

Ever wonder how many runs the excellent Yankee teams of the late '50s and early '60s might have scored if they had had accomplished hitters at the top of the order? Bobby Richardson batted first or second for nearly 80 percent of his 5,783 plate appearances yet had a measly .299 on-base percentage. On the vaunted '61 Yankees—Maris and Mantle, a then-record 240 home runs, 5.07 runs a game—he was the leadoff man, made 533 outs, got on base only 205 times and scored 80 runs. He and Tony Kubek made a lot of outs.

77. John Goryl, Infielder, Chicago Cubs.

John Goryl was your basic '50s–'60s backup infielder: good hands, no bat. Except for 1963. Suddenly the light-hitting Goryl batted .283/.353/.540 for the Minnesota Twins with nine home runs in 174 plate appearances. In the rest of his 212 major league games, he batted 204/.286/.315 with seven homers. It wasn't an expansion year. The American League wasn't having a home run surge (there were actually fewer homers in the league in '63 than in '62). The Twins were not in a new ballpark. The dimensions weren't changed, and no grandstands were built that year that might have affected the flight of the ball. So what got into Goryl? Whatever it was, it didn't stay there: He batted .140/.216/.175 without a single homer in 1964, his last season in the majors.

78. Pedro Ramos, Pitcher, Washington Senators.

There was something about Senators pitchers and Mickey Mantle. (The Senators *were* last or next to last in six seasons of the '50s and never had a winning record, so, yeah.) There was Mantle's titanic home run off Chuck Stobbs, detailed elsewhere. And there was another famous home run, off Pedro Ramos. On May 30, 1956, Ramos hit Mantle with a fastball his first time up. Second time? Mantle crushed a ball that hit the upper-deck façade in right field less than two feet from the top, just missing becoming the first to leave Yankee Stadium on the fly. "It was the best I ever hit a ball left-handed," Mantle said. Ramos would later recount his frequent challenges to Mantle to a footrace; depending on when he was telling the tale, the details (for example, that Mantle wanted to bet large sums) could vary. What didn't was that they never did race. As George Vecsey wrote in *The New York Times* based on his interview with the pitcher, Mantle said: "'Pete, if I beat you, I got nothing to gain. ... If you beat me, I look bad. If I get hurt, I can't play.'" Mantle was basically Babe Ruth against Ramos: .344/.438/.750 lifetime, with 12 home runs in 112 plate appearances.

79. Harry Chiti, Catcher, Kansas City Athletics.

Take a look at Harry Chiti's catcher's mitt. It looks sort of like a huge pancake with a swatch of webbing and some padding around the edges but little flexibility. This was '50s standard, but it was the advanced evolution of the mitt. For decades catcher's mitts were like hard pillows; my dad had what was probably a late '20s or early '30s Mickey Cochrane autograph catcher's mitt that was little more than a pillow with a baseball-size scoop in the center and the teeniest of webbing. You had to catch the ball and immediately cover it with your right hand. (Hence all those catcher hand injuries back in the day.) Longtime catcher Mickey Owen said in 1993 that when he came up in 1937, mitts "were still pretty small, flat and had no shape," according to the Encyclopedia of Baseball Catcher's Equipment. Owen said a designer at Rawlings "made a real change in the depth of the mitt so the ball would really stick."

Card 79: Catcher's mitts like Harry Chiti's had hardly evolved over the decades. "We caught two-handed so the ball wouldn't pop out," a contemporary said.

Earl Battey, a three-time Gold Glove winner in the '60s, used a mitt that Chiti would have been comfortable with. "When I played, we had a pocket but no breaks," he told the Encyclopedia, "and we caught two-handed so the ball wouldn't pop out." That all changed radically with the hinged mitt that Randy Hundley and Johnny Bench made popular in the late '60s, according to a 2010 article in the *SABR Research Journal*. Their gloves were flexed, more like first basemen's mitts, and allowed catchers to catch the ball one-handed. No matter what glove he used, though, Chiti was not so adept with it. He twice led his league in passed balls—the second time while catching only 83 games. And it wasn't because he was catching knuckleballers. There were, in fact, three pitchers on the '58 Athletics who threw a knuckleball, according to The (Mostly) Complete List of Knuckleball Pitchers, but they combined for only 34 innings. Chiti had other defensive shortcomings as well. When the 1962 Mets, who cycled through seven catchers that year, acquired Chiti, John Drebinger of *The New York Times* wrote that he was "not exactly a bullseye operator when it comes to throwing out runners."

80. Minnie Miñoso, Outfielder, Cleveland Indians.

Bill Veeck did a lot of oddball things in baseball, but he did give players of color a chance. He signed the first Black player in the American League, Larry Doby, in 1947. By 1949, after he had signed Orestes (Minnie) Miñoso, the Indians had four

Black players—Miñoso, Doby, Luke Easter and Satchel Paige—and a Mexican, Bobby Ávila, and a first-generation Mexican American, Mike García. Miñoso did not get a real shot in the majors until 1951, when he was 27. Had he retired at 39 (he had 38 futile plate appearances at age 40 and 10 frivolous at-bats at 52 and 56), he would have been a .300 hitter. As it was, he clocked in at .299/.387/.461 with 2,113 hits and 195 home runs despite his late start.

81. Hal Jeffcoat, Pitcher, Cincinnati Redlegs.

There have been some notable conversions of position players to pitcher. Bob Lemon, former infielder, became a Hall of Fame pitcher, and Bucky Walters became a pitcher who won an MVP Award. Trevor Hoffman, Sean Doolittle and Kenley Jansen also made the move to the mound. Those more recent converts became pitchers in the minors, though. Not Hal Jeffcoat. From 1948 to 1953 he was an outfielder, if not a very productive one (a .252 hitter with a sub-.300 on-base percentage and doubles power on a good day). From 1954 to 1959, he was a pitcher, with modest results (39–37, 4.22 ERA, 97 ERA+). Jeffcoat, who had pitched in the minors and was the subject of discussions about moving to the mound before '54—the Cubs did need pitching—played 560 games in the outfield and 245 on the mound. He had 2,131 plate appearances and faced 3,053 batters.

82. Bob Boyd, First Baseman, Baltimore Orioles.

Bob Boyd had one fine nickname: Rope. Or El Ropo when he was playing winter ball in Spanish-speaking locales. He hit line drives everywhere he played. *Crossing the Line* says Boyd got the nickname when he was with the Orioles, tagged by one of the coaches, Lum Harris, who saw him hit line drives repeatedly in spring training. Boyd was signed out of the Negro leagues in 1950 but did not have a full-time role in the majors until 1957, when he was 37. He was fourth in the American League in batting that year, at .318—"I'm laying out those ropes because I'm playing regularly," he said in *Crossing the Line*—and was a .298 career hitter. What he lacked was power. And opportunity.

83. Bob Smith, Pitcher, Pittsburgh Pirates.

When Bob Smith was toiling, not so successfully, in the minor leagues for the Boston Red Sox, the team signed another Bob Smith. Who was also a pitcher. They were teammates briefly in Scranton in 1951, then again for the 1955 season in Louisville and yet again in 1956 in San Francisco, where their statistics were freakishly similar: 8–11, 4.38 for this Bob, 9–10, 4.45 for the other Bob. The Red Sox even had another Bob Smith who pitched for them in the '20s and '30s. The Smith name apparently lends itself to this sort of duplication: In the '80s, the Reds had two pitchers named Mike Smith, so they called them Mississippi Mike and Texas Mike to simplify things.

84. Reno Bertoia, Third Baseman, Washington Senators.

He signed on August 31, 1953, and sat on Detroit's bench until the last game of the year, when the Tigers, trying to draw a crowd at the end of a 60–94 season, started their three 18-year-old "bonus babies"—Bertoia, Al Kaline and pitcher Bob Miller—against the ancient St. Louis Browns pitcher Satchel Paige. (It was billed as the oldest pitcher—Paige at 47—versus the youngest, Miller. Paige earned his final major league victory.) Bertoia struck out against Paige on three pitches and then was spiked on a play at second base and was pulled from the game. Under the bonus rules of the time, Bertoia had to spend the next two seasons in Detroit, and he went to bat only 119 times. His career never took off, and Bertoia thought his wasted years on the bench were one reason. "I think it was the stupidest rule that was ever made," he said in *Baseball's Bonus Babies*.

85. Harry Anderson, Outfielder, Philadelphia Phillies.

Discounting the pandemic-shortened season of 2020, Harry Anderson was the last batter to lead one of the major leagues in strikeouts with fewer than 100. In 1958, he whiffed an NL-leading 95 times. Still, the 26-year-old outfielder hit .301/.373/.524 with 23 home runs, 34 doubles and six triples. It came after a rookie season in which he batted .268/.333/.453 with 17 homers in 118 games. But these were the Phillies: His offense cratered, his defense was never very good, and he was done in the majors in 1961.

86. Bob Keegan, Pitcher, Chicago White Sox.

The 1954 White Sox were pretty good. They won 91 games. But they could not pinch-hit. The Sox were 16 for 124 for the season, a .129 average, and their pinch-hitters started the season 0 for 35. On May 14, Chicago was trailing the Philadelphia Athletics, 1–0, in the fifth inning and had runners on first and second with one out. First baseman Bob Boyd, in a .179 slump, was due to bat, but the Sox sent up a pinch-hitter: Bob Keegan. He was a 33-year-old pitcher in his second year in the majors, but he had gone nine for 28 (all singles) in 1953 and three days earlier was two for three. Keegan singled off Alex Kellner to drive in the tying run, and Chicago went on to win. Keegan had used up his offensive heroics, though: He was four for 60 the rest of the season.

87. Danny O'Connell, Second Baseman, San Francisco Giants.

Major league teams don't always spend money readily, but they spent on Danny O'Connell. After O'Connell hit .314/.393/.481 in Class AAA in 1949, the Pirates doled out $50,000 to acquire him (nearly $630,000 in 2023 dollars). Four years later, the Milwaukee Braves sent $100,000 and six players to Pittsburgh for O'Connell in the hope that he would fill their hole at second base. There was some skepticism that he could. *The Sporting News* reported that the Phillies' president, Bob Carpenter, said: "There is no assurance that O'Connell can play second base. He's no cat at that spot and if he is shifted to third, there is no proof that Ed Mathews will be a success in the outfield. They are going to have their headaches." Even a Pirates teammate, pitcher Bob Friend, noted that O'Connell was one of the slower players on the team. In fact, O'Connell did not hit much in Milwaukee and his defense had holes. When he was traded to the Giants in 1957 for Red Schoendienst, the second baseman Milwaukee had long coveted, Braves pitcher Bob Buhl said, "We had other good second basemen, but they couldn't turn a double play or hit .300 like Red." With O'Connell gone and Schoendienst in place, the Braves won the pennant and the World Series, then won the pennant again the next year.

88. Herb Score, Pitcher, Cleveland Indians.

Herb Score came blazing into the major leagues in 1955, striking out batters at an unprecedented rate; he was the first ERA qualifier to fan more than a batter per inning. But he also walked batters in huge numbers—154 as a rookie, 129 more the next year. This should not have seemed unusual to Cleveland fans, who had watched their pitchers walk 100-plus batters a year for more than half a century. Indians pitchers cracked 100 walks 56 times from 1901 (the first year of the American League) to 1971; the rest of the league's pitchers did so 294 times. Cleveland played 9.5 percent of team's seasons in that span but had 16 percent of the 100-walk seasons. So it was not just Score and Bob Feller walking batter after batter. Sam McDowell, Bob Lemon, Wes Ferrell, Allie Reynolds, Early Wynn—they all had numerous 100-walk seasons for Cleveland. With innings so diminished now, we may not see a 100-walk season again, but Cleveland fans sure saw plenty.

89. Billy Gardner, Second Baseman, Baltimore Orioles.

The SABR Bio Project biographies unearth some fascinating information. For example, Billy Gardner married the 1952 Miss New London, Connecticut, 18-year-old Barbara Carnaroli. His profile says she was named the top female athlete in New London three years in a row and aspired to play professional baseball or basketball. Billy was also from New London but seven years older than Barbara. Hers was an athletic family; her younger brother, Hank, played a season in rookie ball with the Orioles and, according to his obituary, roomed with Boog Powell. Hank also played in Japan. After Gardner became manager of the Minnesota Twins in 1981, he lived in a Super 8 motel at a truck stop outside town for four years, *The Baltimore Sun* reported. "The people are nice to me, I get along great with the drivers, and there's a Denny's nearby," he said.

90. Bill Skowron, First Baseman, New York Yankees.

After World War II, the Big Ten produced a series of hulking first basemen who had gone to college to play another sport. Bill Skowron was a football player—his freshman coach was Hank Stram, later a successful NFL coach—who played blocking back and punted. But he also became an All–Big Ten shortstop in 1950 (comical as that may seem to those who remember his physique in the majors and his nickname, Moose). Ted Kluszewski was an end and kicker on Indiana's Big Ten championship football team in 1945. (Surprisingly, he played center field at IU.) And 6-foot-7 Frank Howard was a basketball All-American at Ohio State, averaging 17.4 points and 13.9 rebounds for his career. Combined, they hit 872 home runs.

91. Herb Moford, Pitcher, Boston Red Sox.

Herb Moford's major league career was nothing to write home about—four teams in four seasons, 5–13, 5.03 ERA in 50 games—but back home in Northern

Kentucky, he did give 'em plenty to write about. When Moford died in 2005, a sportswriter, Punk Griffin, who had been watching local sports for 50 years, remembered an all-star game in which Moford pitched in the early '50s. "Herb struck out 18 straight batters to start the game, and I had never seen anything like that," Griffin said. *The Maysville Ledger Independent* said Griffin also recalled what Moford said was the difference between a minor league hitter and a big leaguer. "If you miss the plate by three inches, a minor leaguer will strike out most times," Moford told him. "A big league hitter will just stand there and laugh at you … you gotta get the ball over the plate." He knew a lot about minor league hitters; Moford pitched 17 seasons in the minors.

92. Dave Philley, First Baseman-Outfielder, Philadelphia Phillies.

Philley of the Phillies—ideal combination, isn't it? I couldn't find a much better meshing of name and team. You did have Bill (1912), Ed (1884), Walter (1947) and William (1894) Brown of the Browns, and Jim York of the New York Yankees (1976) and Grover Cleveland Land of the Cleveland Naps. But no Rocky with the Rockies, no Boston in Boston, no Brewer with the Brewers.

93. Julio Bécquer, First Baseman, Washington Senators.

One scout, Joe Cambria, signed more than 400 players from Cuba to professional contracts from the mid–1930s until his death in 1962, and as many as 20 a year, according to *Joe Cambria: International Super Scout of the Washington Senators*. Julio Bécquer was one of them. It seemed as if 390 of those Cubans played for the Senators. Cambria and the Senators' owner, Clark Griffith, worked together for decades, sending a pipeline of Cubans to Washington and early on skirting baseball's segregation policies by signing light-skinned Cubans. After Jackie Robinson, Cambria signed Cubans of all hues, like Bécquer. But segregation's tentacles still entangled baseball. He missed out on a chance to play for the Chattanooga Lookouts because of his dark skin, said his obituary at RIP Baseball, which added that the Senators then tried to send him to the Richmond Virginians, who declined to take him.

94. Chicago White Sox Team Card.

On the night of September 23, 1959, the White Sox clinched their first pennant since 1919 by winning in Cleveland. A few minutes later, air raid sirens went off all over the city back home, *The Chicago Tribune* reported, sending many people into the streets fearing that a Soviet invasion was under way. (This *was* the Cold War era.) City Hall received 1,100 calls an hour the next day, *The Tribune* reported. And it said Mayor Richard J. Daley explained that the sirens were sounded "in the hilarity and exuberance of the evening. I regret if anyone was inconvenienced, but after 40 years of waiting for a pennant in the American League, I assume that everyone who was watching the telecast was happy about the White Sox victory."

95. Carl Willey, Pitcher, Milwaukee Braves.

The left-hander Carlton Willey had remarkable success against a number of Hall of Famers: Orlando Cepeda, seven for 48, .146; Ernie Banks, nine for 50, .180; Willie Mays, 11 for 50, .220; Richie Ashburn, eight for 34, .235; Stan Musial, eight for

31, .258. And Cepeda, Banks and Mays were right-handed hitters. But guys like Lee Walls, 11 for 23, .478; Clay Dalrymple, six for 13, .462; and Charlie Neal, 15 for 34, .441, owned him.

96. Lou Berberet, Catcher, Detroit Tigers.

The Yankees of the late '40s and early 1950s developed an unbelievable amount of catching talent. Berberet was one of those catchers who, stuck behind Yogi Berra (and eventually Elston Howard) with Ralph Houk on the bench, moved on and made it with another team. Others included Sherm Lollar (acquired by the Yankees by trade, developed, traded, became an All-Star with the Browns and the White Sox), Gus Triandos (traded, became an All-Star with the Orioles), Hank Foiles (signed as an amateur, lost in the Rule 5 draft, became an All-Star with the Pirates). That was all in a half-dozen years or so.

97. Jerry Lynch, Outfielder, Cincinnati Reds.

Nineteen sixty-one was a magical season for Jerry Lynch and the Reds. In his first at-bat of the season, on April 13, he pinch-hit in the bottom of the eighth and broke a 2–2 tie with a three-run homer; the Reds won. Pinch-hitting on June 2, he drove in three runs with a double, although the Reds lost to the Cubs. Pinch-hitting on June 16 in the top of the eighth, he smacked a tie-breaking double, and the Reds beat the Phillies. In his next game, he pinch-hit with one out in the bottom of the ninth and singled in the tying run; the Reds beat the Cardinals in extra innings. On June 27, his pinch-hit triple drove in three runs in the seventh to break a 6–6 tie, and the Reds went on to defeat the Cubs. On July 30, his two-run single as a pinch-hitter put the Reds on top, 5–4, and they held on to win. Cincinnati won its first pennant in 21 years as Lynch hit as almost no other pinch-hitter has: .404/.525/.851 (19 for 47) with five home runs, 12 walks against five strikeouts, and 25 RBIs, which is the most ever for a pinch-hitter. For the season, Lynch hit .307/.407/.624 with 13 homers, 13 doubles and 50 RBIs in 210 plate appearances. Bill James made a case in his *Historical Baseball Abstract* for Lynch being the MVP for the Reds, who were picked to finish sixth. This season was not really an anomaly: Lynch had great seasons as a

Card 97: Jerry Lynch was a pinch-hitter extraordinaire, so proficient (.404/.525/.851 with five homers) that he may have been the MVP of the Reds' 1961 pennant-winners.

pinch-hitter in 1958, '59 and '63 as well. In those four big seasons he hit .382 (47 for 123) with 11 homers and 19 walks. When he retired, Lynch was first in career pinch-hit home runs (18) and second in pinch hits (115). Lynch told *Baseball Digest* he thought Smoky Burgess was the best pinch-hitter ever. "But I was the best clutch hitter because I hit 18 dingers," he said. "I rang the bell 18 times. Hey, if you don't think you're the best, who will?"

98. Arnie Portocarrero, Pitcher, Baltimore Orioles.

The perils of playing winter league ball. In 1954, 22-year-old rookie Arnie Portocarrero led starting pitchers for the Philadelphia Athletics (who finished 51–103–2) in wins (and losses), ERA, strikeouts (and walks), innings pitched and complete games. Then he went to Puerto Rico, his father's homeland, to pitch winter ball and hurt his arm. His career faltered immediately. It calls to mind the experience of Carl Willey, who threw 248 innings in Class AAA in 1957 and then added 112 innings in the Dominican Winter League. His ERA+ then skidded from 132 to 85.

99. Ted Kazanski, Infielder, Philadelphia Phillies.

Ted Kazanski was from Hamtramck, Michigan, and laugh if you will at the name Hamtramck, but it has produced a fair amount of athletic talent. Kazanski (who got a $100,000 bonus from the Phillies), Steve Gromek and Tom Paciorek all had lengthy major league careers. Rudy Tomjanovich was a six-time NBA All-Star who coached the Houston Rockets to two championships. And Peaches Bartkowicz was a pioneering player on the women's tennis tour in the '70s. All from Hamtramck. And if you're looking for one more player with hits, Mitch Ryder (of the Detroit Wheels) was also from Hamtramck.

100. Bob Cerv, Outfielder, Kansas City Athletics.

Arnold Johnson bought the Athletics and moved them to Kansas City from Philadelphia, with the help of the Yankees' owners (from whom he had bought Yankee Stadium a year or so earlier; he then sold it when he purchased the Athletics). The connections remained complicated, except for the simple fact that in 16 deals between the Yankees and the Athletics from 1955 to 1961 (shortly after Johnson died), New York continually fleeced its KC cousins, as *Baseball Almanac* laid out in detail. (Remarkably, the wealthy Yankees got cash in three of the deals.) In 2010, Jeff Zimmerman calculated the Wins Above Replacement that were involved in the transactions between baseball's most successful team and one of its least successful: 64 WAR for the Yankees, 36 for the Athletics. Bob Cerv was on the NY-KC shuttle not once, but twice. (The Yankees even acquired him a third time, from another team.) Cerv said he was excited to be going to Kansas City the first time for the opportunity to play regularly, but his son told *The New York Times* for Cerv's obituary, "He was proud to be a Yankee. That's who he felt he was."

101. Alex Kellner, Pitcher, St. Louis Cardinals.

If Alex Kellner could have pitched entire seasons the way he pitched in April and May, he might have been a perennial All-Star. In 563⅔ innings over 12 seasons, his April–May ERA was 3.54; in all other months, it was 4.80. His control was better (3.16 walks per nine in April–May, 3.74 the rest of the year). He gave up less than a hit per inning in April–May, well over that afterward. He was especially tough in April—a WHIP (walk and hits per innings pitched) at least 10 percent better than any other month, a strikeout/walk ratio 15 percent better than the next-best month. He won 20 games as a Philadelphia Athletics rookie in 1949 (his underlying stats indicate it was a mirage), then *lost* 20 in his second season. In the near namesake competition: George Kell, the longtime high-average/low-power third baseman, hit seven of his 78 home runs off Kellner.

102. Felipe Alou, Outfielder, San Francisco Giants.

You may hear that the Alou brothers were the Giants' starting outfield once upon a time, but it didn't happen. They *did* play in the outfield together three times in September 1963, with Jesus and Matty coming off the bench. When Jesus made his major league debut that September 10, Manager Al Dark had the brothers bat consecutively in the eighth inning—Jesus and Matty as pinch-hitters before Felipe Alou came up. No storybook finish: They went 0 for 3 against Carlton Willey. What a baseball family, though. Felipe, a three-time All-Star who collected 2,101 hits, was also the father of Moisés Alou and future Mets Manager Luis Rojas, the uncle of longtime Expos reliever Mel Rojas and a cousin of Astros reliever José Sosa.

103. Billy Goodman, Third Baseman, Chicago White Sox.

The 1950 Boston Red Sox had some kind of offense. Billy Goodman led the American League in batting at .354, yet he couldn't find a full-time role. Ted Williams played only 89 games because he shattered his elbow in the All-Star Game, but Boston still led the league in batting (.302), runs (1,027, or 6.67 a game; runner-up was 5.9), on-base percentage (.385), slugging (.464) and doubles. They were second in home runs, walks and even triples. The team rang up the fourth-highest total of runs in the 20th century. Five players scored 100 runs; the worst regular hit .294 (and he drove in 120 runs). First baseman Walt Dropo (.322/.378/.583, 34 homers, 144 RBIs) was Rookie of the Year. Center fielder Dom DiMaggio (.328/.414/.452) had the best numbers of his life. Even aging catcher Birdie Tebbetts, a sub-.270 hitter the rest of his career, batted .310. But the Red Sox did not win the pennant. They didn't even finish second. No, despite that offense, Boston was third, four games behind the Yankees. One word: pitching. (Boston was sixth in the eight-team league in ERA, with the most walks allowed.) This came a year after the Red Sox lost the pennant to the Yankees in the last game of the season. *The Saturday Evening Post* wrote in 1951 that the Red Sox could do just about everything "except win pennants." Goodman did a lot of everything in his career, playing more than 300 games each at first, second and third and 100-plus in the outfield. He batted .2996–.300 in the record book.

104. Del Rice, Catcher, Milwaukee Braves.

Del Crandall *and* Del Rice, both catchers, on the same team? They were teammates in Milwaukee for five years, which must have given new meaning to the Wisconsin Dels. Sixteen guys who went by Del have played in the major leagues, and two of them were teammates (and two others also played in the 1950s … and in the National League). Heck, three more Dels were also catchers: Baker, Bates and Wilber. You want your kid to be a National League catcher, name him Del.

105. Lee Walls, Outfielder, Chicago Cubs.

Ballplayers used to have to work in the off-season to make ends meet. Lee Walls did not have your typical ballplayer job: Baseball Reference says he was a maître d'. From Jim Brosnan in *Baseball Players of the 1950s*: "Lee Walls was my roommate with the Cubs. He was quite gregarious and for years during the off-seasons worked as a greeter in Palm Springs. We'd always go to the fanciest restaurants and Lee would smoothly talk us inside without reservations." His glasses were tinted, earning him the nickname Captain Midnight.

106. Hal Woodeshick, Pitcher, Cleveland Indians.

It isn't hard to have a bad record on an expansion team, and Hal Woodeshick sure did have a bad record for the 1962 Houston Colt .45s: 5–16, 4.39 ERA (league average was 3.95). He lost nine of his last 10 decisions, and for the most part he earned those losses. In his five major league seasons after that, Woodeshick never started another game. But even on a bad team, he became a very good reliever. In 1963 he was 11–9 (yes, 20 decisions as a reliever) with 10 saves. His 1.97 ERA (in 114 innings) would have been second only to Sandy Koufax's had he pitched enough to qualify. Reliever usage was so different that he had seven games in which he pitched at least four shutout innings; once he went eight innings in relief, another time seven and two-thirds, a couple of others six innings.

Card 105: Lee Walls had a great nickname—Captain Midnight—because of his tinted glasses.

107. Norm Larker, First Baseman-Outfielder, Los Angeles Dodgers.

Norm Larker knocked Braves shortstop Johnny Logan out of a playoff game in 1962 with a hard slide. Logan said he would never forgive Larker (or forget it). Don Zimmer told *The New York Times* that when he and Larker played together in Japan, Larker ran off three interpreters. Larker once got into a fight with his teammate Bob Shaw, who contended that Larker was blocking his view in the dugout of Cardinals pitcher Bob Gibson, according to his SABR Bio Project profile. With the Houston

Colt .45s, Larker, upset after grounding out, kicked the electric fan that was cooling their dugout one hot night, breaking the fan (and leading teammate Bob Lillis to ask Larker why he had done it, to which Larker replied, "I had to kick *something*."). He once threw 18 bats on the field after being called out on strikes, David Krell wrote in *1962: Baseball and America in the Time of JFK*. His nicknames were Dumbo and Mad Dog, and he despised both names. *The Houston Chronicle* noted that Larker was so angered by the high grass in the Houston ballpark, Colt Stadium, that, believing it was costing him infield hits, he brought his own lawn mower to the ballpark to cut the grass. No surprise: Norm Larker had an ulcer.

108. Zach Monroe, Pitcher, New York Yankees.

Zach Monroe and Johnny James were hard-throwing right-handers who were longtime teammates in the minors (the bulk of four seasons) but never could quite master the strike zone or really make the Yankees in the '50s and early '60s. Monroe did spend half of the 1958 season in New York but otherwise appeared in only three more major league games (and three and a third innings). James was up with the Yankees a little longer but less successfully before tapping out with the expansion Angels. They had short careers but personal longevity—in late 2023, both were still alive: Monroe was 92, James 90, two of the oldest living Yankees.

109. Bob Schmidt, Catcher, San Francisco Giants.

In the minors, Bob Schmidt had never hit much for average, but as a 25-year-old rookie with the San Francisco Giants in 1958, suddenly he was hitting. After going seven for 10 on May 12 and 13, he was batting .323. At the end of the month, he was still batting .304. This was the time to make an impression on All-Star selectors, and Schmidt did, earning a backup role on Manager Fred Haney's NL team, behind Del Crandall and John Roseboro. It helped that no other NL catcher was playing well, including the Redlegs' Ed Bailey, who wound up being a five-time All-Star but was hitting below .200 as late as June 21. By the end of the season, Schmidt (.244, 14 home runs) and Bailey (.250, 11) had similar numbers in a similar number of plate appearances. But Schmidt had nabbed the All-Star spot for 1958. Never again, however.

110. George Witt, Pitcher, Pittsburgh Pirates.

Opposing batters just couldn't hit Red Witt. Through six minor league seasons, his *worst* hits per nine innings was 8.4. Problem was, he walked batters left and right. That is, until 1957, when he cut his walks per nine innings to 2.8 from 5.1. Pitching in the Class AAA Pacific Coast League, he also allowed only 6.9 hits per nine and went 18–7, 2.24. The next year, after seven more Class AAA starts, Witt was in the majors and put up 9–2, 1.61 numbers for the Pirates. In his first start, he beat Sandy Koufax, 2–1 (although he was not yet *Sandy Koufax*). Whatever Witt had found, however, was quickly lost. Beset by arm injuries and wildness, he was 0–7, 6.93 in 1959 and split 1960 between Pittsburgh and AAA. He did get into three games of the 1960 World Series—but only when the Pirates were behind by nine runs, eight runs and 12 runs.

111. Cincinnati Redlegs Team Card.

In 1953 and early '54, Senator Joe McCarthy initiated hearings designed to ferret out the communists he *knew* were lurking in the State Department and elsewhere. The time was known as the Red Scare, and it scared the Reds, who officially changed their name to the Redlegs (or Red Legs) from 1953 to 1959. The team even removed "Reds" from its home jerseys. "It was a way to get away from any association with communists," Rich Walls, executive director of the Reds Hall of Fame, told MLB.com.

112. Billy Consolo, Second Baseman-Shortstop, Boston Red Sox.

Another bonus baby, and Billy Consolo knew that taking the money and spending his first two years on the Red Sox's bench, as required by baseball rules for any amateur signing for more than $4,000, would slow his development. But the money—a reported $60,000—was too good to pass up, Consolo said. (After his death, *The Long Beach* [California] *Press-Telegram* reported this bonus perk: Citing *Baseball America*, it said that the Red Sox landed Consolo only after also arranging to buy a barber shop for his father.) His Boston manager, Lou Boudreau, was candid about the effects of being an 18-year-old bench warmer in the majors. "Consolo should be out playing every day," Boudreau said, according to Consolo's SABR Bio Project biography. "No sense kidding about it. Billy would be much better off with two years in the minors. He'd come back as a great player." He finally got a year in the minors at age 20 (and hit well), but he never did become a great player, or even a good one. In 10 seasons he was a .221/.315/.389 hitter with a 63 OPS+ and a -0.1 WAR.

113. Taylor Phillips, Pitcher, Chicago Cubs.

After Taylor Phillips graduated from high school, he had offers to sign with the defending World Series champion New York Yankees or the Class AA Atlanta Crackers, who the year before were 71–82. Phillips, who lived just outside Atlanta, chose the Crackers. He was farmed out by the minor league team for two years, and when he reached Atlanta in 1952, he still was not making much money, as he recalled to *The Kingsport* (Tennessee) *Times News*. He said the club's owner came into the clubhouse after games, and when Phillips won a game, the owner would slip a $50 or $100 bill into his handshake. "I made more money shaking hands than I did pitching that year," he said, which means he really wasn't making much money as he won only 11 games. In his major league debut, he struck out Willie Mays. But as he told *The Times News*, "Another thing about Willie Mays is he hit his 80th and 100th home runs off me."

114. Earl Battey, Catcher, Chicago White Sox.

The White Sox won the pennant in 1959, their first in 40 years, and did not want to wait to win again. So after the season, they traded away three talented young players who were stalled in Chicago: Earl Battey, 24; first baseman Norm Cash, 25; and outfielder Johnny Callison, 20. Battey immediately won three Gold Gloves and became a four-time All-Star with the Twins; Cash wound up an All-Star four times with the Tigers; and Callison turned out to be a three-time All-Star with doubles, triples and home run power for the Phillies. The White Sox received some talented players in return, but they were all gone after two years. Battey won a pennant with the Twins, Cash won a World Series with the Tigers and Callison was part of the famed 1964 pennant race. Chicago did not win another pennant until 2005.

115. Mickey Vernon, First Baseman, Cleveland Indians.

Mickey Vernon, the longtime Washington Senator, holds the record for most double plays by a first baseman, 2,044. He was no doubt helped by all those baserunners Senators pitchers allowed. In his 14 seasons with the Senators, they had one winning team—at 78–76. Vernon won a batting title at age 28 (.353/.403/.508 with an OPS+ of 160) and again at 35 (.337/.403/.518, 150 OPS+), but he was basically league-average in between. In his *Historical Baseball Abstract*, Bill James wrote, "Vernon is one of those players, like Rico Carty or Frank Howard, who would be in the Hall of Fame if he had just put in an ordinary progression between his high spots."

116. Bob Allison, Outfielder, Washington Senators.

Bob Allison was an impressive athlete—6 foot 3, 220 pounds, fast. The team trainer called him "the strongest man I ever handled." He played football (fullback) and baseball at the University of Kansas, and in 1959, he was the American League Rookie of the Year. He hit 256 home runs and stole in double figures in four of his 13 seasons with the Senators/Twins. But in his early 50s, he began having coordination issues—he had trouble catching a baseball at a 1987 old-timers' game—and eventually he learned he had a form of ataxia, a neurological condition that affects nerve cells in the brain and severely affects coordination, according to a University of Minnesota Medical School profile and an obituary in *The New York Times*. The once-rugged Allison suffered from the disease for eight years, losing his ability to walk, talk, write and feed himself before he died at age 60. He and his family created the Bob Allison Ataxia Research Center at the University of Minnesota. There is still no cure.

117. Johnny Blanchard, Catcher, New York Yankees.

Johnny Blanchard was meant to play in Yankee Stadium. He was a patient, powerful left-handed hitter. But he was a catcher, and ahead of him were Yogi Berra (a Hall of Famer) and Elston Howard (proficient enough to be the 1963 MVP). Blanchard never caught more than 48 games in a season and actually played more often in the outfield than behind the plate. Forty of his 67 career homers came at Yankee Stadium (in 637 plate appearances).

118. John Buzhardt, Pitcher, Chicago Cubs.

It was the harmonica heard 'round the world. The Yankees, winners of four consecutive pennants, were slumping as August 1964 wore on, and after their fourth straight loss to the White Sox, by 5–0, on a hot afternoon in Chicago, they were in third place, four and a half games behind the first-place White Sox and four back of the Orioles. The Yankees' bus became mired in traffic after the game, and infielder Phil Linz, bored in the back of the bus, pulled out his new harmonica and began playing "Mary Had a Little Lamb." Accounts diverge from there, but this is indisputable: Manager Yogi Berra was angry and told Linz to stop. He didn't. Berra told Linz to shove it up his ass. Such was the Yankee temperament. Linz was fined (he also got an endorsement from the Hohner harmonica company). The catalyst for this unhappiness was John Buzhardt, who had pitched a seven-hit shutout. Whether spurred by the harmonica incident or not, the Yankees finished the season 30–11 to win the pennant (although that did not save Berra's job). Buzhardt, meanwhile, did not win another game that season and barely pitched in September. The White Sox won their final nine games but still finished a game behind the Yankees.

Card 118: John Buzhardt shut down the Yankees in the 1964 game that gave baseball the famed Phil Linz harmonica episode.

119. Johnny Callison, Outfielder, Chicago White Sox.

Johnny Callison and Bob Allison had such similar names and similar careers, distinguished by the fact that they were mostly in different leagues and Allison played on better teams. Both were outfielders. Callison was in the majors from 1958 to 1973; Allison, from 1958 to 1970. Each was an All-Star three times. Callison's slash line was .264/.331/.441, with an OPS+ of 115; Allison's was .255/.358/.471, 127. Allison had more home runs (256–226); Callison had more extra-base hits (626–527). Callison was 74 for 125 stealing; Allison was 84 for 134. Callison could "run, throw, field, and hit with power," his manager said. Allison "can run, he can throw, he swings a good bat," a sportswriter reported. Heck, each of them married his high school sweetheart.

120. Chuck Coles, Outfielder, Cincinnati Redlegs.

Topps labeled Chuck Coles a rookie star of 1959, but he never had a chance. The Reds had so many good-hitting outfielders that they played some of them out of position—Frank Robinson at first base, for example, and Frank Thomas at third. The outfield was locked down by 19-year-old Vada Pinson, Gus Bell (30) and Jerry Lynch (28). Coles was 28 himself and had 11 major league at-bats—and two hits—after seven seasons in the minors. He had spent a full season in Class A ball as recently as 1957. Coles never made a major league roster again.

121. Bob Conley, Pitcher, Philadelphia Phillies.

Bob Conley was from Mousie, an unincorporated village in Appalachian Kentucky. The village was named, in 1916, by the postmaster after his younger daughter, who was called Mousie Martin, according to the organizer of the village's centennial. Her older sister was nicknamed Kitty, so it could have been Kitty, Kentucky. (There was, by the way, a Kitty League—for Kentucky-Illinois-Tennessee—through 1955.) On Mousie's Wikipedia page, there is one entry for Notable Person: Bob Conley, who pitched in two games and eight and a third innings, allowing seven runs, for the 1958 Phillies.

122. Bennie Daniels, Pitcher, Pittsburgh Pirates.

When the Brooklyn Dodgers played their last game in Ebbets Field, Bennie Daniels, making his major league debut, was the opposing starter for the Pirates. (He lost, 2–0.) When the expansion Washington Senators played the final game in Griffith Stadium, Daniels was their starter. (He lost, 6–3.) And the next year, when the Senators opened D.C. Stadium, Daniels was again their starter. (He won, 4–1.) It was the only opening game at which President John F. Kennedy threw out the first pitch.

123. Don Dillard, Outfielder, Cleveland Indians.

Talk about an odd game: Look at the one when Hank Aaron had a home run taken away and Don Dillard had one awarded to him. On August 18, 1965, in St. Louis, according to RIP Baseball, Aaron hit a ball over the right-field pavilion roof in the eighth inning but was ruled out by the home-plate umpire, Chris Pelekoudas, who said Aaron had left the batter's box before hitting the ball. Aaron said it was "the worst call I've ever seen." An inning later, Dillard, pinch-hitting, smacked a ball off the fence in right-center field that bounced back onto the field, RIP Baseball said. The Cardinals contended the ball was still in play; the umpires said it bounced off the top of the wall, hit a fan and rebounded onto the field: home run. It was the last of Dillard's 14 major league homers. Aaron had another 362 of his 755 homers to go.

124. Dan Dobbek, Outfielder, Washington Senators.

The Red Sox must have thought they were facing Dangerous Dan Dobbek. On April 22, 1960, they intentionally walked Dobbek, who had been to the plate only 70 times in the major leagues, not once, but twice. Two days later, they intentionally walked Dobbek again. Dobbek, who hit .218/.316/.387 that season, was in fact walked intentionally seven times in 1960 (he walked 35 times in 288 plate appearances), second on the Senators only to Harmon Killebrew. He was walked intentionally only one more time: again on April 22, in 1961.

125. Ron Fairly, First Baseman, Los Angeles Dodgers.

When Gil Hodges finally faded, Norm Larker became the Dodgers' everyday first baseman. But for only a season and a half. Another left-handed-hitting first baseman arrived: Ron Fairly. After breaking in as an outfielder to get his bat in the lineup, Fairly took over at first in 1961. Jim Murray, the great *Los Angeles Times* columnist, asked Larker whether Fairly could play the position. "Can Fairly play first base? Buddy, Fairly can do ANYTHING," Larker said, according to RIP Baseball. "He could pitch if they wanted him to. Or tune the piano. He's the most natural ballplayer I've ever seen. He never does anything wrong." Fairly later played with the Expos, giving Montreal two left-handed-hitting, redheaded first basemen who sometimes masqueraded as outfielders—him and Rusty Staub.

Card 125: How impressive was young Ron Fairly? A teammate, asked if Fairly could play first base, replied, "Buddy, Fairly can do ANYTHING."

126. Eddie Haas, Outfielder, Milwaukee Braves.

Eddie Haas played in 55 major league games over three seasons, but he pinch-hit in 44 of them and pinch-ran in two others. That leaves nine games in which he spent the whole game on the field. Those nine games totaled 22 hours and 35 minutes. He stayed in the game a few times after pinch-hitting. Maybe four more hours on the field, and three hours in the batter's box while pinch-hitting. Round up and that's 30 hours that Haas played major league baseball. He spent 11 years in the minors pursuing his dream, and the payoff was not even a full workweek in any other profession. Haas also was a longtime minor league manager, a coach with the Braves and, for most of a season, the Braves' manager. But the dream is to play in the majors, and Eddie Haas got to fulfill that dream, if only for 30 hours.

127. Kent Hadley, First Baseman, Kansas City Athletics.

In 1958, Kent Hadley led the Class AA Southern Association in home runs. A year later, he was traded with Roger Maris to the Yankees. In 1964—the last year of the Yankees' great midcentury dynasty—Hadley was a hero in Japan, blasting a walk-off home run in Game 4 of the Japan Series, which the Nankai Hawks won in seven games. Hadley had homered in his first game in Japan, in 1961—the first foreigner to do so—and became the first foreign player to hit 100 homers in Japan.

128. Bob Hartman, Pitcher, Milwaukee Braves.

For years, ballplayers who had diabetes did their best to keep it a secret. Ron Santo, for example, kept his diabetes from most of his Cubs teammates for a decade, even, for much of that time, from his roommate on the road. His wife said he feared that his baseball career would end if his diagnosis became known. Bob Hartman couldn't keep his diabetes a secret. He had a diabetic attack on the road when he was a 19-year-old minor leaguer, according to his SABR Bio Project biography. He lost 50 pounds (he'd been 210) before regaining his strength. While with the Braves, he suffered a blackout, apparently related to his diabetes. His wife said she feared the knowledge of Hartman's diabetes would cause teams to consider him a bad risk. He pitched in the majors only briefly in two seasons, but he did last nine years in pro ball. More players have publicly acknowledged their diabetes in recent years—Adam Duvall and Sam Fuld, for example—but players still worry that it will be held against them. Garrett Mitchell, a first-round draft pick of the Brewers in 2020, told The Athletic that he was aware of the skepticism surrounding an athlete with diabetes and that it might have caused him to fall in the draft. Still, he told The Athletic, he viewed his Type 1 diabetes as an advantage, not a challenge, because he has to understand his body so much better.

129. Pancho Herrera, First Baseman, Philadelphia Phillies.
Pancho Herrera could always hit, hit homers and take walks. He also struck out. He fanned 108 times in Class AAA in 1959—a 16.5 percent rate that was abnormally high for the time. As a Phillies rookie in 1960, he set a National League record with 136 strikeouts—at a 23.7 percent rate. (He also hit .281/.348/.455 with 17 homers and 71 RBIs, both team highs. And led NL first basemen in errors. And was second in Rookie of the Year voting.) The next year he whiffed 120 times—with a 26 percent rate. His strikeout rate has long since become commonplace. *Sports Illustrated* reported in 1994 that his 136-strikeout season was not even among the top 140. (Think how many whiffs there have been since then.) But although he continued to hit and homer and walk, and although he was well liked by fans and teammates (especially Latino teammates), his major league days were done. Herrera kept playing in the minors until he was 38, and he even played a few games in the Mexican League at age 40. He was still hitting. And still striking out.

130. Lou Jackson, Outfielder, Chicago Cubs.
Grambling State University is famous for all the players it has sent to the NFL, but it has also produced 15 major league baseball players. Lou Jackson was the first, playing 48 games spaced out over three seasons. Buck O'Neil scouted and signed Jackson after he played one season at Grambling; O'Neil kept his eye on players at historically black colleges and universities, signing Lou Brock out of Southern University, for example. (O'Neil himself had spent a couple of years at an HBCU.) Grambling's baseball graduates are not as numerous as its football progeny, but the university spawned such solid major leaguers as Tommie Agee, Cleon Jones, Ralph Garr, Lynn McGlothen and Gerald Williams.

131. Deron Johnson, Outfielder, New York Yankees.
One lasting, if unfortunate, memory of Willie Mays comes from the 1973 World Series, just as he was about to retire from the game. Mays, a late-inning replacement for the Mets, fell twice in Game 2, his ninth-inning misplay allowing the Athletics' leadoff batter to get on base and set up a tying rally. As *The New York Daily News* wrote: "What can you say about a 42-year old legend who is retiring after this year?

What you can say is that he looked every bit of his 42 years and had people feeling sorry for him as he floundered around under two fly balls in the sun." That leadoff batter was Deron Johnson, who would be better remembered as a right-handed slugger who hit 245 home runs over 16 seasons.

132. Don Lee, Pitcher, Detroit Tigers.

Don Lee and his father, Thornton Lee, both pitched to Ted Williams. Given that Williams batted .344 with 521 home runs in his career, they did not do too badly. Williams was two for seven with a home run and two walks against Don, in 1960; he batted seven for 26 with a double, a triple but no homers against Thornton, from 1939 to 1947. Thornton even struck Williams out three times. Thornton had a much longer career, but he and Don had very similar winning percentages (father, .485; son, .476) and earned run averages (dad, 3.56; son, 3.61).

133. Bob Lillis, Shortstop, Los Angeles Dodgers.

In 1959, Bob Lillis, who had entered the Dodgers' organization in 1951, was a 29-year-old, 5-foot-11, glove-first shortstop who played most of the season at Class AAA Spokane and hit .286/.315/.379. He got called up to Los Angeles. That same year, Maury Wills, who had entered the Dodgers' organization in 1951, was a 26-year-old, 5-foot-11, glove-first shortstop who played a chunk of the season at Class AAA Spokane and hit .313/.387/.391. He also got called up to Los Angeles. Lillis, who had probably earned consideration as a Rookie Star of 1959 by batting .391/.421/.501 in a 20-game call-up in 1958, hit abysmally for Los Angeles in '59 and played only 30 games; Willis was marginally better offensively, but in those back-of-the-baseball-card days, had a batting average that was 31 points higher, and he had proved himself as a base stealer in the minors. Wills wound up playing 83 games for the Dodgers and helped them win the pennant. Three years later, Wills was a star, setting a major league record with 104 stolen bases; Lillis was the third pick in the expansion draft by the Colt .45s, a team so bad that he was its MVP after a .249/.292/.300 season in 1962 in which he had one home run and an OPS+ of 65.

134. Jimmie McDaniel, Outfielder, Pittsburgh Pirates.

It took nine seasons for Jimmie McDaniel to reach Class AAA, but when he got there in 1958, he had quite a season. He hit .293/.388/.604 with 37 home runs at launching-pad Salt Lake City (Dick Stuart hit 31 homers in 80 games). But in 1959, he was cut early in spring training—he was not about to break up an outfield of Roberto Clemente, Bill Virdon and Bob Skinner—as the Pirates were more concerned about another number from 1958: his 101 strikeouts (the National League leader had had 95). McDaniel kept hitting homers at Class AAA, but he started striking out even more—180 times in 1959 (the major league record was 136), followed by seasons of 164, 174 and 135. He never had a chance to strike out in a major league game.

135. Gene Oliver, Catcher-Outfielder, St. Louis Cardinals.

Phil Niekro told *The New York Times* that he revered the Braves' general manager, Paul Richards, because "he even traded Gene Oliver to Philadelphia to get

Bob Uecker, a catcher who could handle my knuckleball." Oliver, a reluctant but unrepentant catcher, had his own take: "There are only three people who can catch knuckleballers—managers, general managers, and sportswriters." Oliver was often quick with a quip. As a Brave, he had a likely double overruled (the umpire called it foul), a home run on the next pitch waved off (the umpire had called time out so the third-base coach, whom he had ejected along with the manager for arguing, could be replaced) and then was called out on strikes, according to his SABR Bio Project profile. "I'm the only player in history to get a double, a home run and a strikeout in the same time at bat," he said.

136. Jim O'Toole, Pitcher, Cincinnati Redlegs.

Jim O'Toole needed only one minor league season—and what a great season it was, 20–8, 2.44 ERA, 280 innings—to make it to Cincinnati. He had five excellent seasons, but by 1969 he was a minor leaguer, struggling to make the expansion Seattle Pilots. So was Jim Bouton, who wrote about their divergent experiences—Bouton, struggling to pitch effectively himself, hung on to his major league dream, while O'Toole wound up pitching for a semipro team, the Ross Eversoles, in the Kentucky Industrial League. Bouton wrote in *Ball Four*: "Jim O'Toole and I started out even in the spring. He wound up with the Ross Eversoles and I with a new lease on life. And as I daydreamed of being fireman of the year in 1970 I wondered what the dreams of Jim O'Toole are like these days. Then I thought, would I ever do that? When it's over for me, would I be hanging on with Ross Eversoles? I went down deep and the answer I came up with was yes. Yes I would. You see, you spend a good piece of your life gripping a baseball and in the end it turns out that it was the other way around the whole time."

137. Dick Ricketts, Pitcher, St. Louis Cardinals.

A surprising number of athletes played in both the NBA (or a forerunner) and the major leagues in the 1940s, 1950s and 1960s. The list includes Gene Conley, Dick Groat, Chuck Connors, Frank Baumholtz, Hank Biasatti, Howie Schultz, Dave Debusschere, Ron Reed … and Dick Ricketts. (Longtime NBA All-Star Bill Sharman made it to Class AAA in baseball.) Ricketts was a 6-foot-7½ basketball All-American at Duquesne (he averaged 20.1 points and 17.3 rebounds as a senior) and was the

Card 137: Dick Ricketts was one of a surprising number of two-way MLB-NBA players in his day. He was the No. 1 pick in the 1955 NBA draft.

No. 1 pick in the 1955 NBA draft, landing with the St. Louis Hawks. He told *The Pittsburgh Post-Gazette* that year that he had a two-year plan to play both pro sports but preferred baseball, where he was an intimidating pitcher. His SABR Bio Project biography says, "An opposing hitter was quoted as saying that facing Ricketts was 'like standing under a roof and having a pitcher throw at you from up there.'" He gave up the NBA in 1958 after three seasons, saying, "I wanted to prove to myself that I could or couldn't play big league baseball." His brother Dave—who also played basketball and baseball at Duquesne—was a catcher in the Cardinals' chain and caught him in Class AAA. Dick made it to the majors only for part of one season—1959, when he went 1–6, 5.92 for a Cardinals team that had another pitcher with a stellar basketball background, Bob Gibson. Coincidentally, Dick Ricketts played the 1959 season at Rochester with Johnny O'Brien, who, with his twin, Eddie, was an All-American basketball player at Seattle University in the early 1950s (and was the first NCAA player to score 1,000 points in a season).

138. John Romano, Catcher, Chicago White Sox.

John Romano, a slugging catcher who had just had a successful season for the White Sox's Class AAA team, knew he needed to improve his defense. Al López, the manager in Chicago, told him so. Walker Cooper, who became his manager in Indianapolis in 1958, showed him how. "The White Sox said the only thing that was holding me back from not going to the big leagues was not knowing how to catch," Romano said, according to his SABR Bio Project biography. "Walker Cooper helped me very much in that regard." They were "very instrumental in me being a good catcher." They were able mentors—López had set a record by catching 1,918 major league games; Cooper caught 1,224 and was an eight-time All-Star—and helped Romano become a competent catcher, earning All-Star status twice himself in a career shortened by injuries.

139. Ed Sadowski, Catcher, Boston Red Sox.

When Ed Sadowski finally made it to the majors in 1960 at the age of 29, he wore No. 8 for the Red Sox. He was selected by the Angels in that winter's expansion draft, leaving No. 8 available to another Red Sox rookie in 1961: Carl Yastrzemski. No one else has worn it since, of course. Two of Sadowski's brothers and a nephew also played in the big leagues, but the Sadowski whom Ed played with in 1963—Bob—was no relation. Sadowski died of ALS—Lou Gehrig's disease—in 1992.

140. Charlie Secrest, Outfielder, Kansas City Athletics.

Charlie Secrest played with Kent Hadley on the 1958 Little Rock Travelers. Hadley (34 home runs) and Secrest (21) were big boppers for the Travelers, but this was out of character for Secrest, who never hit more than six homers in any of his other nine minor league seasons. (He never made the majors.) The '58 Travelers were in the middle of the pack in the Southern Association with 128 homers in 154 games, but few would have known it as the team did not average even 900 paying customers a game. The next year, those Travelers were the Shreveport Sports, and Secrest was a Portland Beaver, homering only twice.

141. Joe Shipley, Pitcher, San Francisco Giants.

Joe Shipley pitched for two dozen teams in the majors, the minors and winter ball over 13 years and couldn't consistently find the plate for any of them. His best walks per nine innings for any team came, oddly enough, with the Giants—nine walks in 20 innings in 1960. He averaged six walks per nine innings in the minors. Felipe Alou is widely quoted saying that Shipley once threw a ball over the screen at Seals Stadium in San Francisco and hit a fan. "I heard he was ordered to hit someone," Alou said. Another legend is that Shipley once hit a minor league batter … in the on-deck circle. Sadly, finding confirmation of these stories is infinitely harder than finding the stories.

142. Dick Stigman, Pitcher, Cleveland Indians.

Cleveland could have had a rotation packed with star left-handers in the 1960s. Dick Stigman came up in 1960, a year before Sam McDowell first pitched in Cleveland and three years before Tommy John arrived. But Stigman was traded to Minnesota before the 1962 season and John was sent to the White Sox in '65. Stigman immediately led the American League in winning percentage (12–5, .705) and John won 286 games elsewhere. Stigman once pitched 10⅓ innings of no-hit ball in the minors, on the same night Harvey Haddix pitched 12 perfect innings for the Pirates before losing in the 13th. Stigman was born in Nimrod, Minnesota. Really.

143. Willie Tasby, Outfielder, Baltimore Orioles.

Before McClymonds High School in Oakland fielded Frank Robinson, Curt Flood and Vada Pinson in the early 1950s, it was Willie Tasby's school. Tasby was only the latest McClymonds Warrior to move on to pro ball when he signed with the St. Louis Browns before the 1950 season. And soon after him came Robinson, a Hall of Famer with 583 home runs and the first Black manager in Major League Baseball; Flood, a defensive stalwart who played a starring role in the players' fight against the owners over labor rights; and Pinson, who combined speed and power over 18 seasons. Tasby never hit those heights but did play six seasons in the majors. (Basketball great Bill Russell also attended McClymonds, and Robinson played with him on the 1952 state championship basketball team. And MC Hammer, who once worked for the Oakland A's, graduated from McClymonds.)

144. Jerry Walker, Pitcher, Baltimore Orioles.

Paul Richards built the Orioles in the late 1950s with an emphasis on young pitching, and Jerry Walker was in the vanguard of that youth movement. He signed with the Orioles out of high school at age 18 and, because of his $20,000 bonus, spent the season in Baltimore, pitching only 27⅔ innings. Two years later, at age 20, he became the youngest pitcher to start an All-Star Game. Baltimore was also pushing young pitchers like Milt Pappas, Steve Barber, Chuck Estrada and Jack Fisher through its system. Walker was one of the unlucky ones whose career was curtailed by injuries, and he missed the Orioles' glory years of the later '60s. Maybe he should have switched to the outfield like Hal Jeffcoat; in 1960, he hit .368/.400/.421, and in 1962, he homered three times.

145. Dom Zanni, Pitcher, San Francisco Giants.

In 1954, Dom Zanni was a hard-throwing 23-year-old for the Sioux City Soos of the Class A Western League, and he was one out away from pitching a no-hitter. The batter in the way was Earl Weaver, the future manager. "I'll never forget Weaver saying, 'Just throw a strike, buddy, and that's the end of your no-hitter,'" Zanni recalled in a 1994 interview with Chuck McAnulla for *Sports Collectors Digest*. "But he just popped it up to second. That's Weaver for you. He would bother you for everything." Weaver, an infielder, hit 38 minor league home runs in 5,196 plate appearances; Zanni, a pitcher, hit 19 minor league home runs in 1,057 plate appearances.

146. Jerry Zimmerman, Catcher, Boston Red Sox.

Major league umpires went on strike for a day in August 1978 in an effort to gain recognition for their union, leaving baseball to fill in with amateur and semi-pro umps. And, for an inning in Toronto, coaches. When the Twins played the Blue Jays, only two amateur umpires were on hand for the start of the game, so Jerry Zimmerman, the Twins' bullpen coach, umpired at third base; Don Leppert, a Blue Jays coach, umpired at second. When a third amateur ump arrived in time for the second inning, Zimmerman and Leppert were back on their benches. It was the first time since 1941 that active players or coaches had acted as umpires, Twins Trivia said.

147. Cubs Clubbers: Long-Banks-Moryn.

The 1958 Chicago Cubs did indeed hit for the power that was the basis for this card. They led the National League in home runs with 182 as shortstop Ernie Banks hit 47, outfielder Walt Moryn hit 26 and first baseman Dale Long hit 20. Two more Cubs knocked out 20-plus homers as well: outfielders Lee Walls (24) and Bobby Thomson (21). The power was short-lived; the '59 Cubs were third in homers with 163, and only Banks surpassed 20 (he hit 45). Long already had a home run distinction—in 1956, he became the first major leaguer to homer in eight consecutive games, for the Pirates.

148. Mike McCormick, Pitcher, San Francisco Giants.

When he was traded to the Giants in December 1966, Mike McCormick joined a pitching staff that included Ray Sadecki, who had been acquired seven months earlier. Both were left-handers. Both had been 17-year-old signees who had received $50,000 bonuses. Both had success at a young age (McCormick won an ERA title at 21, Sadecki won 20 games at 23). With expectations low after troubled 1966 seasons, both had perhaps their best year in 1967 (McCormick was 22–10, 2.85 ERA, 118 ERA+; Sadecki went 12–6, 2.78 ERA, 121 ERA+). Many of their career numbers were also eerily similar, McCormick over 16 seasons and Sadecki, who did pitch more in relief, in 18 seasons.

Player	W-L	Pct.	GS	IP	HR	ERA+
McCormick	134–128	.511	333	2,380	256	96
Sadecki	135–131	.508	328	2,500	240	98

149. Jim Bunning, Pitcher, Detroit Tigers.

Plenty of roads are named after baseball players, from Babe Adams Highway to Zach Wheat Drive. But very few interstates are. Part of Interstate 70 is named for George Brett (in Kansas City, of course) and another section across Missouri is named for Mark McGwire (in St. Louis, naturally). Then there is I-471, a five-and-three-quarter-mile stretch across Northern Kentucky to Cincinnati, named for Jim Bunning. After retiring from baseball, Bunning was elected to the City Council in the Cincinnati suburb of Fort Thomas, Kentucky, and later to the State Senate, the U.S. House of Representatives (six times) and the U.S. Senate (twice). He was a conservative politician, but he was one of the four players who nominated Marvin Miller to become head of their till-that-time relatively tame union, and after baseball he became a player agent, with 30 clients at one point. His reputation was marred by comments he made about a Senate opponent and about Ruth Bader Ginsburg (he apologized). Numerous fellow Republicans turned on him, but he was unbowed. "When you've dealt with Ted Williams and Mickey Mantle and Yogi Berra and Stan Musial," he said, according to his *New York Times* obituary, "the people I'm dealing with are kind of down the scale."

150. Stan Musial, Outfielder-First Baseman, St. Louis Cardinals.

Can you imagine the Yankees trading Mickey Mantle or Joe DiMaggio? The Pirates dealing Roberto Clemente? The Tigers sending away Al Kaline? The Cardinals did in fact contemplate trading Stan Musial. Not once, but three times. In 1956, *The Sporting News* reported that it was investigating talk that the St. Louis general manager, Frank Lane, was "prepared to trade Musial to the Phillies for Robin Roberts," George Vecsey wrote in his book *Stan Musial: An American Life*. The owner, August Busch, apparently rebuffed the idea—although Lane then traded the popular and productive Red Schoendienst, Musial's great friend. In 1959, as recounted by James Giglio in *Musial: From Stash to Stan the Man*, *The Sporting News*—which, based in St. Louis was quite tapped in to the Cardinals—reported that the aging Musial, who was in the midst of his worst major league season to date, would be traded that fall for the aging Yankees catcher Yogi Berra (a St. Louis native). Again, nothing came of it. But the next

Card 150: Stan Musial was a Cardinal for life ... but it almost wasn't that way. The team considered trading him several times.

season, when Musial started slowly, Manager Solly Hemus cut his playing time in embarrassing fashion, Giglio wrote, and Hemus told reporters that Musial had been benched. Stories circulated that Musial was considering retirement, but quiet discussions began about his going to the Pirates. Musial, after all, was from Donora, in the Pittsburgh area, and the Pirates, chasing a pennant, had needs at first base. Pittsburgh was unwilling to give up young players for a 39-year-old, though. Musial began to hit and St. Louis began to win and The Man played another three seasons. All, of course, for the Cardinals.

151. Bobby Malkmus, Second Baseman, Washington Senators.

Dick Stuart bashed 35 home runs in 1961 and got one MVP vote ... the same as Bobby Malkmus, a part-timer who hit .231/.276/.327 while playing all over the infield for the last-place Philadelphia Phillies, who finished 47–107–1. Malkmus didn't have power (seven home runs in 342 plate appearances) and he didn't walk (20 bases on balls) and he didn't steal bases (one, in four attempts). His OPS+ was 62. He didn't hit at all for three months—Malkmus was batting .189 on July 8—and although he picked up the pace, he still hit only .250 (with a mere 12 walks) over the final three months of the season. But he did field well, as he generally did. Still ... an MVP vote?

152. Johnny Klippstein, Pitcher, Los Angeles Dodgers.

Hard-throwing Johnny Klippstein played his first five major league seasons for the Cubs, and he was a Cubs fan to the end. Literally. He died in 2003 while listening to Chicago's 5–4 victory over the Marlins in 11 innings, according to his obituary in *The Chicago Tribune*. "He passed away just after the Cubs scored that fifth run," his son, John, said. "He was listening to the game as we had it on the TV at his bedside, clutching my hand and blinking to let us know he was aware of what was going on. He stuck out one more victory." Those 2003 Cubs, who made it to the NLCS, won a lot more games than Klippstein's Cubs; they were last or next to last in four of his five seasons.

153. Jim Marshall, First Baseman, Chicago Cubs.

The 1958 Cubs weren't very good—fifth-place finishers at 72–82—but from that team came a surprising number of managers: Jim Marshall, Al Dark, Chuck Tanner, Johnny Goryl and El Tappe (part of the Cubs' doomed College of Coaches experiment in 1961 and '62) and the longtime University of Arizona coach Jerry Kindall. Marshall was an itinerant outfielder (eight minor league seasons, five teams in five seasons in the majors, three years in Japan) before becoming a manager in the minors and, for two and a half seasons, with the Cubs. His managing résumé reflects damning consistency: 75–87 in each of his two full years with the Cubs, followed by 71–65, 74–65, 74–73 and 71–71 back in the minors.

154. Ray Herbert, Pitcher, Kansas City Athletics.

Being a ballplayer must really be fun sometimes. Ray Herbert, a journeyman right-hander, was having a magical season for the White Sox in 1962. His record was merely 4–4, 5.04 after 13 starts, but he went 16–5, 2.45 over the final three and a half months. Still, the most fun may have come when Herbert was batting in what would be his 19th victory, a 9–3 win at Boston. In the top of the ninth, Herbert was set to bat against Hal Kolstad, a rookie prone to allowing home runs (11 in 61⅓ innings). Before he batted, Herbert asked the next hitter, Jim Landis, what he knew about Kolstad, which was nothing. Let's let Herbert pick it up, in an interview with the Chicago Baseball Museum: "I said to Jim, 'This kid don't know me, he's going to think this is just a pitcher, and throw me a fastball. I'm going to hit it out of the park.' Sure enough, the guy throws me a straight batting practice fastball and I hit it over the wall in left field. When I get to home plate Jim turns his back on me! I went into the dugout and all the guys turned their backs on me! Jim must have told them what I said and they were giving me the business."

155. Enos Slaughter, Outfielder, New York Yankees.

Read just about any book that details Jackie Robinson's first season in the major leagues and Enos (Country) Slaughter's name will come up. He is often said to have been among the leading proponents of a proposed strike by Cardinals players—a plot not to play against the Dodgers in the teams' first series of the 1947 season. Many St. Louis players insisted no such plot existed, and Slaughter always said he did not contemplate a strike. Later in the season, Slaughter spiked Robinson's right leg on a play at first base. In *Baseball's Great Experiment*, Julius Tygiel writes that observers were mixed on whether Slaughter had spiked Robinson on purpose. "I've never deliberately spiked anyone in my life," Slaughter said then—but when he was inducted into the Hall of Fame in 1985, he said, "I was accused of spiking Jackie Robinson, but I stepped on a lot of players." Dodgers players at the time were convinced. As Tygiel wrote: "Noting that the cut on his [Robinson's] leg was located eight inches above the ankle on the outside of his leg, one player asserted, 'How in the hell could Slaughter hit him way up on the side of the leg like that unless he meant to do it?'" Slaughter was certain that his history with Robinson kept him out of the Hall of Fame for years, before the Veterans Committee voted him in. Coincidence: Robinson's last hit was a home run over Slaughter's head in Game 6 of the 1956 World Series.

156. Ace Hurlers: Pierce-Roberts.

It's unclear how the photo for this card came to be. Billy Pierce, White Sox left-hander, and Robin Roberts, Phillies right-hander, played in different leagues. There was no interleague play. Pierce was on the 1958 AL All-Star team; Roberts was not on the NL team in '58. Chicago held spring training in Arizona, Philadelphia in Florida. They didn't have the same agent, as agents did not exist. Photoshop had not been invented. So how'd this happen?

157. Félix Mantilla, Second Baseman-Shortstop-Outfielder, Milwaukee Braves.

In 1959, Félix Mantilla was listed on his baseball card as 6 feet 1 and 160 pounds. In 2003, Mantilla sure wasn't 160 pounds; he was way north of 200, disguised only marginally by the guayabera shirt he was wearing. I had run a race in Chicago, the San Juan 8K, as part of a Puerto Rican Day celebration, and Mantilla was handing out age-group awards. I stuck around for mine just because I wanted to shake

Mantilla's hand. He no longer looked like an athlete, but he was quite gracious with an adoring crowd.

158. Walt Dropo, First Baseman, Cincinnati Redlegs.

The Boston Red Sox couldn't find a regular first baseman for three decades. From the late 1930s until the late 1960s, Boston did not have the same player start 100 games or more at first in three consecutive seasons. (George Scott broke the drought with a run at first from 1966 to 1968 ... and then was moved to third base.) In 1950, however, it may have looked as if the Red Sox would not have a first-base problem, because of Walt Dropo. He was a 27-year-old rookie, but what a rookie season. He hit .322/.378/.583, with 34 home runs. He led the league in RBIs (144) and total bases (326) despite not being called up from Class AAA until May 2. But 1950 was a year when everyone hit, and in 1951, Dropo didn't, and he was sent to AAA. In June 1952, he was traded, and Boston was on to a revolving door of Billy Goodman, Dick Gernert, Harry Agganis, Norm Zauchin, Mickey Vernon, Pete Runnels, Vic Wertz, Dick Stuart, Lee Thomas and lesser lights. That was right-handers and left-handers, big bashers and slap hitters, youngsters and veterans, a Greek god in Agganis and a Strangeglove in Stuart. And 30 years of first-base futility.

159. Bob Shaw, Pitcher, Chicago White Sox.

Bob Shaw had wonderful seasons with the White Sox, the Braves and the Giants. He beat Sandy Koufax, 1–0, in a World Series game. But he may be best known for someone else's cheating. In the autobiography he wrote with Bob Sudyk, *Me and the Spitter*, Gaylord Perry discussed in detail how he learned the spitball from Shaw in the Giants' spring training in 1964. Perry (or Sudyk) wrote: "I noticed right away that some of his pitches traveled to the plate in a very unnatural way. My eyes near popped from my head. I knew how Tom Edison felt when he discovered the electric light. Bob Shaw promptly became my idol. Shaw threw the illegal spitball, one of the best I've ever seen." Beginning that season, Perry did, too.

160. Dick Groat, Shortstop, Pittsburgh Pirates.

Dick Groat won the National League's MVP Award in 1960 (he hit .325), and he was on World Series champions in Pittsburgh and St. Louis. He played 14 years in the majors and not a day in the minors. But he may have been a better basketball player than baseball player. He was a two-time All-American guard at Duke, where he averaged 25.2 points per game as a junior and 26 as a senior, when he was the college Player of the Year. For a year he juggled baseball and the NBA, where he averaged 11.9 points a game for the Fort Wayne Zollner Pistons. "I loved pro basketball," he said in his SABR Bio Project profile. "Basketball was always my first love, mainly because I played it best and it came easiest to me." Red Auerbach nearly became his coach at Duke—Auerbach was hired in an amorphous role because the head coach had cancer and Duke thought it would need a quick replacement, but the coach pulled through and Auerbach left. Lefty Driesell was also on the Duke team when Groat was starring, and he told Joe Posnanski that he thought Auerbach might have taught Groat the jump shot.

161. Frank Baumann, Pitcher, Boston Red Sox.

Ray Berres was the pitching coach of the White Sox for most of two decades, and there was a reason (besides spacious Comiskey Park) for Chicago's almost unbroken run of good pitching then: Ray Berres. Frank Baumann was traded from Boston to Chicago in midcareer, and, according to his SABR Bio Project biography, he said, "The best coaching I got was from Ray Berres." He also said, "I learned more with Chicago in four days than I did during my five years in Boston." He had won 13 games with the Red Sox; he went 13–6 in his first season with the White Sox and led the American League in ERA (2.67). Baumann was hardly the only pitcher who swore by Berres. Bob Shaw did, too. So did Gary Peters, Tommy John, Joel Horlen, Juan Pizarro and even veterans like Virgil Trucks, Turk Lown and Jerry Staley.

162. Bobby Gene Smith, Outfielder, St. Louis Cardinals.

Baseball-themed cards appeared before the Civil War, according to *The Card: Collectors, Con Men, and the True Story of History's Most Desired Baseball Card*, and the first mass-produced cards appeared in New York City in the 1860s. In the 1880s, *The Card* says, the first cards that fans nowadays would recognize were created. Photos were used, but they tended to be highly posed studio shots. Portraits, not photos, were common in the early decades. As late as 1953, Topps's set comprised beautiful portraits, but the next year photos took over the cards. By 1957, Topps cards all had color photos. Still, as a Bobby Gene Smith card indicates, even in 1959 there was the occasional portrait or massaged photo that looked more like a baseball Monet. Smith, a .243/.284/.331 hitter with a nondescript name, didn't stand out as a ballplayer, but his 1959 card did. So much that the same photo was used on his 1960 card even though by then Smith was a Phillie; the hat was changed (even the color) and the Cardinals name and logo were airbrushed out.

Card 162: This Monet–like Bobby Gene Smith image was used on his 1959 *and* 1960 cards, even though he was traded between seasons. The magic of airbrushing.

163. Sandy Koufax, Pitcher, Los Angeles Dodgers.

I hadn't realized how neatly Sandy Koufax's career broke down into six-year segments—one in which he was basically a league-average pitcher, the other in which he was one of the greatest pitchers ever in the game. Take a look:

Years	W-L	Pct.	ERA	IP	SO/9	BB/9	HR/9
1955–60	36–40	.474	4.10	691.2	8.9	5.3	1.15
1961–66	129–47	.733	2.19	1632.2	9.4	2.3	0.64

Koufax spent his first six seasons pitching in Ebbets Field and the Los Angeles Coliseum (with its left-field fence 251 feet from home plate, although with a 40-foot screen atop it). After pitching in the Coliseum one more year, in 1961, he moved to the Matterhorn-like mound at Dodger Stadium for his final five seasons. The only thing Koufax led the league in during his first five seasons was wild pitches, once. In the final six seasons, he led the league in ERA five times in a row, strikeouts four times, strikeouts per nine innings five times, WHIP four times, complete games twice and shutouts twice. And he was not pitching Jacob deGrom–like short seasons—his final two years, despite an arthritic elbow that forced his retirement, he led the league in batters faced. He won the Cy Young Award three of his final four seasons; in that fourth he was 19–5, 1.74 but finished third in the voting when he started only 29 games because of injuries.

164. Johnny Groth, Outfielder, Detroit Tigers.

Among major leaguers who stole at least 19 bases in their career, Johnny Groth was the worst thief since at least World War II. Probably since before the Depression and maybe back to World War I. Groth, once a Detroit Tigers phenom who quickly leveled out, stole 19 bases and was caught 42 times in his 15-year career. That's a 31.4 percent success rate. One year, he was thrown out 10 times in 12 attempts; another year, nine times in 12 attempts. His managers did not tend to steal a lot, but maybe they tried the hit-and-run while Groth was on base and it just kept failing. Caught stealing numbers are not all available in earlier decades, and it is possible that a couple of players from the teens and '20s, Ray Powell and Zeb Terry, were worse; they stole bases at around a 27 percent clip in the seasons for which the CS data is available. But for some reason their managers never said, "Stop running."

165. Bill Bruton, Outfielder, Milwaukee Braves.

Baseball players fudging their ages has been part of the game for a century or more. Pee Wee Reese and Phil Rizzuto misstated their ages by a year. So did Hoyt Wilhelm. In *Ball Four*, Jim Bouton wrote that his Yankees teammate Roland Sheldon had shaved six years off his age, believing the team would not sign him otherwise. Bill Bruton made a similar decision. He was playing for a semipro team and was scouted by the Boston Braves' Bill Yancey, according to *Crossing the Line*, and Yancey suggested that he make himself younger so he would be attractive to sign. Suddenly the 24-year-old Bruton was 20 and receiving an invitation to the Braves' minor league camp. With a focus on Latino players in recent decades, the practice remained in place, just at younger ages—Miguel Tejada, Rafael Furcal and Bartolo Colón all adjusted their ages as teenagers. It went even further: Danny Almonte was 14 when he pitched in the 2001 Little League World Series as a purported 12-year-old.

166. Destruction Crew: Minnie Miñoso-Rocky Colavito-Larry Doby.

If you look at Larry Doby's card in this set (No. 455), you'll see he is listed as playing for the Detroit Tigers, *not* the Cleveland Indians. Doby did in fact open the season with the Tigers, but he had been traded by Cleveland's general manager, Frank Lane, to Detroit on March 21. So this card was obviously produced before March 21, when he, Rocky Colavito and Minnie Miñoso were still expected to be a force in Cleveland. None of these guys lasted in Cleveland, in fact—Lane traded both Colavito and Miñoso before the 1960 season. Cleveland, which finished second in 1959, wouldn't finish that high again until 1994.

167. Duke Maas, Pitcher, New York Yankees.

The Great American Baseball Card Flipping, Trading and Bubble Gum Book has an entry for Duke Carmel, lamenting the disconnect between his perfect baseball name and his perfectly forgettable baseball career. The authors say that "should you be considering a name such as Babe, Pee Wee, or Rocky for your firstborn son, it would perhaps be best to check out the little rascal's reflexes before you go about making it official." They could have written that about Duke Maas, whose name wasn't really Duke, but Duane; he was called Duke when he was quite young because either he or his father wasn't fond of the name Duane (accounts vary, his SABR Bio Projects biography says). Maas had a wonderful name, too, but an exceedingly ordinary career: 45–44, 4.19, 91 ERA+. And a 15.43 World Series ERA. A perk of being a '50s Yankee: World Series appearances.

168. Carroll Hardy, Outfielder, Cleveland Indians.

Some players carved careers out of being pinch-hitters. Carroll Hardy carved out notoriety. In September 1960, Ted Williams fouled a pitch off his foot in the first inning of a game in Baltimore and had to be replaced. As Hardy recalled to *The Los Angeles Times* in 2009: "They said, 'Hardy, get a bat; you're the hitter.' So I grabbed a bat and ran out there and hit into a double play." No one recognized the uniqueness of that at-bat at the time, Hardy said, but a few months later a Boston sportswriter told him he was the only player to pinch-hit for Williams, who had retired after the 1960 season. (Hardy also replaced Williams in left field on September 28, 1960, after Williams had homered in his final career at-bat: "Hub Fans Bid Kid Adieu.") Hardy's first major league home run came as a pinch-hitter for … Roger Maris, in 1958. And he pinch-hit for Carl Yastrzemski three times in Yaz's rookie year, 1961. (Hardy was two for three.) Hardy was, however, only a .191 batter in his career as a pinch-hitter.

169. Ted Abernathy, Pitcher, Washington Senators.

It was the summer of 1960, and even a young baseball fan could recognize that there was something very different about Ted Abernathy. He was a tall, gangly right-hander scrambling to resurrect his career with Class AAA Louisville, but he was not some over-the-top fireballer in town to come out of the bullpen against my Indianapolis Indians; no, Abernathy was nearly scraping his knuckles on the dirt as he befuddled batters with a submarine delivery. It was not something you saw every day. Or every year. Submariners have a long history in the game, at least back to Carl

Mays (think Ray Chapman). Over the years there have been some other notable submariners—Elden Auker back in the '30s and '40s, star relievers Kent Tekulve (with noteworthy Pirates teams) and Dan Quisenberry (a Royals star) in the '70s and '80s, Mark Eichhorn (one of the last 100-plus-inning relievers, with the Blue Jays). Abernathy was an important part of that time line. Tekulve often noted Abernathy's influence on him (he was a kid in Cincinnati when Abernathy was pitching for the Reds). "Ted was who I copied my delivery from after I decided to move away from my natural sidearm delivery," Tekulve said, according to Abernathy's SABR Bio Project biography. Like many submariners, Abernathy took up the pitch as a last-ditch effort to salvage his career, going from a sidearm delivery to one way, way below sidearm. The salvage project worked: Abernathy led his league in saves twice and in games pitched three times after resurfacing in the majors at age 30. The occasional submariner still pops up—Tyler Rogers led the NL in games pitched in 2021 with the Giants.

170. Gene Woodling, Outfielder, Baltimore Orioles.

Across 17 seasons and with six teams, Gene Woodling was a good and remarkably consistent hitter. His career slash line was .284/.386/.431. In six seasons with the Yankees, he hit .285/.388/.434. In five seasons with the Indians, he hit .280/.380/.430. In four seasons with the Orioles, he hit .280/.387/.424. Heck, as a 39-year-old playing with the second Senators franchise and the Mets, he hit a combined .276/.376/.424. There were two major exceptions: He didn't hit left-handers all that well and he crushed it in his five World Series. In 104 Series plate appearances, Woodling batted .318/.442/.529, with 19 walks and eight strikeouts. (And his teams won all five of those World Series.)

171. Willard Schmidt, Pitcher, Cincinnati Redlegs.

Willard Schmidt had a rough half-hour on April 26, 1959. It began well—called on in the top of the third with the Reds trailing the Braves, 3–0, he induced an inning-ending double play—but then it became bruising. The second batter in the bottom of the third, he was hit by a pitch from Lew Burdette (who would not hit another batter all season). Before the inning was over, with Cincinnati scoring six runs, the Braves were on their third pitcher, Bob Rush, who hit Schmidt again. It was the first time in modern major league history that a batter had been hit in one inning by two different pitchers. (It has happened six times since, according to Bob Lemke, an author and memorabilia expert.) Schmidt's bruising wasn't over. In the top of the fourth, Johnny Logan led off with a line drive that hit Schmidt on his pitching hand, knocking him out of the game.

172. Kansas City Athletics Team Card.

The Athletics played in Kansas City for 13 seasons (1955–67) and never had a winning record. Never came close. Their best winning percentage was .452, their best win total was 74. So the team moved to Oakland in '68 and had the franchise's first winning season since 1949. Now it's 2023 and the Athletics have played in Oakland more seasons than they did in Philadelphia, 56–54. Now, how long will they play in Las Vegas?

173. Bill Monbouquette, Pitcher, Boston Red Sox.

It isn't easy being a good pitcher on a bad team, and that's what Bill Monbouquette was in Boston from 1960 to 1962: 43–38, 3.45 ERA for teams that finished 217–259. Then in 1963 he was a lucky pitcher on a bad team—20–10 with a 3.81 ERA (only a 99 ERA+) as Boston limped to a 76–85 record. Monbouquette led the league in hits allowed and earned runs. Despite compiling a 5.42 ERA in his final 14 starts, he managed a 6–3 record. He benefited from the magnificent season by Dick (The Monster) Radatz, who saved eight of Monbouquette's victories while going 15–6 with 23 saves. In saving those eight wins for Monbo, Radatz allowed five hits and one earned run in 13⅓ innings.

174. Jim Pendleton, Infielder-Outfielder, Pittsburgh Pirates.

Jim Pendleton was swift. He was versatile (he would play every position but catcher and pitcher in the major leagues). But he was a 29-year-old rookie in 1953 playing sporadically for the Braves when he got a rare start on August 30 in the first game of a doubleheader against the lowly Pirates. He walked in the second, homered in the fourth, singled in the fifth, homered in the sixth and again in the seventh—a four-for-five day with three homers, five runs, five RBIs and the start of a heater that carried him through the season. Over his final month, Pendleton batted .367 (40 for 109) with eight doubles, six homers, 21 runs and 18 RBIs. It might have looked as if he had made it, but the next spring Hank Aaron arrived, and Pendleton spent the rest of his career scraping for playing time.

175. Turk Farrell, Pitcher, Philadelphia Phillies.

Perhaps it's the nickname Turk. Get hung with that name and go into baseball and things can get weird. Richard Joseph (Turk) Farrell was a hard-throwing right-hander whose dad was called Big Turk; the son growing up to be 6 foot 4 and 215 pounds (or so), you couldn't really call him Little Turk. He was a ringleader of hard-drinking carousers on the Phillies called the Dalton Gang. He was renowned for pranks, like dumping ice water on someone. During spring training in Arizona with the Houston Colt .45s, *Hardball Times* related, he enjoyed shooting snakes and rabbits on his walk to the ballpark and was known to leave dead rattlesnakes in a car he had borrowed. Next to him, Steven John (Turk) Wendell was merely quaint. A reliever in the 1990s and 2000s, Wendell wore a necklace of animal claws and teeth, chewed black licorice and brushed his teeth between innings. He insisted that the umpire roll the ball to him on the mound. He leaped over the foul line going on and off the field. Before his first pitch, he would wave to his center fielder, who had to wave back. Good thing these guys were never teammates.

176. Preston Ward, First Baseman-Third Baseman, Kansas City Athletics.

Preston Ward's career numbers in the majors were not much—.253/.326/.380 with 50 home runs—but as a teenager he looked as if he might be something special. He turned pro at age 16 during World War II. In 1946 at 17, he hit .325 with a .426 on-base percentage in the Piedmont League. He batted .325 again when he was 19, with 17 home runs, 21 triples and 30 doubles. He certainly impressed the Dodgers, who had won the pennant in 1947 but made him their Opening Day first baseman in 1948. Not for long, however; he hit an empty .260 and was shipped out to Mobile while some guy named Gil Hodges took over at first base. After being a starter on a defending champion, he became a utility player on a succession of bad teams. He was hitting .338 for the Indians in 1958 when he was traded to Kansas City along with Roger Maris. After the 1959 season, Maris was dealt to the Yankees … but Preston Ward's career was over.

177. Johnny Briggs, Pitcher, Chicago Cubs.

Two players named John Briggs have made it to the major leagues, and they were nothing alike. This John Briggs was a slender white pitcher from California, who entered pro ball out of high school and played mostly in the 1950s. The other John Briggs was a powerful Black outfielder from New Jersey who had spent a couple of years at Seton Hall University and played from 1964 to 1975. This John Briggs couldn't control the strike zone (4.5 walks per nine innings in the majors) and gave up a fair number of home runs (23 in his 165⅔ innings), leading to a career of 59 games over five seasons marred by a 5.00 ERA. The other John Briggs hit for power and took his share of walks while lasting 12 years in the majors and forging a 121 OPS+.

178. Rubén Amaro, Shortstop, Philadelphia Phillies.

In 1964, Rubén Amaro won a Gold Glove despite playing fewer than half of the Phillies' games at shortstop (79) and 42 percent of the innings, according to his SABR Bio Project biography. Bobby Wine, who had won the Gold Glove in 1963, had the majority of the starts and 52 percent of the innings (and was *third* in the '64 Gold Glove voting, which was done by the league's players). Their defensive numbers were quite similar: Fielding percentage—Amaro, .971; Wine, .965. Range factor—Amaro, 4.87; Wine, 4.87. Double plays per nine innings—Amaro, 0.646; Wine, 0.653. Amaro was said to have better range, Wine a better arm. Unfortunately for the Phillies, neither had a decent bat.

179. Don Rudolph, Pitcher, Chicago White Sox.

Don Rudolph's renown was far greater than warranted for a pitcher who was 18–32, 4.00 with four franchises over six seasons. Fans knew Rudolph

Card 179: Don Rudolph was renowned not for his life on the mound but his wife on the stage. She was a burlesque dancer.

wasn't a very good pitcher, but they also knew his wife was a burlesque dancer, with the stage name Patti Waggin. (Like many a ballplayer, Patricia Hardwick had fudged her age; born in 1926, she said she was born in 1934. And Don sort of used a stage name, too; his first name was actually Frederick.) Rudolph first saw her at a club in Colorado Springs when he was a minor leaguer, according to an article at *Hardball Times*, but she would not go on a date with him. He saw her again in the off-season in his hometown, Baltimore, and this time she said yes. They married in 1955, two years before his major league debut, and word eventually leaked about his wife. Rudolph did not display discomfort about his wife's profession and even helped as her manager and, when needed, as off-stage help. (I recall that once, when he was a minor leaguer in Indianapolis, the papers reported that she was performing in town.) She responded to letters from fans, which she later compiled in a book, *Fan Letters to a Stripper*. Patti retired from her chosen profession in the early '60s; Don retired from his in the mid-'60s.

180. Yogi Berra, Catcher, New York Yankees.

Yogi Berra looked funny, and he talked funny, but he was serious about playing. He caught at least 120 games eight years in a row—the first catcher to manage that. (Five catchers have done so since he retired in 1965.) He is 20th in career games caught, although he averaged more innings per game than all but three of the 19 players ahead of him. In his eight-year stretch of keeping Yankee backups on the bench, Berra played in 90 percent of the team's games. Although the common narrative was that he struggled to become a good catcher, Berra threw out 49 percent of would-be base stealers in his career, including 52 percent in his eight-year run as a literal everyday catcher. And he could hit a little.

181. Bob Porterfield, Pitcher, Pittsburgh Pirates.

Calvin Coolidge became president on August 2, 1923, upon the death of Warren Harding. Erwin Cooledge (Bob) Porterfield was born eight days later, so maybe Cooledge was a misspelled recognition of the new commander in chief. Porterfield served in World War II but later told what Gary Bedingfield at *Baseball in Wartime* called "an elaborate story about combat jumps with the 82nd Airborne Division at the Battle of the Bulge, which were reported in many newspapers and other publications during his career. In reality, he spent most of his service time with the 13th Airborne Division who were sent to France in 1945, but were never in combat." It fits—his high school coach said Porterfield fibbed about his high school baseball exploits, too, according to his SABR Bio Project biography. This is the truth: He was 22–10 for the 76–76 Senators in 1953.

182. Milt Graff, Infielder, Kansas City Athletics.

Others may have wanted the Willie Mays card or the Mickey Mantle card, but the one I really wanted after months of collecting was the Milt Graff card. After I found untold numbers of Gary Geiger and Don Demeter and Bob Giallombardo cards, Milt Graff was the final acquisition for my 572-card set. His career was undistinguished—a .181 season as a rookie, followed by five games and a single at-bat the next year. But he had a long career in baseball, mostly with the Pirates. He served in the front office, as an accountant, the traveling secretary and the director of stadium operations when Three Rivers Stadium opened in 1970, and as an infield coach. As a scout, his obituary in *The Pittsburgh Post-Gazette* said, Graff helped devise the report on the Orioles for the 1979 World Series, which the Pirates won.

183. Stu Miller, Pitcher, San Francisco Giants.

Warren Spahn used to say: "Hitting is timing. Pitching is upsetting timing." And Stu Miller upset batters' timing. The little guy (maybe 5 foot 8 and 150 early in his career) never threw hard, but he struck out a surprising number of batters—6.2 per nine innings for his career—because he changed speed on his pitches so well. His lack of velocity entranced sportswriters. "It's doubtful that Miller could throw a baseball through a wet paper sack," wrote Tex Maule of *Sports Illustrated*. "He's got three speeds of pitches—slow, slower and reverse," Jim Murray of *The Los Angeles Times* wrote. However he did it, Miller led his league in ERA once and saves twice, and he was third in career saves when he retired.

184. Harvey Haddix, Pitcher, Cincinnati Redlegs.

You can't pitch 12 perfect innings in one game and not be known for that for the rest of your life, and that was the case for Harvey Haddix. On May 26, 1959, pitching for the Pirates, he retired the first 36 Braves he faced before giving up a run in the bottom of the 13th. But that was merely the most impressive piece of a fantastic two-week run for Haddix. On May 16, he allowed two earned runs, seven hits and no walks with eight strikeouts in a loss to the Cubs. Five days later, he gave up 10 hits but no walks, with seven strikeouts, in a complete-game victory over the Cardinals. Then came the perfect game that wasn't quite perfect: 12⅔ innings, one unearned run, one hit, one walk (intentional), with eight strikeouts. A week later, he threw an eight-hit shutout with two walks and six strikeouts to beat the Cardinals. His two weeks in summary: 38⅔ innings, four earned runs, 26 hits, four walks, 26 strikeouts, a 0.93 ERA, a 0.78 WHIP and, remarkably, only a 2–2 record. But one intimate dance with immortality.

185. Jim Busby, Outfielder, Boston Red Sox.

Jim Busby was a full-time center fielder for only about six seasons, but he is 50th on the career list for outfield putouts, led the league in putouts three years in a row and has three of the top 26 seasons for putouts (12th, 20th, 26th). It helped that he played in some of the most expansive center fields of his era, but he was also fleet. Arthur Daley of *The New York Times* quoted Casey Stengel saying this about Busby in his outfield-covering prime: "That guy there catches singles off his shoe-tops and steals second off pitchouts." His steals don't resonate the way the putouts do—the early '50s were pretty much a no-fly zone for base stealers, and he topped out at 26—but Busby was in the top five in the league in thefts four times. One indicator that he could run: Busby was used as a pinch-runner 68 times from ages 31 to 35.

186. Mudcat Grant, Pitcher, Cleveland Indians.

Jim Grant literally wrote the book on some of the top African American pitchers. He and two co-authors published *The Black Aces: Baseball's Only African-American Twenty-Game Winners* in 2005, profiling the 13 pitchers—Grant being one of them—to do so. Two others have done so since: C.C. Sabathia, in 2010, and David Price, in 2012. Given the paucity of Black pitchers now and that only 11 pitchers in all have won 20 games in the 11 seasons since, we may have seen the last African American 20-game winner. In 1965, when Grant was 21–7 for the Twins, he also won two games and hit a three-run homer in the World Series.

187. Bubba Phillips, Third Baseman-Outfielder, Chicago White Sox.

Mudcat Grant was given his nickname when other players at a tryout camp thought he was from Mississippi and began calling him Mississippi Mudcat, to his chagrin. He wasn't from Mississippi, but Bubba Phillips was, and he reveled in his nickname, which his brother had given him. Hal Lebovitz of the *Cleveland Plain Dealer* wrote that Phillips called himself the Rebel. Phillips and Grant were teammates in Cleveland from 1960 to 1962, and one wonders about the clubhouse dynamics between a man fond of his Southern heritage and another who remembered the Klan terrorizing his neighborhood when he was a child.

188. Juan Pizarro, Pitcher, Milwaukee Braves.

Early in my card-collecting days, I acquired a 1957 Juan Pizarro card and was astounded by his record in his first professional season: As a 19-year-old, he went 23–6, 1.77 with 318 strikeouts in 274 innings at Class A Jacksonville. Yet he never became a star with the Braves, nor did another young pitcher, Joey Jay. Little used, they were only sporadically effective, and after the 1960 season Milwaukee traded both away. Jay immediately went 21–10, 3.53, and he helped the Reds win the pennant and followed that up with a 21–14, 3.76 season. Pizarro spent the next four seasons with the White Sox compiling a 61–38, 2.93 record, averaging an excellent-for-its-day 7.2 strikeouts per nine innings. In his book *I Had a Hammer: The Hank Aaron Story*, Aaron said of the Braves, who kept coming up short after winning pennants in 1957 and '58: "I've always felt that we would have won some more championships if we had hung onto Pizarro and Jay. We needed young pitchers to take over for Spahn, Burdette, and Buhl, and we never came up with them." He added, "I'm not sure I ever saw a pitcher with more ability than Pizarro had when he came to us out of Puerto Rico at the age of nineteen."

189. Neil Chrisley, Outfielder, Detroit Tigers.

His full name was Barbra O'Neil Chrisley, and rest assured he is the only major leaguer with the given name Barbra. He is perhaps the second best of the five major leaguers who played at Newberry College in South Carolina, which is very faint praise. Chrisley's bWAR on offense for his .210/.275/.349, 69 OPS+ career was -1.2. Outfielder Billy Rhiel (.266/.323/.387, 78 OPS+ in 200 games for a 0.1 WAR) leads the Newberry alums, who also include pitchers Al Shealy (5.71 ERA in 123 innings), Cal Cooper (one inning, five runs in his only major league game) and Zack Kelly, who began his major league career at age 27 in 2022 by allowing two runs in three innings over three games.

190. Bill Virdon, Outfielder, Pittsburgh Pirates.

Bill Virdon had a respectable playing career: Rookie of the Year, Gold Glove winner, World Series champion. But Virdon became better known as the first Yankees manager George Steinbrenner fired. The quiet Virdon was not supposed to be the manager in the first place; Steinbrenner wanted Dick Williams, who had quit the Athletics because he had wearied of owner Charlie Finley's meddling. But Finley and Steinbrenner could not agree on a deal for Williams, and Virdon, who had won a division title with the Pirates in 1972, was hired. That 1974 season, the Yankees stayed in contention in the AL East until the final day—they finished two games out of first—and Virdon was named Manager of the Year. But with the team scuffling along at 53–51 the next season, Steinbrenner had Virdon fired—and on came fiery Billy Martin for the first time as Yankees manager.

191. Russ Kemmerer, Pitcher, Washington Senators.

The expansion Houston Colt .45s were glad to be in the major leagues, but not everything about the Colt .45s was major league. Russ Kemmerer recalled that the players were given a cowboy suit to wear on the road—"one of the things we learned to hate." "They were royal blue suits and Texan boots that were blue with an orange design in them," he said in a 2008 interview with the baseball blogger Nick Diunte. "You wore a white shirt that had blue stripes with an orange tie and a ten gallon hat. You wore it on the road. When we went to New York, they said, 'Hey, the rodeo is in town!' The first thing we'd do, to the man, we'd throw them things down and put on regular clothes when we're in public." Makes the Astros' later rainbow uniforms sound tasteful.

192. Charlie Beamon, Pitcher, Baltimore Orioles.

Three years into his professional career, Charlie Beamon was assigned—demoted, really—to the Stockton Ports of the Class C California League and ran up a 16–0 record in nine weeks in 1955. "Going to the Cal League was like a good horse dropping down in class," Beamon said, according to a 2007 article on MiLB.com. He won all 15 starts—all complete games—and a game in relief. He yielded only 80 hits and one homer in 139 innings, fashioning a 1.36 ERA with a hard sinker and a slider. "He broke more bats than they had wood to make," his teammate Ernie Broglio said. It earned Beamon a promotion to Class AAA Oakland, where he won his first start; given that he had won his final two games in 1954, his winning streak was 19. The run was over, however, and he finished up 2–8, 4.81 in Oakland. He had had an earlier streak, though—8–0 as a high school senior, pitching for the McClymonds High team in Oakland that featured Frank Robinson.

193. Sammy Taylor, Catcher, Chicago Cubs.

Sammy Taylor played for a Cubs team that had a College of Coaches and the original "Can't anybody here play this game?" Mets, so it was no surprise that he was involved in one very unusual play, on June 30, 1959. Here's RIP Baseball's account: "Stan Musial was at bat, and the 3–1 pitch from Bob Anderson bounced off Taylor and umpire Vic Delmore and rolled to the backstop. Musial ran to first for the walk. Taylor, instead of retrieving the ball, argued that Musial had fouled it off. That ball was picked up by the Cardinals batboy who handed it to field announcer Pat Pieper, who realized it was in play and dropped it. Meanwhile, Delmore took out a new ball and handed it to Anderson. Musial, seeing that nobody had retrieved the original ball, took off for second base. Anderson threw the new ball toward second but fired it into the outfield instead. Musial saw the ball headed to center field and ran to third. He was surprised to be tagged out by shortstop Ernie Banks, who had the original ball that had been tracked down by third baseman Al Dark. It was ultimately determined that since Musial was tagged with the original ball, he was out."

194. Jim Brosnan, Pitcher, St. Louis Cardinals.

It is hard to contemplate Jim Brosnan without also thinking about Jim Bouton. Aside from the similarity in names, both were baseball diarists. Brosnan wrote *The Long Season* and followed up with *Pennant Race*, while Bouton co-wrote *Ball Four* a decade later with subsequent updates. Both were relief pitchers, traded in midseason, writing in the final year of a decade (1959 and 1969) from a novel perspective in the clubhouse. Both were in many ways outsiders there, although Brosnan was even more so. Brosnan was more professorial, Bouton more pranksterish. Brosnan is more reflective, relying on his own voice to describe life in baseball; Bouton is more circumspective, liberally quoting his teammates in their antics and angst. When Brosnan wrote *The Long Season*, there was no template for such a book, which Bouton clearly had; he also had the help of a co-author and editor, Leonard Shecter. The sensibilities of the books differ in part because of the times in which they were observing and writing; you could no more have written *Ball Four* in 1959 as it was published in 1970 than you could have made the movie *Midnight Cowboy* as it was filmed in 1968. Brosnan wanted to be a writer, and he became one. Bouton wanted to be a ballplayer, and he became a raconteur (among many other things). Baseball literature—sports literature, really—was never the same after Brosnan and Bouton.

Card 194: Jim Brosnan broke ground with his baseball diary, *The Long Season*. Jim Bouton flourished in similar terrain a decade later with *Ball Four*.

195. Rip Repulski, Outfielder, Los Angeles Dodgers.

When Rip Repulski, Ray Jablonski and Steve Bilko, young players in their first full seasons in the major leagues, joined forces on the 1953 Cardinals, they were called the Polish Falcons. It was a reference to their heritage and to a longtime fraternal and sports organization of the same name that in the 1920s and 1930s began sponsoring baseball teams in towns across the country, according to the author Richard (Pete) Peterson. (This came even after Polish immigration shrank drastically after 1911.) By 1940, Peterson said, 10 percent of major leaguers were Polish American. The 1950s Polish Falcons were not the first group of Cardinals standouts of Polish heritage; excellent St. Louis teams of the 1940s included the Polish Americans Stan Musial, Whitey Kurowski and Ted Wilks.

196. Billy Moran, Second Baseman, Cleveland Indians.

Baseball has not always looked fondly on the educational pursuits of its players. Take Billy Moran. He began attending Georgia Tech in the off-season in 1952 but flunked out, he said in an interview for his SABR Bio Project profile, because of engineering physics and engineering calculus. When he was in the Army, stationed in Georgia, in 1955 and 1956, he resumed night classes at Georgia Tech. Then in 1960, he asked the Indians if he could report to spring training 10 days late so he could complete his classes. According to RIP Baseball, General Manager Frank Lane wouldn't agree to it. "If that dumb so-and-so thinks getting an education is more important than playing baseball, he'll not report to Tucson at all," Lane said, *The Akron Beacon Journal* reported in a 1966 article. Sure enough, Cleveland sent Moran to Class AAA, and he did not return to the majors until the next season with the expansion Angels. He did get his degree, in 1963—Angels owner Gene Autry reportedly attended his graduation—although RIP Baseball said Moran "joked that he took so long to complete his classes that one of the instructors in his class was a former classmate."

197. Ray Semproch, Pitcher, Philadelphia Phillies.

After five seasons in the minor leagues, Ray Semproch had had only one really good year, but here he was before the major leagues' first of two All-Star Games in 1959, tied for the National League lead in victories with a 10–5 record. His ERA was excellent, too—3.17, in a season in which the league ERA would be 3.95. After Semproch won the opener of a doubleheader on July 6, the Phillies had won six straight and were a surprising 37–36. Then it all fell apart. Philadelphia lost nine of its first 11 games after All-Star I—Semproch was drilled in one of the losses—and fired the manager during the freefall. The Phillies tumbled to 32–49 in the second half, and Semproch stumbled to a 3–6 record and 5.08 ERA with 106 hits allowed in 83⅓ innings. Three years later he was out of baseball.

198. Jim Davenport, Third Baseman, San Francisco Giants.

Jim Davenport and Willie Kirkland were born six months apart in the same small town, Siluria, Alabama (population 736 in 1960), and wound up as teammates on the first Giants team in San Francisco in 1958. They were even in San Francisco's first Opening Day lineup. Davenport got to San Francisco via Thompson High

School in Alabaster, Alabama, while Kirkland had moved on to Detroit. They were teammates in San Francisco for only three years; the Giants had Willie Mays, Felipe Alou and the unlikely pairing of Orlando Cepeda and Willie McCovey in the outfield, and Kirkland was traded. Davenport, however, spent half a century with the Giants as a player, coach, manager, minor league manager and front-office employee.

199. Leo Kiely, Pitcher, Boston Red Sox.

Leo Kiely was nicknamed the Black Cat, and he was hardly the only pitcher of the era with a feline nickname. There were Harry (the Cat) Brecheen and Harvey (the Kitten) Haddix (so nicknamed, Bill James wrote, because he reminded people of Brecheen, his teammate). Kiely earned his nickname because he started taking a toy black cat to the Red Sox's bullpen, although Bill Lewers in *Six Decades of Baseball: A Personal Narrative* notes that Kiely had dark, heavy eyebrows. Kiely was a man of many nicknames, according to his SABR Bio Project profile, including Blackie, Kiki and Le-Ki.

200. Warren Giles, National League President.

Warren Giles was a highly successful minor league executive, resurrected the debt-laden Cincinnati Reds during the Depression as their general manager (they won pennants in 1939 and 1940 and the World Series in '40) and was president of the National League for 18 years in an era when the leagues were very much distinct entities. And he was almost baseball's commissioner. After the leagues' owners would not renew Commissioner Happy Chandler's contract in 1951, their search included Giles, still with the Reds; Ford Frick, the NL president; and Generals Dwight Eisenhower and Douglas MacArthur. The vote quickly came down to Giles and Frick, and after 17 ballots, according to Giles's *New York Times* obituary, he withdrew his name from consideration, calling the stalemate "harmful to the game." He added that "my first interest in baseball is the welfare of baseball itself." Five days later, he became the NL president.

201. Tom Acker, Pitcher, Cincinnati Redlegs.

Tom Acker wanted to pitch. But on his own terms. After the Redlegs traded him to Kansas City, the Athletics sent him to Class AAA Richmond. He went. Then the A's wanted him to move to their team in Dallas–Fort Worth. He went home, to Fair Lawn, New Jersey, saying he did not want to move his family so far, according to RIP Baseball. After the season the A's assigned him to Shreveport, Louisiana, and Acker retired. But only from professional baseball. He joined the semipro Metropolitan League in New Jersey, first for a team in Paterson and then for seven years with a new team, the Emerson-Westwood Merchants. Early in the next decade, Jim Bouton also pitched for the Merchants.

202. Roger Maris, Outfielder, Kansas City Athletics.

In 1957, Cleveland had an outfield to dream on: Roger Maris, a 22-year-old rookie; 23-year-old Rocky Colavito, who would hit 25 home runs that season; and the veteran Gene Wooding, who hit .321 with 19 homers. So the inveterate wheeler-dealer Frank Lane traded away Woodling. In another trade, in came the veteran Minnie Miñoso, so in 1958, the outfield was Maris, who would hit 28 homers that season; Colavito, who would hit 41 and lead the league in slugging percentage; and Miñoso, who hit .302 with 24 homers. Maris didn't last the season; he was traded to Kansas City. Colavito (a league-leading 42 homers) and Miñoso (21, and with two more excellent years in the tank after this one) survived one more season in Cleveland before Lane sent them packing, too. Maris (who came up as a center fielder), Colavito and Miñoso also all had real defensive assets. The returns for that potentially great outfield, basically, were Woodie Held, who became a low-average, power-hitting fixture at shortstop; Vic Power, a flashy but fading first baseman with limited power; a budding catching star, John Romano; and singles-hitting Harvey Kuenn, who was then moved along after a year. Cleveland had seen enough and forced out Lane, who got his just desserts: He signed on with the new owner of the Athletics … Charlie O. Finley.

203. Ozzie Virgil, Third Baseman, Detroit Tigers.

A total of 895 players from the Dominican Republic had played Major League Baseball through 2023, from Fernando Abad to Aneurys Zabala. The first, however, was Ozzie Virgil. He came up in the majors with the Giants in 1956 but was traded to the Tigers in 1958, when Detroit was one of two teams, along with the Red Sox, that still had not integrated. The team's longtime owner, Walter Briggs, had refused to sign Black players even as his team foundered for years. Briggs died in 1952, and the eventual owner, Fred Knorr, "believed in integration on principle and soon helped contribute $75,000 to develop 17 Black players in Detroit's minor-league system," according to an article by the Foundation for Economic Freedom. That change was not immediately evident to Virgil when Detroit acquired him. "I knew that the Tigers did not have any Black players on their roster nor had never invited one to spring training," Virgil told *Michigan History Magazine*. "I wondered what they were going to do with me." He recalled that his reception was cool on multiple fronts, including among African Americans. "They thought of me more as a Dominican Republic player instead of a Negro," he said in the journal of the African American Registry. "That bothered me." Perhaps he won over some fans in his first game in Detroit, in what was still known as Briggs Stadium: Virgil went five for five.

204. Casey Wise, second baseman, Milwaukee Braves.

Look at his card and you know that Casey Wise would not hit in the current era of exit velocity and launch angle. Hands separated, choked well up on the bat—this is not a formula for taming 100-mph fastballs. But let's face it, Wise did not thrive in the 1950s, either. He had trials with three organizations over four seasons, and his career slash line in 352 plate appearances was .174/.243/.240. His career OPS+ was 42. He hit three home runs (curiously, two came in the same game in 1960). He had hit well in the minors, but never with any power, averaging one home run every 48 games. According to his SABR Bio Project biography, in midcareer he had a very equivocal response to the query "If you had it all to do over, would you play professional baseball" from the National Baseball Hall of Fame: "I don't know."

205. Don Larsen, Pitcher, New York Yankees.

The baseball world knows about Don Larsen and his perfect game in the 1956 World Series, so let's look at how he came to be a Yankee. Larsen was 24 years old and walking more batters than he struck out in 1954, his second year in the majors, when he went 3–21 for the Orioles. But he was a key component of a 17-player trade between the Orioles and the Yankees in the off-season, a deal so complicated it took two weeks to complete even after it was announced. Other principals were Bob Turley and Billy Hunter (the Yankees saw Phil Rizzuto fading fast) headed to New York and Gus Triandos and Gene Woodling off to Baltimore. It is unclear why the trade involved so many other players—filler, mostly—but Yankees general manager George Weiss told *The New York Times*, "When we got Turley and Larsen, we plugged the biggest weakness of the Yankee club—pitching." This came, of course, after the Yankees had won 103 games but failed to win the pennant for the first time since 1948. Casey Stengel told United Press that the Yankees needed to develop a younger pitching staff—Allie Reynolds, 37, and Eddie Lopat, 36, had anchored the rotation and Harry Byrd, about to turn 30, had been a bust after being acquired in an 11-player trade with the Athletics a year earlier. Despite Larsen's disastrous '54 season, *The Times*'s article on the trade said that "most baseball men are agreed that he has the equipment to become one of the game's top hurlers." He didn't—Larsen never won more than 11 games for the Yankees or pitched more than 179⅔ innings. But the Yankees won the next four AL pennants.

Card 206: Carl Furillo and Steve Garvey both wore No. 6 for the Dodgers for years, and their numbers at bat were eerily similar, too.

206. Carl Furillo, Outfielder, Los Angeles Dodgers.

Carl Furillo wore No. 6 for the Dodgers for 15 seasons; Steve Garvey wore No. 6 for the Dodgers for 14 seasons. Many of their career numbers with the team were quite similar:

Player	G	PA	H	HR	BA	OBP	SLG	OPS+	WAR
Furillo	1806	7022	1910	192	.299	.355	.458	112	34.6
Garvey	1727	7027	1968	211	.301	.337	.459	117	38.0

In many other respects, they were quite different. Furillo was an outfielder known for his strong arm, Garvey a first baseman known for his weak arm (after coming up as a third baseman known for his erratic arm). Although each received MVP votes in eight seasons, Furillo was a lesser star on great teams, Garvey an in-the-spotlight star on excellent teams. Garvey was an All-Star eight times as a Dodger, Furillo only twice. And off the field, they were very different. Furillo was a rough, blue-collar guy, often feeling unappreciated. Garvey was a polished college guy whose accomplishments may have been overappreciated in his day.

207. George Strickland, Infielder, Cleveland Indians.

Teams sometimes say they intend to win with pitching and defense, but that is often hollow talk. Take the Cleveland teams of George Strickland, a good-field, no-hit shortstop. In 1954, Cleveland won 111 games even though Strickland hit .213/.314/.313 with a 72 OPS+. The team led the league in ERA, strikeouts and WHIP by large margins—but it also was second in runs scored and slugging and first in home runs and managed a 102 OPS+. Two years later, when Strickland hit .211/.299/.292, 56 OPS+, in a lesser role, Cleveland was again first in ERA, strikeouts and WHIP—but won only 88 games as it sank to fifth in runs and slugging and cratered to an 88 OPS+. The team was second in fielding percentage and easily first in defensive efficiency, but that wasn't enough either. You gotta score runs. And George Strickland couldn't help them do it.

208. Willie Jones, Third Baseman, Philadelphia Phillies.

How does a third baseman get putouts? Pop-ups. Line drives. Forceouts. The occasional tag on a steal or on a throw from the outfield. Willie Jones had a lot of putouts, by a third baseman's standards. Jones, whose name you probably don't recognize unless it's as Willie (Puddin' Head) Jones, is 11th on the career list for third baseman putouts, after a 15-year career that ended in 1961. (Third baseman putouts lag far behind those of other infielders—the record total at third is 2,697; at shortstop, 5,139; at second, 6,552.) The third-base list is populated mostly by 1880s–90s players, Deadball-era players or players from the '20s; only six of the top 20 played substantially after World War II. Putouts per game by third basemen have fallen over the decades. In the top 20, the best putouts/game ratio starts at 1.51, by Billy Nash (1884–98), followed by 1.43 by Jimmy Austin (1909–29) and 1.41 by Jimmy Collins (1895–1908). Jones was unusually busy making putouts in his era, at 1.27 per game, far ahead of contemporaries in the career top 20 like Brooks Robinson, Eddie Yost and Eddie Mathews. More recent great third basemen have been even less likely to score putouts—Adrián Beltré, No. 7 in the career totals, averaged only 0.80 putouts per game, and Mike Schmidt (like Jones, a longtime Phillie), No. 30, averaged only 0.72. Base runners per game have not fluctuated wildly since 1901, when the American League began play, and double plays in 2021 were roughly what they were in 1941. The big change in outs, of course, has been strikeouts. In 2023, each team averaged 8.7 strikeouts per game, up 22.5 percent since 2011 (7.1) and nearly 30 percent since 2001 (6.7). No ball in play, no chance for a putout. Puddin' Head Jones seems safe at No. 11.

209. Lenny Green, Outfielder, Baltimore Orioles.

When Lenny Green played for Baltimore, he also held down a part-time job (when the Orioles were at home): Beginning in 1958, he had his own daily sports radio program. He worked for WUST, whose name derived from its original location in Washington, U Street. WUST had begun in 1947 as a 250-watt station—which means its signal did not go far—focused on R&B. WUST, 1120 on your AM dial, has survived, and now it is a 50,000-watt station—but only during the daytime. At night it drops to 50 watts so it doesn't interfere with the dominant 1120 station in the country, KMOX in St. Louis.

210. Ed Bailey, Catcher, Cincinnati Redlegs.

Ed Bailey was part of a sizable Southern white contingent on the mid-'50s Reds—he was from Strawberry Plains, Tennessee—but he did not have a constricted world view. At a spring training game in Tampa, Florida, according to both *The Great Experiment* and *Crossing the Line*, Bailey and his teammate Brooks Lawrence, a Black pitcher, were removed from the lineup and went up into the stands to watch the rest of the game together. Now, in 1955, local officials had ordered Black players on the Pirates who were not in uniform for their first exhibition game to sit in the section roped off for Black fans. On this day, Bailey sat on the "White" side of the rope and Lawrence sat next to him on the "Black" side. "Boy, this is stupid," Bailey said, both books report. "I'm gonna change this." He removed the rope, and Lawrence said it never went back up. As a player, Bailey was similar to Del Crandall, another left-handed-hitting catcher: a little more power, a little more on-base skill, a little less defensive proficiency and longevity. Fittingly, they were traded for each other in 1963.

211. Bob Blaylock, Pitcher, St. Louis Cardinals.

What Bob Blaylock apparently needed was a major league team in Oklahoma. As an 18-year-old pitching for Ardmore in the Class D Sooner State League, he was 9–1 with a 3.49 ERA (despite 7.5 walks per nine innings). Six years later, pitching for Class AAA Tulsa, Blaylock went 10–1, 2.56. That's a 19–2 record and 2.98 ERA pitching for Oklahoma teams; the rest of his minor league career was 57–73, 3.83. The Cardinals did not relocate from St. Louis, and Blaylock managed only 50 innings for them with a 1–7, 4.42 record.

212. Fence Busters: Hank Aaron-Eddie Mathews.

Which two players hit the most home runs as teammates? Not Ruth and Gehrig, not Mays and McCovey. It's Hank Aaron and Eddie Mathews, who combined for 863 home runs as Braves teammates over 13 seasons. Aaron hit 442, Mathews 421. (Mays and McCovey totaled 800 homers together as Giants, Ruth and Gehrig 772 as Yankees.) As Kenneth Matinale pointed out at Radical Baseball, Aaron and Mathews had a lot more at-bats—more than 2,300 more than Mays/McCovey and more than 4,000 more than Ruth/Gehrig—but 863 is a lot of homers.

213. Jim Rivera, Outfielder, Chicago White Sox.

Jim Rivera most likely would not get a chance to play pro ball today. While in the Army in 1944, he was charged with raping the daughter of an officer at a dance; he was convicted of attempted rape and sent to federal prison in Atlanta. While there he played baseball on a prison team and caught the attention of the owner of the local minor league team, the Crackers, who signed Rivera when he was paroled after five years, in 1949. Three years later he was in the majors, a 30-year-old rookie. He was not a shrinking violet. *The Fort Wayne* (Indiana) *News-Sentinel* reported these tales from a 2012 interview with Rivera, who owned a restaurant in nearby Angola: "He once chided President John F. Kennedy for an illegible autograph on a souvenir baseball, telling him, 'You certainly have to do better than this, John.' Another time, he boasted to former first lady Bess Truman after beating her hometown Kansas City team, 'I'm sure sorry my home run beat your club, but it was a hell of a wallop, eh, Bess?'" He was brash with baseball executives, too. Rivera recalled arranging a deal with the White Sox's general manager, Frank Lane, for a $100 bonus for every base he stole; Lane would get $100 back every time Rivera was caught, however. Rivera stole 25 bases that season ... but he was caught 16 times, so he netted only $900.

214. Marcelino Solis, Pitcher, Chicago Cubs.

Of course you can't trust everything you read on the back of a baseball card, as proved by Marcelino Solis's 1959 card, which says, "The amazing Mr. Solis has pinpoint control." Hmmm. In his first season in Organized Baseball, he walked 50 batters in 69 innings in Class C. The next year, same level, he walked 121 batters in 209 innings. He lost two years to injuries, but in 1956, he walked 100 batters in 154 innings in two Mexican leagues. A year later, still in Mexico, he walked 123 batters in 196 innings. At this point, Solis was 26 years old, had never pitched above the modern equivalent of Low A ball in the United States and had walked ... let's do the math, 5.6 walks per nine innings. The Cubs for some reason decided to sign him and send him to Class AA Fort Worth, where he *did* have almost pinpoint control: 2.1 walks per nine innings, a 15–2 record and a 2.44 ERA. He was called up to Chicago, where the problem was hits allowed and a 6.06 ERA. He never pitched in the majors again, and one website says a 1959 card autographed by Solis himself is one of the hardest gets for '50s cards.

215. Jim Lemon, Outfielder, Washington Senators.

Griffith Stadium in Washington marred many a slugger's career, but it gave life to Jim Lemon's. The Senators inched in the left-field fence in 1955 and moved it in about 15 more feet in 1956, just in time for Lemon's emergence, at age 28, as a full-time player. He hit 27 home runs (and teammate Roy Sievers added 29) for a team whose record had stood at 22 until 1954. Lemon went on to average 28 homers in his five full seasons playing in Griffith Stadium, which he used to full advantage: .275/.344/.524. In all other ballparks, he hit .252/.326/.414.

216. Andre Rodgers, Shortstop, San Francisco Giants.

Their backgrounds and eras were quite different, but in many ways Andre Rodgers was an early version of Shawon Dunston. Both were strong-armed, error-prone shortstops who couldn't lay off breaking pitches but made their major league debut at 22. Rodgers, who grew up playing cricket, not baseball, and became the first player from the Bahamas in the major leagues, hit .249/.328/.365, with an OPS of .694 and an OPS+ of 90. Dunston, coming up three decades later, hit .269/.296/.416, with an OPS of .712 and an OPS+ of 89. Baseball Reference lists Rodgers with 6.2 Wins Above Replacement in 854 games, Dunston 11.5 WAR in 1,814 games.

Card 216: Andre Rodgers was the first major leaguer from the Bahamas and grew up playing cricket. His game was much like that of Shawon Dunston.

217. Carl Erskine, Pitcher, Los Angeles Dodgers.

Perhaps the most touching section of *The Boys of Summer* is Roger Kahn's description of Carl Erskine's loving interactions with his son Jimmy, who was born with Down syndrome the year after Erskine retired from baseball. Youngsters with Down syndrome at that time were often institutionalized, but the Erskines raised Jimmy at home with their other three kids. Carl became an active advocate for educational opportunities for developmentally disabled people and for the Special Olympics. He was 95—and Jimmy was 62, with unusual longevity for someone with Down syndrome—when a documentary, *The Best We've Got: The Carl Erskine Story*, had its premiere in August 2022. "The true beauty of the film will be what Carl has done, quietly but so powerfully, to integrate society and make all feel accepted and welcome," said Ted Green, the filmmaker behind the documentary. Dr. Richard Schreiner, who met Erskine in the 1980s at a support conference for parents of children with Down syndrome, said of Erskine and his wife, Betty, "What they did, their model of raising Jimmy, it was just phenomenal."

218. Román Mejías, Outfielder, Pittsburgh Pirates.

On Opening Day in 1955, the Pirates' starting right fielder was a 24-year-old rookie named Román Mejías, who had a strong arm, speed, some pop and a penchant for hitting—two .300-plus seasons and one 55-game hitting streak in the minors. He went one for three with a walk, and the next day he homered. In the third game of the season, he went 0 for 4, and the Pirates were 0–3. The next game, the Pirates had a new right fielder: 20-year-old Roberto Clemente, who made his first major league start and never came out of the lineup. Pittsburgh experimented pretty liberally with Latino outfielders in the mid-'50s—Carlos Bernier and Felipe Montemayor in 1953; Luis Marquez in 1954; and Mejías, Clemente and Montemayor in '55—but only Clemente had a substantial career.

219. George Zuverink, Pitcher, Baltimore Orioles.

When George Zuverink filled out a questionnaire for the American Baseball Bureau in 1946, his first minor league season, he listed as his ambition "to be the first major league player from Holland, Michigan." He missed by nearly 40 years—an infielder named Bill Morley who is listed from the town played two games for the 1913 Washington Senators—but Zuverink has been the best player from Holland, Michigan, with a 32–36 record, 3.54 ERA and 40 saves over eight seasons. Then again, there have been only three players from Holland, Michigan (Andy Van Hekken pitched five games for the 2002 Tigers). Eleven players, by the way, have been born in the European Holland.

220. Frank Malzone, Third Baseman, Boston Red Sox.

Frank Malzone could field. When the Gold Glove awards were introduced in 1957—one award given at each position covering both leagues—Malzone won for third base. He won a Gold Glove each of the next two seasons, too, when each league gave out an award, before Brooks Robinson began his string of 16 consecutive Gold Gloves. No other Boston third baseman has won the award. Pinky Higgins, his longtime manager and a former Red Sox third baseman himself, told *The Saturday Evening Post* in 1957: "We're not only happy with Malzone; we're practically hysterical about him. I couldn't carry his glove. Neither could anyone else I can remember. He's the best third baseman I've ever seen."

221. Bob Bowman, Outfielder, Philadelphia Phillies.

The 1958 Phillies were a last-place team, but they could hit; they were first in the league in batting average. And they could really pinch-hit; the team's pinch-hitters batted .311/.367/.544, tying the National League record with 64 pinch hits. They also had 11 pinch-hit home runs. Bob Bowman was a major reason for that. He was 13 for 32, with a .406/.429/.781 line and three home runs as a pinch-hitter. Teammate Dave Philley went 18 for 44 for a .409/.469/.591 line, and Rip Repulski added four pinch-hit homers and Wally Post three. Bowman pinch-hit just as often in 1959, but, as frequently happens with pinch-hitters, he didn't hit well (.219/.286/.313) and his major league career was over.

222. Bobby Shantz, Pitcher, New York Yankees.

It was December 1960, and Cardinals general manager Bing Devine coveted Bobby Shantz. Shantz, a 5-foot-6-inch left-handed reliever, had just been taken in the expansion draft by the new Washington Senators. Now the Cardinals and the Pirates were circling the Senators for Shantz, and St. Louis eventually offered three players for him, *The Sporting News* reported: either pitcher Ron Kline or outfielder

Walt Moryn; one of a batch of minor leaguers; and a disgruntled, 25-year-old right-hander—Bob Gibson. "I wanted Shantz to cement our bullpen as the second man behind Lindy McDaniel, just as the Pirates wanted him behind Roy Face," Devine told *The Sporting News*. To get Shantz, he was willing to give up Gibson, who was at odds with manager Solly Hemus and had posted unimpressive 3–6, 5.61 numbers in 86⅔ innings in his second big-league season. Washington didn't want Gibson, though, and swapped Shantz to Pittsburgh for three players who wound up with marginal careers. Still in St. Louis, Gibson went 13–12, 3.24 in 211⅓ innings; Shantz was 6–3, 3.32 in 89⅓ innings. Then Shantz was once again exposed to an expansion draft and was off to Houston, where he pitched only three games before Devine finally landed the reliever he so wanted. Gibson furthered his workhorse excellence in 1962, while Devine decided he didn't need Shantz so much after all—and sent him to the Cubs as part of the price for Lou Brock.

223. St. Louis Cardinals Team Card.

It's one thing to acquire talent, it's another to acquire the right talent. The 1959 Cardinals had three hard-hitting, left-handed-hitting first basemen: Stan Musial, Bill White and Joe Cunningham. In deference to his age, Musial, 38, played 90 games at first, which forced White and Cunningham into the outfield. Cunningham (.345) and White (.302) hit but played subpar defense in the outfield, and their presence kept defensive stalwart Curt Flood on the bench. And the Cardinals finished seventh, next to last. It took two more seasons (and third- and fifth-place finishes) before St. Louis undid the logjam.

224. Claude Osteen, Pitcher, Cincinnati Redlegs.

As a rotation fixture for the expansion Washington Senators, Claude Osteen had plenty of hard-luck losses. Then came his good fortune: a trade to the Dodgers. But the losses kept mounting. In his first four seasons in Los Angeles, Osteen went 15–15, 17–14, 17–17 and 12–18 (leading the league in losses) while compiling an ERA for those years of 2.98. That fourth season was 1968, the Year of the Pitcher, but it was not an auspicious year for Osteen, whose 3.08 ERA was worse than the league average. As Cary Osborne noted in an MLB blog, the Dodgers, who were last in the league in runs scored at 2.9 per game, scored no runs for Osteen five times that season, one run six times and two runs 11 times. He was 5–16 in those games despite a 3.33 ERA. Interestingly, Osteen's best years in Los Angeles came *after* the mound was lowered, beginning in 1969.

225. Johnny Logan, Shortstop, Milwaukee Braves.

Yogi-isms are well known. Loganisms should be, too. The book *Hard-Luck Harvey Haddix and the Greatest Game Ever Lost* rolls out a series of malapropisms from Logan, the fine-fielding shortstop on the tough Braves teams of the '50s. While making an acceptance speech, the book reports, he said, "I'm very, very speechless." And he said, "It's a pleasure to share the rostrum with Stan Musial, one of baseball's great immorals." Logan's SABR Bio Project profile adds more, including this bit of history: "Rome wasn't born in a day." And it adds: "When a teammate referred to a mutual acquaintance, Johnny said, 'I know the name, but I can't replace the face.'" Even if, much as with Yogi-isms, Logan didn't really say everything he is said to have said, it's fun to think he might have.

Card 225: Johnny Logan could match Yogi Berra for malapropisms. "It's a pleasure to share the rostrum with Stan Musial, one of baseball's great immorals."

226. Art Ceccarelli, Pitcher, Chicago Cubs.

And now, a Ceccarelli-ism, from Baseball Reference. Art Ceccarelli pitched one season for the Cubs, but he apparently wasn't overly fond of Wrigley Field, saying: "It wears pitchers down. The winds are unbelievable. Willie Kirkland once hit a home run off me that Ernie Banks called for at shortstop." This is just the kind of baseball story that can turn out to be a tall tale, but Kirkland did indeed homer off Ceccarelli at Wrigley on a breezy day, a three-run shot in the third inning of a game on August 13, 1959. It was one of eight homers as the Cubs won, 20–9, on a day with 10-mph winds.

227. Hal Smith, Catcher-Third Baseman, Kansas City Athletics.

It is fitting that a pitcher and a catcher would team up off the field, too. Hal Smith, then part of the Pirates' catching platoon, and ace reliever Roy Face became a musical act. Smith once made $2,500 a month for four months playing guitar and singing with Face in clubs, according to his SABR Bio Project biography—a healthy sum when he was making $25,000 a year. They even put out a country album, *2 Bucs at the Holiday House*. Smith's SABR bio says that after the Pirates won the World Series in 1960, they played *The Ed Sullivan Show*; an Associated Press retrospective in 2020 says they also played on Perry Como's show. Smith wrote some songs, too, including one with the lament, "My curveball weren't breakin'/my fastball, they's takin'/Oh how they hit me tonight."

228. Don Gross, Pitcher, Pittsburgh Pirates.

Joe L. Brown called it the worst trade he made in his 21 years as general manager of the Pirates: sending Bob Purkey to the Reds for Don Gross. They had similar nondescript seasons in 1957—Purkey was 11-14, 3.86 (ERA+ of 99) in 179⅔ innings for Pittsburgh, Gross was 7-9, 4.31 (ERA+ of 95) in 148⅓ innings for Cincinnati. Purkey was two years older, but Gross had a long history of injuries and a modest history of success. Purkey went on to become the Reds' ace, with a 103-76 record and an

ERA of 3.49 (ERA+ of 112) in seven seasons. Gross, meanwhile, was shunted to relief and threw only 113 innings over three seasons for the Pirates. Gross's 1959 card pictures him with a bat in his hands, and who decided on that? He was a .106 hitter in the major leagues and once injured a finger practicing bunting against a pitching machine.

229. Vic Power, First Baseman-Third Baseman, Cleveland Indians.

Vic Power was known for his glove, not his speed, but he stole home twice in one game—with the team's best hitters at the plate. In the bottom of the eighth inning against the Tigers on August 14, 1958, Power was on third with two out and Minnie Miñoso at bat when the third-base coach, Eddie Stanky, told Power to "go if you can get the jump." He did. The game went to extra innings, and in the bottom of the 10th, Power was back on third, bases loaded and two out and Rocky Colavito at bat. Stanky told Power to be cautious this time, *The Toledo Blade*'s account said, but Power danced off the bag and then took off—sliding in so easily that *The Blade* said catcher Charley Lau made only a token tag. "Just go," was Power's explanation. It was the first time in 47 years that a player had stolen home twice in a game. Power had only one other steal all year. But eight of his career 45 steals were of home. Power had the Twins' first steal of home—with Harmon Killebrew at the plate—in 1962. And he once stole home twice in a spring training game (again with the power-hitting Colavito batting).

230. Bill Fischer, Pitcher, Washington Senators.

The 1959 Senators were awful (63–91), but they had a number of pitchers who became serviceable relievers elsewhere. Fischer was one of them, although he was a starter that season for Washington. He mostly came out of the bullpen in succeeding seasons for Detroit and Kansas City. Russ Kemmerer, Tex Clevenger and Hal Woodeshick all became relievers elsewhere, and the Senators also had Dick Hyde, a solid reliever who actually played most of his career with the team.

231. Ellis Burton, Outfielder, St. Louis Cardinals.

Ellis Burton did not hit many home runs, but they were special. In August 1963, the switch-hitting Burton homered for the Cubs from both sides of the plate against the Braves. The next year, again against the Braves in a September game, Burton once more homered from both sides of the plate. (In a 1961 game for the Class AAA Toronto Maple Leafs, he homered from both sides of the plate in the same inning.) Burton also hit a walk-off grand slam in 1963 against Houston, which had dumped him in spring training. "There's no team in the big leagues I want to beat as bad as this one," he told *The Chicago Tribune*.

232. Eddie Kasko, Shortstop-Third Baseman, Cincinnati Redlegs.

For a guy with such thick glasses, Eddie Kasko had vision. As a manager of the Red Sox, "he discovered that Carlton Fisk and Dwight Evans were more than capable everyday players, converted Bill 'Spaceman' Lee from bullpen also-ran to a starter, and helped make Luis Tiant one of the most memorable and dominant pitchers of the 1970s," the Random Baseball blog said. After being fired as manager, he became a Red Sox scout and then head of scouting. As RIP Baseball noted, he helped draft and develop Mo Vaughn, Jeff Bagwell, Ellis Burks, Dennis (Oil Can) Boyd, Mike Greenwell and Roger Clemens. Those efforts got Kasko, who hit .213 in his one season playing in Boston, into the Red Sox Hall of Fame.

233. Paul Foytack, Pitcher, Detroit Tigers.

Paul Foytack excelled at memorable home runs. In 1956, Mickey Mantle sent a Foytack pitch over the right-field roof—not the fence, the roof—at Briggs Stadium. It was only the second time a fair ball had sailed out of the stadium. Four years later, Mantle punished Foytack again, launching a fastball over the roof, across Trumbull Avenue and into Brooks Lumber Yard across the street—a blast so prodigious that a reconstruction of it in 1985 came up with an estimate of 643 feet in the air. Then in April 1961, Foytack yielded Roger Maris's first home run of his 61-homer season. In a 2007 interview with *The New York Times*, Foytack joked that Maris owed him. "I told Roger he should have sent me $400 a month after that," he said. "If it wasn't for me, he wouldn't have hit 61." The best was yet to come: Pitching in relief for the Angels in 1963, Foytack gave up back-to-back-to-back-to-back home runs to Cleveland, becoming the first pitcher to give up four consecutive home runs. Foytack's SABR Bio Project biography gives this account of manager Bill Rigney's visit to the mound after No. 4: "According to Foytack, upon arriving Rigney said, 'Well, Paul, what do you think?' 'Gee, Bill,' I said, 'I think I am in pretty good shape. There's nobody on base.'"

234. Chuck Tanner, Outfielder, Chicago Cubs.

When Chuck Tanner made it to the majors in 1955, he did not have much of a role. The Braves had the 21-year-old Hank Aaron, swift center fielder Billy Bruton and the solid veterans Bobby Thomson and Andy Pafko in the outfield. First base was foreclosed by the thumpers Joe Adcock and George Crowe. Yet among those sluggers, it was Tanner who, on the first big-league pitch he saw, homered, as a pinch-hitter on Opening Day. That first pitch was his season's highlight—career's highlight, pretty much. Dogged by Achilles problems (and his .261/.323/.388 career slash line), he retired as a player at age 33. He hit only 21 home runs. But that first one was memorable. Only 31 players have homered on their first pitch. Curiously, 16 of them have done so since 2000; from the inception of baseball in the 1800s through 1999, only 15 had. Even more curiously, eight of these first-pitch sluggers were pitchers.

235. Valmy Thomas, Catcher, Philadelphia Phillies.

Valmy Thomas became the first player from the Virgin Islands to play in the major leagues, in the same game in which Andre Rodgers became the first Bahamian to play in the majors—on April 16, 1957. Rodgers was the Opening Day shortstop for the Giants, while his teammate—and road roommate—Thomas came on to catch in the sixth inning. In his final minor league season, 1962, Thomas was critically wounded—shot twice in the chest—by the other man in a love triangle, according to his SABR Bio Project profile. His assailant then killed himself.

236. Ted Bowsfield, Pitcher, Boston Red Sox.

Ballplayers are always looking for an advantage, and Ted Bowsfield thought he had found one. Before the 1959 season, his second in the majors, Bowsfield built a pitching tunnel—he told *The Minneapolis Tribune* at the time that it was like a wind tunnel—at home in British Columbia so he could pitch through the frigid winter and arrive in spring training in great shape. In an interview for his SABR Bio Project profile, he called that tunnel "the worst mistake I ever made in my life." He had not built it wide enough, altered his motion and "from that time on," he said, "I was basically pitching with a sore arm." He did not make the same mistake the next winter—he pitched in Venezuela.

237. Run Preventers: Gil McDougald-Bob Turley-Bobby Richardson.

The 1958 Yankees certainly did prevent runs. They led the league in fewest runs per game, earned run average and double plays turned, and they were second in total fielding runs above average and fewest home runs allowed. Turley played his part, with a 2.97 ERA, and McDougald was third among American League second basemen in double plays despite starting only 113 games at second. Richardson was a part-timer in '58 but played a majority of games at second in 1959 as McDougald became Casey Stengel's Swiss Army knife infielder.

Card 238: Gene Baker was part of the Pirates' influx of minority players, and he is believed to have been Organized Baseball's first Black manager, in Class D in 1961.

238. Gene Baker, Second Baseman, Pittsburgh Pirates.

It was 1953, six years after Jackie Robinson, before the Pirates had a player of color on their roster—Carlos Bernier, an outfielder from Puerto Rico, who was joined briefly by Felipe Montemayor, an outfielder from Mexico. Pittsburgh was only the fourth of the eight National League teams to integrate. But once they started, the Pirates did integrate, and most other teams did not integrate as thoroughly. An African American player, Curt Roberts, was their starting second baseman (and Sam Jethroe played two games) in 1954, and Luis Marquez of Puerto Rico played some. In 1955, Roberts and four Latino players—including 20-year-old Roberto Clemente—were on the roster. In 1956, Roberts and four Latino players were Pirates. Gene Baker came over from the Cubs in 1957 and was joined by two other Black players and three Latino teammates. In 1958—the year the Tigers finally integrated, with a

Dominican player—the Pirates had four Black players and two Latinos. They added another Black player, for a total of five, in 1959—the year the Red Sox at last integrated, the final major league team to do so. Perhaps Pittsburgh eventually integrated so well as part of the legacy of Branch Rickey, who was their general manager from 1950 to 1955. Maybe it was because they were so bad that they concluded that talent (and cheaper talent at that) mattered most. Maybe there was local acceptance, too; the city had been home to two of the best Negro league teams, the Homestead Grays and the Pittsburgh Crawfords. The Pirates' willingness to play so many Blacks and Latinos only grew under Rickey's successor, Joe L. Brown; in 1967, they became the first team to play eight players of color at once—only the starting pitcher was white in their June 17 game. Four years later, Pittsburgh fielded the first all-minority lineup, on September 1. Baker had had his own role in the Pirates' development of minorities' roles. He was believed to be Organized Baseball's first African American manager when he was named player-manager of Class D Batavia in 1961, and the next year he was a player-coach for the Pirates' Class AAA team. And in 1963 the Pirates made him the second Black coach in Major League Baseball, according to his SABR Bio Project biography. He even managed part of one game, after manager Danny Murtaugh and another coach, Danny Ozark, were ejected.

239. Bob Trowbridge, Pitcher, Milwaukee Braves.

Nothing in his career speaks of the Hall of Fame, but there is a hazy link to a Hall of Famer in Bob Trowbridge's background. The mother of the Hall of Famer Eddie Collins was born Mary Meade Trowbridge (and Collins's middle name was Trowbridge). The family has a long history in the United States, arriving from England as early as 1637, according to *History of the Trowbridge Family in America*. The genealogy, unfortunately, provides no link between Mary Meade and Bob, but Collins and Trowbridge, although of different generations, were born only 30 miles apart in New York State.

240. Hank Bauer, Outfielder, New York Yankees.

Casey Stengel certainly had plenty of talent when he managed the Yankees from 1949 to 1960, but he also pulled strings in a way that other managers did not. One of his moves was to make Hank Bauer a leadoff hitter in 1954. Now, Bauer was seven years into his career and about to turn 32, and his *New York Times* obituary described him this way: "a muscular 6 feet and 202 pounds, he played baseball with a fullback's ferocity." He was not the limp middle infielder who frequently batted leadoff in that era, nor was he a base-stealing threat (Bauer swiped 50 bases in his career). In his first six seasons with the Yankees, he was the leadoff man in 7.7 percent of his plate appearances; in his final six seasons in New York, he batted leadoff in 60 percent of them, and he made his presence known. "When Hank came down the base path," the Red Sox infielder Johnny Pesky said in the *Times* obituary, "the whole earth trembled."

241. Billy Muffett, Pitcher, San Francisco Giants.

At the beginning of his professional career, Billy Muffett looked nothing like a future pitching coach. He walked 154 batters in 164 innings as an 18-year-old pitching for the Helena (Arkansas) Seaporters in the Cotton States League. In his first five years in pro ball, he averaged 126 walks a year and never fewer than 5.0 per nine innings. He made it to St. Louis eight years after entering pro ball, but his career never flourished. As a pitcher. As a pitching coach, however, he spent 18 years in the majors with the Cardinals, the Angels and the Tigers, plus about another decade as a minor league coach. His pitchers in the majors included Bob Gibson, a very young Steve Carlton, Nolan Ryan, a very young Frank Tanana, and Jack Morris and Dan Petry.

242. Ron Samford, Shortstop, Washington Senators.

Ron Samford started at second base on one of the best winter league teams of the 1950s. In the winter of 1954–55, the starting outfield for the Santurce Crabbers was Willie Mays (just off an MVP season), 20-year-old Roberto Clemente (about to make his major league debut) and Bob Thurman, a powerful veteran of the Negro leagues. The league MVP, however, was Crabbers shortstop Don Zimmer, who had an OPS of .971, according to a longtime SABR member, Michael Bradley. Other top players included the former Negro leaguers Bus Clarkson, an infielder who led the team in RBIs (and hit .294 in Class AAA at age 40), and George Crowe. The pitching staff included Sad Sam Jones and Ruben Gomez. The team won both the Puerto Rican Winter League and the Caribbean Series. "With a couple more pitchers," Samford said in a 2021 article published in *Forbes* after his death, "I feel we could have won a pennant in the National League."

243. Marv Grissom, Pitcher, St. Louis Cardinals.

Marv Grissom had an excellent vantage point from which to watch The Catch—Willie Mays's improbable snag of Vic Wertz's line drive in the eighth inning of Game 1 of the 1954 World Series. Grissom was in the Giants' bullpen, left there when Leo Durocher called on Don Liddle to face Wertz. But Grissom had little time to celebrate The Catch, because Durocher now picked him to get out of the mess that was still on the bases—runners on first and third and one out in a tie game. Liddle is said to have told Grissom when he came on to replace him, "I got my man," although it took a ball that carried 450 feet, according to *The New York Times*. Now Grissom would have to retire Dale Mitchell (five years later, the last batter in Don Larsen's perfect Series game). Grissom, a 36-year-old right-handed reliever having the year of his career, relied on a fastball and, according to Arnold Hano in his delightful *A Day in the Bleachers*, an account of the game, a screwball he had only recently picked up. "I'll win 20 games if Grissom's arm holds up," Hano reports that Sal Maglie said of Grissom. None of his pitches worked against Mitchell, however—Grissom threw four straight balls, loading the bases. But Grissom struck out pinch-hitter Dave Pope on what a teammate said was a screwball that fooled Pope; Hano said the called third strike looked "a trifle high." Jim Hegan then lofted a fly to left that threatened to just make it to the stands in the short porch in the Polo Grounds' left field, but Hano wrote that a gentle breeze kept the ball in play: third out. Grissom then had to get through a nervous ninth: A two-base error by Monte Irvin with two out and an intentional walk brought up Al Rosen, the American League MVP in 1953. He sent another fly ball toward Irvin—the fifth in six batters—but Irvin made the play, and it was still 2–2. Grissom was called on again in the 10th, and up stepped Wertz, whose only out on the day was Mays's miraculous catch. He came through with another hard-hit ball, a double, and Cleveland had the go-ahead run in scoring position with no one out. After a sacrifice bunt, Grissom walked Pope—once again, runners on first and third, one out. Then two: Pinch-hitter Bill Glynn struck out. The game was now at a point it never would have been a half-century later. Grissom was well into his third inning of relief and had gone through the lineup more than once, but he was still pitching. And with a Series opener on the line, he would face Bob Lemon, Cleveland's starting pitcher, still in the game in the 10th inning and coming to bat. Lemon was a good-hitting pitcher (.232 for his career, with 37 home runs), yet Cleveland had one potential pinch-hitter remaining, Wally Westlake, who had hit .263 with power as a part-timer that year. But manager Al López stuck with Lemon, and he smacked a line drive—right at the first baseman. Grissom had finished two and two-thirds unlikely scoreless innings, and when Dusty Rhodes hit his famous pinch-hit home run in the bottom of the 10th, Grissom was a World Series winner. As *The Times* reported: "He's got it in here," Maglie said of Grissom, pointing to his heart. "He's always in there with that old will to win, and *that* helps a lot."

244. Dick Gray, Third Baseman, Los Angeles Dodgers.

On their way out of Brooklyn, the Dodgers developed a problem at third base. They cycled through six third basemen in Brooklyn in 1957, but Dick Gray was the Los Angeles Dodgers' Opening Day third baseman in 1958. He looked like a solution through 12 games—Gray was batting .382 with three home runs and nine RBIs—but then he went into a 7-for-60 slump. By the end of the season, the Dodgers had used seven third basemen, and Gray was traded away the next year. The instability lingered for 15 years, and reports about the number of third basemen the Dodgers had played were frequent. Jim Gilliam was a semi-regular for a few years, but from 1958 through 1972, a Dodger played third base at least 100 games in a season only three times. Then the wait was over: Ron Cey played at least 100 games at third each of the next eight seasons.

245. Ned Garver, Pitcher, Kansas City Athletics.

When Ned Garver signed with an affiliate of the St. Louis Browns before spring training in 1944, it could not have been apparent what he would face: losing, losing, losing. The Browns were beginning the only pennant-winning season in their history, and it would be one of three winning seasons in four years. By the time Garver made it to the majors in 1948, however, he was a good pitcher and the Browns were the worst team in the American League. He forged a 14-year career, and although his record looks pedestrian—129–157—his winning percentage of .451 was 40 points better than his teams' record in games in which he did not have a decision. To pick a comparison pretty much at random: Don Drysdale's winning percentage was .557; the rest of the Dodgers' pitchers was .568. Advantage: Garver, by a lot. In 1951, Garver became the first AL pitcher to win 20 games on a team that lost 100—a 20–12 standout on a 52–102 team. That means the rest of the Browns' pitchers won only 26 percent of their games that year. Ouch.

246. J.W. Porter, Catcher-Outfielder, Washington Senators.

J.W. was his given name, his wife was called Zee and the obituary from his family said he had been born in Bugscuffle, Oklahoma. But the hype about J.W. Porter as a teenage ballplayer in Oakland was no joke. "Certainly, there has never been another high school star in the Bay Area who has attracted as much attention from major league scouts," *The Oakland Tribune* wrote in 1950. He received a $67,500 bonus. He had a plaque installed at the Baseball Hall of Fame for his exploits in the American Legion tournament (where a teammate was a 14-year-old third baseman named Frank Robinson). Porter never could live up to all that, but he did brush up against the stars. As detailed in his obituary in *The Palm Beach* (California) *Post*, he pinch-hit for Roger Maris (and homered); he caught Bob Gibson in Gibson's rookie season; and in his final major league game, he replaced Stan Musial at first base. He even shined the shoes of a Browns teammate, Satchel Paige.

247. Don Ferrarese, Pitcher, Cleveland Indians.

Don Ferrarese's career record—19–36, a .346 winning percentage—got me wondering about the worst won-lost records in baseball history. A .346 winning percentage equates to a 56–106 record in a full modern season for a team, so it's clearly bad. But with a cutoff of 50 career decisions, there are 58 pitchers with worse records than Ferrarese's. The pitchers are from all eras, although only four pitched this century. The two just worse than Ferrarese were basically contemporaries, Tracy Stallard (.345) and Pete Burnside (.346). The worst record: Ike Pearson's 13–50, .206, from 1939 to 1948 for the Phillies and the White Sox. Pearson's record was actually much worse until his final two seasons, when he went 3–3; he had gone 10–47, a .175 percentage, in his first four seasons. This list of pitchers with the worst records does have some of the best names, however, including Dolly Gray, Happy Townsend, Beany Jacobson, Snipe Hansen, Buster Brown, Kaiser Wilhelm, Clise Dudley (full name Elzie Clise Dudley) and my favorite, Egyptian Healy, presumably because he was born in Cairo, Illinois.

248. Boston Red Sox Team Card.

This was, it seems likely, the last team card with only white players for a Major League Baseball franchise. The Red Sox, the final team in the majors to integrate, called up Pumpsie Green on July 21, 1959, well after the photo for this card was taken. It was the Red Sox who were the problem, not the city of Boston. The Boston Braves integrated in 1950. So did the Boston Celtics. The Boston Bruins did so in 1958. Boston College athletics had integrated in the late 1930s.

249. Bobby Adams, Third Baseman, Chicago Cubs.

The Cubs had been so bad for so long—14 consecutive seasons without a winning record—that their owner, Phil Wrigley, decided to eliminate the position of manager and institute what came to be called the College of Coaches for the 1961 season. "If it works, it'll be a good idea," Wrigley said at the news conference announcing the move. "Managers are expendable. I believe there should be relief managers just like relief pitchers." And El Tappe, one of the coaches, said, "We certainly cannot do much worse trying a new system than we have done for many years under the old," according to the Ernie Banks biography *Let's Play Two*. Bobby Adams was part of the original eight coaches, who, Wrigley indicated, would take turns as the head coach but also rotate down to the Cubs' minor league teams to ensure systematic teaching of plays, signs, et cetera. Tappe told *The Chicago Tribune* that he wrote "an institutional playbook" so that as players moved up, they "didn't have to learn anything new." Such a framework was lauded elsewhere—the Dodgers instituted something similar in the '50s at their Dodgertown camp in Florida, and the Oriole Way was a playbook much like the one Tappe suggested. But the Dodgers and the Orioles, with a traditional manager in charge, were successful; the Cubs, with their conveyor belt of head coaches, were not. Ultimately, only four of the first College of Coaches became head coaches; Adams and the rest served as coaches who floated between the majors and the minors. None of the head coaches could stop the losing. Vedie Himsl was 10-21-1 in two stints, Harry Craft was 7-9 in two turns in the seat, Tappe was 42-54-1 in three tries and Lou Klein was 5-6 in his two weeks as head coach. Chicago actually improved on 1960's record, but it was still only 64-90-2. The players did not like the College—Don Zimmer loudly criticized it after the season ended, and he was left exposed to the expansion draft—but, undaunted, Wrigley brought the College back in 1962. Adams was still among the coaches (so, eventually, was the former Negro league veteran Buck O'Neil, who was thus the first Black coach in the majors) but not one of the head coaches. Tappe and Klein had their chances again, but newcomer Charlie Metro managed the final 112 games (for a 43-69 record). Other coaches, however, still moved up and down between the majors and the minors. Metro was no more popular than the rotating head coaches were. A SABR account of the College said Metro barred players from having golf clubs in the locker room; called some players and coaches (whom he did not name) "happy losers"; and even tried to ban shaving in the clubhouse. Metro was fired, and a new head coach, Bob Kennedy, was hired. The Cubs improved, but not enough, and after the 1965 season, Leo Durocher was hired. But not as the head coach. "If no announcement has been made of what my title is, I'm making it here and now," he said, according to *Leo Durocher: Baseball's Prodigal Son*. "I'm the manager. I'm not a head coach. *I'm the manager.*" Adams did get his chance to manage in 1962—with the Cubs' affiliate in the Arizona Instructional League.

250. Billy O'Dell, Pitcher, Baltimore Orioles.

Billy O'Dell leaped from college directly to the majors and never played in the minors. He won 19 games for a pennant-winning team. In his 30s, he reinvented himself as a reliever, saving 29 games over two seasons while appearing in 123 games and throwing 224 innings. But at age 33, he became fatigued and dropped from 180 pounds to 148, according to Baseball Reference. He later told *The Baltimore Sun* he thought the fatigue might have been from his heavy use and then what he thought was the flu. Tests, however, eventually showed he had Addison's disease, which affects the adrenal glands. Cortisone shots helped, but he was ineffective in 1967 with the Pirates and was released after the season. His problems were far from over. O'Dell told *The Sun* that he was hospitalized five or six times over the next five years—he had dangerously low blood pressure, which is a common complication of Addison's—and had to retire on disability at age 41. "It was tough at first, really depressing," he said. "Sometimes you wonder if it's worth going on." It was. With improved medication, he lived to the age of 85.

251. Cletis Boyer, Infielder, New York Yankees.

Cletis ("Clete"), Ken and Cloyd Boyer all had long careers in professional baseball with considerable stints in the majors. But they had four other brothers who also played pro ball. The Boyers, who grew up in a small town in Missouri, also had seven sisters (one of whom would die in infancy), which would indicate that their mother, Mabel, was very tired. Mabel Boyer told *Time* magazine in 1962, "Everybody tells me that each of my boys turns out a little better than the next older one." This wasn't true, but it did not prevent teams from signing Boyers—especially the Cardinals, who wound up with five of them. Here's the roster of Boyer brothers: *Cloyd:* pitcher, born in 1927, played 17 seasons of pro ball, five in the majors (20–23, 4.73 ERA). He spent 10 seasons at Class AAA, the last five in Indianapolis. *Wayne:* pitcher and outfielder, born in 1929. He was signed at age 16 by a Class D team in the Georgia-Alabama League before moving to the Cardinals' organization. He was 14–18, with an ERA north of 5.00, and hit .239 with one home run in 207 plate appearances. *Ken:* third baseman, born in 1931. The family star, he played 15 years in the majors, hit .288/.349/.462 with 282 home runs and was a seven-time All-Star and the National League MVP in 1964. *Lynn:* first baseman, born in 1935. He played two seasons, batting .225/.326/.343 with 10 home runs. He was 16 for 18 stealing. *Clete:* third baseman, born in 1937. He played 16 seasons in the majors and four in Japan and was considered an exemplary defender who lost out on Gold Gloves because of Brooks Robinson; he finally won one, at age 32, only after moving to the National League. He batted .244/.299/.372 with 162 home runs. He was involved in an extraordinary run of off-the-field events (bonus baby, a signing as an amateur by the Kansas City Athletics that was widely seen as a ruse for the Yankees to land him; gambling accusations; his move to Japan). *Ron:* third baseman, born in 1944. He played one season in the White Sox's organization and then seven in the Yankees' but didn't hit anywhere:

Card 251: Clete Boyer was one of seven brothers who played pro ball. He won pennants in New York and a Gold Glove in Atlanta and he enjoyed a four-year run in Japan.

.215/.306/.306 for his career. He batted above .200 only twice. **Len:** third baseman, born in 1946. He played seven seasons for Cardinals farm teams, with a career .226/.317/.326 line. His best season: .249/.354/.368 in the Class A Carolina League. Looking at the numbers, it's apparent that the Boyer brothers, other than Ken, struggled at bat, but at one point it looked as if Clete might hit well, too. Speaking of Clete to *Time* in 1962, Yogi Berra said, "When you see anybody hit two homers into the upper deck in Washington, he ain't what you would call an ordinary hitter." Unfortunately, he was.

252. Ray Boone, Third Baseman, Chicago White Sox.

Baseball is the family business for the Boones, too. Ray Boone played for 13 seasons in the majors and was the father of Bob, who caught for 19 years, and a grandfather of Aaron, an infielder for 12 years (and later the Yankees' manager), and Bret, a second baseman for 14 years. Ray was the best hitter in the family, but he had the least postseason opportunity: one at-bat, in the 1948 World Series. (He struck out.) At least he did get a World Series ring.

253. Seth Morehead, Pitcher, Philadelphia Phillies.

Seth Morehead was the last pitcher to face the Brooklyn Dodgers. On September 29, 1957, Morehead, a 22-year-old rookie, got his first start of the season as Brooklyn played its final game, in Philadelphia, before moving to Los Angeles. Morehead held the Dodgers to one unearned run and four hits, and the Phillies won, 2–1, to finish the season at .500, 77–77. Such wins were scarce for Morehead, whom Reds manager Birdie Tebbetts once said had "the potential to be a 25-game winner," according to Morehead's SABR Bio Project biography. He didn't even win 25 games in his career, finishing 5–19, 4.81. He had a fatal heart attack shortly before his 28th birthday.

254. Zeke Bella, Outfielder, Kansas City Athletics.

The cachet of being a major leaguer can last long after a major league career is over. Or didn't amount to much. Zeke Bella was a .334 hitter in the minors but managed only 104 plate appearances and a .196 average in the majors over two seasons. Yet back home in Greenwich, Connecticut, he was, even decades later, considered one of the best athletes ever produced in town. He was a member of the first class of the Greenwich High School Sports Hall of Fame, not long before his death in 2013, along with the Pro Football Hall of Fame quarterback Steve Young. "I'm grateful for his inspiring me to be better," Young, who was three decades younger, said at the induction ceremony. "He was an important part of the rich athletic tradition in Greenwich." Bella became a high school and Babe Ruth League umpire, and his obituary in *The Greenwich Time* quoted Dan Gasparino, who played catcher at Greenwich High (Class of '78) and later signed with the Yankees, saying that while umpiring Bella would give him pointers. At his Hall of Fame induction, one of the current baseball tri-captains said, "Six decades of baseball players—all influenced by Zeke in some fashion—were that much better."

255. Del Ennis, Outfielder, Cincinnati Redlegs.

Del Ennis had just about everything it took to be an idol for Phillies fans. He was from Philadelphia, came up in the organization and hit as soon as he reached the majors. When he was traded away after 11 seasons, he held the team's career record for home runs, with 259 (he is still third, behind only Mike Schmidt and Ryan Howard). He was streaky at bat but hustled. His defense wasn't bad. He earned MVP votes in seven seasons in Philadelphia. And the fans booed and booed. Robin Roberts, the Phillies' ace, wrote in *The Whiz Kids and the 1950 Pennant* that Ennis "was probably subjected to more booing by Philadelphia fans than any player in team history." Ennis recalled that in a 1955 game, he homered in his first three at-bats. "I popped up the fourth time with runners on base and the fans liked to boo me out of the park," he said in *The Whiz Kids*. (He popped out in his second at-bat, but still.) The book *The 50 Greatest Players in Philadelphia Phillies History* says that even Ennis's grandchildren were asked why he was booed so much. "When there was a lot written about Mike Schmidt being booed, Del couldn't believe it," the book says. "He'd say: 'They think that's booing? That's nothing.'" He was a shrewd negotiator, though, as recounted in his *New York Times* obituary: "I had it put in my contract that I'd get paid an extra $5,000 for 105 RBIs, $10,000 for 110 RBIs, $15,000 for 115 RBIs and $20,000 for 120 or more RBIs. Three times I would collect the biggest bonus."

256. Jerry Davie, Pitcher, Detroit Tigers.

His big-league career did not amount to much, but Jerry Davie had a spectacular first season in pro ball. He was 17–3 with a 2.63 ERA for Jamestown in the Class D PONY League. Two of his Jamestown teammates in 1951 earned much greater renown. First was Charley Lau, who after a nondescript career as a catcher became a famed hitting coach (and a well-paid one; he was the first coach with a $100,000 contract). And the 18-year-old shortstop who hit .219 would go on to a lucrative career, just not in baseball: Eight years later, Mike Ilitch opened a pizza joint in Garden City, Michigan—and named it Little Caesar's. Billionaire Ilitch later owned the Tigers himself (and the Detroit Red Wings).

257. Leon Wagner, Outfielder, San Francisco Giants.

Daddy Wags brought a lot of levity to baseball with his effervescent approach and hip wiggles at bat (and consternation to his managers and general managers for his inability to field well). When he was traded by the Angels from Los Angeles to Cleveland, he was quite unhappy, saying, "Nothing against Cleveland—but I'd rather have been traded somewhere in the United States," according to his *Los Angeles Times* obituary. While in Los Angeles, he had opened a clothing store with the slogan "Get your rags from Daddy Wags." Few people did, apparently, and *The Times* said the Angels helped him stave off foreclosure with loans. He was a prodigious home run hitter (211 playing really only seven full seasons), but his defense was lacking. *Hardball Times* wrote that "his defensive play bordered on the clownish. He had hands like pitchforks, took bad routes to fly balls, and threw weakly with an awkward motion." After his playing career, he had a supporting role in the movie *The Bingo Long Traveling All-Stars and Motor Kings*. But soon everything soured. His businesses faltered, he and his wife were wounded by intruders in a break-in, and he was burdened by substance abuse, *Hardball Times* said. He became homeless, and his *L.A. Times* obituary noted that he died in an electrical shed next to a dumpster that he had converted into a place to live.

258. Fred Kipp, Pitcher, Los Angeles Dodgers.

Fred Kipp made it to the majors from the middle of nowhere, which is little exaggeration: He was from Piqua (pronounced Pick-way), an unincorporated area of eastern Kansas that these days has fewer than 100 people. He is the second most famous person born there. The great comic actor Buster Keaton was born in Piqua, but he wasn't really *from* there; his parents were vaudeville performers, traveling with Harry Houdini, who got stuck in Piqua because of a storm. And that's where Myra Keaton gave birth to Buster, who was quickly no longer in Piqua. There is a Buster Keaton museum in Piqua, though, and the town's website proudly proclaims that it "is the only town in the state to have a life-sized statue of St. Isadore, the Patron Saint of Farmers."

259. Jim Pisoni, Outfielder, Milwaukee Braves.

Imagine you're Jim Pisoni, 19 years old, signed by a hometown team, the St. Louis Browns, to play baseball. You're a city kid but are shipped off to play for the Mayfield Clothiers, in a town of 9,000 in southwestern Kentucky, in the Class D Kitty League (that's for Kentucky-Illinois-Tennessee). Your team is terrible—it will go 38–86, 45 games out of first place. You are one of the youngest players on the team, but at least you are the best of the lot. Of your 25 teammates, only one will reach the major leagues. That's George O'Donnell, a pitcher whose career will amount to 87⅓ innings on a Pirates team that will go 53–101. Playing for a .290 team, what keeps your hopes up? The dream, no doubt. Pisoni did make it to the majors in 1953, playing in three of the Browns' final four games as a team in St. Louis. Typically, they lost them all.

260. Early Wynn, Pitcher, Chicago White Sox.

When Early Wynn was asked if he would throw at his own mother, he said, "It would depend on how well she was hitting," his *New York Times* obituary reported. How about his grandmother? "I'd have to," he replied. "My grandma could really hit the curveball." And his son? Well, Joe Early Wynn was once at Yankee Stadium, where his father was throwing him batting practice, as Roger Kahn recounts in *A Season in the Sun*. Joe Early hit a long line drive to left-center field, and Early threw the next pitch at his cheekbone, sending his son sprawling. "You shouldn't crowd me," Wynn said. He felt entitled to throw at, or near, batters. "Every hitter I face is a man trying to take money out of my pocket," he said, according to *The Times*. "Every hitter is an enemy." Hitters knew what was coming, too. "That SOB is so mean he would [expletive] knock you down in the dugout," Mickey Mantle said, according to *Sports Illustrated*. Wynn was a Southern boy, from Alabama, but he protected all of his teammates, including his Black teammates. "Whenever Early pitched, we didn't have any problems getting knocked down," Larry Doby said of himself and his Black teammates in Cleveland. "Early, he would start at the top of the opposing lineup and go right down to the bottom. They threw at me, he'd throw at them." Wynn said that when he was a rookie with the Senators in 1939, manager Bucky Harris told him to knock down every hitter once he got two strikes on them or he would be fined $25, at a time when he was earning $350 a month. So he did. Funny thing is, Wynn did not hit very many hitters. In a career spanning 23 seasons, he hit only 64 batters, which barely puts him in the top 300. Bob Gibson was like that, too, although he tagged more hitters than Wynn did. A man feared for his willingness to throw inside, Gibson hit 102 batters—tied for 89th on the career list. Sal Maglie, who also said he would throw at his grandmother, hit only 44 batters. Some of their contemporaries known for throwing inside *did* hit batters, though. Don Drysdale, for example, lived up to his reputation by hitting them 154 times.

Card 260: Early Wynn said he might throw at his grandmother—she "could really hit the curveball"—and did throw at his son.

261. Gene Stephens, Outfielder, Boston Red Sox.

Gene Stephens was known as "Ted Williams's caddy" because his primary role in seven-plus seasons with the Red Sox was to be Williams's late-inning defensive replacement in left field. From 1955 to 1959, Stephens averaged 112 games a season but only 1.88 plate appearances per game. Yet he shares a major league batting record, with three hits in a single inning. On June 18, 1953—while Williams was serving in Korea—Boston scored 17 runs in the seventh inning against Detroit. Stephens singled off Steve Gromek, doubled off Dick Weik and singled off Earl Harrist. It was his only three-hit game of the season. Stephens was the only twentieth-century player to accumulate three hits in an inning. Johnny Damon matched the feat in 2003, and three teammates, Fred Pfeffer, Tom Burns and Ned Williamson, did it in 1883—in the same inning in the same game. The Chicago White Stockings (later Cubs) scored 18 runs in that inning and beat the Detroit Wolverines, 26–6.

262. Hitters' Foes: Johnny Podres-Clem Labine-Don Drysdale.

These three pitchers were not exactly formidable in 1958, which raises the question: Why this card? Johnny Podres was 13–15, 3.72 ERA; Don Drysdale, 12–13, 4.17; and Clem Labine, 6–6, 4.15. In their first year in Los Angeles, the Dodgers were last in the league in ERA and finished seventh in the standings. Podres and Labine were not vastly better in 1959, but Drysdale did improve and the Dodgers, despite winning only 88 games, were the NL champions.

263. Bud Daley, Pitcher, Kansas City Athletics.

Bud Daley and Roger Maris just couldn't stay apart, playing together on four teams. The first time was in 1956 at Class AAA Indianapolis, an excellent team (92–62, 24 players who made it to the majors) for whom Maris was a very good 21-year-old (.293/.356/.494) and Daley was a spectacular 24-year-old (11–1, 2.31 ERA) in a half-season. The next year, they were both promoted to Cleveland, where Maris was solid and Daley (2–8, 4.43) was not. A year later, Daley was traded to Baltimore right before the season, but two weeks after that he was sent to Kansas City without having appeared in a regular-season game. That June, Cleveland dealt Maris to Kansas City. Teammates again. But only briefly, as Maris was on the KC-to-New York shuttle in December 1959. Daley rejoined him, however, in mid–1961 and recorded the final out of the Yankees' World Series–clinching victory over the Reds. Daley said he misjudged Maris's career arc in *Where Have You Gone?*, a book about ex-Yankees: "I didn't think he would hit a lot of home runs. Nobody did. He just had that beautiful line-drive swing. I thought he would be a high-average hitter. That all changed, I guess, when he came to New York."

264. Chico Carrasquel, Shortstop, Baltimore Orioles.

Alfonso Carrasquel—he was nicknamed Chico by minor league teammates in Fort Worth in 1949—was not the first Venezuelan to play in the major leagues. That was his Uncle Alex. But he was the third, and he was the first in the enduring line of All-Star shortstops from Venezuela (126 Venezuelans have played shortstop in the major leagues), earning All-Star berths in 1951 and 1953 to 1955. The White Sox then traded him so they could insert another Venezuelan at shortstop: Luis Aparicio, who, upon Carrasquel's death, said, "Chico was my hero and mentor." A dozen Venezuelan shortstops have made an All-Star team, including Omar Vizquel, Dave Concepción and Ozzie Guillén. Like his countrymen, Carrasquel could play defense. "Oh, he could move. To his left, to his right," White Sox star Billy Pierce told *The Chicago Tribune*. "Could come in on a ball. Had a great arm." He also had style and flash, although his SABR Bio Project biography says critics thought his effort was inconsistent. When he died in 2005, Venezuela announced two days of mourning for him.

265. Ron Kline, Pitcher, Pittsburgh Pirates.

Ron Kline managed to hold onto a job in the major leagues for a decade while baseball was figuring out what job he really should be performing. Kline was mostly a starter for that decade, compiling a 68–107 (.389) record with a 4.14 ERA. Two of those seasons he led the National League in losses, although by many measures those were his best years to date. He cycled through the Pirates, the Cardinals, the expansion-year Angels and the Tigers with no real improvement. But the Tigers had put him in the bullpen, and in his second season as a full-time reliever, Kline finally blossomed. Over his final eight seasons he started only once and put together a 46–37 (.554) record and a 2.83 ERA, aided by lowering his home run rate from 1.02 per nine innings to 0.75. He pitched until he was 38.

266. Woodie Held, Shortstop-Outfielder, Cleveland Indians.

The best-hitting shortstop in the American League from 1959 to 1965 was Woodie Held, who spent all but the last of those seasons in Cleveland. Although he made a fair number of errors (as did many of his cards, which called him Woody), his defensive numbers were above average, too. Yet he never made an All-Star team, although lighter-hitting shortstops or those with anomalous seasons like Tony Kubek, Dick Howser, Zoilo Versailles, Eddie Bressoud and Dick McAuliffe did. For that seven-year span, Held hit .253/.347/.447 for a 119 OPS+ while averaging just over 20 homers a season despite high strikeout totals for his era. Luis Aparicio and Ron Hansen had more WAR, by Baseball Reference, than Held did from 1959 to 1965 thanks to their defensive chops, but Held was a darn good player. Also versatile: He was adept at third base and in the outfield.

267. John Romonosky, Pitcher, Washington Senators.

Wally Yonamine, a Japanese American who was born in Hawaii, became an unlikely football standout who played a season with the San Francisco 49ers. An injury curtailed his football career, but he had also been playing baseball in a league in Hawaii and wound up playing Class C ball in 1950 for the Salt Lake City Bees. He hit .335, but his future was in Japan, where he starred for 12 seasons. He would go on to hit .311 with a little pop and some speed. But before he left Salt Lake City, he was given an appreciation night before his final game, against the Pocatello Cardinals. One of the special events, according to *Wally Yonamine: The Man Who Changed Japanese Baseball*, was a match race around the bases with Pocatello's John Romonosky, who, although a pitcher, was considered one of the fastest men in the Pioneer League. He was fast enough on this night, racing around the bases in 14.0 seconds to Yonamine's 14.3. The next year, Yonamine was hitting .354 for the Yomiuri Giants; Romonosky was 3–8 in the Class C California League. After 38 years in Japanese baseball, Yonamine was enshrined in the Japanese Baseball Hall of Fame. Romonosky kicked around the minors for years, mostly below Class AAA, but was 3–4, 3.15 in 32 games in the majors.

268. Tito Francona, Outfielder, Detroit Tigers.

In 1954, Cleveland's Bobby Ávila won the American League batting title when he hit .341, even though Ted Williams finished at .345. The standard of the day, however, was 400 at-bats, and Williams had only 389—he missed some games, but he walked 136 times and had 526 plate appearances. Boston fans were incensed, and before long baseball quietly devised a new qualifying standard: 3.1 plate appearances per game, or 477 overall at the time (it's 502 now). Few people paid attention. Then in late 1959, Tito Francona was leading the AL in batting but had only 398 at-bats with two games to play. As *The Plain Dealer* wrote later, some Cleveland fans could not figure out why manager Joe Gordon wasn't pushing to play Francona. They remembered the Avila case, where 400 at-bats was the magic number. Francona, a trade acquisition just before the season started, wound up with only 399 ABs—one short, to many fans' thinking—but what he really needed was the 477 plate appearances, and he wasn't close. He finished with 443 and a .363 batting average. And Harvey Kuenn, a .353 hitter, had a batting title.

269. Jack Meyer, Pitcher, Philadelphia Phillies.
Ernie Banks was having quite a year against the Phillies in 1958. In the third inning of the Cubs' June 4 game against Philadelphia in the Friendly Confines, Banks hit his fourth homer of the season off Phillies pitchers in five games. But when he stepped in against reliever Jack Meyer in the fourth inning, Banks had no chance to homer again—Meyer threw at him with the first three pitches, then hit him with the fourth. According to Meyer's SABR Bio Project profile, the umpire Leo Dascoli "suggested that the new rule requiring safety head gear had led to an increase in beanballs." The National League did have a rule, instituted in 1956, mandating headgear for batters—either a batting helmet or inserts in a cap, which had been used by a few players since the early '40s. Dascoli's theory was provocative, but, as it turns out, not provable. Hit batters in the NL actually went down in 1956, by 18.5 percent. They then returned to the pre-batting helmet norms in 1957. The American League did not mandate helmets or inserts until 1958, and its experience was similar—a drop in hit batters the first year, and then a return to the norm. Batting helmets only—no inserts—were not made mandatory in the majors until 1971, and then only for new players; those already in the majors could still bat without an actual batting helmet. Red Sox catcher Bob Montgomery was the last grandfathered player to use inserts in his cap, in 1979. As for Meyer, Banks was the only batter he hit in 1958, in 90⅓ innings. Maybe he was fed up with Banks tattooing Phillies pitchers (he in fact homered again later in that June 4 game). Or maybe Meyer was the one player in baseball who didn't like Ernie Banks.

270. Gil Hodges, First Baseman, Los Angeles Dodgers.
Maybe Gil Hodges should have retired after the 1959 season; it might have improved his chances for making the Hall of Fame. After that season, Hodges had been instrumental in the Dodgers' winning two World Series championships and had been on seven pennant-winning teams. His career line was .277/.365/.495 with 345 home runs—11th on the career list at the time. But Hodges played three more seasons and a smidgen of a fourth, leaving Hall of Fame voters with memories of a .228/.312/.389 demise. That included two seasons tarred by playing for the expansion Mets, to the tune of a 49–125 record. After decades of politicking by others, Hodges did make the Hall in 2022, but 50 years after his death.

271. Orlando Peña, Pitcher, Cincinnati Redlegs.
Old Metropolitan Stadium in Minneapolis was a good hitters' park. Especially when Orlando Peña came to town. Peña was a starter and reliever for the Athletics, the Tigers and the Indians from 1962 to 1967, and Twins hitters relished seeing him in Minneapolis, putting up a .280/.349/.541 line, with an OPS+ of 144. That was the highest OPS+ at any ballpark in which he faced at least 30 batters, including

Fenway Park. He allowed 14 home runs in 252 plate appearances at the Met. The Twins had some excellent hitters in those years—Harmon Killebrew, Tony Oliva and Don Mincher all roughed up Peña—but so did the Orioles and the Yankees for much of that period, and he was far better at Memorial Stadium and Yankee Stadium. Nineteen sixty-four was an especially bad year for Peña at Metropolitan Stadium, as he yielded a .344/.379/.754 line, with seven homers for the 66 Twins batters he faced. Those are almost Barry Bonds-at-his-best numbers.

272. Jerry Lumpe, Third Baseman, New York Yankees.

By 1959, the Yankees had an infield logjam. Gil McDougald and Tony Kubek were sharing shortstop. McDougald and Clete Boyer were playing third. McDougald was also logging time at second, but mostly so were Bobby Richardson and Jerry Lumpe. Richardson and Lumpe began the season with similar major league experience and success, but in 1959, Richardson was hitting—he finished at .301, although with few walks and minimal power—and Lumpe was not. Richardson also was two years younger. So in May, Lumpe was traded to Kansas City. The Yankees won the pennant every year from 1960 to '64 with Richardson playing second and batting leadoff, while Lumpe was mostly batting second or third for Kansas City teams that never played better than .451 ball. But Lumpe was the better hitter. Lumpe's career line was .268/.325/.356, with an OPS+ of 87; Richardson's was .266/.299/.335, with an OPS+ of 77. (Although those Yankee teams won, Richardson was always a drag on the offense with that low on-base percentage; Lumpe was on base, on average, 17 or 18 more times a year.) Lumpe had some slightly better defensive numbers. In 1,100 games at second base, he had a fielding percentage of .984, 14 fielding runs above average and a range factor per nine innings of 5.23 and defensive WAR of 4.6; Richardson was .979/13/5.12 with a dWAR of 4.9 in 1,339 games at second. Richardson did take part in many more double plays. But those excellent Yankee teams might have been a teeny bit better with Jerry Lumpe batting.

273. Joey Jay, Pitcher, Milwaukee Braves.

Joey Jay was the first former Little Leaguer to play in the major leagues, when he made his debut with the Braves in 1953 at age 17. Five years earlier, he had been playing first base in

Card 273: Joey Jay was the first major leaguer who had played in Little League, which he sharply criticized years later.

the Middletown, Connecticut, Little League. His feelings about Little League were not positive. A 1970 report by the National Education Association, as detailed by UPI, said Jay agreed with psychologists who said that Little League put too much pressure on players and that the program was too ambitious and had too much parental supervision. "I am certainly not in sympathy with the Little League program the way it has developed," he was quoted saying in the report. "Perhaps it was not intended to be this way, but it is not serving the purposes it claims to be and I don't think it is helping baseball." Jay distanced himself from baseball generally after retiring. According to an article in *The Middletown Press*, Jay said that it was "infantile to keep thinking about the game." He added: "I don't live in the past, like most ballplayers. When I made the break, it was clean and forever."

274. Jerry Kindall, Infielder, Chicago Cubs.
Jerry Kindall had labored through eight major league seasons, all with losing teams. In 1965, finally, he was the regular second baseman for a very good Twins team ... until he injured a leg and couldn't regain the job. The Twins made the World Series, but Kindall never got in a game. Still, he knew something about championships. He had been the shortstop on the University of Minnesota's College World Series champions in 1956. And as the head coach, he led the University of Arizona to three NCAA titles, in 1976, 1980 and 1986. His players earned first-team All-America honors 34 times, including another guy who knows something about championships: Terry Francona.

275. Jack Sanford, Pitcher, San Francisco Giants.
If Willie McCovey's line drive had gone over Bobby Richardson's head, not into his glove, Jack Sanford would be a well-remembered World Series hero. Instead, he was the losing pitcher in Game 7 in 1962 as the Yankees defeated the Giants, 1–0, when McCovey's shot with two out and runners on second and third became the final out, not a game-winning, two-run base hit. The only run Sanford gave up came on a fifth-inning double play with the bases loaded. Sanford and the Yankees' Ralph Terry faced off three times over the course of the Series. Sanford threw a three-hit shutout to win Game 2, 2–0—he called it "the best game I ever pitched"—and struck out 10 in Game 5, but lost when he yielded a three-run home run to Tom Tresh. Then came Game 7 and McCovey's oh-so-close line drive. "I dream about it every night," Sanford said years later, according to his *New York Times* obituary. "It never goes away."

276. Pete Daley, Catcher, Boston Red Sox.
Catcher Pete Daley and pitcher Bud Daley, no relation, came into the league the same year, 1955. They faced each other infrequently—11 times, with Pete, a .239 career hitter with a .297 on-base percentage, having unusual success with two singles, a double, a home run and a walk against Bud. Then in 1960, they became teammates and batterymates with the Athletics. Bud pitched to Pete 14 times, and once more, Bud struggled, to a 5–8 record with a 5.03 ERA, while pitching to Pete, who batted .309 (17 for 55) with two homers in those games. They did have two big games

together: On Aug. 7, Bud allowed only two earned runs in beating the Yankees, while Pete went two for five with an RBI. Then on September 26, Pete went two for four with a homer while Bud was throwing a four-hitter to beat Cleveland, 6–1.

277. Turk Lown, Pitcher, Chicago White Sox.

Starting in 1959, the White Sox under manager Al López put together some impressively strong bullpens. Turk Lown and Jerry Staley, veterans with starter pedigrees before becoming relievers, first teamed up in 1958 but excelled in '59 for a White Sox team that could pitch but couldn't score. In his book *Early Wynn, the Go-Go Sox and the 1959 World Series*, Lew Freedman wrote that López, "assessing the age of his starting staff and being cautious with a ball club that was not high scoring, was ahead of his time in his use of Staley and Lown." Lown was 9–2 with, retroactively, 15 saves, most in the American League, and a 2.89 ERA in 93⅓ innings; Staley was 8–5 and also had 15 saves and a 2.24 ERA in 116⅓ innings. Lown had a down year in 1960, but the next season he was superb again. Then Eddie Fisher came along, and then Hoyt Wilhelm and Jim Brosnan, and then Don Mossi. Until 1959 (especially when he had the great rotation in Cleveland), López was below the league average in pitchers used per game; from 1959 to 1962, he was above the league average. The White Sox averaged 88 wins while finishing sixth, second, third and sixth in runs scored.

278. Chuck Essegian, Outfielder, St. Louis Cardinals.

Chuck Essegian and Larry Sherry both graduated from Fairfax High School in Los Angeles, but four years apart, so they were never high school teammates. In 1959, however, they were both vital if unexpected cogs in the Dodgers' World Series victory over the White Sox. Neither began the season in Los Angeles. Essegian was in the St. Louis organization before the Cardinals traded him to the Dodgers in mid–June. Still, he was sent to Class AAA and did not make it to Los Angeles until early August after Duke Snider and Carl Furillo sustained injuries. Sherry was having a middling season as a starting pitcher at Class AAA before he was called up, making his first appearance on July 4. Essegian did not play much; he had only 50 plate appearances. But he hit .318 as a pinch-hitter—seven for 18 with three doubles—and that's how he made his name in the World Series. The Dodgers lost Game 1 and were trailing, 2–1, with two outs in the seventh inning of Game 2 before manager Walt Alston had a hunch Essegian might homer. He did indeed hit a bomb to tie the score, and Los Angeles went on to win the game. In Game 6, he hit another home run, and the Dodgers won the Series. Essegian had four at-bats—all as a pinch-hitter. "I think those home runs probably hurt my career," he told *The Los Angeles Times* in 2006. "You know, you kind of get labeled as a certain kind of player. If you're a pinch-hitter, you're a pinch-hitter because you're not good enough to play every day." His home runs would not have mattered, however, if not for the stellar relief pitching of Sherry, who was not converted to a full-time reliever until mid–September. In the Series, he won two games, saved two games and allowed only one run in 12⅔ innings—the most innings of any Dodgers pitcher. "He was just superb," Essegian said. "They couldn't touch him."

279. Ernie Johnson, Pitcher, Baltimore Orioles.

Ernie Johnson finished his playing career with a season in Baltimore, but he was a Brave, always a Brave. He signed with the Boston Braves out of high school in 1942, made the big club in 1950 and accompanied the team to Milwaukee in 1953. After he retired, he stayed in Milwaukee and sold life insurance and also was host of a TV show called *Play Ball*—his SABR Bio Project biography says he and his guests would talk and drink milk. Before long, he joined the Braves' front office and their broadcast team. In 1965, with the team still in Milwaukee but planning to move to Atlanta the next year, Johnson broadcast 70 games on radio and TV for an Atlanta station, WSB. When Ted Turner's new station, WTBS, took over the broadcasts, Johnson was in the booth, where he stayed until 1989, when a special night for his retirement drew 42,000 fans for a team that was averaging 12,000, *The Atlanta Journal-Constitution* reported. He soon returned in a part-time role for another decade. Turner's "superstation" made national figures out of the Braves' broadcast team, which developed tentacles throughout sports broadcasting. Johnson's son, Ernie Jr., joined the Braves crew in the mid-1990s but earned his own national niche on TNT's NBA broadcasts. One of Ernie Sr.'s broadcast partners was Skip Caray, son of Harry and father of Chip. When Johnson finally retired after the 1999 season, his son, then 43, told his father on-air, "When I grow up, I want to be just like you."

280. Frank Bolling, Second Baseman, Detroit Tigers.

The Braves had the best offense in baseball in 1964. They led the National League (and the majors) in runs and also in batting average, on-base percentage and slugging percentage while finishing second in home runs. But the Braves' second basemen hit so poorly that they tried Hank Aaron at second. The Braves hoped Frank Bolling would hit, despite a .244/.299/.312 line in 1963 that followed two All-Star seasons. He slumped badly after mid-May in 1964 and wound up batting .199/.245/.278 with an OPS+ of 47. His most frequent replacement, Woody Woodward, hit .209/.260/.243 with an OPS+ of 43. Stuck around .500, the Braves moved Aaron to second base for 11 games, most of them in August. (He was a second baseman when he signed out of the Negro leagues and played 27 games at second in 1955, his second season in Milwaukee, but had played only two games there since.) Milwaukee eventually shifted shortstop Denis Menke to second for the last half of September and got hot, finishing the season 14–5. Too little, too late: The Braves wound up in fifth place.

281. Walt Craddock, Pitcher, Kansas City Athletics.

Walt Craddock's major league career didn't have many highlights—he was 0-7 with a 6.49 ERA in 29 games and 61 innings—but the first time he faced Ted Williams, he struck him out. Then again, the next inning he hit Williams with a pitch. Williams was the only major league batter Craddock ever hit.

282. R C Stevens, First Baseman, Pittsburgh Pirates.

In the post–World War II era, scouting ballplayers was, let's say, inexact. In an autobiographical essay he wrote for a website honoring Colquitt County, Georgia, graduates of the local Black schools, R C Stevens (no first or middle names or periods, just R C) said that Branch Rickey, then the general manager of the Pirates, wrote to his coach at Moultrie High School for Negro Youth asking for the names of prospects. (Rickey wrote such letters to coaches at Black high schools throughout the South.) The coach recommended Stevens; a Pirates scout went to Moultrie, Georgia, to check him out; and Stevens attended a couple of Pirates tryouts. Pittsburgh liked him, Stevens signed immediately and the 17-year-old country boy was off to Batavia, New York. His SABR Bio Project profile says his manager at Batavia offered to pay him $19.50 for a new glove if he hit four home runs in two weeks. He got the glove. Then the manager made a similar deal for new spikes—four homers in two weeks. A fan got wind that Stevens needed spikes, though, and took up a collection and, for $20.04, Stevens got the spikes.

283. Russ Heman, Pitcher, Cleveland Indians.

As I began researching Russ Heman, I could not remember one thing about him. Then I saw his card and remembered: I must have had 20 of these cards, which would be one for every major league inning he pitched. He did, however, pitch the first no-hitter for the San Diego Padres. It was the minor league San Diego Padres, though, as he blanked the Vancouver Mounties, 2–0, on May 7, 1959. Al Worthington (1961) and Sammy Ellis (1962) subsequently pitched no-hitters for the minor league Padres, but the major league team did not have one until 2021, when Joe Musgrove notched a no-no in the franchise's 53rd season. Heman should have been a submarine pitcher; his father, Rudy, was a well-regarded fast-pitch softball pitcher in the 1930s.

284. Steve Korcheck, Catcher, Washington Senators.

Very few ballplayers wore glasses on the field in the 1950s, but for several years the Senators had not one but two catchers who wore glasses: Clint Courtney and Steve Korcheck. Courtney could hit a little; Korcheck could not. He managed a .159/.196/.214 line with no home runs in 155 plate appearances over four seasons as the third-string catcher, a role that no longer exists. (He had chosen baseball over pro football, where he was a third-round draft pick of the San Francisco 49ers and could have delivered some hits as a 6-foot-1, 205-pound center.) His professorial look worked better in subsequent careers: Korcheck, who earned bachelor's, master's and doctoral degrees from George Washington University, was an instructor at the Kansas City Royals Baseball Academy in the early 1970s and was president of Manatee Community College in Florida from 1980 to 1997.

285. Joe Cunningham, First Baseman, St. Louis Cardinals.

Joe Cunningham was known to hustle, and that's what he was doing as he tried to beat out a ground ball on June 3, 1963. Cunningham, the White Sox's first baseman, stepped on his opposing number's foot, fell and broke his collarbone. Chicago was in second place, two games behind the Yankees, when he got hurt. When he returned on September 2, the White Sox were still in second, but 10½ games back. The rookie Tommy McCraw—like Cunningham, a left-handed hitter with minimal power—stepped in but couldn't match Cunningham's standards (.291/.403/.417 for his career). After Cunningham returned in September, batting .383 with a .500 on-base percentage, Chicago went 17–9, but they barely made up any ground on the Yankees.

286. Dean Stone, Pitcher, Boston Red Sox.

Dean Stone won an All-Star Game without, officially, facing a batter. Here's how it happened: Stone, a Senators left-hander, was called in to get the American League out of an eighth-inning jam with the National League leading the 1954 game by a run. Runners were on first and third, and Duke Snider was coming to bat, with Stan Musial on deck. The Baseball Happenings blog says the third-base coach, Leo Durocher, was monitoring Stone's warm-up throws and setting up the runner, Red Schoendienst, to try to steal home. Schoendienst took off on the third pitch, Stone threw home, Yogi Berra applied the tag, and the runner was called out, despite NL arguments that Stone had balked. Because the play would be a caught stealing, Stone's pitch total was recorded as zero. The AL rallied in the bottom of the eighth, Virgil Trucks pitched the ninth and Stone had an All-Star Game victory.

287. Don Zimmer, Shortstop-Third Baseman, Los Angeles Dodgers.

In a little over a decade beginning in the late '40s, Western Hills High School in Cincinnati pumped out a half-dozen future major leaguers (and that doesn't include Jim Frey, who hit .305 over a long minor league career and became a big-league manager). The best of the ballplayers may have been Don Zimmer, even though Pete Rose was among those former Mustangs. Zimmer could hit, he could run, he had power, he was versatile defensively and he was supremely self-confident. And at Western Hills, ballplayers were all around him. Frey was a teammate. Catcher Russ Nixon came along a few years later, then pitcher Dick Drott, then pitcher Art Mahaffey, then Rose, then fine-fielding shortstop Ed Brinkman. Four of them became All-Stars; four managed in the major leagues. Rose, of course, became the Hit King. Zimmer became a Hit by Pitch King, with two serious injuries (fractured skull, fractured cheekbone) damaging his career. Western Hills has always been a baseball power—it has produced major leaguers from the 1930s to the 2000s and has won five Ohio state championships—but luminaries from other dimensions also came from the school, including Rosemary Clooney (George's aunt and a star in her own right), the singer Andy Williams, the football star Jack (Hacksaw) Reynolds and Will Reynolds (creator of the Slush Puppie).

288. Dutch Dotterer, Catcher, Cincinnati Redlegs.

As a minor leaguer in 1954, Henry (Dutch) Dotterer, Jr. (his father was also called Dutch) earned $500 when he caught a ball dropped 575 feet from a helicopter, according to his obituary in *The Los Angeles Times*. He played 11 years of pro ball, but he was far from one-dimensional. After leaving baseball, he taught bilingual education for nearly two decades at Santa Ana (California) High School, where he also was the chess club adviser, *The L.A. Times* wrote. After leaving there, *The Times* reported, he returned to his hometown of Syracuse, New York, and opened a bookstore. "Dutch was the kind of guy you could talk baseball with or the origins of the universe," Frank Alvarado, the athletic director at Santa Ana High, said.

289. Johnny Kucks, Pitcher, Kansas City Athletics.

The Yankees won 10 pennants and seven World Series championships during Casey Stengel's 12-year tenure, but he was sometimes dismissed as a manager who was blessed with the team's many stars and resources. (Which it certainly had.) But Stengel added dimension, platooning adroitly and finding pitching from unexpected sources almost every year. Young and journeyman pitchers frequently performed as they never had before or would again, and Stengel used numerous veterans in ways to recover lost performance. And for all their stars and deep pockets, the Yankees needed to maximize victories—they won their first four pennants under Stengel by one, three, five and two games. Here's a look at some of the surprising pitching success stories under Stengel.

1949: Fred Sanford, who the year before lost 21 games for the Browns, went 7–3, 3.87 as a spot starter and reliever. Clearly his best season. The Yankees edged out the Red Sox by a game.

1950: Tom Ferrick, a 35-year-old near the end as a career reliever, finished 8–4, 3.65 with nine saves after coming over from the Browns in June. A 21-year-old rookie, Ed Ford, was a sensation at 9–1, 2.81, but he was no fluke and became the star known as Whitey. The Yankees won the pennant by three games.

1951: Joe Ostrowski, another 1950 pickup from the Browns, came out of the bullpen to go 6–4, 3.49, with six saves in his next-to-last major league season. The Yankees won by five games.

1952: Discarded by the Braves the year before for ineffectiveness, Johnny Sain started and relieved for the Yankees, for an 11–6, 3.46 mark with seven saves at age 34. This was the first of three top-flight seasons out of the bullpen for the failed Braves starter. The Yankees won by two games.

1953: Jim McDonald, another ex–Brown, threw a career high in innings and went 9–7. Stengel, who was not averse to using his starters in key relief spots, really leaned on 36-year-old Allie Reynolds out of the pen; he was 13–7 (only 15 starts), 3.41, with 13 saves. The Yankees won their fifth pennant (and World Series) in a row, by eight and a half games.

1954: Stengel got a 20–6, 3.26 season out of the rookie Bob Grim and an 11–5, 3.34 effort from Tom Morgan as this Yankees team won 103 games, their high under Stengel. Cleveland, however, won 111.

1955: Tommy Byrne had the best season of his career at 35 and earned double-digit victories for the first time in five years, going 16–5, 3.15 for a 120 ERA+. Another reclamation project, the ex–Phillie Jim Konstanty, was 7–2 with 12 saves. The Yankees regained the pennant, by three games.

1956: Here we get to Johnny Kucks, who, in his second season, went 18–9. He never won more than eight games in any other season. And Tom Sturdivant, in *his* second season, put up a record of 16–8, 3.30 ERA and five saves. The Yankees won by nine games.

1957: Sturdivant was a known quantity because of 1956, following up with a 16–6, 2.54 season. But in the other eight years of his career, he was 27–37. Grim, who had pitched infrequently for two years, became a full-time reliever and was 12–8, 2.63 with 19 saves. The Yankees won by eight games.

1958: No particular magic this year, although Bob Turley finally lived up to his promise with a 21–7, 2.97 season. The Yankees won by 10 games.

1959: Duke Maas, 30 years old, had the season of his life—14–8, five saves—but the Yankees fell apart and finished in third place, 25 games out of first.

1960: Jim Coates was 13–3–40 percent of his career victories—and Luis Arroyo solidified the bullpen after being called up from the minors at age 33, going 5–1 with seven saves and a 2.88 ERA in 29 games. The Yankees won by eight games, although the lead was only one on September 16.

And after losing the World Series, Stengel was fired. The Yankees continued to unearth unlikely pitching gems for a while (Ralph Terry, Jim Bouton). So maybe it wasn't Stengel. Maybe it was his pitching coach, Jim Turner. Or maybe it was Ralph Houk, a third-string catcher who clearly would have been working closely with the pitchers for much of that run (Terry and Bouton flourished after Houk replaced Stengel). Or maybe it was catcher Yogi Berra, whom Stengel called "my assistant." Whoever deserves the credit, Stengel's Yankees came up with pitching performances no one ever would have predicted.

290. Wes Covington, Outfielder, Milwaukee Braves.

If only Wes Covington could have hit left-handed pitching. Against right-handers, Covington was an All-Star: a .288/.344/.490 line with 122 homers—one every 23 plate appearances. Against lefties, he was helpless: a .219/.292/.316 line with nine homers—one every 49 plate appearances. At no time was this more obvious than in the Braves' two pennant-winning seasons:

1957	BA/OBP/SLG	HR	PA/HR
vs. RH	.298/.348/.578	19	16.1
vs. LH	.208/.295/.321	2	32.5

1958	BA/OBP/SLG	HR	PA/HR
vs. RH	.366/.413/.715	23	10.4
vs. LH	.192/.250/.236	1	61.0

He kept being platooned and was vocal in his displeasure while with Philadelphia, where he hit .205 from 1962 to 1965 under Gene Mauch, who was fond of platooning. The Phillies folded in '64, Covington popped off, and *The Philadelphia Daily News* wrote, "Nobody wants to listen to a mean, tough grumbler when that grumbler is hitting .220."

291. Pitching Partners: Pedro Ramos-Camilo Pascual.

The belief was that if Pedro Ramos and Camilo Pascual could ever get free of the lowly Senators, they would be stars. Ramos was finally sprung; Pascual was not. But it was Pascual who became the star. He was very good his last two seasons in

Washington, then continued his excellence when the team moved to Minnesota in 1961 and found its footing. From 1959 to 1965, he was 109–69 (.612) with a 3.07 ERA. Pascual led the league in shutouts three years out of four and, riding his big curveball, strikeouts three consecutive years. He got off to a hot start in '65 before injuries curtailed his season, but he finally pitched for a pennant winner. Ramos, meanwhile, was traded to Cleveland in 1962 after leading the league in losses four years in a row. He never found success as a starter, although he did have two-plus decent seasons as a reliever for the Yankees—but in the end, after they were an also-ran.

292. Dick Williams, Third Baseman-Outfielder, Kansas City Athletics.

By some measures, Dick Williams, a 30-year-old infielder-outfielder, had his best season as a player for the Athletics in 1959. So did Whitey Herzog, a 27-year-old outfielder. But they made their mark, of course, as managers. Williams won four pennants and two World Series titles. He constructed a 1,571–1,451 record (.520) while managing six teams over 21 seasons. Herzog won three pennants and a World Series championship. He built a 1,281–1,125 record (.532) while managing four teams over 18 seasons. Those A's actually had another future major league manager who, in one respect, had an even better record: Joe Morgan (not the Hall of Famer Joe Morgan) put together a .535 winning percentage as manager of the Red Sox for three and a half seasons. He won two division titles but never captured a pennant.

293. Ray Moore, Pitcher, Chicago White Sox.

Ballplayers have earned some unusual bonuses over the years. Some of the A's in 1972 picked up $300 each for growing mustaches. Roy Oswalt of the Astros was promised the bulldozer he had always wanted if he won Game 6 of the NLCS in 2005. (He did.) Joe DiMaggio was said to have been in line for a $10,000 bonus—just over $200,000 in 2023 dollars—from the Heinz ketchup company in 1941 if he extended his hitting streak to 57 games. (He didn't.) Then there was the bonus that White Sox owner Bill Veeck offered Ray Moore in 1959, according to *Go-Go to Glory: The 1959 Chicago White Sox*. Veeck said he would give Moore a Bluetick Coonhound puppy if Moore won his start on June 1. Moore gave up only three hits and three runs as the Sox lost, 3–1—but Veeck gave him the dog anyway. He was called Young Blue, as one of Moore's coon hounds back home was named Old Blue.

294. Hank Foiles, Catcher, Pittsburgh Pirates.

One of my running friends mentioned in passing that she was Hank Foiles's cousin. I remembered Hank Foiles. Did I know, she asked, that Hank was the first major leaguer to wear contact lenses in a game? I did not, but he was. It was 1958 when a hometown optometrist, Joe Goldberg, provided Foiles with his contacts. In Goldberg's obituary in *The Virginian-Pilot* in Norfolk, Foiles said his uncorrected eyesight was next to "nil. And that's pretty tough when you're trying to hit a ball coming in at 80 to 100 miles per hour." A few catchers wore glasses, but Foiles said: "They'd get all bent up or fog up on you. And playing in the rain? Forget it. They didn't come with no windshield wipers." He told *The Virginian-Pilot* that Goldberg made 15 or 16 pairs of lenses for him, some tinted—yellow worked best in Yankee

Stadium's shadows. Curiously, Goldberg's own vision was terrible—"something like 20/1300," his daughter said.

295. Billy Martin, Second Baseman, Cleveland Indians.

Billy Martin's baseball life turned into a Not Welcome Mat. Here is Martin's career, in 31 transactions over 42 years: *1946:* Signed by the Class D Idaho Falls Russets. *1947:* Purchased by the Oakland Oaks (Pacific Coast League). *October 13, 1949:* Traded by Oakland to the Yankees. *June 15, 1957:* Traded by the Yankees to the Athletics (after the infamous Copacabana incident). *November 20, 1957:* Traded by the Athletics to the Tigers. *November 20, 1958:* Traded by the Tigers to the Indians. *December 15, 1959:* Traded by the Indians to the Reds. *December 3, 1960:* Purchased by the Braves from the Reds. *June 1, 1961:* Traded by the Braves to the Twins. *April 3, 1962:* Released by the Twins. *1962:* Hired as a scout by the Twins. *1965:* Named third-base coach by the Twins. *June 1968:* Named manager of the Denver Bears (Twins affiliate). *October 11, 1968:* Hired as manager by the Twins. *October 13, 1969:* Fired by the Twins. *October 7, 1970:* Hired as manager by the Tigers. *September 2, 1973:* Fired by the Tigers. *September 8, 1973:* Hired as manager by the Rangers. *July 21, 1975:* Fired by the Rangers. *August 2, 1975:* Hired as manager by the Yankees (No. 1). *July 24, 1978:* Resigned under pressure from the Yankees (after his "One's a born liar; one's convicted" comment). *June 19, 1979:* Rehired as manager of the Yankees (No. 2). *October 28, 1979:* Fired by the Yankees (after a fight with a marshmallow salesman). *February 22, 1980:* Hired as manager by the Athletics. *October 20, 1982:* Released from his contract by the Athletics. *January 11, 1983:* Hired as manager by the Yankees (No. 3). *December 16, 1983:* Replaced as manager of the Yankees and named a special adviser to George Steinbrenner. *April 28, 1985:* Hired as manager of the Yankees (No. 4). *October 27, 1985:* Replaced as manager and given other, unspecified duties. *October 19, 1987:* Hired as manager by the Yankees (No. 5). *June 24, 1988:* Fired by the Yankees. He died in a car crash in the early hours of December 25, 1989. I'd say R.I.P., Billy, but it seems doubtful that Billy Martin ever rested peacefully.

Card 295: Billy Martin's résumé over 42 years in the game was unlike any other in baseball.

296. Ernie Broglio, Pitcher, St. Louis Cardinals.

Ernie Broglio's fate was to become the punchline for jokes about bad trades after the Cubs dealt for him in June 1964, sending Lou Brock to St. Louis. Brock became a Hall of Famer and won two World Series rings; Broglio, bedeviled by injuries, went 7–19, 5.40 for the Cubs and then was out of baseball. But to be fair, Broglio was the prize in another lopsided trade six years earlier, when the Cubs stole him from the Giants. Broglio had just finished 17–4 in Class AAA when he was sent, with end-of-the-line reliever Marv Grissom, to Chicago for catcher Hobie Landrith (unaccomplished enough to be exposed in the 1962 expansion draft), nondescript reliever Billy Muffett and career minor leaguer Benny Valenzuela (15 major league plate appearances). Those three combined for 2.9 Wins Above Replacement the rest of their careers; Broglio had 7.1 in 1960 alone with a sparkling 21–9, 2.74 season. And he came back three years later with 6.1 WAR for his 18–8, 2.99 season. That's the pitcher the Cubs hoped they were getting for that young outfielder with a .257 batting average and .306 on-base percentage.

297. Jackie Brandt, Outfielder, San Francisco Giants.

Plenty of ballplayers have been called flakes, but Jackie Brandt was apparently the first. A Cardinals teammate, Wally Moon, said of him, "Brandt is so wild his brains sometimes fall out of his head, flaking off his body." His new and forever nickname: Flakey. He once told sportswriters in spring training that he was going to play with "harder nonchalance," *The Baltimore Sun* said. He made basket catches and base-running blunders. Why? He said that the faster he ran, the more his "eyeballs jumped up and down." He made no-look throws back to the infield. As *The Sun* recounted, Orioles manager Hank Bauer asked him how he managed to misplay a fly ball. "He said, 'I lost it in the jet stream,'" Bauer said. At the end of one season, general manager Lee MacPhail saw Brandt cleaning out his locker and said, "Have a good winter, Jack," to which Brandt replied: "I always have good winters. It's the summers that give me trouble."

298. Tex Clevenger, Pitcher, Washington Senators.

The Senators were unexpectedly approaching .500 in midseason in 1959. After Camilo Pascual pitched a shutout in the first game of a doubleheader on July 19, they were 43–46. Then, the Senators being the Senators, they lost 18 games in a row. It was only when they gave Tex Clevenger his first start of the season, on August 5, in the second game of a doubleheader, that they rediscovered what winning was like—Clevenger pitched a seven-hit shutout against Cleveland, with no walks and eight strikeouts. He started six more games that season and threw another shutout. They were the only shutouts of his career. His nickname notwithstanding, he was from California, not Texas. He never played for a team in Texas. But while in the Red Sox organization, a teammate thought he resembled Boston pitcher Tex Hughson.

299. Billy Klaus, Shortstop, Baltimore Orioles.

Billy Klaus was one of those scrappy middle infielders whose move into managing comes as no surprise. But he wound up managing one of the truly bad minor league teams of the '60s, the 1967 York White Roses. York went 43–95, 30½ games out of first place, and was one of only two teams in the eight-team Eastern League that did not finish above .500. The team hit .217/.302/.276 with 27 home runs, roughly one every five games. The White Roses scored 351 runs (2.54 per game) and allowed 469. They were shut out 29 times and no-hit four times. The team leader in RBIs had 34. They were also last in the league in fielding. One pitcher was 0–16. It was not all Klaus's fault—he was replaced when the team was 17–44 (.279), and the roster was hardly stocked with future big-league stars; Del Unser was the best player, and he hit .231/.314/.322. And it was a brutal year for offense in the Eastern League, where batters averaged an unsightly .228/.314/.301, apparently anticipating the next season's Year of the Pitcher. That sad season did not end Klaus's managing career, but after three more years with a .374 winning percentage, Klaus was soon painting houses in the Blue Ridge Mountains.

300. Richie Ashburn, Outfielder, Philadelphia Phillies.

Richie Ashburn is in the Hall of Fame because he could hit (.308 career average), take walks (.396 on-base percentage), run (234 stolen bases, twice led the league in triples) and play wide-ranging defense in center field (led the league in putouts nine times, most of those years while Willie Mays was playing). But what he is most remembered for is one play that turned the 1950 National League pennant race. On the last day of the season, the Phillies held a one-game lead over the Dodgers when the teams met in Brooklyn. In a 1–1 game with no outs in the bottom of the ninth, the Dodgers' Cal Abrams was on second base when Duke Snider singled. Ashburn fielded the line drive on one hop. (Some accounts suggest Ashburn was playing even shallower than usual, anticipating a bunt, but Ashburn said otherwise, that he was certain Snider, who led the league in total bases, would not be bunting.) Now, Ashburn "was not known to have a strong throwing arm," Phillies ace Robin Roberts recalled in *The Whiz Kids and the 1950 Pennant*. Even Ashburn acknowledged "I did not have a great arm," although he insisted "I did not have a bad arm." But he positioned himself well, charged balls and, after the Dodgers' third-base coach, Milt Stock, waved Abrams home, Ashburn threw past the cutoff man and Abrams was out easily at the plate. A three-run homer in the top of the 10th pushed the Phillies to the pennant. The accurate throw home was not uncharacteristic; Ashburn, unimposing arm and all, led the league in assists three times. And in *The Whiz Kids*, he remembered this about Milt Stock. The Dodgers fired him and he became the third-base coach for the Cardinals. In one game against St. Louis with Stock coaching third, Ashburn said: "If memory serves me right, I threw out three guys from center field. He never thought I could throw, I guess."

301. Earl Averill, Third Baseman, Chicago Cubs.

Fourteen sons of Hall of Famers have played Major League Baseball, including Earl Averill, son of Earl Averill (but not Jr. and Sr.—it was Howard Earl Averill, père, and Earl Douglas Averill, fils). Most of the sons had nondescript careers. In fact, Vladimir Guerrero, Jr., already has the best son-of–Hall of Famer career. After five seasons (one of them pandemic-abbreviated), he had accumulated 15.2 Wins Above Replacement. Here's the whole list (through 2023):

Vladimir Guerrero, Jr., 15.2 WAR
Dick Sisler (George), 7.2
Cavan Biggio (Craig), 7.0
Dale Berra (Yogi), 5.4
Tony Gwynn, Jr., 5.1
Earl Averill (Earl), 3.6
Dave Sisler (George), 3.0

Eduardo Pérez (Tony), 0.9
Tim Raines, Jr., 0.2
Charlie Lindstrom (Freddie), 0.1
Ed Walsh (Ed), 0.1
Earle Mack (Connie), -0.1
Queenie O'Rourke (Orator Jim), -0.2
Eddie Collins, Jr., -0.8

Averill apprenticed mostly as a catcher in the minors but played mostly third base in his first two brief stints in the majors, with the Indians and the Cubs. His defense at third (.885 fielding percentage) sent him back behind the plate; his offense eventually sent him back to the minors.

302. Don Mossi, Pitcher, Detroit Tigers.

There is no escaping Don Mossi's appearance. *The Bill James Historical Baseball Abstract*, a (mostly) very serious book, mentions it with an article headlined "The Man Who Invented Winning Ugly." *The Great American Baseball Card Flipping, Trading and Bubble Gum Book*, a decidedly not serious book, focused in on Mossi's appearance, noting "his loving-cup ears and the dark hulking presence of one newly dead or resurrected." His obituary in *The Detroit Free Press* used the headline "Former pitcher Don Mossi, 'complete five-tool ugly player,' dies at 90." His *Detroit News* obit mentioned his nicknames: The Sphinx and Ears. So we're on the record here. But Mossi was also a darn fine reliever in Cleveland before becoming, at age 30, a creditable starter in Detroit (52–37, 3.45 ERA in his first four seasons in the rotation). He was also an adept fielder (only three errors in 311 career chances). That's an attractive package.

303. Marty Keough, Outfielder, Boston Red Sox.

Baseball came to Japan in 1872 (for context, that was four years before the National League was formed), and professional games began in the 1920s. When the first professional league began play there in 1936, the rosters included three Americans, the first of more than 1,000 foreigners to play in Japan through 2023. In 1968, Marty Keough was part of an influx of Americans to the Japanese leagues, playing a season with the Nankai Hawks. He took his family along, including his 12-year-old son, Matt—who, after his own major league career, took the mound for the Hanshin Tigers in 1987. That made Marty and Matt the first father-son ex–major leaguers to play professionally in Japan. Marty played a single season—"One year for me was plenty," he said—but Matt, one of Oakland's "Five Aces" in the early '80s, pitched four seasons for Hanshin.

304. Chicago Cubs Team Card.

The Cubs became a national team, as did the Braves, after the advent of cable superstations for the 1979 season. Having a national audience on TV dovetailed with their becoming a national attraction at the ballpark, with swarms of tourists joining the beer-loving Wrigley Field regulars, whom manager Lee Elia once described this way: "85 percent of the [expletive] world is working. The other 15 percent comes out here." It is easy to forget that for years the White Sox, not the Cubs, owned the Chicago market. From 1951 to 1967, the White Sox outdrew the Cubs every year but one. The White Sox resumed being a better draw for four straight years in the early '80s, before cable-TV exposure cemented Wrigley as a destination. Better teams, a refurbished stadium and a spruced-up neighborhood have made a difference in recent decades; every year from 1993 through 2022, the Cubs drew more fans than the White Sox.

305. Curt Raydon, Pitcher, Pittsburgh Pirates.
Curt Raydon was about as sure an out as you could find in the major leagues in his one season in the bigs, 1958. He was hitless in his first 36 at-bats, striking out 25 times. Then, in the next-to-last at-bat of his career, he singled off Tom Acker. He reverted to form six days later: He struck out in his final appearance in a major league batter's box. Raydon finished 1 for 38, for a .026 batting average (and slugging percentage). Somehow, however, he walked six times—twice in one game. The lone RBI of his career came on a squeeze bunt.

306. Jim Gilliam, Second Baseman-Outfielder, Los Angeles Dodgers.
The Dodgers have retired 10 numbers—nine of them belonging to Hall of Fame players or managers. The 10th is Jim Gilliam's No. 19. His career numbers don't explain why, but manager Walt Alston did when Gilliam, then a Dodgers coach, died the day after Los Angeles won the National League pennant in 1978, after suffering a brain hemorrhage. "Jim was the best No. 2 hitter I ever saw," Alston told *The Washington Post*'s Tom Boswell. "When Maury Wills was stealing all those bases"—he stole a then-record 104 in 1962—"Gilliam was taking strikes, getting himself in the hole at the plate, giving himself up to move Wills from second to third. Junior was the perfect team player who'd sacrifice batting average to help the club." And he would play anywhere. Although primarily a fine-fielding second baseman, Gilliam also played third, first and all three outfield positions. He made such a stellar defensive play at third in Game 7 of the 1965 World Series that the Baseball Hall of Fame requested his glove.

307. Curt Barclay, Pitcher, San Francisco Giants.
The Giants-Dodgers rivalry in New York was so old that it predated the Dodgers; they were the Bridegrooms when the teams first met, in 1889. There could be no Subway Series, as there was no subway. The best rivalry since sliced bread? No, as Ben Hoffman noted in *The New York Times*, it began four decades before sliced bread was invented. The rivalry was, however, heated. "When the Dodgers played the Giants," Pee Wee Reese said in *New York City Baseball*, "it was the most important game in your life. There will never be another rivalry like that again." Now, here it was, September 8, 1957, and the long rivalry was coming to an end in New York; the Giants had announced that they were moving to San Francisco, and it was broadly believed that the Dodgers were moving to Los Angeles. For their final meeting as New York teams, the rookie Curt Barclay took the mound at the Polo Grounds before a crowd

of 22,376. The Giants won, 3–2, as Barclay, capping what would be the finest stretch of his major league career, allowed two runs in six and a third innings to earn his fourth consecutive victory. The next time the teams met, it was San Francisco versus Los Angeles, in the cavernous Los Angeles Coliseum, on April 15, 1959. Barclay won one more game in his career: that April 17 against Los Angeles.

308. Norm Siebern, Outfielder, New York Yankees.

After the 1959 season, their worst in 34 years, the Yankees were actively looking to shake up the team. On December 11, they succeeded, pulling off a franchise-changing (and baseball history-changing), seven-player deal with the Athletics (surprise, surprise) in which the principals were Roger Maris heading east and Norm Siebern heading west. Maris was a 25-year-old left-handed hitter who had just finished his third season in the majors; Siebern was a 26-year-old left-handed hitter who had just finished *his* third season in the majors. *The New York Times*, in its account of the trade, called Maris "potentially an outfield star of major magnitude"; Siebern, "a 'potentially great' outfielder who with the Yankees never quite made it." Maris was hitting like Mickey Mantle in late July 1959 (344/.405/.602 with 14 home runs) before slumping, with only two homers in his last 55 games. *The Times* said his season was diminished by appendicitis. Siebern, whom *The Times* said was still bothered by a knee injury from two years earlier, hit poorly for two months before hitting consistently, although with limited pop. Siebern was criticized for defensive lapses in the 1958 World Series but was good enough to win a Gold Glove that year. We know how this trade worked out, but it was not so apparent at the time that it would benefit the Yankees (and Maris) so greatly. Here's a comparison of the players the two seasons before and after the trade:

Card 308: Norm Siebern was traded for Roger Maris. It was not as lopsided a deal as you may think. (Except for those home runs!)

1958	BA/OBP/SLG	HR	OPS+	1959	BA/OBP/SLG	HR	OPS+
Maris	.240/.295/.431	28	97	Maris	.273/.359/.464	16	123
Siebern	.300.388/.454	11	136	Siebern	.271/.341/.403	11	108

1960	BA/OBP/SLG	HR	OPS+	1961	BA/OBP/SLG	HR	OPS+
Maris	.283/.371/.581	39	160	Maris	.269/.372/.620	61	167
Siebern	.279/.366/.471	19	125	Siebern	.296/.384/.475	18	129

Siebern, an on-base machine unlike anyone else on the Yankees except Mantle, played at an All-Star level after the trade (although he did not actually make the All-Star team until 1962, the first of three selections). Maris, a power-hitting machine unlike anyone else on the Yankees except Mantle—and in 1961, in all of baseball—played at an MVP level. Yankee Stadium was not a boon for Maris except for his home runs; the Stadium had been a drag on Siebern's output. Here are their career numbers at Yankee Stadium and Municipal Stadium in Kansas City:

Maris	PA	HR	BA/OBP/SLG	Siebern	PA	HR	BA/OBP/SLG
NY	1718	98	.259/.346/.503	NY	815	18	.259/.342/.383
KC	773	35	.282/.377/.513	KC	1450	42	.293/.383/.467

The Yankees gambled on swapping a solid-hitting outfielder—a young Hank Bauer, by the numbers—for a power-hitting outfielder they must have sensed was ideal for their ballpark. Stripped of the other players, this was essentially what Bill James has called a "challenge trade." And the Yankees won. One last comparison: their career numbers, which show how closely their offensive value matched—except for Maris's vast edge in home run power.

Player	PA	HR	BA/OBP/SLG	OPS+
Maris	5847	275	.260/.345/.476	127
Siebern	5269	132	.272/.369/.423	118

Both were traded away again—Maris to the Cardinals, Siebern to the Orioles before he began a peripatetic career. Their teams actually met in the 1967 Series: Maris starred for the Cardinals while Siebern pinch-hit for the Red Sox. One last similarity: Each retired after the '68 season.

309. Sal Maglie, Pitcher, St. Louis Cardinals.

In 1950, Sal Maglie was 33 years old and had 84⅓ innings of major league experience. He had struggled to get into baseball, had struggled in the minor leagues, had sat out two seasons during World War II to work in a defense plant, had spent two seasons playing in Mexico and was barred by Major League Baseball for doing so. There was little reason to expect much from Maglie. And then for the next three years, playing for the Giants, he was one of the best pitchers in baseball—a 59–18 record with a 2.86 ERA (he had seasons of 18–4, 2.73; 23–6, 2.93; 18–8, 2.92). He had 13 shutouts and even six saves. "During those years, if I wanted a ballgame won, I wanted Sal Maglie pitching," his Giants teammate Monte Irvin said in Maglie's *Los Angeles Times* obituary. He was known for his heavy stubble, a hard-breaking curve and a willingness to throw at hitters enough to back them off the plate, with a glare that indicated his intent. His first wife, Kathleen Maglie, had difficulty understanding why the baseball world thought her husband was such a hard guy. "He isn't tough at all," she was quoted saying in his *New York Times* obituary. "He lets his beard grow before a game so he'll look fierce. I used to wonder what people were talking about when they said he scowled ferociously at the batters. Then I stayed home one day and watched him on TV. I hardly knew him." Despite chronic back problems that limited his use, Maglie was still an effective pitcher at age 40.

310. Luis Aparicio, Shortstop, Chicago White Sox.

The White Sox were unlike any other American League team in the 1950s; they would actually have players try to steal a base. In 1950, the league leader was Dom DiMaggio with 15 steals; the entire eight-team league stole 278 bases. From 1951 to 1961, Chicago led the league in stolen bases every year, and it wasn't close, and the Sox had nearly 24 percent of the steals in the league. From 1951 to 1962, the AL's individual leader in stolen bases played for the White Sox every year but one. Chicago was hardly running wild compared to other eras—its peak was 122 thefts—but the team ran enough to be called the Go-Go Sox. And Luis Aparicio was a major reason. He led the AL in steals his first seven years in Chicago, although with totals of only 21, 28 and 29 his first three seasons. He took off in the pennant-winning season of '59 with 56 steals, and at a great success rate—81 percent. He was not a good hitter (.266/.311/.343) and not really a very good leadoff hitter (he never scored 100 runs or led the league). He often did not even lead his team in runs; as Bill James noted in his *Historical Baseball Abstract*, teammates who were plodders, like Curt Blefary, Joe Cunningham and George Scott, scored more runs in some seasons than Aparicio. But he changed perceptions of how the game could be played.

311. Norm Zauchin, First Baseman, Washington Senators.

Norm Zauchin stood 6 foot 4, and as a high schooler he had aspirations of playing professional basketball. He chose baseball instead, signing with the Red Sox, and as an 18-year-old first baseman he hit .353/.447/.672 with 33 home runs in 120 games in Class D. But Boston decided it had enough first basemen in its system, according to Zauchin's SABR Bio Project biography, so it spent spring training in 1949 converting him to a ... catcher. Now, the average listed height of a starting catcher in the American League that year was 5–11; in the National League it was 6–0. There was one catcher as tall as 6–3, the Braves' Del Crandall. The best catcher in the AL was the 5–7 Yogi Berra; in the NL, the 5–9 Roy Campanella. (Even now, none of the top 30 players in career games caught is 6–4.) But Boston persisted, even with Zauchin making the leap from Class D to Class AAA Louisville. He caught two regular-season games for Louisville, then was sent down to Class A Scranton, where he played four more games before he was sent down *again,* to Class C San Jose, where he became a first baseman again. He never caught another game.

312. Don Newcombe, Pitcher, Cincinnati Redlegs.

History can compress reality, so it is easy to forget that Don Newcombe and Roy Campanella also played major roles in baseball's integration. They signed with the Brooklyn Dodgers five months after Jackie Robinson did and joined the minor leagues in 1946, the same year Robinson did. While Robinson was on the cusp of the major leagues at Class AAA Montreal, however, Newcombe and Campanella wound up at Class B Nashua, New Hampshire. That was a last-resort assignment. The Dodgers' Class AA teams were in segregated Mobile, Alabama, and Fort Worth, Texas, as Jules Tygiel detailed in *Baseball's Great Experiment*, while three of their Class B teams were in segregated states. The team in Danville, Illinois, did not want them, Tygiel said, which left Nashua—a town with no Black residents. Branch Rickey's grand experiment might have faltered, but Nashua management took on Newcombe, who turned 20 that summer, and Campanella (who as a 25-year-old Negro leagues star could clearly have played at a higher level). Their careers were delayed a bit when the Dodgers decided not to have Newcombe and Campanella report to spring training in Florida that first year because of problems Robinson had faced there. They had minimal difficulties in Nashua or the New England League. Newcombe went 14–4, 2.91, and Campanella batted .290/.393/.477 with 13 homers in a league that sapped power. The next year, when Robinson broke the racial barrier in the majors, Campanella was starring at Montreal, but the Dodgers held Newcombe back in Nashua, saying he needed to work on his curve. He responded by going 19–6, 2.91, and two years later he was the National League Rookie of the Year.

313. Frank House, Catcher, Kansas City Athletics.
Harmon Killebrew told a great story about Frank House and Killebrew's first career home run. The scene: late June 1955, the second season for Killebrew, a struggling 18-year-old with the Senators. When he came up against the Tigers' Billy Hoeft in the fifth inning, he was batting .077—2 for 26, both of his hits singles. We'll let Killebrew pick up the tale, as told in *Baseball's Bonus Babies*: "Frank House was the catcher—Pig House—and he said, 'Kid, we're gonna throw you a fastball.' I didn't know whether he was telling me the truth or lying, but, sure enough, here comes the fastball and I hit it 476 feet. When I ran around the bases, came in at home plate, and touched home, he said, 'Kid, that's the last time we'll ever tell you what's coming.'" Killebrew didn't need much help; that was the first of 573 homers. And House could afford to be generous; the Tigers were leading 13–0 in a game they won 18–7.

314. Don Cardwell, Pitcher, Philadelphia Phillies.
The 1969 Miracle Mets earned that nickname—a team that had never finished better than 16 games under .500 in its first seven seasons captured the World Series. Don Cardwell was a good example why. At age 33 he was the veteran presence in a rotation that included Tom Seaver (24), Jerry Koosman (26), Gary Gentry (22) and Jim McAndrew (25), but he had previously had marginal success. His record was 92–125 with a 3.89 ERA, even while pitching in the hitting-depressed late '60s. Cardwell began the 1969 season by losing his first four decisions. At the end of June he was 2–8; at the end of July he was 3–9, and his ERA had been steadily climbing for two months. Then came the Cardwell part of the miracle. He won both of his decisions in August while compiling a 1.84 ERA and moving back into the rotation. He won his first three starts in September as the Mets pulled away from the Cubs. In the second game of a September 12 doubleheader, he drove in the only run as the Mets won, 1–0. (Koosman had driven in the only run in winning the opener, 1–0.) Only a meaningless two-inning start on the last day of the season fluffed up his ERA for September to 1.80. Cardwell finished 8–10 with a 3.01 ERA and a career-best 121 ERA+, and the Mets won the pennant by eight games. "Tom Seaver told me: 'We really looked up to you. You were the strong point of our young club,'" Cardwell said in a 2002 interview with *The Chicago Sun-Times*. "They probably thought that if I could do it at my age, they could do it at theirs."

315. Joe Adcock, First Baseman, Milwaukee Braves.

Joe Adcock was a fearsome right-handed power hitter for the Braves. He slugged .500 or better seven years in a row and eight out of nine. In 10 seasons with Milwaukee, he averaged 24 home runs despite playing a full season's worth of games only half the time. Adcock lost about a season's worth of games to injuries, but he lost even more to platooning. His playing time was sacrificed to get the left-handed-hitting Frank Torre in the lineup. (Adcock also shifted to left field some so Torre could play—clearly not a move made for defensive purposes.) The numbers raise questions about the platooning. Adcock actually hit right-handers a little better than lefties, and he hit them both well. And Torre, a lefty swinger, actually hit left-handers a little better than righties. Torre kept his spot in the lineup in the Braves' pennant-winning seasons, 1957 and '58, by hitting for average (.272 and .309) although with no power. Adcock's playing time was crimped by injuries in 1957 and by platooning in '58, even though he hit .280/.339/.520 over the two seasons, with 31 home runs in 580 plate appearances. The platoon was costing the Braves power (assuming they could have found an adequate left fielder) for the sake of a small boost in on-base percentage. With Hank Aaron and Eddie Mathews in the lineup, perhaps the Braves thought it was a good tradeoff, but Adcock, who was 23rd on the career home run list with 336 when he retired in 1966, might have reached 400 had he stayed healthy and not been platooned so often.

316. Ralph Lumenti, Pitcher, Washington Senators.

On September 2, 1957, Ralph Lumenti, a 20-year-old pitcher from the University of Massachusetts, Amherst, signed with the Senators for $35,000. Five days later, he was pitching against the Yankees; he threw a scoreless ninth and struck out Harry (Suitcase) Simpson. On September 12, he went seven innings against the Athletics, yielding only three hits and two runs while striking out five. Manager Cookie Lavagetto said: "He was wonderful. You would have thought he had been pitching 20 years. This boy is a real find." Lumenti earned a mention in *Sports Illustrated*'s 1958 preseason look at the Senators: "The pitching staff could certainly benefit if Ralph proves he was worth his bonus." He made the rotation and won his third start, allowing the Tigers one run in five and a third innings, although he gave up four hits and six walks. By late May, he was in the bullpen. By the end of June, he was in the minors, having walked 36 batters and allowed 20 earned runs in 21 innings. At age 25, he was out of baseball.

317. N.L. Hitting Kings: Richie Ashburn-Willie Mays.

On September 24, 1958, Willie Mays led Richie Ashburn in the race for the National League batting title, .346 to .344. Mays had the next day off; Ashburn the next two. On Friday the 27th, Mays went hitless in three at-bats against the Cardinals, while Ashburn went two for four against the Pirates; now Ashburn was in the lead, .345 to .344. On that Saturday, Mays managed two singles in five at-bats, putting him at .345; but Ashburn countered with a three-for-five day, including two opposite-field singles, and was hitting .347. So the batting title went down to the last day, and Mays came up big—three for five with a double and a homer; his last at-bat of the season was a line out to center field. Ashburn, however, wrapped up the title with a three-for-four day (including an opposite-field single and an infield single), edging out Mays, .350 to .347. Mays had gone eight for his last 16, but Ashburn went eight for his last 13. Mays never batted above .319 again; Ashburn hit .300 only once in his final four seasons.

318. Rocky Bridges, Shortstop, Detroit Tigers.

Card 318: Rocky Bridges took a teammate's advice and began chewing tobacco in an effort to make the majors, as the telltale bulge in his cheek proves.

The lasting image of Rocky Bridges is with his cheek packed with chewing tobacco. He, Nellie Fox and Bill Tuttle were all known for their chaws in the '50s and '60s, with baseball cards to prove it. Bridges was so renowned for his cheek full of chaw that a 1962 photo shows him with a female reporter for *The Valley Times*, a San Fernando Valley newspaper, and a pouch of Beech-Nut captioned, "Rocky Bridges teaches tobacco chewing." Bridges said a minor league teammate told him he would never make the majors unless he smoked and chewed, so he did both (cigars off the field, chaw on it). Tobacco use persisted in the game—look up photos of George Brett or Lenny Dykstra, for example—but Major League Baseball finally banned the use of smokeless tobacco in 2016 for all players entering the league. That meant current major leaguers who used were grandfathered in, so you may still see a major league ballplayer with the telltale distended jaw.

319. Dave Hillman, Pitcher, Chicago Cubs.

Darius Dutton Hillman, of Dungannon, Virginia—call him Dave—spent eight seasons in the major leagues and never played for a winning team. The closest he came was in 1962, when he opened the season with the Reds, who went on to post a 98–64 record. But they began the season 1–3, at which point Hillman was sent to the New York Mets, who had already sunk to 1–11 in their inaugural season. Those Mets finished 40–120, but Hillman was long gone. He last appeared in a 16–3 loss to the fellow expansionists, the Houston Colt .45s, on June 22. He was optioned to Syracuse, but his career was over. Hillman had done his part for his losing teams, posting a single winning record (3–2 for the '61 Red Sox).

320. Bob Skinner, Outfielder, Pittsburgh Pirates.

There have been dozens of father-son combinations who have played in the major leagues, but only five have both managed in the majors. Bob Skinner, a longtime Pirates outfielder, and Joel Skinner, a veteran American League catcher, were the second. Bob replaced Gene Mauch as the Phillies' manager in midseason 1968. He had no more success in overseeing Dick Allen than Mauch had and resigned in August 1969, citing conflicts over Allen. Skinner managed only one more major league game—as the interim skipper for the woeful 1977 Padres. They won, leaving him with a 92–123 record (.428). Joel had an even shorter managerial career, finishing out the 2002 season for Cleveland with a 35–41 record (.461). The other father-son managers? George and Dave Sisler, Felipe Alou and Luis Rojas, Buddy and David Bell, and Bob and Aaron Boone.

321. Bob Giallombardo, Pitcher, Los Angeles Dodgers.

Sandy Koufax and Bob Giallombardo, lean left-handed pitchers, were born 18 months apart and wound up at Lafayette High School in Brooklyn at the same time. But they never played high school ball together. Koufax did not go out for baseball until his senior year—he played first base at Lafayette—and Giallombardo tried out for the team but didn't make it. As he recalled in a 2009 interview, he struck out 14 or 15 batters in an exhibition game, but it wasn't enough. "The coach said, 'You're not quite ready,'" Giallombardo said. "I was laughing at him. They classified Koufax as too wild and that he'd never make it as a pitcher." Both signed with the Brooklyn Dodgers, and in 1958 they were teammates in Los Angeles. Giallombardo, only 21, won his fourth start, limiting the Reds to seven hits and one earned run in eight and a third innings. Two weeks later, he was sent back to Class AAA, never to return. He hurt his arm in winter ball, had surgery and lost his fastball. "Once they cut me," he said in 2009, "it wasn't the same."

322. Harry Hanebrink, Infielder, Milwaukee Braves.

If you saw only Harry Hanebrink's bare minor league statistics, you might think he was a power-hitting infielder who never quite developed. He hit 16 home runs at Class C Eau Claire in his first season in professional baseball, and later, he thumped 20 and 24 at Class AAA Wichita. But Hanebrink, who was listed at 6 feet and 165 pounds and batted left-handed, was no slugger; instead, he was the beneficiary of accommodating ballparks. It was 312 feet down the right-field line in Eau Claire; same thing in Wichita. Eau Claire led its league in homers; Wichita was second only to the mile-high Denver Bears in both of Hanebrink's seasons in the American Association. He hit 60 homers in those three seasons, 53 in his other 11 years in pro ball.

323. Frank Sullivan, Pitcher, Boston Red Sox.

In December 1960, the Red Sox traded 6-foot-7-inch pitcher Frank Sullivan to the Phillies for 6-foot-8 pitcher Gene Conley. Frank Lane, a longtime general manager, was asked who won the trade. "The Red Sox by an inch," he replied. Conley was also a backup center for the Celtics—he had come up with the Boston Braves—but

Sullivan had his own history with the Celtics. Sullivan wrote in his autobiography, *Life Is More Than Nine Innings*, that when Bill Russell joined the Celtics for the 1956–57 season, Jack Nichols was his backup. But Nichols was also going to dental school and often had to miss practice. A college teammate of Nichols's was Sammy White, who was also a Red Sox catcher, and he suggested Sullivan as a fill-in for Celtics practice. Sullivan wrote that "every time I was chosen to be on one team in practice, the other team clapped." Red Auerbach used him throughout the preseason and asked Sullivan to consider being a two-sport player, as Conley was, but, Sullivan wrote, "I told him I was already maxed."

324. Don Demeter, Outfielder, Los Angeles Dodgers.

Don Demeter never won a Gold Glove, but he did set an impressive fielding record—266 consecutive games in the outfield without being charged with an error. (Not counted: his errors at third base.) The streak began in 1962 and continued until July 9, 1965, when it ended with the help of Charlie O. Finley and a dog. Finley, the Athletics' owner, had instituted a gimmick in which dogs trained to aid the Kansas City grounds crew would carry out bases in their mouths between innings. In the fifth inning, Mike Hershberger lined a two-out single to center that Demeter caught on a hop, but the grounds crew apparently thought he had snagged it in the air for the third out and unleashed the dogs. "I scooped the ball up and threw into second base to hold the runner, and the dog ran through our shortstop Dick McAuliffe's legs," Demeter said, according to his *New York Times* obituary. "Dick looked down at the dog and missed the ball I threw him, advancing the runner, and they gave me the error." The streak would not have lasted much longer anyway; Demeter made another outfield error before the season ended.

325. Ken Boyer, Third Baseman, St. Louis Cardinals.

It was clear pretty quickly that Ken Boyer was a hard-hitting, good-fielding third baseman. But the Cardinals did some curious things with him. In the minors, they tried to develop him as a pitcher *and* a third baseman. In his first year, in Class D, he walked more batters than he struck out, while batting 15 for 33 with three home runs. The experiment persisted another year, but when his pitching deteriorated and he hit .342 with nine homers in 240 at-bats, the Cardinals left him at third base. When he was a rookie in St. Louis, the Cardinals concluded he was a base-stealing threat. (The managers that year, Eddie Stanky and Harry Walker, both tended to be above average in stolen base attempts.) Boyer did steal 29 bases (in 39 attempts) the year before, but he was no Vince Coleman, swiping 22 bases for the Cardinals while being caught 17 times. It was typical of the team—St. Louis succeeded on only 52 percent of its attempts, although that was better than its won-lost record (.441). In came a new manager, Fred Hutchinson, and the Runnin' Redbirds came to a halt. But the Cardinals tried a new wrinkle in 1957, Boyer's third season, moving him to center field. His SABR Bio Project biography said Boyer suggested the move so that Eddie Kasko could slide into the lineup at third base. Kasko's defensive numbers at third were not as good as Boyer's, and he did not hit nearly as well. Boyer, meanwhile, playing between lackluster defenders in left (Wally Moon) and right (Del Ennis), led NL center fielders in putouts. That experiment lasted a single season: St. Louis acquired Curt Flood to play center and moved Boyer back to third base, where he immediately won the first of five Gold Gloves.

326. Marv Throneberry, First Baseman-Outfielder, New York Yankees.

After Marv Throneberry died in 1994, George Vecsey of *The New York Times* called him "the ultimate Met," and it was not for starring exploits on the 1962 Metropolitans. "Marv missed bases. Marv dropped throws. Marv threw to wrong bases. Marv missed signs," Vecsey wrote, making him the symbol of a 40–120 team. He was called Marvelous Marv, and fans took to him. Four of them wore T-shirts printed with V, R, A, M and !—VRAM! or Marv spelled backward. Fans would chant, "Raspberry, Strawberry, we love Throneberry." He was good-natured about how bad he was, but Throneberry really had been a top power-hitting prospect. He hit 16 homers in 88 games in his first season in the minors; the next year he hit 30 in a full season. From ages 21 to 23, playing in Denver, he led the Class AAA American Association in homers with 36, 42 and 40. But he struck out too much, walked too little, didn't hit enough and couldn't catch the ball when he needed to. Marvin Eugene Throneberry—yes, M.E.T.—was born to be a Met.

327. Gary Bell, Pitcher, Cleveland Indians.

Seven weeks into the 1967 season, Gary Bell was 1–5 with a 3.71 ERA, which wasn't very good in 1967. His Cleveland team sat at .500 but was bound for an eighth-place finish. Then he received an unlikely reprieve—Bell was traded to the Red Sox, who hadn't won a pennant in 21 years and were barely above .500 themselves. Those were the Impossible Dream Red Sox, though, and Bell was an important reason the dream came true. He won five of his first six decisions to help keep Boston afloat. Beginning in mid–August, he again won five of six decisions, and the Red Sox moved from fourth place to second, a half-game out of first. The lead pinballed the rest of the way among the Red Sox, the Tigers, the Twins and the White Sox, with Boston claiming the lead on the next-to-last day of the season; Bell had the save. He finished 12–8, 3.16 for the Red Sox, who won the pennant by a single game. Baseball glory can be fleeting, however; two years later, Bell couldn't stick with the moribund expansion Seattle Pilots—Bell said his fastball had died—and was cast off to the White Sox, where he was even worse. On October 6, the day the first American League Championship Series ended, so did his major league career.

328. Lou Skizas, Outfielder, Chicago White Sox.

He was called the Nervous Greek. The Greek part was obvious. If you saw him bat, the Nervous part was, too. Lou Skizas had an elaborate ritual before every at-bat. As *The Sporting News* described it in 1955, he would drop the bat in the batter's box and cover it with dirt. Then he would wipe the bat off on his pants, drawing it between his legs. Then he would kiss the fat end of the bat. Then he would reach into a rear pocket, at least three times; the suspicion was that he had a good-luck charm there, but Skizas insisted he was not superstitious. Now he was ready to bat, but even his stance was unorthodox. He kept his left heel off the ground until the pitch arrived to ensure he kept his weight on his back foot. He was a pretty good hitter, at best an indifferent fielder and, Casey Stengel said, "a guy who fires managers." But he was plenty smart, earning a Ph.D. in biology and teaching for years at the University of Illinois.

329. Detroit Tigers Team Card.

This is a team picture of vanilla. (And that's not just because the Tigers were so late in integrating—1958.) Detroit was a contender in 1950, winning 95 games but finishing three games back of the Yankees. A collapse followed, including a 50–104 season in 1952, before the team got stuck in consistent mediocrity. Beginning in 1955, Detroit went 79–75, 82–72, 78–76, 77–77, 76–78 and 71–83 to get them to 1960. Finally, the Tigers got back in a pennant race in 1961, but their 101-win team was again no match for the Yankees. Detroit did not sink to the depths of the '50s afterward, but it got stuck in a not-good-enough rut: 85–76, 79–83, 85–77, 89–73, 88–74, 91–71. And then, the Tigers' world turned colorful: 103 wins in 1968, an American League pennant and their first World Series title since 1945.

330. Gus Triandos, Catcher, Baltimore Orioles.

Gus Triandos was slow. Joe Posnanski called him "famously slow" and described the difference between a slow ballplayer and a famously slow one. A slow ballplayer might not be noticed if he hustles, Posnanski wrote. "But the famously slow ballplayer—he has nowhere to hide. And that was Gus Triandos." His obituary in *The Baltimore Sun* described Triandos as "a swarthy, slow-footed catcher." Heck, in one interview with Ed Attanasio of the blog This Great Game, Triandos himself noted three times that "I couldn't run." Triandos famously stole only one base in his 13-year career, on his only attempt. It came in the last inning of the last game of the 1958 season. Catchers are notorious for being slow. Posnanski wrote for MLB.com that "the slowest measurement known to man is a 'Molina' and that all players can be measured against it." A YouTube video is headlined "Bengie Molina Is the Slowest Man in Baseball, and that was seven years before his career ended. Bill James said in his *Historical Baseball Abstract*—written after Triandos but before Molina—that hulking catcher Ernie Lombardi, late in his

Card 330: Gus Triandos was in a long, slow line of catchers who couldn't run. "Famously slow," one writer accurately said. But he was perfect as a base stealer.

career, was "surely the slowest man ever to play baseball well." And a former Houston Astros ball boy contended that a ball boy went into the clubhouse one day with a box for catcher Ed Herrmann and told him: "Here you go, Ed. Something you can beat in a foot race." Inside the box? A garden slug.

331. Steve Boros, Infielder, Detroit Tigers.

Steve Boros touched a lot of bases in baseball, at least metaphorically. He was a college star (third-team All-American at Michigan). A bonus baby ($26,000). A minor league MVP (with a .317/.404/.576 season in Class AAA with 30 home runs and 22 steals). A major leaguer for parts of seven seasons. A minor league manager. A major league coach specializing in base running (he used a stopwatch on the field, a rarity at the time). A major league manager (he succeeded Billy Martin in Oakland and Dick Williams in San Diego and failed at both stops; he was said to be too nice). He was a coach in Oakland in 1983—well before *Moneyball*—when he helped the Athletics introduce computers in the clubhouse. His *Los Angeles Times* obituary noted this about the brightest moment in Boros's time as a Dodgers scout, a report on the Athletics before the 1988 World Series: "Among the traits that Boros and fellow scouts Mel Didier and Jerry Stephenson noticed: Oakland relief ace Dennis Eckersley tended to throw a backdoor slider on 3–2 counts to left-handed hitters." Didier mentioned it to Kirk Gibson before Game 1, and with a 3–2 count against Eckersley in the ninth inning, that's what Gibson hit for a game-winning home run.

332. Ray Monzant, Pitcher, San Francisco Giants.

There was not much to distinguish Ramón Monzant's baseball career. In fact, he was so undistinguished that in 1958, Topps inadvertently put Monzant's image on the card for his teammate Mike McCormick. One tipoff that it's the wrong guy: Monzant was right-handed, McCormick was left-handed. That really was Monzant on the '58 Monzant card, though. The '59 card, too.

333. Harry Simpson, Outfielder, Kansas City Athletics.

The name Suitcase Simpson has been part of American culture for more than a century. It first appeared with a character—so named because of his big feet—in a long-running cartoon, *Toonerville Folks*, that began in 1908 and lasted until 1955. By that time, Harry (Suitcase) Simpson had picked up the nickname, which, he acknowledged in the *1951 Cleveland Indians Sketch Book*, came from the cartoon. Harry also had big feet. (Some accounts say Simpson picked up the nickname because he played for so many different teams, but he did not, in fact, move around inordinately.) Simpson's professional career ended in 1964, but his name was not forgotten. In 1997, the Jesse Stone series by Robert B. Parker, about a small-town police chief in Massachusetts (and ex–minor league shortstop), included a young cop, Luther Simpson, who was nicknamed Suitcase by his fourth-grade gym teacher. Luther didn't know there had been a ballplayer named Suitcase Simpson. Harry Simpson said he did not much care for the nickname at first, but he got used to it. Back home in Dalton, Georgia, however, no one called him Suitcase; he was Goodie. A 2009 article in *The Dalton Daily Citizen News*, reporting on a new memorial to

Simpson, said, "He earned that moniker for his willingness to help his friends and neighbors in Dalton." It is a delight to note that Suitcase Simpson faced off against Satchel Paige 18 times—and Suitcase owned him, with five hits (for a .385 average) and five walks.

334. Glen Hobbie, Pitcher, Chicago Cubs.

Sometimes things work out even when things don't work out as planned. Such was the case for the Cardinals in 1964, when, foundering two months into the season, they made changes they hoped would turn the season around. The season did turn, but not for the reasons they anticipated. After a loss in its first game in June, St. Louis stood 25–21. General manager Bing Devine thought he might be able to upgrade his pitching staff, so he swapped 37-year-old left-hander Lew Burdette, who had been used sparingly in relief, to the Cubs for 27-year-old right-hander Glen Hobbie, a once-promising starter whose career had been stymied by injuries. Hobbie immediately paid off. He allowed a single run in seven and a third innings in his first start, three days after the trade, although the bullpen blew the victory. In his next start, Hobbie pitched a two-hitter as the Cardinals won, 2–1. Two days later, St. Louis fell below .500 for the first time since Opening Day as Ernie Broglio pitched so-so. On June 15, the day of Hobbie's third start for the Cardinals and with St. Louis falling increasingly behind the leaders Philadelphia and San Francisco, Devine made an even bigger deal, again with the Cubs—Broglio and others for Lou Brock and others. Hobbie looked like an answer in the rotation that Broglio had not been, and St. Louis had averaged only 2.25 runs in the previous 13 games, so its offense needed a boost. Hobbie was not the answer, as it turned out—he ran up a 6.11 ERA in 11 more games and was banished to Class AAA—but Bob Gibson, Ray Sadecki and Curt Simmons were excellent in the rotation and Brock was fantastic. The maneuvering for pitching amounted to very little, except that it brought in Brock, who amounted to a lot. And Hobbie did win one game … and the Cardinals won the pennant by one game.

335. Johnny Temple, Second Baseman, Cincinnati Redlegs.

It was an article of faith in my Little League that Johnny Temple was a sly hitter who was content to get hit by a pitch by turning his back into it rather than trying to get out of the way. It was a way to test an umpire's willingness to enforce a rule, known as 5.05(b)(2), which says a batter hit by a pitch will be awarded first base unless "the batter makes no attempt to avoid being touched by the ball." We called it the Johnny Temple rule, and it was along the continuum of efforts to circumvent the rules that include what we now refer to as framing pitches. (Perhaps we should call this the Aledmys Díaz rule after his futile attempt to get a hit-by-pitch in the 2022 World Series.) Odd thing is, Johnny Temple was almost never hit by a pitch—only 13 times in 13 years. So how did we hear about the Johnny Temple rule?

336. Billy Loes, Pitcher, Baltimore Orioles.

Shortly after Christmas in 1966, *The New York Times* published a one-paragraph article about a robbery at Billy Loes's home in the borough of Queens. The article said that five armed men knocked on the door of his home and asked, "Where's the card game?" Loes said they had the wrong place, but the robbers went in anyway, one of them shoving a shotgun against his belly, and took "$120 in cash, some jewelry, and mementoes of Mr. Loes's baseball career." Barebones, straightforward *Times* account. But after Loes's death in 2010, *The New York Daily News*'s Bill Madden published a much more colorful tale. Madden quoted Tom Villante, a former advertising executive who he said served as "an unofficial Dodger alumni director." Madden wrote that Villante said Loes, whom he had met in his Brooklyn Dodger days, was known for hosting card games with large sums of money. In this account, the shotgun was held to Loes's head while the robbers ransacked his home, taking his 1955 World Series ring and other valuables. But, Madden wrote, "before departing, Loes asked them: 'Do me a favor? Would you mind setting fire to the place on your way out so I can collect the insurance money?'"

337. George Crowe, First Baseman, St. Louis Cardinals.

Basketball has been king in Indiana for more than a century. *The Indianapolis Star* created the country's first Mr. Basketball honor in 1939 and awarded it to a 6-foot-2-inch powerhouse from Franklin, a small town south of Indianapolis: George Crowe. Indiana had a tortured racial history—the Indiana State Library notes the Ku Klux Klan's rise "to prominence in Indiana politics and society after World War I" and refers to the Klan's role in the election of the governor in 1924. Which makes Crowe's selection just 15 years later all the more remarkable. Crowe played professional baseball and basketball on segregated teams (he and Jackie Robinson were hoops teammates) before those pro sports integrated. He made it to the majors as a 31-year-old slugger, but he was unable to secure a regular spot in a lineup until he was 36. He responded by hitting 31 home runs and slugging .504 in 133 games for the Reds. Crowe became a mentor to young Black players while in St. Louis. A team-first approach was in his DNA—his Franklin High School team lost the state championship in his Mr. Basketball season, to his great disappointment. "He always said he would have much rather won the state championship and someone else be Mr. Basketball," his nephew Brad Crowe said. George's brother Ray was a basketball luminary in his own right, coaching state champion teams and Oscar Robertson at Crispus Attucks High School in Indianapolis.

338. Sparky Anderson, Second Baseman, Philadelphia Phillies.

George (Sparky) Anderson was fired from his first managing job, with a Class AAA team of the Braves. But Bob Howsam, general manager of the Cardinals, was, perhaps inexplicably, in Anderson's corner. When Howsam needed a last-minute manager at Class A Rock Hill the next year, he hired Anderson, against the advice of his farm director. Anderson's second team finished 59–63 and was last in the league in hitting and runs scored and next-to-last in slugging. (That team, to no surprise of future pitchers of a manager nicknamed Captain Hook, was also last in complete games.) But Anderson had been given an untalented team—only two players made it to the majors, for a combined 99 games. He was named manager at St. Petersburg the next season, and the team won 22 games in a row. Howsam went on to become general manager of the Reds and once again hired Anderson to manage a Class A team.

Two years later, in 1970, "Sparky Who"—that was a headline name in *The Cincinnati Enquirer*—became manager of the Reds, who won pennants in his first and third years and World Series in years six and seven. If Howsam "doesn't hire me" to manage in the low minors, Anderson told *The Los Angeles Times*, "chances are I never manage in the big leagues."

339. Roy Face, Pitcher, Pittsburgh Pirates.

"No player is in more demand—or in shorter supply—these days than a good relief pitcher. So exacting is the job that there are even specialists among specialists; some come into a game early, some in the middle innings and some late. Face is one of those who take a nap for the first six innings. As a late (or 'short') man he is one of the glamour boys of the relief corps. He does not pitch much, but if he gives up even one run, it usually is a calamity." That basic outline of a top reliever could be written now, but it was actually written by *Sports Illustrated* about Elroy Face in 1963. Figured retroactively (saves were not an official statistic until 1969), Face was the career leader in saves then. And games finished. And games won by a reliever (aided by his remarkable 18–1 season in 1959 and 22-game winning streak over two seasons). He also was the first pitcher to earn three saves in a World Series, doing so for the Pirates in 1960.

340. Roy Sievers, Outfielder, Washington Senators.

There was something about Roy Sievers's swing. His *Washington Post* obituary said it was "often described as one of the prettiest in baseball." It was modeled after the swing of Joe Medwick, a star of Sievers's hometown St. Louis Cardinals. The swing was so good that it was even used, with some Hollywood sleight-of-hand, in *Damn Yankees*, a film fable about a middle-aged man who trades his soul to the devil to help the hapless Washington Senators (Sievers's team in real life) overcome the damn Yankees to win the pennant. Sievers was a double for the star, Tab Hunter, but his elegant swing was not quite right for Hunter—he was left-handed, Sievers right-handed. To make the swing work, the St. Louis Sports Hall of Fame said, Sievers wore a mirror image uniform and the film was reversed in production.

341. Tom Qualters, Pitcher, Chicago White Sox.

Of all the examples of how the "bonus baby" rule hindered the development of what baseball had deemed the best amateur talent, Tom Qualters stands out. The first bonus rule was instituted in 1946, rescinded because of its unpopularity in 1950, but reinstated, with a $4,000 ceiling on signing bonuses, in 1953. The Phillies signed Qualters for $40,000—about $450,000 in 2023 dollars—in June 1953, after he graduated from high school. Under the bonus rules, he had to remain on the roster for two years or be made available to any other team. Over the rest of the '53 season, a professional ballplayer in name only, he pitched one inning. And gave up six runs. The next year was worse. Qualters was on the active roster the entire season and never played in a single game. "I had *no* business being in the major leagues," he told Brent Kelley for *Baseball's Bonus Babies*, but the Phillies also made no effort to develop him. Qualters said all he did was pitch batting practice (and he wasn't even allowed to *take* batting practice, frozen out by other pitchers). "For some reason, the management in Philadelphia had this theory that if I went out there and got beat up, that it would ruin me," he said in an interview with Nick Diunte, a baseball card expert, adding, "The thing that really hurt me so bad was we'd be in a game getting beat 12–2 and they wouldn't even let me pitch." he said. Such mop-up stints were how bonus babies like Sandy Koufax earned some experience. "All I was doing was taking up space for someone who was a major league player," Qualters said. Many of his teammates resented that (and his money; he drew the nickname Moneybags). When his two-year sentence was up, Qualters was sent to a Class D team, and while he eventually returned to the big leagues, there was no payoff for his big bonus: not one decision in 34 games and 52⅔ innings with a 5.64 ERA. "That was about the worst rule they could have ever done," Qualters said. Baseball finally came to its senses and eliminated the rule after the 1957 season, but after bonuses for amateurs soared over the next few years, the owners tried another tactic to curb costs: They instituted the amateur draft in 1965.

342. Ray Jablonski, Third Baseman, San Francisco Giants.

A St. Louis Cardinals history says that as a third baseman, Ray Jablonski "had the skills of a designated hitter" and that he "couldn't field or throw well." He was a versatile defender—he didn't field or throw well anywhere. He made 31 errors in 67 games as a Class D shortstop. The next year, he was error-prone at shortstop and in the outfield. In his third year, in Class A, he struggled as a second baseman. He was moved to third base and fielded even worse than he had at second (21 errors in 105 games). But he could hit line drives, and St. Louis made him its starter at third base in 1953. With on-base machines batting ahead of him—hi, Stan Musial—Jablonski drove in 100 runs each of his first two seasons, the first Cardinal to do that. He still couldn't field—he led the league in errors both years—and with Ken Boyer arriving, Jablonski was expendable. Playing a power-hitting position, he totaled more errors than homers.

343. Billy Hoeft, Pitcher, Detroit Tigers.

In 1954, Billy Hoeft led the American League in strikeout-to-walk ratio at 1.93. Now, that was low even for its era; the major league leader for most of the 1950s had a ratio comfortably above 3 to 1, with the National League running consistently higher than the American League. But it would be incomprehensibly low in 2022: The major league leader, the Phillies' Aaron Nola, had a strikeout-to-walk ratio of 8.10. No. 10 on the list was Shohei Ohtani at 4.98. The *average* K/BB ratio in 2022 was far superior to Hoeft's, at 2.75. The last time the league average was as low as Hoeft's league-leading 1.93 was 2002. Different game.

344. Russ Nixon, Catcher, Cleveland Indians.

It's hard to tell, but it does not look as if Russ Nixon is actually giving a sign in the photo on his card. Unless it's a fist, often used to signal for a pitchout. Catchers' signals to pitchers have a long history. A Society for American Baseball Research article about ballplayers who were deaf and the origin of hand signals indicates that pitchers and catchers for a deaf team called the College Nine used "short, expressive signals" to communicate in the mid–1860s. The article also says Henry Chadwick reported that by the 1870s, catchers were already signaling pitch type and location to pitchers. With recent concerns about sign stealing, Major League Baseball now allows electronic signaling between catchers and pitchers. The devices have nine sign choices, which would have saved Nixon a lot of waggling.

Card 344: Russ Nixon may have been flashing a sign, a tactic that is reported to have started in the 1860s among deaf players.

345. Gil McDougald, Second Baseman, New York Yankees.

Gil McDougald was a very good player on very good Yankees teams in the 1950s, but he became known, more than anything else, for one line drive he hit. It smashed into the face of the young Cleveland ace Herb Score in 1957, seriously injuring his eye. Score returned to baseball, but he was never the same pitcher (although he insisted an arm injury, not the eye injury, was the cause of his demise). Oddly, as his *New York Times* obituary noted, McDougald suffered serious physical problems from a line drive that hit him, too. That occurred in 1955, when a line drive hit him just above the left ear during batting practice. He soon lost his hearing in that ear, a 1996 *Sport Illustrated* profile said, and then the hearing in his other ear began to diminish until he was basically deaf and largely withdrew from social and business life. He did not reveal this publicly until 1994, in an interview with *The Times*. An otolaryngologist heard about it, wound up examining McDougald and recommended a cochlear implant. It worked, and in 1995 McDougald could hear again. He said it was "certainly a surprise." One of his daughters was bolder. "It's a miracle," she said. McDougald, once a near recluse, became a vocal advocate for the hearing-impaired. "When you see the progress, particularly with little children, it's so satisfying," he told *Sports Illustrated*. "It's like hitting a home run with the bases loaded."

346. Batter Bafflers: Tom Brewer-Dave Sisler.

Perhaps there should have been only 571 cards in Topps's 1959 set: Dave Sisler had not baffled much of anyone in 1958. He had the worst ERA of his career (4.94). His hits and walks per inning ratio was an unsightly 1.58. He allowed 22 home runs in 149⅓ innings—about one every seven innings. He walked more batters than he struck out. In 1959, he baffled only the Red Sox, who gave up on him after three games and six and a third innings, trading him to Detroit.

347. Bob Buhl, Pitcher, Milwaukee Braves.

The Braves teams of the '50s were lucky to have such a standout No. 3 starter in Bob Buhl, who was 109–72 with a 3.27 ERA (110 ERA+) in his time with the team—basically nine seasons. The top Similarity Score for Buhl on Baseball Reference is Dave Stieb, the excellent Blue Jays starter, and the top 10 also includes Virgil Trucks, Rick Sutcliffe, Dave Stewart, Bob Forsch, Kevin Appier, Hal Schumacher and Rick Rhoden—pitchers any team would be happy to have on the mound. But Buhl had few comps as a bad hitter. In 15 major league seasons, he had *one* with a positive OPS+. It was 11. Remember, 100 is league average. He went 0 for 70 in 1962, all but one at-bat with the Cubs (although he did manage six walks and one sacrifice fly), and wound up with an 0-for-87 stretch over three seasons. The streak finally ended on May 8, 1963, with a run-scoring single against the Pirates. "When I was going through my hitless streak," he told the historian Danny Peary for *We Played the Game*, "I didn't feel any pressure. Everybody knew I couldn't hit. The infielder was backing up, caught his spikes and fell down and the ball fell. They called time to give me the damn ball. I was embarrassed."

348. Ted Lepcio, Infielder, Boston Red Sox.

He received a $60,000 bonus from the Red Sox to play ball, but Ted Lepcio had modest goals. "The only thing I prayed for was to be a major-league player and it came true," he told *The Observer-Dispatch* in Utica, New York, his hometown, in 2016. "I didn't crash any records, but I played 10 years in the major leagues and that's something to be proud of." In 1952, the Red Sox decided on an all-rookie double-play combination: Lepcio at second base—a position he had never played—and Jimmy Piersall at shortstop—also a position he had never played. (No surprise, Boston finished in sixth place.) Lepcio said the first game of his career was his most memorable; he wound up with the ball after President Harry S Truman threw out the ceremonial first pitch.

349. Hoyt Wilhelm, Pitcher, Baltimore Orioles.

Hoyt Wilhelm was the first reliever elected to the Hall of Fame, and if it weren't for the knuckleball, he would not have made it. Wilhelm said he learned about the knuckler when he was 12 years old and read a newspaper article about the Senators and their four-man rotation of pitchers who threw the pitch, according to his *New York Times* obituary. He taught himself the knuckler by throwing a tennis ball and then used it in high school, through seven long years in the minors and 21 in the majors. He played until he was 16 days shy of 50. When he pitched for the Orioles in 1959, his catchers set a record with 49 passed balls. The next year, his manager, Paul Richards, introduced an oversize catcher's mitt. "I used to tell the catchers, 'After I turn it loose, it's your responsibility,'" Wilhelm said, according to his *Washington Post* obit. He became a minor league pitching coach for the Yankees, and the fireballer Dave Righetti recalled Wilhelm's mentoring at Class AA West Haven in 1979. "He didn't try to teach me the knuckler," he said in Wilhelm's Associated Press obituary. "He just told me, 'Just throw that ball, boy.'"

350. Ernie Banks, Shortstop, Chicago Cubs.

For nine years, Ernie Banks played like a Hall of Fame shortstop. For the next 10 years, racked by knee injuries, he played like a competent-hitting first baseman. Here's how those Banks eras compare:

Years	PA	AB	H	HR	RBI	BB	SO	BA	OBP	SLG	OPS+
'53–'61	5206	4670	1335	298	858	452	577	.290	.353	.552	138
'62–'71	5190	4751	1228	214	778	311	659	.259	.307	.448	106

Further examples of how Banks slowed: His doubles and triples fell 15 percent, his runs scored 26 percent. Still, from 1962, when Banks was 31, to 1968, when he was 37, he averaged 25 home runs a year and had an OPS+ above 100 in six of seven seasons. But beginning in 1966, new manager Leo Durocher wanted Mr. Cub gone and did not hide it. In *Let's Play Two*, Ron Rapoport writes that Durocher wanted Banks seen as just another player and did not want Banks stealing his thunder. Pitcher Ferguson Jenkins counted five first basemen Durocher used, futilely, to replace Banks. (Rapoport counted even more.) Durocher would say to reporters, Rapoport wrote: "Why don't you knock off that Mr. Cub stuff? The guy's wearing out. He can't go on forever." And Banks didn't, though his uncertain playing time did not help. Rapoport said of Durocher's use of the aging Banks as a fall guy: "This is what it had come to, Banks realized. He had become a bad example Durocher was using to motivate younger players." Blake Cullen, the Cubs' longtime traveling secretary, told Rapoport: "Leo wanted to be No. 1 in Chicago. That's all there was to it." Durocher got his wish, in a way—Banks was through in 1971 at age 40. But Durocher was fired midway through the next season.

351. Earl Torgeson, First Baseman, Chicago White Sox.

Earl Torgeson was a Boston Braves rookie in 1947, and what a player it looked as if he would be. A rangy, 6-foot-3 first baseman, he batted .281/.403/.481, with 20 doubles, six triples and 16 home runs in 487 plate appearances. He walked 82 times. He stole 11 bases. He played until 1961, but Torgeson came close to that kind of season only once, in 1950. He became renowned for his willingness to scrap—with opponents, with teammates. He was the rare player who wore glasses on the field, and early on he figured out he should take his glasses off before getting into a fight during a game. The Baseball Hall of Fame estimates he was involved in 50 fights, fracases and melees.

352. Robin Roberts, Pitcher, Philadelphia Phillies.

Robin Roberts was a Hall of Fame pitcher. He led the Whiz Kid Phillies to their first pennant in 35 years. But his lasting impact in baseball came off the field, as he was a formative figure in the Players Association and played a key role in hiring Marvin Miller as its executive director. Roberts became his team's player representative to the fledgling Players Association in 1952 and was quickly involved in negotiations to increase the players' pension fund, according to his SABR Bio Project biography. Before the World Series in 1964, knowing that baseball was about to settle on a new television contract and another battle over pension money would be brewing, Roberts persuaded the union to hire a full-time executive director. That turned out to be Miller, whose negotiations changed the balance of power in the game. Bill James said in his *Historical Baseball Abstract* that Roberts was one of the most respected players in the game, citing what Curt Flood wrote: that "in an era of social unrest, the manager might well be chosen among former players qualified by intellect to deal not only with God and the press but with the team. … To name only four, Jackie Robinson, Bill White, Robin Roberts and George Crowe are eminently capable of overcoming the benightedness and confusion that wreck so many clubs."

353. Curt Flood, Outfielder, St. Louis Cardinals.

The infamous reserve clause was introduced into baseball players' contracts in 1879—just three years after the first professional league was founded—and by 1887 was formally included in all player contracts, as the economists Jennifer Ashcraft and Craig Depken noted. It was the owners' means of binding players to their teams—in perpetuity, according to the owners. The clause was about 200 words, but its substance was embedded in these 64 words: "If prior to the March 1 next succeeding said December 20, the Player and the Club have not agreed upon the terms of such contract, then on or before 10 days after said March 1, the Club shall have the right by written notice to the Player at said address to renew this contract for the period of one year on the same terms…." You might read that to mean a contract was for one year (unless otherwise specified); the owners read that to mean a contract was for one year but that they could renew the contract themselves, thus binding the player to another year. And on and on. The players eventually chafed at the owners' interpretation, but the owners would not relent. Not even when Curt Flood, a three-time All-Star and seven-time Gold Glove center fielder for the Cardinals, sued Major League Baseball over the reserve clause, citing violations of antitrust law. The Cardinals had traded Flood to the Phillies, and he did not want to go. Flood enlisted the help of the Players Association, although its executive director, Marvin Miller, warned

Card 353: Curt Flood was warned that he might jeopardize his career if he fought the reserve clause. He did fight, and he did lose. But the players eventually won.

that he was likely to lose … and likely to jeopardize his career. Miller was correct on both counts. Flood, who sat out the 1970 season (forgoing his salary—$90,000 in 1969, or about $733,000 in 2023 dollars), lost in United States District Court, where, as his *New York Times* obituary pointed out, the judge suggested that the sides negotiate. The owners would not. Flood appealed all the way to the United States Supreme Court, where he still lost. But, emboldened, the players' union continued to fight the reserve clause, and the matter went to binding arbitration. This time the players did not lose, as the arbitrator, Peter Seitz, ruled in 1975 that if players fulfilled their contract and did not sign a new one, they were free agents. Even though he had lost his battle, Flood had set the stage for the players to begin to even the playing field in their negotiations with team owners. And baseball was never the same. The minimum major league salary in 2023 was $720,000, the average $4.9 million.

354. Pete Burnside, Pitcher, Detroit Tigers.
Ward Willits, Pete Burnside's maternal grandfather, had a significant stake in American architecture: He commissioned Frank Lloyd Wright to build him a home in the Chicago suburb of Highland Park. The house, designed in 1901 and built the next year, "represents a radical step forward in Wright's emerging design maturity and is considered his first true Prairie house." The Prairie School of architecture was "rooted in nature, with a sense of place, but also incorporated modern elements, like flat planes and stylized ornamentation," the Chicago Architecture Center wrote. Willits, a foundry executive, lived in the home until 1954, the year before Burnside made his major league debut. Burnside's SABR Bio Project profile said he apparently inherited $3 million from his maternal grandfather. But not the Frank Lloyd Wright house.

355. Jim Piersall, Outfielder, Cleveland Indians.
It can't match "Headless Body in Topless Bar," the 1983 *New York Post* classic, but the headline in *The New York Times* after Jimmy Piersall hit his 100th career home run and backpedaled his way around the bases in 1963 is a gem of its own: "ymmiJ llasreiP of the Mets (Who Else?) Makes Backward Run After Hitting 100th Homer." Piersall's actions were often unexpected and sometimes uncontrollable; he was treated in his rookie season in a psychiatric hospital (grist for an autobiography and the film *Fear Strikes Out*). *The Washington Post* noted in his obituary that Piersall "argued with umpires, fought opposing players, climbed a flagpole during a game." It added that he once spanked a teammate's four-year-old son in the dugout. He mimicked the distinctive running gait of his teammate Dom DiMaggio and, the Associated Press reported, mocked the unusual pitching motion of Satchel Paige. "I'm the gooney bird that walked to the bank," he told *The Plain Dealer* of Cleveland in 2001. "I'm doing better than most of those guys who said I was crazy."

356. Bob Mabe, pitcher, Cincinnati Redlegs.
Baseball Almanac says Bob Mabe lost sight in his right eye in a childhood accident, quoting the historian Michael B. Ackerman. Mabe pitched well in the minors—he was 21–10 in 1956 and then added three victories in the playoffs for Class

AA Houston—but struggled in the majors. He was not the only ballplayer who had sight in only one eye. In writing about Whammy Douglas, a pitcher in the '50s who lost his right eye at age 11, MiLB.com said he was one of eight major leaguers to have played with one eye. Another was Tom Sunkel, whose blindness because of a cataract earned him a 4-F deferment in World War II, and he finished with a 9–15, 4.53 record in 220⅓ innings over six seasons. Dodgers left-hander Julio Urías is partially blind in his left eye. Juan Sandoval, a longtime minor leaguer, was hit in the eye by three shotgun pellets and lost his sight in 2006 but he kept pitching until 2020.

357. Dick Stuart, First Baseman, Pittsburgh Pirates.

Baseball Reference lists nicknames on each of its players' pages, and Dick Stuart's has all the ones that are a testament to his otherworldly bad defense: Dr. Strangeglove, the Boston Strangler, Stonefingers, the Man with the Iron Glove. His defense was tolerated because he could hit home runs. In fact, Stuart has one of the seven best single-season home run totals in professional baseball—66, hit in 1956 in the Class A Western League, in 141 games. (It was a big year for minor league home run hitters: Ken Guettler hit 62 in the Texas League and Forrest [Frosty] Kennedy hit 60 in the Southwest League. Four other players hit at least 50.) Here are the 60-plus home run seasons:

Minor Leagues	*Major Leagues*
72—Joe Bauman, 1953, Longhorn League (C)	73—Barry Bonds, 2001
69—Joe Hauser, 1933, American Association (AA)	70—Mark McGwire, 1998
69—Bob Crues, 1948, West Texas–New Mexico League (C)	66—Sammy Sosa, 1998
66—Dick Stuart, 1956, Western League (A)	65—Mark McGwire, 1999
64—Bob Lennon, 1954, Southern Association (AA)	64—Sammy Sosa, 2001
63—Joe Hauser, 1930, American Association (AA)	63—Sammy Sosa, 1999
62—Moose Clabaugh, 1926, East Texas League (C)	62—Aaron Judge, 2022
62—Ken Guettler, 1956, Texas League (AA)	61—Roger Maris, 1961
60—Tony Lazzeri, 1925, Pacific Coast League (AA)	60—Babe Ruth, 1927
60—Frosty Kennedy, 1956, Southwest League (B)	

Stuart did match his spectacularly good offensive season in '56 with a spectacularly bad defensive season—he made 17 errors in 36 games at first base and 13 in 108 games in the outfield.

358. Ralph Terry, Pitcher, Kansas City Athletics.

Ralph Terry first worked with Johnny Sain in 1959, when he was a struggling young starter for the Athletics and Sain was a first-year pitching coach. The results were not particularly good for either of them, but Terry had the good fortune of being traded in midseason to the Yankees. Two years later, Sain moved to New York, and both he and Terry began to establish themselves. Terry, who had given up the World Series–losing home run to Bill Mazeroski in 1960, had his first excellent season in 1961—16–3 with a 3.13 ERA—and credited Sain with improving his breaking ball. Terry was outstanding again in 1962, finishing 23–12, 3.19 and winning Game 7 of the World Series, 1–0. Terry then became increasingly ineffective and Sain became increasingly peripatetic but still successful. Over 15 more seasons, Sain coaxed highlight seasons out of veterans (Whitey Ford, Jim Kaat) and especially youngsters and pitchers with little history of success (Jim Bouton, Bill Stafford, Roland Sheldon, Al Downing, Luis Arroyo, Hal Reniff, Mudcat Grant, Al Worthington, Wilbur Wood, Stan Bahnsen). Fifteen of his pitchers won 20 games; 10 led the league in victories. Five of his teams led the league in earned run average. Sain rarely lasted long—he wanted to run the staff *his* way, not the manager's way, and he lost those battles—but in *Ball Four* Bouton called him "the greatest pitching coach who ever lived." Kaat called Sain's firing by the Twins "the Great Mistake," *Sports Illustrated* reported. Terry, meanwhile, had left baseball and had become a coach of sorts himself—he was a head golf pro at several clubs and started a program to teach golf to kids at a public course in Larned, Kansas; 45 of them went on to play college golf.

359. Bill White, First Baseman-Outfielder, San Francisco Giants.

Bill White was an excellent-hitting, Gold Glove–dominating first baseman who kept popping up in the wrong place at the wrong time. He came up with the Giants, but they also were developing two Hall of Fame first basemen, first Orlando Cepeda and then Willie McCovey, so they traded White to the Cardinals. There he lost playing time at first to another Hall of Famer, Stan Musial, and a similar hitter, Joe Cunningham. He finally did establish himself at first base in St. Louis, but then the Cardinals acquired Cepeda and sent White to Philadelphia. As his career was winding down, the Phillies traded him away so they could move Dick Allen to first. White became the first Black broadcaster for a major league franchise (teaming with Phil Rizzuto for years to call Yankees games) and then became the first Black league president, overseeing the National League. Once again, his timing eventually went awry—Commissioner Bud Selig wanted to eliminate the league presidents. So White quit.

360. Al Kaline, Outfielder, Detroit Tigers.

Al Kaline and Mickey Mantle were perhaps the two best all-around players in the American League in the '50s (Minnie Miñoso would have a case). Oddly, both developed osteomyelitis, a swelling or inflammation of the bone, as youngsters—Kaline in his left foot, Mantle in his left shin. Kaline's ailment developed when he was eight, and he had two inches of bone removed from his foot. He was left with an unpleasant scar and a couple of malformed toes that affected his gait when he ran. Mantle's osteomyelitis developed when he was 14 after he was kicked in his shin while playing football, and there were fears his leg would have to be amputated. Both excelled despite chronic pain. Kaline and Mantle were really nothing alike as players, but they did have similarities in batting average. Both were career .309 hitters in 1964. Kaline wound up at .297 for his career, Mantle at .298. Kaline slipped below .300 in his next-to-last season (1972), Mantle in his last year (1968).

361. Willard Nixon, Pitcher, Boston Red Sox.

Willard Nixon was an archetype for Shohei Ohtani in the Southeastern Conference and minor leagues in the 1940s. As a sophomore at Auburn, he set a conference record by striking out 145 batters—including 20 in one game against Mississippi to set another conference record. His season strikeout mark lasted for 39 years, before Derek Lilliquist broke it. Nixon also batted .448 that season, according to his SABR Bio Project profile. He then went 11–5, 14–7 and 11–2 in the minors, while batting .345 (at Class AA in 1949) and .346 (at Class AAA in 1950). Alas, he was ordinary in his nine years in the major leagues—69–72 with a 98 ERA+ on the mound, .242/.305/.296 in the batter's box.

362. Dolan Nichols, Pitcher, Chicago Cubs.

You can connect the dots between Dolan Nichols and the King and some royalty of fiction. Nichols grew up in Tupelo, Mississippi, just a few years before Elvis Presley was born there, and he later played minor league ball in Memphis, where Presley relocated. Although Nichols grew up in Tupelo, he was born in Tishomingo, Mississippi, the setting for the great Elmore Leonard's novel *Tishomingo Blues*, about a daredevil high diver who witnesses a mob hit from his platform on an 80-foot tower. That leaves the book with more hits than Nichols had in the majors (he was 0 for 5).

363. Bobby Ávila, Second Baseman-Third Baseman, Baltimore Orioles.

Baseball has a long history in Mexico. The game has been played there since at least the 1880s, and its premier professional league was founded nearly a century ago. In the mid-1940s, the Pasquel brothers launched what they intended as a third major league, poaching 18 players from Major League Baseball (while also signing several Negro league veterans); despite the high-profile signings, however, the league faltered after the 1947 season. Teams from Monterrey were the first international teams to win the Little League World Series, in 1957 and '58. But Mexican players did not get a foothold in the major leagues until Bobby Ávila became a star second baseman with Cleveland. He was the third Mexican-born player in the bigs, according to Baseball Reference, although the first two—outfielder Mel Almada and infielder Chile Gómez—actually went to high school in the United States. After a rocky rookie season in 1949, Ávila hit .307/.377/.417 over the next five seasons, including a league-leading .341 batting average in the Indians' pennant-winning season of 1954. It was the first batting title won by a Latino, and he was the first Mexican player to make an All-Star team. He is still third in career WAR among the 147 Mexican major leaguers through 2023, with 28.4, following only pitchers Fernando Valenzuela (41.5) and Teddy Higuera (30.3). "Everybody knows who Avila was in Mexico," Valenzuela said in Ávila's obituary in *The Los Angeles Times*. "He was an inspiration, of course, for Mexican ballplayers to follow to the States and play in the major leagues."

364. Danny McDevitt, Pitcher, Los Angeles Dodgers.

Fielding was not what prevented Danny McDevitt from having a successful major league career. No, that was control. He averaged 5.2 walks per nine innings in the major leagues—and that was an improvement over his minor league number, 7.1. (In his first minor league season, he walked 76 batters in 43 innings—15.9 per nine innings! No wonder the Yankees released him.) But in addition to displaying bad control, McDevitt also played bad defense. His major league fielding percentage was an abysmal .899. And again, that was better than his minor league performance: an unreal .817 for the years Baseball Reference has statistics. Yet McDevitt has a spot in Dodger history. He started, and won, the Dodgers' last game in Brooklyn, and in Ebbets Field, a 2–0 victory on September 24, 1957. Remarkably, he walked only one batter. And did not make an error.

365. Gus Bell, Outfielder, Cincinnati Redlegs.

Buddy Bell had a longer career than his father, Gus, 2,405 games to 1,741 and 18 seasons to 15. But their statistics, per 162 games as compiled by Baseball Reference, are strikingly similar:

Player	AB	R	H	2B	3B	HR	RBI	BB	SO	BA/OBP/SLG	OPS+
Gus	603	80	170	29	6	19	80	44	59	.281/.330/.445	103
Buddy	606	78	169	29	4	14	74	56	52	.279/.341/.406	109

Gus made four All-Star teams, Buddy five. Gus received MVP votes once, Buddy five times. Each played for four franchises, including Cincinnati. Buddy never played a postseason game, but Gus did play in the 1961 World Series. He went 0 for 3 in three pinch-hitting appearances.

366. Humberto Robinson, Pitcher, Milwaukee Braves.

Forty years after the Black Sox scandal, a co-owner of a bar and restaurant in Philadelphia tried to bribe Phillies pitcher Humberto Robinson, offering him $1,500 to throw a game. When gamblers moved to fix the 1919 World Series involving the White Sox and the Reds, they roped in Chicago's two star pitchers, Eddie Cicotte and Lefty Williams, who between them had won 52 games that season. When Harold (Boomie) Friedman wanted to fix a game of a September 22, 1959, doubleheader between the Phillies and the Reds (nice coincidence), he turned to Robinson, who had won one game that season. According to court documents in Friedman's appeal of his conviction, he approached Robinson in the Rittenhouse Hotel and offered $1,500 if Robinson, who had frequented Friedman's bar, would lose the game. Robinson told him no, and when he returned to his companions at the hotel he was

Card 366: Humberto Robinson had won one game all season when a gambler tried to induce him to fix a game. Instead, he pitched well and got the win. The gambler got prison time.

noticeably upset, the court documents say. Friedman went to Robinson's hotel room the next day, repeated the offer and flashed two or three hundred dollars in cash. Robinson again said no. Robinson went to the ballpark and told his teammate Rubén Gómez about the bribe offer, the documents say, and, according to a SABR account, Gómez urged him to tell the manager, Eddie Sawyer. Robinson said no to that, too, and pitched the game, but a United Press International article says he told Sawyer in the fifth inning and again after the game. (Robinson allowed two runs and three hits in seven innings before being removed for a pinch-hitter. He picked up the win.) Word of the bribe was passed up the food chain to Commissioner Ford Frick and then to the Philadelphia police. Friedman's defense was that he was merely trying to lend money to Robinson, who had been robbed the evening of September 21 (the pitcher reported it to the police). Friedman's lawyer pointed out how ludicrous it would be to try to fix a game with a pitcher who had won only once, but the jury was not swayed. Friedman was convicted and sentenced to two to five years in prison. (And he lost his appeal.) Robinson, meanwhile, was lauded by Frick, but his major league career lasted only one more season. And he never won another game.

367. Cal Neeman, Catcher, Chicago Cubs.

Maybe the 1957 Cubs knew something the baseball world didn't know. Or maybe this is a reason they finished 62–92: The players named a rookie catcher, Cal Neeman, the team's most valuable player. Neeman did set a National League record for games played by a rookie catcher (122) and might have set the major league record had he not missed three weeks in September with an injury. He hit .258/.298/.376 with an OPS+ of 81. But MVP? Of the Cubs' 10 most regular players, six had a better OPS+ than Neeman. And his teammates did include Ernie Banks, who hit 43 home runs, drove in 102 runs, scored 113 (75 percent more than the next-best Cub) and batted .285/.360/.579 with an OPS+ of 149. Neeman played only part-time in his second year, but his career totals then were .258/.308/.411 with 22 homers in 671 plate appearances, so he was a valuable Cub even if not *most* valuable. His offensive value vanished, though—he hit .168/.242/.275 with eight homers in 429 plate appearances over his final five seasons.

368. Don Mueller, Outfielder, Chicago White Sox.

Baseball Almanac has compiled a list of the best strikeout ratios for hitters, based on at least 1,000 games and 1,000 at-bats. Don Mueller, whom writers called Mandrake the Magician for his ability to hit 'em where they ain't, is 10th on the list of strikeout avoiders, none of whom, to little surprise, has played in the last half-century. They include Hall of Famers and slap hitters and batters who played against Babe Ruth but not, as you might imagine, power hitters. Here are the top 10:

Player	K Ratio	HR	SLG	OPS+	WAR
1. Joe Sewell	1.6%	49	.413	109	54.7
2. Lloyd Waner	2.2%	27	.393	99	29.6
3. Nellie Fox	2.3%	35	.363	94	49.5
4. Tommy Holmes	2.4%	88	.432	122	35.5

Player	K Ratio	HR	SLG	OPS+	WAR
5. Andy High	3.0%	44	.388	93	12.5
6. Sam Rice	3.0%	34	.427	112	54.4
7. Frankie Frisch	3.0%	105	.434	110	71.8
8. Dale Mitchell	3.0%	41	.416	114	19.5
9. Frank McCormick	3.3%	128	.434	118	31.9
10. Don Mueller	3.3%	65	.390	89	4.1

As you can see, Mueller was the least productive hitter of the group, magician reputation aside. He walked barely more than he struck out and had skimpy power despite playing home games in a home run haven, the Polo Grounds. (At that, 50 of his 65 dingers came at home.)

369. Dick Tomanek, Pitcher, Kansas City Athletics.

Dick Tomanek and Stan Pitula were both highly regarded young pitchers in the Cleveland organization. They had been teammates in 1956 with Class AAA Indianapolis and then again the next year in Cleveland. Tomanek's stuff, one of his managers said, was second on the staff to ace Herb Score's, and Pitula was considered a potential replacement for Score after he was hit by a line drive. Tomanek, though, went on to have an underwhelming career. He walked too many batters and managed a 10–10 record and 4.95 ERA in 231 career innings. Pitula's career was both underwhelming and tragic. He badly injured his elbow on a pitch to Roy Sievers in July 1957, and although he labored in the minors through 1961, he never pitched another major league game. He wound up working as a machinist, but in 1965, his baseball days having ended badly and his marriage dissolving, he was found dead in his car. The death was ruled suicide.

370. Pete Runnels, Second Baseman, Boston Red Sox.

Pete Runnels, a slap-hitting, left-handed batter, came up as a middle infielder who moved to first base. His contemporary—and eventual teammate—Billy Goodman, a slap-hitting, left-handed batter, came up as a first baseman who moved to the middle infield (and third base). But they were offensive clones statistically. Here's how Baseball Reference breaks down their 162-game averages:

Player	AB	R	H	2B	3B	HR	RBI	BB	SO	BA/OBP/SLG	OPS+
Runnels	574	79	167	25	6	4	57	76	56	.291/.375/.378	107
Goodman	563	81	169	30	4	2	59	67	33	.299/.365/.378	99

Neither was a base-stealing threat (Runnels was 0 for 10 trying one season) and not distinguished with the glove. But Runnels won two batting titles and lost out on a third to his teammate Ted Williams on the last day of the season, and Goodman won a title of his own. They were about 80 percent the hitter that a similar player, Rod Carew, was, but that still made them pretty good.

371. Dick Brodowski, Pitcher, Cleveland Indians.

Dick Brodowski began his professional career with 21 games at third base for the Class D Marion Red Sox. Then injuries jumbled the pitching staff, so his manager asked him to pitch, according to Brodowski's SABR Bio Project biography. He hit .276 with 20 extra-base hits in 185 at-bats that season, but it paled in comparison to his newfound role: He went 21–5, 2.60 on the mound. The next year he batted .290 (11 for 40, with nine RBIs) while going 7–1, 3.40 as a pitcher in Class AAA and earning a call-up, at age 19, to Boston. He was drafted into the Army and pretty much played baseball—but as a second baseman. After his discharge, his baseball career stalled, but he hit well for a pitcher, even in the majors—.242 with a couple of homers. Managers in the '50s were not reluctant to tap pitchers to pinch-hit, but somehow Brodowski never got the call.

372. Jim Hegan, Catcher, Philadelphia Phillies.

Jim Hegan was the starting catcher in Cleveland for a decade, during which the staff led the American League in earned run average six times. Now, Hegan *was* handling a star-laden staff—three future Hall of Famers (Bob Feller, Bob Lemon and Early Wynn) and another excellent starter (Mike García)—and for the final six of those seasons, the manager was the highly regarded ex-catcher Al López. Hegan earned their respect. The hard-throwing Feller, not the easiest guy to catch, told Bob Dolgan of the Cleveland *Plain Dealer*: "He was the best defensive catcher I ever had. He had a great arm and great mechanics. You couldn't throw a ball past him." Lemon told Dolgan: "When I first started pitching, I used to shake him off sometimes. Invariably, they'd get a hit. So, I stopped shaking him off." Faith in Hegan's pitch-calling was not immediate, though. In 1947, Hegan's first full season as a starter, player-manager Lou Boudreau insisted that he call the pitches and relay them to Hegan. Neither the pitchers nor Hegan liked that arrangement, and before the next season, Boudreau relented and Hegan called the pitches. The Indians led the league in ERA and won the pennant. He was durable (one season he started 146 of 154 games) and was a five-time All-Star despite considerable inadequacies as a hitter (a .228/.295/.344 batting line and a 74 OPS+)—a more-decorated Martín Maldonado of his day, including a prominent role on World Series teams.

373. Herb Plews, Second Baseman-Third Baseman, Washington Senators.

Herb Plews had a theory about the 1955 Denver Bears. They were a Class AAA team of the Yankees, shifted from Kansas City, where, as the Blues, they had played for decades. But when the Philadelphia Athletics moved to KC for the 1955 season, the Blues had to go—and they went to Denver, supplanting a venerable Class A Western League team also called the Bears. "I think the Yankees wanted to have a good club in here for the first year in Triple-A," Plews told *The Denver Post* in 2012. "We outdrew the Washington Senators in the American League in attendance." Indeed, they did—by 710 fans. You wouldn't know it from his major league career (much of it spent, coincidentally, in the attendance abyss of Washington), but Plews was one of the stud players on the '55 Bears, batting .302 with a .400 on-base percentage.

374. Art Ditmar, Pitcher, New York Yankees.

Casey Stengel had a knack for wringing the best out of Yankee pitchers with little pedigree, but his handling of his staff late in the 1960 season and the World Series was a bit curious. Whitey Ford had struggled while dealing with arm issues late in the season and Art Ditmar, another of the Yankees' Kansas City refugees, had been the team's best pitcher—15–9 with a 3.06 ERA. The Yankees could not pull away from the upstart Orioles until the last two weeks of the season, but Stengel still had the chance to set up his rotation for the World Series against the Pirates. On September 26, John Drebinger of *The New York Times* said Stengel's announced starters to finish up the season made it likely that Ford would start the World Series opener on October 5. Ford pitched five decent innings in Game 152 on September 28. Ditmar pitched four innings on September 29 and Ford threw two in the finale on September 30. It still appeared, Drebinger reported, that Ford would be the Game 1 starter on October 5, having pitched seven innings in the previous week. Instead, Stengel tapped Ditmar. Stengel's rationale, as Robert Creamer laid out in *Stengel: His Life and Times*, was that there was no good reason to use Ford against the Pirates' ace, Vern Law, in Game 1. Ditmar was plenty good enough, and Ford could then be counted on to win against a lesser Pirates starter. But Ditmar did not get out of the first inning. Even then, Stengel did not start Ford in Game 2. Some accounts have said Stengel worried about the left-handed Ford facing the Pirates' right-handed hitters in Forbes Field, although it was 365 feet to the left-field foul pole and Pittsburgh had only one batter who had hit more than 16 homers. The Yankees romped in Game 2 anyway, and then Ford, pitching in the accommodating Yankee Stadium, threw a shutout as the Yankees went ahead 10–0 early in Game 3. (Even with a rested bullpen, Stengel had Ford pitch the entire game.) Pittsburgh came back to lead the Series, three games to two—Ditmar didn't get out of the *second* inning in Game 5—and at last Stengel leaned on Ford for Game 6. Pitching on short rest, he threw another shutout. Game 7 was the Mazeroski game, but to get to that moment, Stengel went a little too long with sore-armed Bobby Shantz (the Pirates got to him in his fifth inning of relief) and Ralph Terry warmed up in the bullpen five times, Creamer wrote, before delivering the fateful pitch to Maz. Stengel had asked Ford to warm up, but, Creamer related, Ford—who *had* pitched nine innings the day before—said he could not loosen up. In a 1973 interview that Creamer quotes, Stengel knew he had messed up his use of Ford: "I shoulda pitched him the first game and I'da had

Card 374: Art Ditmar, not Whitey Ford, started Game 1 of the 1960 World Series, a decision Casey Stengel came to regret.

him to relieve in the last game." It might have saved his job; Stengel was forced out five days after Game 7.

375. Bob Nieman, Outfielder, Baltimore Orioles.

An OPS+ of 132 is good. Really good. Compile a career OPS+ of 132 and you are likely a multi-time All-Star (José Canseco, Rocky Colavito, Jim Edmonds, Juan González, Tommy Henrich, Matt Holliday, J.D. Martinez, Rafael Palmeiro, Ken Singleton, George Springer, Mo Vaughn), maybe even a Hall of Famer (Tony Gwynn, Joe Morgan). Or maybe you're Bob Nieman. Nieman was a left fielder in need of a DH spot who crushed left-handers (.312/.397/.540) over 12 seasons. He had respectable power and took walks. But Nieman was slow (10 for 40 stealing), lacked polish or an arm in the outfield (his SABR Bio Project profile says that when he was a scout, he would reportedly say of a weak-throwing player, "He's got a Nieman arm") and could not stay healthy. But when he was in the lineup, he could hit.

376. Hal Naragon, Catcher, Cleveland Indians.

Hal Naragon made his mark not as a catcher but as a bullpen coach. A bullpen coach alongside Johnny Sain. When Sain became the Twins' pitching coach in 1965, Naragon was named the bullpen coach. Minnesota won the pennant. The team backslid in 1966, and manager Sam Mele ousted Sain and Naragon, saying they had sabotaged him. That did not make Twins pitchers happy. Jim Kaat wrote an open letter that said: "Every move John Sain and Hal Naragon talked about, or attempted to do, was in the best interest of the Minnesota Twins baseball club and to attempt to improve our position. To me that is not disloyalty.... Hal Naragon was the last instrument of communication between Mr. Mele and the players. Now there is a complete division." Sain and Naragon went to the Tigers, who fought for the pennant down to the last day in 1967 and won it (and the World Series) in 1968. A Detroit sportswriter, Watson Spoelstra, wrote, "There's no question that Sain and his close friend and associate, coach Hal Naragon, know about as much as anyone on pitching." Sain praised Naragon, too, according to RIP Baseball, saying, "Naragon has done an unbelievable job and I've often been given credit that he deserves." The Tigers slipped in 1969, however. Sain was gone after another falling-out with a manager, and Naragon left baseball. For good. When the White Sox hired Sain in 1971, Naragon stayed home and ultimately ran a sporting goods store.

377. Johnny Antonelli, Pitcher, San Francisco Giants.

His Boston Braves teammates so resented 18-year-old Johnny Antonelli, who had received a $52,000 bonus that required him to be on the major league roster in 1948, that they wouldn't vote him a World Series share. After he finally established himself at 23, Warren Spahn said that, with three left-handers in the rotation, the Braves had one too many, according to Antonelli's SABR Bio Project biography— and that Antonelli should be bumped. He became a star after a trade to the New York Giants, but after the team moved to San Francisco, he alienated fans by trashing Seals Stadium, the team's home for their first two seasons there. "Put it in the paper that this is a [bleep] ballpark," he told reporters after a 1959 game, according to

RIP Baseball, adding: "A pitcher should be paid double for working here. Worst ballpark in America. Every time you stand up there, you've got to beat the hitter and a 30-mile-an-hour wind." The fans booed him at his next start, apparently believing he had badmouthed the city of San Francisco. After he had a successful seven-year run in which Antonelli went 114–89 with a 3.09 ERA and a 127 ERA+, his career unraveled. Eventually his contract was sold to the expansion Mets, but he quit baseball. "I'm tired of traveling and I want to be home with my family," he said, according to RIP Baseball, and it was a good call. He went home to Rochester, New York, where he was beloved and ran a Firestone dealership for decades before he got fed up one more time. "He had become frustrated with Bridgestone, the company that bought out Firestone, and called it quits," *The Rochester Democrat & Chronicle* said.

378. Gail Harris, First Baseman, Detroit Tigers.

The second player listed under the Similarity Scores for Gail Harris is Marv Throneberry. This can't be good. Their career numbers, per Baseball Reference:

Player	AB	R	H	2B	3B	HR	RBI	BB	SO	BA/OBP/SLG	OPS+
Harris	1331	159	320	38	15	51	189	106	194	.240/.304/.406	88
Throneberry	1186	143	281	37	8	53	170	130	295	.237/.311/.416	96

Both were left-handed hitters. Both reached the majors in 1955. Both were inadequate fielders. Harris was out of the game at 29, Throneberry at 30. Harris's major league career ended on May 3, Throneberry's on May 5. But Marv had the nickname. And the beer ads.

379. Bob Miller, Pitcher, St. Louis Cardinals.

The '50s were a confusing time to be a major league pitcher named Bob Miller. There were three of them, and all three were almost exclusively relievers. Two of them reached the majors as teenagers and were teammates on the 1962 Mets—this Bob Miller (whom we'll call Bob L.) and Bob G. Bob L. recovered from a 1–12, 4.89 season with the Mets to pitch 11 more seasons in the majors; Bob G. did not rebound from a 2–2, 7.08 stint with the Mets that ended his career. After losing his first 12 decisions in '62, Bob L. won the Mets' next-to-last game, beating the Cubs, 2–1. Bob L. then executed a remarkable turnaround. After pitching for a Mets team that went 40–120, he was traded to the Dodgers and immediately went 10–8, 2.89 for a World Series champion.

380. Hank Aaron, Outfielder, Milwaukee Braves.

In one season or another, Hank Aaron led the National League in games played, runs scored, hits, doubles, home runs, runs batted in, batting average, slugging percentage, total bases, times on base, intentional walks, even sacrifice flies. Those are just the conventional stats; he also led the league in such modern metrics as OPS, OPS+, runs created and batting runs. That's his bat. His glove? He led the league at some point in putouts, assists, double plays and fielding percentage for a right fielder. (And total zone runs and range factor.) He also won three Gold Gloves while playing the same position as Roberto Clemente. On the bases, Aaron was not a league leader, but he *was* in the top 10 in stolen bases eight times and the top 10 in triples five times. He really could do everything well. Which he knew. In his marvelous book *The Baseball 100*, Joe Posnanski quotes Aaron saying: "You know, if I had to pay to go see somebody play for one game, I wouldn't pay to see Hank Aaron. I wasn't flashy. I didn't start fights. I didn't rush out to the mound every time a pitch came near me. I didn't hustle after fly balls that were 20 rows back in the seats. But if I had to pay to see someone play in a three-game series, I'd rather see me." He was worth watching.

381. Mike Baxes, Infielder, Kansas City Athletics.

Mike Baxes spent parts of seven seasons in Class AAA, five of them in the Pacific Coast League. The PCL was still an anomaly, playing seasons far longer than in any other pro league. In 1950, the San Francisco Seals team, for which Baxes played briefly, endured a 200-game season. (The Seals were a perfectly average team: 100–100 record, 998 runs scored, 996 allowed.) That's nearly a third longer than the major league season then, and it's nearly 50 percent longer than a full-season minor league team plays now. But baseball, especially in the minors, was different then. In 1949, Baxes was an 18-year-old on the Class C Phoenix Senators of the Arizona-Texas League. Phoenix averaged 7.41 runs a game, and the entire league averaged 7.05. A year earlier, teams in the West Texas League averaged 8.16 runs a game (that's where Bob Crues hit 69 home runs). As a point of comparison, the highest average for the league for runs per game in MLB is 5.49, in 1930. It had to have been difficult to evaluate minor leaguers in some of the hitting environments of that era.

382. Curt Simmons, Pitcher, Philadelphia Phillies.

The Phillies became infamous for their 1964 collapse, squandering a six-and-a-half-game lead with 12 games to play to lose the pennant by a game. But they had done nearly the same thing 14 years earlier, in part because of Uncle Sam. Curt Simmons was a 21-year-old left-hander having an excellent season when he learned that his National Guard unit had been called to duty—making him the first major leaguer called to duty for the Korean War, according to *The Whiz Kids and the 1950 Pennant*. His call-up was delayed, but Simmons—with a 17–8 record and 3.40 ERA—reported on September 10 with the Phillies up six and a half games with 19 to play. The first time through the rotation without Simmons, the Phillies were flawless, winning four straight. Philadelphia then split the next four games and was ahead by seven and a half games with 11 to go. Then the '50 fold began—the Phillies lost 10 of 12 games, slashing their advantage over the Dodgers to a single game heading into the final game, in Brooklyn. The Phillies won, averting a playoff and baseball infamy. Simmons, who had not pitched in three and a half weeks, actually got a pass from his Guard unit for the World Series, but the rosters were already set and he could not be activated. All he got to do was pitch batting practice.

383. Words of Wisdom: Don Larsen-Casey Stengel.

In *Stengel: His Life and Times*, Robert Creamer describes Casey Stengel's light hand when it came to disciplining players. Stengel sometimes looked at the checks for hotel breakfasts when the Yankees were on the road. "It's those guys who have double tomato juice and black coffee who've gone out to mail letters at three in the morning," Stengel said. One year—before his perfect game fame—Don Larsen ran his car into a telephone pole at 5 a.m., Creamer wrote, and Stengel joked about his mailing a letter. Stengel did not hand out any punishment, Creamer said, "aside from making Larsen work a little harder in the team's practice sessions." Words of wisdom, apparently.

384. Dave Sisler, Pitcher, Boston Red Sox.

Dave Sisler and Chris Young aren't just the two best pitchers to come out of Princeton University. They were also good basketball players for successful Tigers teams before they chose baseball for good. The 6-foot-4 Sisler averaged 9.8 points a game over two seasons in which Princeton went 31-18, in 1950-51 and 1951-52. The 6-foot-10 Young averaged 13.4 points as Princeton went 41-19 in 1998-99 and 1999-2000. Sisler was lured away from his final basketball season with a $40,000 bonus from the Red Sox, and he wound up 38-44 with a 4.33 ERA in 247 games in the majors—all records for a Princeton pitcher until Young came along and went 79-67, 3.95. Ross Ohlendorf, who is 6 foot 4, almost became the third Princeton basketball-major league pitcher combo, attending in hopes of playing both sports. But he decided two sports and an engineering major were too much. Good call: He made more than $6 million in baseball.

385. Sherm Lollar, Catcher, Chicago White Sox.

Teams kept giving up on Sherm Lollar. In Cleveland, he was stuck behind Jim Hegan, saw little action and asked to be sent back to the minors so he could play. Cleveland did just that but did not like his attitude—Lollar "displayed insufficient dash and spirit," one writer said—and traded him to the Yankees. Where he sat behind Yogi Berra. The Yankees preferred Gus Niarhos as a backup and traded Lollar to the St. Louis Browns. There, he became an All-Star. But the Browns were bad (52-102 in 1952) and not very smart and traded him to the White Sox for, among others, Niarhos. In Chicago, Lollar really blossomed, under two former catchers—first, Paul Richards, and then, Al López. He was a six-time All-Star with the White Sox, became a power hitter despite the dampening effects of Comiskey Park, won Gold Gloves in the first three years they were given and retired with the best career fielding percentage for a catcher.

386. Jim Delsing, Outfielder, Washington Senators.

You could count on one fact in an obituary of Jim Delsing: He once pinch-ran for the smallest player in Major League Baseball history. Yes, Delsing replaced 3-foot-7-inch Eddie Gaedel after Gaedel walked as the Browns played the Tigers in 1951. Delsing went three for four and scored a run in the first game of an August 19 doubleheader, and he was upset when he was not in the starting lineup for Game 2. "I went up to Zack Taylor, who was manager, and he said: 'Cool it. You'll be all right.'" Delsing didn't understand, as he and the rest of the Browns did not know what the Browns' owner, Bill Veeck, had in store for the second game. Only when Gaedel walked to lead off the bottom of the first and Taylor said, "Now go run for

Gaedel" did the pieces fall into place. "We never knew what was going on," Delsing told *The New York Times* in 2001. "Something was going on almost every day. This was another of Mr. Veeck's promotions."

387. Don Drysdale, Pitcher, Los Angeles Dodgers.

List the landmark figures in ballplayers' push to earn what they believed they deserved. Robin Roberts. Marvin Miller. Curt Flood. Andy Messersmith and Dave McNally. Peter Seitz. But don't overlook Ginger Drysdale. In the winter after the 1965 season—one in which they had combined to win 49 games and lead the Dodgers to another World Series championship—Don Drysdale and Sandy Koufax met for dinner and discovered that the Dodgers' general manager, Buzzie Bavasi, had been lying to them in contract negotiations, misrepresenting each player's salary to the other. So Ginger Drysdale, Don's wife at the time, made this bold proposal, wrote Jane Leavy in *Sandy Koufax: A Lefty's Legacy*: "If Buzzie is going to compare the two of you, why don't you just walk in there together?" At the time, contracts were for a year. Agents were not allowed to aid the players in negotiations. Salaries were not so publicly known as they are now, so players blindly walked in by themselves. That is, until Drysdale and Koufax took up Ginger's suggestion and told Bavasi that they would both sign or neither would. What they wanted was to split $1 million over three years—$167,000 a year each, or roughly $1.5 million in 2023 dollars—at a time when Mickey Mantle, the biggest name in the game, was making $100,000. The two Dodgers also had the nerve to be taking advice from an entertainment lawyer. It's not as if the Dodgers didn't have the money. As Bill James noted in his *Historical Baseball Abstract*, the team made a profit of more than $4.3 million in 1962 (nearly $43 million in 2023 dollars), according to court documents. Since then, Los Angeles had won two more pennants and had drawn more than 2.5 million fans to Dodger Stadium in 1965; the Dodgers were not paupers. Still, they resorted to the various tactics of the era to portray Drysdale and Koufax negatively, but the players held out well into spring training before finally agreeing to one-year deals—$125,000 for Koufax (who had already decided that 1966 would be his final season) and $110,000 for Drysdale. As Michael Fallon wrote in *Dodgerland*, "The Koufax-Drysdale

Card 387: Don Drysdale joined with teammate Sandy Koufax in an unprecedented contract negotiation that was emboldened by Drysdale's wife.

holdout had planted an important seed: There was value in collective bargaining." Don Sutton, who became a Dodgers standout himself, understood. "Baseball players today owe a lot to Curt Flood and Andy Messersmith and Dave McNally," he said in *Sandy Koufax*. "But Flood, Messersmith and McNally owed a lot to Koufax and Drysdale. Because they were the first guys who really took a stand. This was the first challenge to the structure of baseball."

388. Bob Will, Outfielder, Chicago Cubs.

Was Bob Will some long-lost cousin of the political commentator George Will? Both are from Illinois (Bob, from suburban Chicago, was born in 1931; George, from Champaign, was born 10 years later). Bob wore glasses; so does George. Bob labored through the Cubs' farm system and played parts of six seasons in Chicago; George has been a long-suffering Cubs fan. Bob was an "all-star storyteller," said the author Tom Owens, who corresponded with him. George, of course, has been writing for newspapers about politics for decades. Bob was left-handed, and George ... well, he is a renowned conservative, but he did say he was leaving the Republican Party in 2016.

389. Joe Nuxhall, Pitcher, Cincinnati Redlegs.

Joe Nuxhall spent 38 seasons (and more than 6,000 games) as a radio broadcaster for the Reds. He developed a signature signoff that became so ingrained in Reds culture that it wound up being illuminated across the team's administration building: "This is the old left-hander, rounding third and heading for home." What he was first known for, though, was being the *young* left-hander—the youngest player, in fact, in a major league game. That was during World War II, when, at the age of 15 years, 10 months and 11 days, he pitched two-thirds of a very shaky inning against the Cardinals, allowing five hits, two walks, five runs and one wild pitch, three months before he began high school. Nuxhall retired in 1966 and moved into the broadcast booth in 1967, just a couple of years after another longtime pitcher, Waite Hoyt, had retired as a Reds announcer. Hoyt was almost a 15-year-old major leaguer himself. The Giants signed him in 1915, when he was a 15-year-old sophomore at Erasmus High School in Brooklyn. As it turned out, Hoyt pitched only batting practice that season, according to his *New York Times* obituary, but he was pitching in the minors at 16 and in the majors—for good—at 18.

390. Orlando Cepeda, First Baseman, San Francisco Giants.

Here are three players who became Hall of Famers and their rookie seasons, all at age 20, in the 1950s:

Player	PA	R	H	2B	3B	HR	RBI	BB	SO	BA/OBP/SLG	OPS+
Player A	524	59	127	22	5	20	68	57	60	.274/.356/.472	120
Player B	509	58	131	27	6	13	69	28	39	.280/.322/.447	104
Player C	644	88	188	38	4	25	96	29	84	.312/.342/.512	125

You may well know the identities: Player A is Willie Mays, B is Hank Aaron and C is Orlando Cepeda. All were excellent rookies—Mays and Cepeda were voted

Rookie of the Year, while Aaron was fourth, losing votes no doubt because of a broken ankle—but Cepeda clearly had the best season. Obviously, he did not also have the best career. He did not share the defensive value of Mays and Aaron, and knee injuries robbed him of playing time. But his power game also did not flourish as he aged, as it did for Aaron and Mays. Cepeda had 222 home runs through age 26—just over half of his career playing time—and 157 afterward. Mays had 167 homers through age 26 (he lost a year to the service) and 499 afterward. And Aaron was 219/536. Tough comparisons!

391. Milt Pappas, Pitcher, Baltimore Orioles.

Major league organizations are always doing cost-benefit analysis with their players. Sometimes they underestimate the costs. Sixteen pitchers since the Deadball Era have won at least 150 major league games before they turned 30. Milt Pappas was one of them. Only four of them won as many as 100 games after they turned 30. Milt Pappas was not one of them. Here's how the 16 pitchers fared before and after age 30:

Pitcher	W Before 30	W After 30	Total Wins
Hal Newhouser	190	17	207
Jim Hunter	184	40	224
Robin Roberts	179	107	286
Don Drysdale	177	32	209
Bob Feller	177	89	266
Wes Ferrell	175	18	193
Waite Hoyt	165	72	237
Mel Harder	159	64	223
Dwight Gooden	157	37	194
Bert Blyleven	156	131	287
Lefty Gomez	153	36	189
Milt Pappas	153	56	209
Jim Palmer	152	116	268
Ken Holtzman	151	23	174
Greg Maddux	151	204	355
Vida Blue	150	59	209

392. Whitey Herzog, Outfielder, Kansas City Athletics.

Whitey Herzog began learning what it would take to be a winning manager when he was an outfielder in the New York Yankees' organization. "I'll bet Casey Stengel walked me down the third-base line 75 times a day teaching me that good base running boils down to anticipation and knowledge of the defense," he said in a 2010 *New York Times* article. His takeaway: "You can steal a lot of runs." Which Herzog tried to do, most of them as a manager of the Royals and the Cardinals. He was far above the league average in steal attempts of second; even more of third. He wasn't much for bunting, but he used pitchers and pinch-runners more than his peers. Jim Kaat, a Cardinals reliever under Herzog, told *The Times*, "From the fifth or sixth inning on, when he got into his little cocoon, he was the best at putting pitchers in the position where they had an advantage." Herzog was a manager from

1973 to 1990 and had only five losing records, a résumé that earned him a spot in the Hall of Fame. "He's the best manager I ever played for as a field manager and a tactician," Keith Hernandez told *The Times*, an assessment that came even after Herzog had contentiously traded him away from St. Louis.

393. Frank Lary, Pitcher, Detroit Tigers.

Mel Parnell of the Red Sox was dubbed the "Yankee killer" after he defeated the Yankees in all five of his starts against them in 1953—four of them shutouts. Boston's Willard Nixon beat the Yankees four times in 1954 and again in '55 and then laid down 27⅓ consecutive scoreless innings against New York in 1956: Yankee killer. Years later, Randy Johnson went 5–0 against New York in the postseason. But *the Yankee Killer*? That was Frank Lary. Pitching for nondescript Tigers teams, he was 27–10 against the Yankees from 1955 to '61, a stretch in which the Yankees played .615 ball and won six pennants in seven years. From 1957 to '59, Lary owned a 13–1 record against the Yankees, with seven wins in 1958 alone. "He really was a different pitcher against the Yankees," teammate Al Kaline said, and he was right. For his career, Lary was 28–13 with a 3.32 ERA against the Yankees; against everyone else, 100–103, 3.69.

394. Randy Jackson, Third Baseman, Cleveland Indians.

Perhaps it should be no surprise that the 1959 Topps card for Handsome Ransom Jackson—Randy's first name really was Ransom—would be a photo portrait. After all, if you are good-looking enough to be called Handsome, you'd have a portrait. But Jackson's 1958 card was also a portrait. As was his card for 1956. And 1954. And 1952. Even his 1953 and 1955 Bowman cards, posed action, display Jackson's handsome face quite well. Jackson, however, insisted in his 2016 memoir, *Handsome Ransom Jackson: Accidental Big Leaguer*, that there was more rhyme than reason for the name: "The nickname has less to do with looks and more to do with a sportswriter looking for something to rhyme with Ransom."

395. Elston Howard, Catcher-Outfielder, New York Yankees.

When the Yankees signed Elston Howard away from the Negro leagues in 1950, he was an outfielder. He remained an outfielder through two

Card 394: Randy Jackson insisted there was more rhyme than reason for his nickname, Handsome Ransom. He used it in the title of his autobiography anyway.

years in the Army (he played ball instead of being shipped to Korea) and another minor league season. Then in 1954, the Yankees decided to make Howard a catcher. Now, Yogi Berra was just coming off a season in which he was second in the MVP voting and was only 29—but Howard, at age 25, was turned into a catcher. *Yogi Berra: Eternal Yankee* by Allen Barra notes that catcher was "the position at which he was least likely to become a starter with the parent club," which still had not had a Black player on the major league roster. Howard's 1954 season was so good that it was all but impossible to keep him in the minors in 1955, but he needed polishing as a catcher—and got it, as Berra had, from the Hall of Famer Bill Dickey. Berra also quickly befriended Howard, even though it was evident he might be competition. Injuries (his own and teammates') moved Howard back to the outfield with some regularity, but eventually, Barra wrote, "at this point in their respective careers, he [Berra] knew, Elston Howard had become a better catcher—Yogi had worked overtime to help make that true." Arlene Howard, Elston's widow, told Barra that Elston had appreciated "the way Yogi and Bill Dickey had worked with him to develop his catching skills. Elston said being a Yankee catcher was like being in a special fraternity." Howard eventually paid it forward, helping to tutor a young Thurman Munson. Dickey to Berra to Howard to Munson—that was half a century of catching excellence, with the players ensuring their successors were ready for it.

396. Bob Rush, Pitcher, Milwaukee Braves.

Bob Rush always makes me think of Rick Reuschel. Reuschel was probably better, but their stories were pretty much the same: big right-handers who played many years for many bad Cubs teams and finally saw what the postseason was like when they landed with other teams later in their careers. Here's what their Cubs careers looked like, not counting Reuschel's second, short Cubs stint:

Player	GS	W-L	IP	CG	SH	SV	HR/9	WHIP	ERA	ERA+
Rush, 1948–57	292	110–140	2132.2	112	13	7	0.6	1.298	3.71	109
Reuschel, 1972–81	313	125–114	2091.1	63	7	3	0.6	1.301	3.43	116

They were even alike as hitters: Rush batted .179/.210/.231 for the Cubs with four home runs in 782 plate appearances; Reuschel was .169/.199/.222 with four homers in 856 plate appearances.

397. Washington Senators Team Card.

These Senators were bound for their third consecutive last-place finish and fourth in five years, at 63–91. Washington was 357–567, a .386 clip, for the final six seasons of the decade. But the team was moving toward being good. Harmon Killebrew, a 23-year-old miscast as a third baseman, hit 42 home runs in 1959 and drove in 105 runs, with a .516 slugging percentage and a 137 OPS+. Outfielder Bob Allison, at 24, hit 30 homers and had a 122 OPS+. Shortstop Zoilo Versalles got his feet wet in the majors at 19. The rotation was fronted by Camilo Pascual and Pedro Ramos; Russ Kemmerer was bumping along as an 8–17 starter who would find success as reliever. Further additions helped the team become a contender in 1962 (91–71, second place), but as the rechristened Minnesota Twins, and in 1965 they won the pennant. Squint and you could see that success coming in 1959.

398. Wally Post, Outfielder, Philadelphia Phillies.

There *has* been documented voting fraud, stuffed ballot boxes. It was 1957 and in Cincinnati. The fans in town, taking advantage of the lax rules surrounding voting for the All-Star Game, voted seven Reds into the starting lineup. Seven Reds from a team that was 44–36 at the All-Star break. As Bill James recounts in his *Historical Baseball Abstract*, the ballot-box stuffing was abetted by *The Cincinnati Times-Star*, "a newspaper that printed ballots already filled out and the address of where to send them." One of the beneficiaries was Wally Post, who in the previous two seasons had hit 40 and 36 home runs but in 1957 was clearly not an All-Star. Commissioner Ford Frick bumped Post and Gus Bell for, um, Willie Mays and Hank Aaron. Post never was an All-Star in a very fine 15-year career, but he was so beloved in his hometown, St. Henry, Ohio, that they are still playing a charity golf event in his name.

399. Larry Jackson, Pitcher, Chicago Cubs.

Larry Jackson had just finished the 1968 season with the Phillies' best ERA— 2.77, good for a 109 ERA+ even in the Year of the Pitcher—but he was 37 and two teams were being added in both the National and American Leagues for 1969. So Philadelphia, a seventh-place team, decided not to protect him from the expansion draft. Jackson, an Idaho native, told the Phillies that if they did not trade him to a West Coast team, he would retire, according to his SABR Bio Project biography. The Phillies demurred, the Montreal Expos drafted him and Jackson did retire. The Expos may have thought it was a negotiating ploy, but it wasn't. Jackson never played again, retiring with a 194–183 record and a 3.40 ERA and a 113 ERA+ despite playing mostly for mediocre teams. (His career numbers were pretty similar to those of Milt Pappas, who was 209–164, 3.40, 110 ERA+ in a similar number of innings.) Jackson's 194 victories match the totals of Dwight Gooden and David Cone, and all three had minor league seasons that you will not see again. Jackson was 28–4, 2.85 with 351 strikeouts in *300* innings at age 21. Gooden was 19–4, 2.50 with 300 strikeouts in 191 innings at age 18. And Cone was 16–3, 2.08 in 177 innings when he was 18. They were babying him, I guess.

400. Jackie Jensen, Outfielder, Boston Red Sox.

When Jackie Jensen entered pro baseball, most travel was still by train. No team was farther west than St. Louis. But air travel became more frequent, especially after teams started relocating farther and farther west. This became a problem for Jensen, who had come up to the Yankees in 1950. Flying had always unsettled him, but his "merely irritating fear of flying had escalated into a demoralizing phobia," *Sports Illustrated* wrote in 1975. He once drove 700 miles from Boston to Detroit to avoid flying, *SI* said. He resorted to taking sleeping pills to manage his anxiety, and *SI* said Red Sox teammates sometimes had to haul a "semi-comatose" Jensen onto planes. He had treatment that did not solve the problem. But he is far from alone; many other high-profile ballplayers have also feared flying. Jim Bouton wrote in *Ball Four* about Tommy Davis's fear during a flight in a thunderstorm. Mike Trout acknowledged his own fears and said, "I do not like turbulence." Dustin Pedroia told Gordon Edes of ESPN in 2011: "Yeah, I don't like flying, but I deal with it. I have to. Otherwise, I have to pick a new job." Jensen did. He retired in 1960—his marriage was also crumbling—but came back in 1961. A month into the season, he skipped a flight to Kansas City and left the team. A week or so later, he was back, but at the end of the season, he retired for good. And he still feared flying.

401. Ron Blackburn, Pitcher, Pittsburgh Pirates.

Mount Airy, North Carolina, a town of a few thousand on the Virginia border, has been the birthplace of a surprising number of people of renown. A couple of baseball players, including Ron Blackburn, who had a brief career with the Pirates. An NFL player. Frank Beamer, the longtime successful football coach at Virginia Tech. Donna Fargo, who recorded a No. 1 country song in 1973, *The Happiest Girl in the Whole USA*. But no one from Mount Airy was as famous as Andy Griffith, the hometown boy who starred for eight years in *The Andy Griffith Show*. The show's locale, Mayberry, was said to have been modeled on Mount Airy, and Mount Airy has capitalized on the connection by recreating some of its downtown as Mayberry. There is Floyd's barber shop. Wally's service station. The Mayberry courthouse. The actress who played Thelma Lou moved there from Los Angeles in 2007 and signed autographs once a month for years. And every September, there is the Mayberry Days Festival, which remains one of North Carolina's largest festivals even though *The Andy Griffith Show* stopped being filmed more than half a century ago.

402. Héctor López, Second Baseman-Third Baseman, Kansas City Athletics.

Héctor López always insisted he was a pretty good defensive player, but plenty of people insisted otherwise. One, in fact, was his manager with the Yankees, Casey Stengel, who liked López's bat and his versatility (he eventually played every position but pitcher and catcher) but was uneasy about his fielding. (López committed 17 errors in 73 games in his first half-season in New York after being acquired from the Athletics.) He drove in 93 runs in 1959, and Stengel cited that fact as the reason he kept trotting López out on the field. "If I bench him, I bench 93 runs," Stengel said, according to López's *New York Times* obituary, "but I would like better fieldin' outta my 93 runs." His defensive problems began early—he made 61 errors in 127 games in his first minor league season, as a shortstop, then 51 more the next year. He made at least 20 errors in five major league seasons. He earned the nickname Héctor (What a Pair of Hands) López, wrote the *New York Times* columnist George Vecsey, because of his "exciting duels with ground balls."

403. Clem Labine, Pitcher, Los Angeles Dodgers.

Most pitchers in the '50s wanted to be starters—complete games were, as Ewell Blackwell noted in *We Played the Game*, where the money was. Clem Labine was different. He wanted to relieve. "I always thought Clem would've had a great career as a starting pitcher," his Dodgers teammate Carl Erskine said after Labine died. "But he told me: 'I don't want to start. I liked the pressure of coming into the game with everything on the line.'" Yet two of his biggest performances came as a starter. In 1951, he pitched a 10-0 shutout against the Giants in Game 2 of the Dodgers' three-game playoff series. (Labine and Erskine were in the bullpen for Game 3 when Ralph Branca got the fateful call and gave up Bobby Thomson's pennant-winning homer.) Then in 1956, the day after Don Larsen had pitched a perfect game in the World Series to give the Yankees a 3-2 Series lead, the Dodgers turned to Labine to avert elimination, even though he had started only three games all season (and was knocked out in the second inning of one of them). In Game 6, Labine pitched a 10-inning shutout for a 1-0 victory. But Branca said Labine had "the right equipment to be a reliever" and not just his sinker and curve. "He also had courage," Branca told *Sports Illustrated*. "He really welcomed the challenge of being a reliever. He was a tough bird who loved to be in a crucial spot."

404. Hank Sauer, Outfielder, San Francisco Giants.
Stan Musial led the National League in 1952 in batting average (.336), slugging percentage (.538), runs (105) and hits (196), but he did not win the Most Valuable Player Award. No, he was fifth. Jackie Robinson batted .308, had a .440 on-base percentage, scored 104 runs and hit 19 home runs as a second baseman, and his team won the pennant, but he was not named the MVP. No, he was seventh. Robin Roberts had a 28-7 record and a 2.59 ERA while pitching 330 innings, but he was not the MVP either, not even in those pre–Cy Young Award days. No, he was second. Hank Sauer, a powerful but plodding outfielder for the fifth-place Cubs, was the MVP. He led the league in homers (37) and RBIs (121), and that was pretty much Sauer's contribution as he became the first MVP winner from a second-division club. (He was not being paid for his defense.) In *The Baseball 100,* Joe Posnanski recounts the response to the award from Oscar Fraley of United Press International: "Anybody who knows the difference between a bunt and a punt must be completely flabbergasted by the selection of Hank Sauer in the National League. Most of the voters obviously never heard of Robin Roberts." In his *Historical Baseball Abstract*, Bill James wrote that Sauer—he called him a "sluggardly slugger"—"is often cited as one of the worst all-around players to win the award."

405. Roy McMillan, Shortstop, Cincinnati Redlegs.
Cardinals manager Eddie Stanky, a longtime second baseman, once said of Roy McMillan, "Hitting a ball toward Roy is like hitting it down a sewer," according to McMillan's *New York Times* obituary. Billy Jurges, who briefly managed McMillan with the Reds and was a star infielder himself in the 1920s and '30s, called him "as fine a shortstop as I've ever seen—any time, anywhere." The numbers back him up: McMillan led his league's shortstops in assists, double plays turned, fielding percentage and range factor four times each and putouts three times. He won the Gold Glove each of the first three years it was awarded. His career might have looked even better had he been able to hit, but he is just outside the top 10 in career defensive WAR, per Baseball Reference, for shortstops whose careers were substantially after integration. Here's a look at the top 11 in dWAR, with their innings at shortstop and, just for fun, their OPS+. Most of these guys weren't playing for their offense.

Player	dWAR	SS Innings	OPS+
1. Ozzie Smith	44.2	21,785.2	87
2. Mark Belanger	39.5	15,335.1	68
3. Cal Ripken, Jr.	35.7	20,232.0	112
4. Luis Aparicio	31.9	22,408.2	82
5. Omar Vizquel	29.5	22,960.2	82
6. Andrelton Simmons	28.5	10,338.1	87
7. Pee Wee Reese	25.6	17,707.1	99
8. Ozzie Guillén	23.0	15,802.2	69
9. Phil Rizzuto	23.0	13,650.2	93
10. Alan Trammell	22.8	18,270.0	110
11. Roy McMillan	21.7	16,970.2	72

A couple of footnotes: The dWAR for some of the players above includes other positions (like Ripken at third), but they were primarily shortstops. And Simmons's numbers are through the 2022 season. Look at how high his dWAR is despite playing half as many innings as Smith, Ripken, Aparicio and Vizquel. Belanger's dWAR per innings played is also phenomenal.

406. Solly Drake, Outfielder, Los Angeles Dodgers.

Ballplayers and religion have been intertwined for most of the game's history. Billy Sunday, a 19th-century outfielder, became America's best-known evangelist in the early 20th century. Decades later, Vernon Law, known as Deacon, and Lindy McDaniel were quite public about their faith. In more recent years, Cecil Cooper taught Bible classes after his playing career, and Josh Willingham became a campus minister at a school in Alabama. Solly Drake had an even more substantial involvement in religion. Drake, a light-hitting outfielder (he was 0 for 22 as a pinch-hitter in 1959), completed an undergraduate degree after entering pro ball and ultimately became a minister. Known by then as Solomon, he served at Greater Ebenezer Missionary Baptist Church in Los Angeles for 34 years. He was a mentor to younger pastors, too. "He's been like a physical, living and spiritual GPS for me," one of them said after his death, according to *The Los Angeles Sentinel*. Solly and his younger brother Sammy were the first African American brothers to play in the majors in the 20th century. (If Solly was a futile pinch-hitter, Sammy was a futile pinch-runner—he pinch-ran 21 times and never stole a base.) After baseball, Drake became Prudential Insurance's first Black representative west of the Mississippi, in 1963, prompting some white agents to quit in protest, *The Sentinel* said. Drake became an award-winning rep and stayed for 20 years before moving to the pulpit full-time.

407. Moe Drabowsky, Pitcher, Chicago Cubs.

Ah, the Prince of Pranks. Moe Drabowsky was the master of the hot foot—surreptitiously lighting someone's shoelaces on fire. Could be a teammate. A coach. A reporter. Bill Chuck, a baseball blogger, wrote that Drabowsky lit up Jim Elliot, a *Baltimore Sun* reporter, so often that Elliot resorted to looking at his shoes during interviews. So Drabowsky then lit his notebook. His Orioles teammate Boog Powell said, "If there were 20 guys sitting on the bench, Moe would crawl on his belly under 19 of them to give the last guy a hot foot." He put a snake in Luis Aparicio's glove and another one in a breadbasket at a sports luncheon, giving Brooks Robinson a considerable surprise. He once used the bullpen phone in Kansas City to dial the Athletics' bullpen and, impersonating Kansas City manager Al Dark, ordered a pitcher to start warming up. Jim Brosnan, a roommate for a while, remembered that Drabowsky would use the bullpen phone to order pizza. That was nothing, though. Jim Bouton wrote in *Ball Four*: "Moe picked up the phone, called a number in Hong Kong, and ordered a Chinese dinner. 'To go.'" Powell told John Eisenberg for *From 33rd Street to Camden Yards: An Oral History of the Baltimore Orioles*, "Obviously, Moe's parents never let him have toys when he was little, so he had a lot of catching up to do." He never would have gotten away with all of it had he not been able to pitch a little—Drabowsky lasted 17 seasons in the major leagues.

408. Keystone Combo: Nellie Fox-Luis Aparicio.

Nellie Fox and Luis Aparicio played together on the White Sox for six seasons. The first year, 1956, the Gold Gloves had not yet been created. In 1957—when the award covered both leagues—Fox won the Gold Glove for second basemen, but Aparicio did not win at shortstop; Roy McMillan of the Reds did. (Aparicio might have won had there been an AL award; he did lead AL shortstops in assists.) Beginning in 1958, when there were separate awards for each league, Aparicio won the next five Gold Gloves, while Fox won two more. "Here is a club trying to win on pitching and defense and little power," George Kell, a former All-Star third baseman, told *Sports Illustrated* during the pennant-winning 1959 season. "Their double-play combination of Fox and Aparicio is the most important factor in Chicago's strength. They are the best in baseball. Chicago could hardly win without them."

Card 409: Gus Zernial managed a date—a photo shoot, really—with Marilyn Monroe well before she met Joe DiMaggio. "Man," he said, "could a girl be any prettier?"

409. Gus Zernial, Outfielder, Detroit Tigers.

Gus Zernial was a slugger, but he hit 124 fewer home runs than Joe DiMaggio. He never came close to playing in a postseason game; DiMaggio played in 51 (all World Series games, of course). But Gus Zernial had his arms around Marilyn Monroe before Joe DiMaggio did. Zernial lived in Hollywood in the off-season, and in 1951, he told Danny Peary for *We Played the Game*, some press agents wanted some ballplayers to "pose with a rising young starlet. She was a lovely, well-proportioned young lady." Marilyn Monroe. "I thought, 'Man, could a girl be any prettier?'" Zernial told Peary. He and the other players posed with Monroe, who was wearing high heels and short shorts, for publicity photos—his wife was not thrilled—but that was the extent of his contact with her. Later, Zernial's White Sox went to New York for a series at the same time Monroe was going to the city, which sparked some news coverage. Zernial said, "Joe DiMaggio had never met Marilyn, but when he saw the magazine he made a comment like, 'Why does a rookie like Zernial get to take a layout with someone like her?'" One thing led to another, and DiMaggio and Monroe met, then married in 1954 ... and divorced in 1955. Zernial, meanwhile, was married to his wife, Marla Jean Sims, for nearly 50 years.

410. Billy Pierce, Pitcher, Chicago White Sox.

The White Sox had waited 40 years for a World Series. Billy Pierce had waited 14. And then Pierce, Chicago's ace left-hander for nearly a decade, never started a game in the 1959 Series. Manager Al López started 39-year-old Early Wynn, who would win the Cy Young Award, three times in six games; Pierce pitched four innings of relief over three games. López may have wanted to avoid starting Pierce, a lefty, in the Los Angeles Coliseum, which was 251 feet down the left-field foul line (although with a 40-foot screen). He may have worried about a hip injury that sidelined Pierce for three weeks in August and September. The longtime Chicago sportswriter Bill Gleason had a theory: "My experience with Lopez was that he had pets. For some reason, Pierce fell out of favor with him." Pierce's teammate Al Smith suggested there was something odd going on. "We all knew why Lopez didn't pitch him, but we never told anyone and I won't say now," Smith said in *We Played the Game*. "I will say that I thought he should have pitched." Pierce thought so, too, although he was diplomatic, even years later. "If I'd say I wasn't unhappy that after all my years in Chicago I wasn't given a chance to start a game in our first Series, I'd be a fool," he told Danny Peary, adding, "It was one of those things where one man calls the shots and no one else can do anything about it."

411. Whitey Lockman, First Baseman-Outfielder, Baltimore Orioles.

When Whitey Lockman was a scared 18-year-old rookie with the Giants, his manager, Mel Ott, helped steady him. When Lockman returned after the war and became a full-time player in 1948, Ott was still the manager. Ott was a renowned Giants slugger, but he was also a renowned agreeable fellow—the individual Leo Durocher was referring to when he said, "Nice guys finish last." Here's how that came about, according to Durocher in his book *Nice Guys Finish Last*: Durocher, then with the Dodgers, was talking to some newspapermen and explaining his affection for the play of Eddie Stanky, known as the Brat, when "just at that point, the Giants, led by Mel Ott, began to come out of their dugout to take their warm-up. Without missing a beat, I said, 'Take a look at that Number Four there. A nicer guy never drew breath than that man there.' I called off his players' names as they came marching up the steps behind him,

'Walker Cooper, Mize, Marshall, Kerr, Gordon, Thomson. Take a look at them. All nice guys. They'll finish last. Nice guys. Finish last.'" Which the Giants did in fact do in 1946. They were in fourth place when Ott was fired on July 15, 1948—and Durocher, the antithesis of a nice guy, was hired to replace him. Durocher did little better then (41–38 versus 37–38) but did lead the Giants to pennants in 1951 and '54. He had worn out his welcome after the 1955 season, however. He had a tumultuous tenure as a coach for the Dodgers under Walter Alston, whom he itched to replace, but finally got another chance to manage with the Cubs, in 1966. Chicago quickly improved, as Durocher's teams tended to do, but they never won a title and Durocher was fired in midseason in 1972—and replaced by a nice guy, Whitey Lockman.

412. Stan Lopata, Catcher, Philadelphia Phillies.

Detroit and its suburbs produced a bumper crop of excellent amateur catchers in the mid- to late 1940s—at least five players who were signed then went on to catch for at least 10 seasons in the majors. Stan Lopata was the best of them, although he shared the Phillies' catching job with Andy Seminick for much of his career. He was struggling as a hitter in 1954 when Rogers Hornsby gave him a batting tip, according to Lopata's SABR Bio Project biography. Lopata changed his stance and the arc of his career. Over the next four seasons he batted .264/.358/.510, with 86 home runs and an OPS+ of 130. He had his defensive troubles—he led NL catchers in stolen bases allowed twice and passed balls once, and his career percentage for throwing out base stealers was an anemic 28 percent, compared with the league average of 41. But he put his Detroit contemporaries to shame as a hitter. Here's a look:

Player, Signed	Years	BA/OBP/SLG	HR	OPS+
Stan Lopata, 1946	13	.251/.351/.452	116	114
Frank House, 1949	10	.248/.302/.363	47	79
Joe Ginsberg, 1944	13	.241/.332/.320	20	79
Harry Chiti, 1950	10	.238/.294/.365	41	77
Hobie Landrith, 1949	14	.233/.320/.327	34	75

Bill Freehan came along about a decade later and outdid them all.

413. Camilo Pascual, Pitcher, Washington Senators.

Camilo Pascual, it was said, threw two pitches—a fastball and a curveball. Not just any curveball. It was "the most feared curveball in the American League for 18 years," said Ted Williams (who solved it anyway, for a .395/.537/.684 line in 54 plate appearances; geez, he could hit). Pascual, who pitched for the Senators and their successors, the Twins, for 13 seasons, was just leaving the game (and striking out hitters with his curve) when another great curveballer came to Minnesota: Bert Blyleven. Blyleven grew up watching Sandy Koufax at Dodger Stadium, Tyler Kepner wrote in *K: A History of Baseball in Ten Pitches*, and was captivated. "Even from the upper deck, Blyleven could see the vicious drop on the Koufax curve," Kepner wrote. Blyleven used his own vicious drop for 22 seasons, 11 with the Twins. "You didn't hit it," Reggie Jackson said, according to Kepner. "He had to hang it to hit it." Between Pascual and Blyleven, Minnesota fans got to see knee-buckling curves for a quarter of a century.

414. Dale Long, First Baseman, Chicago Cubs.

Only 28 left-handers have played catcher in the major leagues. Dale Long was one of them. For five outs. It might have been more, though, had a Branch Rickey experiment worked out. In spring training 1951, Rickey decided to try Long, a rookie first baseman, behind the plate—to get his bat in the lineup and, *Sports Illustrated* suggested, for a little PR for a bad team. Long recalled giving the wrong sign right away in his first exhibition game—he thought he'd called for a curve and was surprised by a fastball—and never caught in a regular-season game that year. But in 1958, he caught twice. On August 20, the starter, Sammy Taylor, was pinch-hit for in the eighth inning; Cal Neeman replaced him in the ninth but was ejected. The third-string catcher, Moe Thacker, was out with a knee injury. Enter Long, wearing his first baseman's mitt, to catch the final two outs, making him the first lefty catcher since 1902. Then on September 21, Taylor was sent out to pinch-hit for Neeman in the eighth, but when the Dodgers changed pitchers, an outfielder pinch-hit for Taylor, leaving the Cubs with no catcher. Long to the rescue: He caught the ninth, although he did have a passed ball. That was the last game at catcher for Long, but not for a lefty catcher. Mike Squires caught an inning in each of two games for the White Sox in 1980, and Benny Distefano caught six innings over three games for the Pirates in 1989.

Card 414: Dale Long became one of the few left-handed catchers in the game. Catching in his first exhibition game, he gave the wrong sign and whoops, here came a fastball.

415. Bill Mazeroski, Second Baseman, Pittsburgh Pirates.

How unlikely was Bill Mazeroski's walk-off home run against Yankees right-hander Ralph Terry to win the 1960 World Series? Maz had hit only two homers in the final two and a half months of the season (off righty Stan Williams and off lefty Warren Spahn). His slugging percentage against right-handers that season was .349. He had hit one home run leading off an inning that season in 186 plate appearances. The 1960 season was not a flukily bad one for Mazeroski. He homered about once every 24 games at home in his career and hit more than twice as many homers on the road as at home. He hit only 44 homers in 1,004 games at Forbes Field. But he homered when it mattered.

416. Haywood Sullivan, Catcher, Boston Red Sox.

Haywood Sullivan was mostly a backup catcher for the Red Sox and the Athletics, but he made an unusual transition—he became a part-owner of the team in Boston. This was not without precedent, certainly in earlier decades. Albert Spalding, Ned Hanlon and John Montgomery Ward were players who acquired ownership interests in early decades of the game. Charles Comiskey, Clark Griffith and, most famously, Connie Mack did, too, owning teams well into the 20th century. Christy Mathewson had a small ownership interest. And so did Branch Rickey. Decades later, Nolan Ryan owned a piece of the Astros. But Sullivan's move from player to front office to ownership was unusual and had some unusually notable aspects. He had helped resurrect the Red Sox into the 1967 pennant winner as head of player development, and as general manager he oversaw the acquisition of talent for Boston's mid-'70s teams. He also oversaw the team's dismantling, fouling up a routine contract mailing to Carlton Fisk that allowed him to become a free agent, trading away Fred Lynn and Rick Burleson and drafting his son Marc, a catcher who would go on to hit .186, with a second-round pick. He stepped into an ownership role after Tom Yawkey died, becoming one leg of a triumvirate that included Yawkey's widow, Jean, and a former Red Sox trainer, Buddy Leroux. Sullivan paid for his slice of the team by mortgaging his house and borrowing $100,000. The team unraveled (see moves above) and rebounded (see 1986 pennant winner), but ownership discord led to battles in court and the papers, and ultimately Sullivan was out. He did, however, walk away with $33 million.

417. Virgil Trucks, Pitcher, New York Yankees.

Virgil Trucks was one of the hardest throwers in baseball—he contended that military radar once clocked his fastball at 105 miles an hour, according to his *New York Times* obituary. He had perhaps the best season of any pitcher in the American League in 1949. And he had perhaps the oddest season of any pitcher anywhere in 1952. Pitching for the last-place Tigers (they would finish 50-104), Trucks labored through a 5-19 season with a 3.97 ERA—but also pitched two no-hitters and a one-hitter in which the first batter singled. And he won them all by 1-0. (He nearly pitched another shutout, giving up a single unearned run.) Detroit averaged only 2.65 runs in Trucks's 29 starts and scored two or fewer in 15 of them. He was only the third pitcher to throw two no-hitters in a season.

418. Gino Cimoli, Outfielder, St. Louis Cardinals.

Gino Cimoli had spent two years in the major leagues with the Dodgers without ever being their leadoff hitter. That changed in 1958 when the Dodgers opened their first season in Los Angeles, with a road game in San Francisco—the major leagues' first regular-season game on the West Coast. Manager Walter Alston did Cimoli, a San Francisco native, a favor and had him bat leadoff in that first game. So Cimoli had a historic first at-bat ... and, as it turned out, a historic first strikeout.

419. Milwaukee Braves Team Card.

In 1959, the Braves were on the verge of doing something no National League team had done since World War II—win three consecutive pennants. It was a wild race. The Giants led the Braves and the Dodgers by two games with eight to play but then lost three in a row at home to Los Angeles. San Francisco finished its season with a 1–7 run while its rivals each went 6–2. Heading into the final weekend, Los Angeles led Milwaukee by a game but lost to the Cubs on that Saturday while the Braves beat the Phillies. With the pennant at stake the next day, both the Braves and the Dodgers won, setting up a best-of-three playoff series to determine the NL champion. Los Angeles won Game 1 in Milwaukee. The Braves were set up to win Game 2 in Los Angeles but gave up three runs in the ninth to force extra innings, where the Dodgers won in the 12th. Los Angeles won that World Series and played in three more by 1966; the Braves never returned to the Series until 1991, long after they had left for Atlanta.

420. Rocky Colavito, Outfielder, Cleveland Indians.
Rocky Colavito was the favorite player of just about everyone in Cleveland. Everyone except the new general manager, Frank Lane. He took over the role in November 1957 and immediately swung a trade for Minnie Miñoso. That was one of 31 trades involving 76 players Lane made in his first season. Miñoso would join Colavito, who had just hit 25 home runs as a 23-year-old, and Roger Maris, coming off his rookie season in which he homered 14 times at age 22, in the Cleveland outfield. But, as spelled out in *The Curse of Rocky Colavito*, Lane tried to trade Colavito to Washington early in 1958 and failed, then tried to deal him to Kansas City and failed again. He did swap Maris to Kansas City in midseason. Colavito finished the '58 season hitting .303 with 41 home runs and 113 RBIs, and he was third in the MVP voting. He had a nasty contract dispute with Lane—*The Curse* quotes Colavito as saying Lane lied to him—but Colavito rang up 42 homers and 111 RBIs in 1959 and was fourth in the MVP balloting. Lane traded him anyway, to Detroit, for singles-hitting Harvey Kuenn. And then he traded away Miñoso. Cleveland had an outfield of three near–Hall of Famers, two of them about to enter their primes and the third still quite productive, and quickly had none of them. Cleveland's 1960 outfield? Kuenn, Tito Francona and Jimmy Piersall. In 1961, when Maris bashed 61 homers and Colavito hit 45, Cleveland outfielders hit 72.

421. Herm Wehmeier, pitcher, Detroit Tigers.
Herm Wehmeier was a major league journeyman who did not strike out many batters, but his son Jeff was a tall, lanky, hard-throwing right-hander, even at age 14. I know this because the team from Our Lady of Lourdes that I played on met his team in the late stages of the Indianapolis 14-and-under baseball tournament, with a chance to play at Bush Stadium, the Class AAA ballpark in town, on the line. Four years later, in 1971, Jeff Wehmeier, with five high school no-hitters under his belt, would be the No. 16 pick in the baseball draft, one spot after Jim Rice and 13 ahead of George Brett, but his career would fizzle out after three minor league seasons because of control problems. I can attest to those control problems, because he inexplicably hit my bat with a fastball that resulted in a line-drive single over the second baseman's head. If you were giving up a single to me—I finished the season nine for 35, the best I *ever* hit—your major league future was definitely in question.

422. Hobie Landrith, Catcher, San Francisco Giants.

After 60 seasons with eight teams, the American League, responding to threats of a competing third major league, expanded by two teams in 1961; the National League followed suit the next year. The AL expansion teams were stocked by a draft of players from the existing teams, which could protect 25 players on the 40-man roster and 18 players on the 25-man roster. Predictably, those new AL teams were not very capable; the Senators finished 10th, although the Angels did beat out the Athletics for eighth place. That was not good enough for the NL owners, who tinkered with the rules for their draft, making it easier to expose aging or unproductive players and hide young talent. "I figured the lists of players would be bad, but they're worse than I thought they would be," Houston's general manager, Paul Richards, said in *The Sporting News*. Which brings us to Hobie Landrith, who was the Mets' first pick in the NL expansion draft (the No. 1 pick overall, by Houston, was shortstop Eddie Bressoud, who was promptly traded for another shortstop). Landrith had played 12 seasons at that point, hitting .233 with 28 home runs. He had also led NL catchers in errors twice despite not playing even 100 games in either season. So why pick Landrith? "You gotta start with a catcher or you'll have all passed balls," Mets manager Casey Stengel said. Landrith provided passed balls anyway—three in 21 games before he was traded to the Orioles to complete their deal … for Marv Throneberry.

423. Bob Grim, Pitcher, Kansas City Athletics.

Yankee players have won fewer Rookie of the Year awards than you may imagine. Nine Yankees have been voted ROY since the award was begun in 1947—nine in 76 seasons, for a team that has won 26 pennants in that time. The Athletics have had eight Rookies of the Year (and six pennants) and the Senators/Twins have had seven ROY (and three pennants). Bob Grim was the second Yankee to be named Rookie of the Year, after going 20–6, 3.26 in 1954, a season in which he started only 20 games and pitched 199 innings. Eight of his wins came in his 17 relief appearances, a harbinger of the role he would eventually settle into; Grim would start only 40 of the final 231 games he appeared in. He had the least distinguished career of any Yankee Rookie of the Year. The list also includes Gil McDougald, 1951; Tony Kubek, 1957; Tom Tresh, 1962; Stan Bahnsen, 1968; Thurman Munson, 1970; Dave Righetti, 1981; Derek Jeter, 1996; and Aaron Judge, 2017.

424. Ken Aspromonte, Second Baseman, Washington Senators.

In 1973, Ken Aspromonte was in his second season as manager of the Cleveland Indians and I was an intern, working mostly as an editor, in the sports department of the city's morning newspaper, *The Plain Dealer*. It was a difficult summer for both Aspromonte, overseeing a talented but very young team, and the players churning through loss after loss; Cleveland was 7–21 in June and 11–20 in July. After one summer loss, *The Plain Dealer*'s beat reporter filed his story in which a quote from Aspromonte referred to George Hendrick, a mercurial but productive center fielder who was Black, as a "boy." This produced debate on the copy desk. Should we run the quote as filed, knowing it might well spark a controversy, or alter it in the belief that Aspromonte meant no harm in using the term? The copy desk chief finally ruled that the quote should be tweaked, sparing Aspromonte a potential confrontation with one of his best players. It may well have been an innocent remark or it may have reflected tensions on the team. Aspromonte was fired after the 1974 season, and Cleveland named the major leagues' first Black manager, Frank Robinson, who had been acquired as a player late in the season. In his book *Frank: The First*, written with Dave Anderson of *The New York Times*, Robinson said: "Shortly after I joined the Cleveland Indians for the last three weeks of the 1974 season, I realized this was a ball club in trouble. The dugout was virtually segregated. On one side was the manager, Ken Aspromonte, with almost all the white players. On the other side was Larry Doby, a Black coach, with all the Black players. I sat here and there, mostly in the middle. Any ball club that's split along racial lines like that had to be in trouble." It was: Cleveland lost 15 of its final 21 games.

Card 424: A remark about one of his players by Ken Aspromonte, then the Indians' manager, prompted an ethics debate in the newsroom of a Cleveland newspaper.

425. Del Crandall, Catcher, Milwaukee Braves.

Casey Stengel once said, "They say some of my stars drink whiskey, but I have found that ones who drink milkshakes don't win many ball games." Maybe this misunderstanding of ballplayers is why Stengel's Yankees lost the 1957 World Series to the Milwaukee Braves, whose catcher was that non-drinker Del Crandall. In *We Played the Game*, Johnny Antonelli, a Braves pitcher, said Crandall was his best friend, and "we were called the Milk Shake twins because we drank milk shakes and the other players drank what they wanted." Another Braves pitcher, Bob Buhl, said the players called Crandall "Jack Armstrong, the All-American Boy. He would never do anything wrong. For instance, he didn't drink." But he could play. Crandall was an 11-time All-Star. And sorry, Casey, but his Braves won a lot of games.

426. Jerry Staley, Pitcher, Chicago White Sox.

Gerald Staley, a pitcher in the '40s, '50s and '60s, was known during his career mostly as Gerry, although he preferred Jerry. Same with Gerald Priddy, a second baseman in the '40s and '50s. But Jerry Staley and Jerry Priddy were very different men. Staley was a dependable starter who, after a midcareer slump, became a dependable reliever. After baseball, he spent 17 years as superintendent of parks in Clark County,

Washington. He was inducted into the Washington State Horseshoe Pitching Association Hall of Fame and died at 87. But Priddy? He was known as a "clubhouse lawyer" during his career—baseball code for "troublemaker." (The reference was even in his obituary.) The Yankees got rid of him, the Senators got rid of him, the Browns got rid of him. After baseball he was convicted of extortion and died at 60.

427. Charlie Neal, Second Baseman-Shortstop, Los Angeles Dodgers.

Charlie Neal was the shortstop who pushed Pee Wee Reese to third base. Then he became the second baseman who pushed Jim Gilliam to left field. Then he became the Dodger who pushed the Mets to, effectively, spend $250,000 to acquire him. First the Mets laid out $125,000 to take outfielder Lee Walls in the expansion draft in late 1961; then they sent Walls and $125,000 to the Dodgers for Neal, according to Jimmy Breslin's *Can't Anybody Here Play This Game?* Neal had hit 30 doubles, 11 triples and 19 home runs while stealing 17 bases in 1959 when the Dodgers won the pennant, but in 1961 he had one of the worst seasons of any National League regular: an OPS+ of 66 in 377 plate appearances. That explains his availability, if not his price tag. He had some shining moments with the Mets, including on June 17, 1962. That day, Marv Throneberry tripled in two runs in the first inning but was called out because he had missed first base. And second base. "Well, I know he touched third," Casey Stengel said, "because he's standing on it." Briefly. Neal batted next and homered to deep left field. As *The New York Times* reported, Stengel emerged from the dugout and pointed to each of the four bases as Neal made his home run trot. Unfortunately, Neal had many more Metsian moments, and before the '63 season he was traded for catcher Jesse Gonder. Remember Stengel's line about passed balls? Gonder led the league with 21 in 1964.

428. Buc Hill Aces: Ron Kline-Bob Friend-Vern Law-Roy Face.

Topps could be generous in its characterizations on its specialty cards. "Ace" was a kind word for Pirates pitchers at the time; the team was 62-92 in 1957 before improving to 84-70 and a second-place finish in 1958. Friend, Law and Face *were* the best pitchers those two years. Friend was 36-32, 3.53 ERA, 109 ERA+; Law, 24-20, 3.46, 111; and Face, the top reliever, 9-8, 30 saves, 2.99, 134. Ron Kline? He was 22-32, 3.76, 102. Later, he did sort of become the Roy Face for the post-expansion Senators.

429. Bobby Thomson, Outfielder, Chicago Cubs.

Few people remember Bobby Thomson for anything more than one swing, "the Shot Heard 'Round the World." But his nine years with the Giants were quite good. Then he turned 30. And was traded. A look at his numbers with the Giants and with four other teams:

Team	G	PA	H	HR	RBI	BB	SO	BA/OBP/SLG	OPS+
Giants	1135	4634	1171	189	704	360	477	.277/.332/.462	116
Per 162	132	550	140	23	873	43	55		
Others	725	2564	586	83	360	218	366	.255/.320/.418	98
Per 162	104	366	84	12	51	31	52		

For context, players with a career OPS+ of 116 include Robbie Alomar, Dusty Baker, Adrián Beltré, Ken Boyer, Barry Larkin, Lee May, Thurman Munson, Joc Pederson, Gus Zernial and Ryan Zimmerman. (Pederson surprised me, too.) The Braves landed Thomson in 1954, thinking he would add a big bat to their lineup, but he broke his right ankle in spring training. The saving grace for the Braves? They decided to go with a rookie instead: Hank Aaron.

430. Whitey Ford, Pitcher, New York Yankees.

Until he was 37 years old, Whitey Ford never had even a mediocre season. Yet Casey Stengel used the young Ford much differently than Ralph Houk used the aging Ford. Perhaps because Ford had some arm injuries in 1957, '59 and '60, Stengel used Ford with some restraint (although he did call on Ford out of the bullpen from time to time; that was Stengel's M.O. for his top starters). Houk, who replaced Stengel in 1961, rode Ford much harder. Here's what Ford's average seasons looked like under Stengel (1950–60, with two years out for military service) and under Houk (and Yogi Berra for a season) from 1961 to 1965:

Manager	W-L	Pct.	GS	IP	WHIP	BB	SO	ERA	ERA+
Stengel	15–7	.692	26	195	1.253	88	111	2.70	137
Houk/Berra	18–7	.722	37	260	1.156	65	178	2.85	127

Ford was 31 when Houk became his manager, but he shouldered a much heavier workload—more starts, more innings. He also allowed one fewer base runner per game and struck out one more batter. He had his only two 20-win seasons under Houk (25–4, 24–7). Johnny Sain said that the difference as a pitcher was that Ford "started sinking the ball and throwing more of a controlled breaking ball." And a lot more innings.

431. Whammy Douglas, Pitcher, Cincinnati Redlegs.

Charles William Douglas lost his right eye when he was 11, roughhousing with other kids in North Carolina, and wound up with a glass eye. That much is certain. How he came to be called Whammy is not. In an article on MiLB.com in 2008, Douglas said that because he was striking out so many hitters in semipro ball, he began to be called Whammy. He previously told a reporter in spring training one year that he thought it was because he would "wham" the ball when he played ping-pong as a kid. But other versions of his naming tale say that in the low minors opposing batters saw the glass eye and his overpowering fastball and concluded he was putting a whammy on them. A cartoon character named Evil Eye Fleegle put the whammy on people, so. … Whatever the origin, he was Whammy throughout his baseball career.

432. Smoky Burgess, Catcher, Pittsburgh Pirates.

There are three basic types of Smoky Burgess stories. 1. He was quiet, affable, religious and did not drink. 2. He was by no means lean, as testimonials in *We Played the Game* indicate. Frank Baumholtz called him "pudgy." Jim Fridley referred to his "potbelly." Bob Buhl said that "Burgess was chubby and couldn't squat all the way down." 3. He was an unreal pinch-hitter and could hit any time, even, apparently, on winter holidays. Dick Schofield said: "Smoky could hit a fastball on Jan. 1.

He liked to pick his spots and catch when he wanted to, but he could hit as well as anyone in baseball." And Tom Cheney said: "They always said he could get out of bed Christmas morning and single. I've never seen anything like it. He could hit liners or seeing-eye balls that dribbled through the infield." When he retired, Burgess held the major league record for pinch hits with 145. His pinch-hitting numbers were in fact remarkable: .285/.376/.434 in 590 plate appearances. (Manny Mota, who took his record for career pinch hits, was in the same ballpark: .300/.375/.368. Mota was rotund at the end of his career, too.)

433. Billy Harrell, Infielder, St. Louis Cardinals.

Billy Harrell and Larry Raines were Black middle infielders, born 20 months apart, who took distinctive routes to professional baseball, became teammates in the minors and the majors and, despite obvious defensive prowess, could never hit enough to stick. Harrell was a Siena College graduate with a stronger basketball pedigree—he turned down entreaties from the NBA and the Harlem Globetrotters—and entered pro baseball in 1952, signing with Cleveland. Raines took the unusual path to pro ball of signing with a Japanese team, the Hankyu Braves, in 1953 while on leave from the military. After two successful seasons, he too signed with Cleveland. Harrell and Raines were primarily shortstops (Harrell also played outfield, Raines also played second) and shared time in 1956 at Indianapolis and in 1957 with the big club. The Cleveland manager, Kerby Farrell, said that Harrell had "such tremendous hands, he could play the infield without a glove," according to his SABR Bio Project profile. But he had the "no hit" part of the eternal baseball equation, batting .231/.283/.327 with an OPS+ of 67 in the majors. Same problem for Raines, who batted .253/.308/.332 with a 75 OPS+.

434. Hal Griggs, Pitcher, Washington Senators.

The back of this card has a cartoon with the caption "Hal has some trouble with control." Some? In his first season in the minors, Hal Griggs walked 155 batters. In his second, he walked 145. In his third, 162—but at least he finally pushed his hits per nine innings below 10. He walked more than 100 batters in each of his next three seasons, still, understandably, in the minors. At least in 1956, Griggs walked fewer than 100 opponents—but because he pitched only 99 innings for the Senators. The next year, he was back in the minors and back to walking more than 100. In 1958 he walked "only" 4.5 batters per nine innings, but that went with a 2–11 record and a 5.52 ERA. *The Great American Baseball Card Flipping, Trading, and Bubble Gum Book* says: "Hal Griggs was to pitching as Wayne Causey was to hitting. That is to say—nothing."

435. Frank Robinson, Outfielder, Cincinnati Redlegs.

When I played CYO ball in 1967 and 1968, the coolest players doctored their colored baseball socks so they rode higher and showed more of the white sock underneath. The coolest kids actually wore "sanitaries" (which have their own long history) under their colored socks, socks that were whiter, brighter and thinner and infinitely better looking than the typical sweat socks most of us wore. This look—white undersock, high-cut stirrups—was universally called "the Robinson look," for Frank Robinson, who had the highest stirrups we knew about. The American League knew about his stirrups, too. It created a rule in 1967—the year after Robinson's Triple Crown season with the Orioles—that limited how high the stirrups could go, as laid out by Paul Lukas at Uni Watch. Lukas, aided by research by the brothers Will and Fred Shoken, recounts the history of the rule, as reported by *The Baltimore Sun*; Robinson's unhappiness with it; the potential repercussions for violations (a $25 fine for the first offense, then $50); an umpire's protestation that the crews would only be reporting violations to the league, not fining ballplayers; Robinson's response (captured in a series of photos, a nod toward compliance); and the eventual disappearance of high-cuts as an issue (Robinson and many other players went on to display *lots* of white under their stirrups). It wasn't just teenage ballplayers who loved the look. Here's what Jim Bouton wrote in *Ball Four* about high-cuts, which he thought Robinson might have initiated: "The higher your stirrups, the cooler you are. Your legs look long and cool instead of dumpy and hot." High-cut stirrups have gone out of fashion with most players—the pajama look is in vogue now—but Frank Robinson, you were the coolest.

Card 435: Frank Robinson's high-cut stirrups were the epitome of cool in the mid-'60s, although the American League briefly took issue with his fashion forwardness.

436. Granny Hamner, Shortstop, Philadelphia Phillies.
In the first edition of his *Historical Baseball Abstract*, published in 1985, Bill James theorized that "it is generally true that power-hitting shortstops get a bad rap as defensive players" because of the disconnect between the images of an agile fielder and a powerful slugger. His case in point was Ernie Banks, but he mentioned Granny Hamner as among the group. Hamner was no Banks, but he reached double figures in home runs five times. Although *Total Baseball* rates Hamner as a very poor defensive player, he led National League shortstops in assists once, putouts three times and double plays turned three times. James wrote that had the Gold Glove been awarded then, Hamner would have been the likely NL winner in 1950, '51 and '52 (and Pee Wee Reese and Al Dark were around). He had a bad reputation for the double play, but James pointed out in his *New Historical Baseball Abstract*, published in 2001, that it did not account for the facts that those Phillies teams had fly-ball pitchers, especially Robin Roberts, and walked few batters, so the opportunities for double plays were fewer. "In fact, far from being a *poor* double play infield," James

wrote, "it was actually a fairly good infield at turning the double play, when they had the opportunity to do so." Hamner had a strong arm—he also pitched some—and teammate Andy Seminick said, "When he played short, he was the best at that time at making a relay throw to third or home."

437. Ike Delock, Pitcher, Boston Red Sox.

Lesley Visser grew up in Massachusetts, covered the Red Sox as a pioneering sportswriter for *The Boston Globe* and moved on to CBS Sports, where her work got her into the Sports Broadcasting Hall of Fame. Ted Williams was the star of the early Red Sox teams she followed, but the player she was most enamored of was Ike Delock. "I noticed one day that he looked at me and sort of waved from the bullpen," she said in a 2018 interview. "He became my favorite right there. I still have his baseball card." And she had a memorable meeting with Delock, as related by RIP Baseball. "As a matter of fact," she said in a 1991 interview, "my friends gave me a bachelorette party the night before my wedding [to the broadcaster Dick Stockton], and they flew in Ike Delock. Twenty-five women and Ike Delock! How great was that!"

438. Sam Esposito, Shortstop-Third Baseman, Chicago White Sox.

Sammy Esposito once scored 81 points in a high school basketball game in Chicago and averaged 30 points a game his junior and senior seasons. That earned him a scholarship to Indiana University, where in his first varsity season, 1951–52, he averaged 7.0 points a game as a 5-foot-9 guard. "He was lightning quick, had great hands, and was very smart with the basketball. He was a terrific passer and could use his athletic ability to break down the defense and create shots for himself and his teammates," Jason Hiner wrote in *Mac's Boys: Branch McCracken and the Legendary 1953 Hurryin' Hoosiers.* Esposito was not around for those 1953 Hoosiers, though. He accepted a deal worth $50,000 from the White Sox—and missed out on IU's 1953 NCAA basketball championship.

439. Brooks Robinson, Third Baseman, Baltimore Orioles.

It was Rawlings, the baseball glove manufacturer, that created the Gold Glove Awards, for the best defensive player at each position, in 1957. It was not the first or the last time a company invented an award and put its name on it (the Chalmers Award, named for a car company, was an MVP award starting in 1911; Rolaids, the antacids people, came up with the Rolaids Relief Man Award for the top reliever, in 1976). The Gold Glove Awards the first year covered both leagues, just as the Rookie of the Year Award did for its first two years, 1947 and 1948. Managers and coaches were given the votes, and they, just as fans would have, may have been influenced by reputation. But some of those reputations—like Brooks Robinson's—were well earned. Robinson was a bonus baby who was in the majors at 18, 19 and 20, although neither his bat nor his glove was major-league ready. But when he settled in comfortably at third base, there was no one like him. He won his first Gold Glove Award when Dwight Eisenhower was president (1960) and won every one into Gerald Ford's presidency (1975)—16 consecutive years, most overall of any position player. (Greg Maddux won 18 as a pitcher, and Jim Kaat, 17.) He beat out formidable competition. Frank

Malzone had won the first three Gold Gloves before Robinson's streak began. Clete Boyer was an excellent third baseman but couldn't win a Gold Glove until he moved to the National League. Aurelio Rodríguez, a superb fielder, finally ended Robinson's death grip on the award in 1976, but it was his 10th season. Robinson ensured his reputation with World Series heroics, but he built it day by day—he led AL third basemen in fielding percentage 11 times, assists eight times, range factor four times and putouts and double plays three times each, and he played every day. Joe Posnanski, in *The Baseball 100*, quotes Frank Robinson on Brooks: "I used to stand in the outfield like a fan and watch him make play after play. I used to think, 'Wow, I can't believe this.'"

440. Lew Burdette, Pitcher, Milwaukee Braves.

This card became a darling of collectors for a couple of reasons. First, his name was Lew, not Lou, as it says on the card—actually, Selva Lewis Burdette, Jr. He was Lew on his 1956 and 1957 cards, but for some reason Lou after that. More important, however, Burdette was a right-handed pitcher, not a left-hander, as this card would make you believe. It was his little prank. "This was one of the first times a player deliberately fooled a photographer and then anyone else at Topps who may have proofed this card," *Sports Collectors Daily* wrote. But not the last time a card displayed a major gaffe. Aurelio Rodríguez's 1969 Topps card shows an Angels batboy, not Rodríguez. Joe Koppe's 1964 card has him with a glove on the wrong hand. Billy Martin's 1972 card as manager of the Tigers shows him flipping off the photographer while leaning on a bat. (The White Sox's Frank Thomas later had cards that looked as if he might be giving someone the finger.) And Billy Ripken's 1989 Fleer card clearly shows an obscenity written on the knob of his bat.

441. John Roseboro, Catcher, Los Angeles Dodgers.

For decades the myths used to keep Black players out of Organized Baseball included that they were not intelligent enough and that they wilted under pressure. When baseball finally integrated, however, one of the first Black players was a catcher, Roy Campanella. And by 1959, the year all major league teams were finally integrated, there were three Black catchers among the 16 starters—John Roseboro, an All-Star in four seasons who was the trusted batterymate of the great Dodger pitching staffs of the '60s; Elston Howard, who would be an All-Star in nine seasons and won an MVP award; and Earl Battey, who became a Gold Glove–winning backstop with the Twins. Plus there was another Black catcher, the Virgin Islands native Valmy Thomas, who was a backup with the Phillies. While hardly an overwhelming number, it was four of the 61 players who caught in the majors in 1959. Curiously, only two African American players were among the 150 major league catchers on the 30 teams in 2022—Chuckie Robinson of the Reds and Bo Naylor of the Guardians, and they combined for only 60 plate appearances.

442. Ray Narleski, Pitcher, Detroit Tigers.

Ray Narleski was a hard-throwing right-hander from the East Coast and Don Mossi a control artist lefty from the West Coast, but their careers tracked each other's. They were born two months apart and began playing pro ball in 1949, though they did not become teammates until they were rookies in Cleveland in 1954. Starters in the minors, they were turned into relievers in Cleveland, the "buck stops here" brigade behind the famed rotation that the team rode to the pennant. Narleski and Mossi were anchors of the bullpen for three years before they both got what they wanted—some chances to start—in 1957. Narleski was in and out of the rotation in 1958, with mixed success, while Mossi was sent back to the bullpen, with mixed success. That November they were traded—together—to Detroit, where their careers really diverged at last. Narleski was mostly a struggling reliever whose career was derailed after one more season by a back injury, Mossi a solid starter for several years. Narleski pitched semipro ball after retiring, but he never got over hard feelings about pro ball. "I am bitter about a couple of things," he told the writer Russ Schneider—being used primarily as a reliever and, he felt, being shortchanged on salary. "If that's having an attitude, so be it, I had one."

443. Daryl Spencer, Second Baseman, San Francisco Giants.
Daryl Spencer developed a reputation. In the United States and in Japan. He was a big (6 foot 2), strong middle infielder who made opposing middle infielders look out for him. "The guy I would consider the most notorious slider in the league was Daryl Spencer," Dick Groat told Danny Peary for *We Played the Game*. He added: "He'd cut you. He would spike more middle infielders than anybody." In his *New Historical Baseball Abstract*, Bill James, paraphrasing a *Sport* magazine article, wrote that Spencer "had become so unpopular around the league that people would go out of their way to plow into him on a double play. This had eventually driven Spencer to Japan." Spencer played seven seasons in Japan, where he was a slugging star nicknamed The Monster, but he was still known as a terror on the basepaths. "The burly infielder had no compunction about flattening a second baseman to break up a double play," Robert Whiting wrote in *The Chrysanthemum and the Bat*, adding, "His style was what Americans admire: 'rough and aggressive,' but in Japan it lost him points." Whiting recounts incidents at every base that helped Spencer earn a reputation as "a dirty player." But Spencer was far from the caricature of the Ugly American (or the Tom Selleck character in *Mr. Baseball*). "Spencer was outspoken and independent—traits which are not admired in Japan—but Spencer tried to be a part of the team," Whiting wrote. "He learned to play mahjong and eat Japanese food"—even the raw egg in sukiyaki. And Spencer developed another reputation, for corresponding thoughtfully with autograph seekers who asked about his career as a ballplayer.

444. Ron Hansen, Shortstop, Baltimore Orioles.
When Ron Hansen pulled off an unassisted triple play for the Senators on July 30, 1968, it had been 41 years since a player had managed the feat. The Senators were so impressed they traded Hansen three days later. The unassisted triple play is, however, very unusual—less frequent, for example, than a perfect game. Here are the 15 unassisted triple plays in major league history.

August 23, 2009: Eric Bruntlett, Phillies second baseman, vs. the Mets. (Ended the game.)

May 12, 2008: Asdrúbal Cabrera, Indians second baseman, vs. the Blue Jays. (Hansen happened to be at this game, working as an advance scout for the Phillies.)
April 29, 2007: Troy Tulowitzki, Rockies shortstop, vs. the Braves.
August 10, 2003: Rafael Furcal, Braves shortstop, vs. the Cardinals.
May 29, 2000: Randy Velarde, Athletics second baseman, vs. the Yankees.
July 8, 1994: John Valentin, Red Sox shortstop, vs. the Mariners.
September 20, 1992: Mickey Morandini, Phillies shortstop, vs. the Pirates.
July 28, 1968: Ron Hansen, Senators shortstop, vs. the Indians.
May 31, 1927: Johnny Neun, Tigers first baseman, vs. the Indians. (Last first baseman to do so.)
May 30, 1927: Jimmy Cooney, Cubs shortstop, vs. the Pirates. (Yes, back-to-back days ... and then none for 41 years.)
May 7, 1925: Glenn Wright, Pirates shortstop, vs. the Cardinals. (Jimmy Cooney was one of the base runners.)
October 6, 1923: Ernie Padgett, Braves shortstop, vs. the Phillies. (Final game of the season.)
September 14, 1923: George Burns, Red Sox first baseman, vs. the Indians.
October 10, 1920: Bill Wambsganss, Indians second baseman, vs. the Dodgers. (World Series.)
July 19, 1909: Neal Ball, Naps (later Indians) shortstop, vs. the Red Sox.

445. Cal McLish, Pitcher, Cleveland Indians.

Cal McLish. Short, punchy. Calvin Coolidge Julius Caesar Tuskahoma McLish. Incredibly long, inscrutable. "There were eight kids in the family, and I was No. 7 and my dad didn't get to name one of them before me," McLish told *The Oklahoman* in 1999. "So he evidently tried to catch up." His dad, John, must have worn himself out, as the youngest McLish, born four years after Cal, was Edward Harlan. Cal was born in 1925 and Calvin Coolidge was the president ... but John McLish was a Democrat, according to Cal's SABR Bio Project profile, while Coolidge was a Republican. Julius Caesar? The McLish family was not Roman. Or Italian. Tuskahoma is a Choctaw word and John McLish was part Choctaw, and Tuskahoma is also a small town in Oklahoma ... but 200 miles from Anadarko, where McLish grew up. McLish speculated in an interview for *This Side of Cooperstown* that his father had named him for a president, an emperor and an Indian chief ... but why remains a mystery.

446. Rocky Nelson, First Baseman, Pittsburgh Pirates.

Rocky Nelson, like his contemporary Steve Bilko, tore up Class AAA pitching in the '50s. Bilko's power was expected; he *looked* like a power hitter. Nelson did not, and through eight minor league seasons, he *was* not. At age 28, he was with the Dodgers' Class AAA team in Montreal when manager Walter Alston suggested he chase home runs. And that's when Nelson developed the peculiar stance that made him a minor league sensation. He told *The Montreal Gazette* in 1987 that he experimented in batting practice for several days and "that's how I came up with that crazy stance. I was sitting back as though I was in a rocking chair. Usually, you get set, pivot and then swing. I was just taking out the pivot." Jim Murray, the *Los Angeles Times* sports columnist, said the stance was "right out of a lithograph from the archives of baseball—right foot at right angles to the left foot, knees bent. It was so archaic that a magazine once devoted a whole, fascinating story to it on the notion it was obscene to have this kind of a stance without a handlebar mustache to go with it." It worked, though. Nelson won the Triple Crown in the International League in 1955 and '58. He was the league's MVP in 1953, '55 and '58. He led the league in homers three times and hit .394 once. But, like Bilko, he couldn't hit in the majors until late in his career, and then not long enough or well enough. Pictures of his batting stance are hard to find, but Nelson's is in a line with other oddities like the stances of Dick McAuliffe, Rod Carew, Brian Downing and Craig Counsell.

447. Bob Anderson, Pitcher, Chicago Cubs.

Bob Anderson was an ordinary pitcher over seven major league seasons, and he was not quite league average as a fielder. But in 1961, Anderson led National League pitchers in double plays turned, with seven. For context, Greg Maddux, who won a record 18 Gold Gloves, turned as many as seven double plays only twice, in far more innings than Anderson pitched. Jim Kaat won 17 Gold Gloves and was above six DPs only once (with eight). Zack Greinke has collected six Gold Gloves and did turn 12 double plays one season, but in only one of his other 19 seasons has he had more than six. Heck, Mike Mussina won seven Gold Gloves and never turned more than five DPs in a season. For his career, Anderson had 14 double plays—and 13 errors.

448. Vada Pinson, Outfielder, Cincinnati Redlegs.

Baseball Reference says the player most similar to Vada Pinson at age 20 was Mike Trout. Trout was clearly better, but to be in the same conversation indicates that Pinson was a special player at 20. For the next six years, the most similar player to him was César Cedeño, who seemed to be on a Hall of Fame track until he tore up his knee at age 27. Pinson and Cedeño, both speedy center fielders with power, emerged in the majors at an incredibly young age, 19, were standouts at 20, remained highly successful through 26 and then lost the luster from their careers, which ended in their mid–30s. Here's how they stacked up through age 26:

Player	PA	R	H	2B	3B	HR	SB/CS	BA/OBP/SLG	OPS+
Pinson	4229	661	1177	216	61	125	139/47	.302/.349/.485	123
Cedeno	4265	689	1265	257	41	135	374/112	.292/.350/.466	131

Pinson was very fast but came up at a time when steals were not highly valued. He also played in a better hitters' park in his early years. (Crosley Field versus the Astrodome? No comparison.) Bill James wrote in his *New Historical Baseball Abstract* that Pinson was actually two years older than believed, so perhaps his decline in his 30s is more understandable.

449. Tom Gorman, Pitcher, Kansas City Athletics.

Three Tom Gormans have pitched in the major leagues. This Tom Gorman was the most accomplished, compiling a 36–36 record with a 3.77 ERA (105 ERA+) in 689⅓ innings. His best season came in 1955, when he won seven games and saved 18 for the Athletics. He also pitched in two World Series for the Yankees. The most recent Tom Gorman was also a reliever, with a 12–10, 4.34 mark (84 ERA+) for four teams over seven seasons in the '80s. The first Tom Gorman mustered only one season, for the 1939 Giants, with five innings across four games. But he was a National League umpire for 25 years. After he died in 1986, he was buried, per his request, in his umpire's uniform with a ball-and-strike indicator in his hand—set to 3 and 2.

450. Eddie Mathews, third baseman, Milwaukee Braves.

Early on, Eddie Mathews, not his teammate Hank Aaron, loomed as the challenger to Babe Ruth. At age 23 he already had three 40-homer seasons. During the season he was 29, Mathews closed to halfway to Ruth's record of 714 home runs. Aaron did not get there until the season he was 30. But by then, Aaron

Card 450: Eddie Mathews had 33 more home runs at age 30 than Hank Aaron did at the same age. But we know who became the home run king.

was making up ground on Mathews, as you can see in the table below. When each player was 31, Mathews had outhomered Aaron by 24, 422–398. At age 32, his lead was down to three. At age 33, Aaron finally had more homers than Mathews, whose career ended at 36. By that age, Aaron had 592 homers and Mathews 512 (fifth on the career list when he retired)—and Aaron had 163 more homers in his bats. The progressions for Barry Bonds and Alex Rodriguez are also here to show how quickly ARod accumulated home runs—at age 30 he had nearly a 100-homer lead over Aaron—and how Bonds changed the home run race in his mid– to late 30s. Mathews was betrayed by back injuries. Aaron was aided by his move to a ballpark in Atlanta at age 32 and his durability and consistency. Bonds and Rodriguez benefited … well, that's a discussion for another day.

Age	Mathews Season/Total	Aaron Season/Total	Bonds Season/Total	Rodriguez Season/Total
19	--	--	--	5/5
20	25/25	13/13	--	36/41
21	47/72	27/40	16/16	23/64
22	40/112	26/66	25/41	42/106
23	41/153	44/110	24/65	42/148

Age	Mathews Season/Total	Aaron Season/Total	Bonds Season/Total	Rodriguez Season/Total
24	37/190	30/140	19/84	41/189
25	32/222	39/179	33/117	52/241
26	31/253	40/219	25/142	57/298
27	46/299	34/253	34/176	47/345
28	39/338	45/298	46/222	36/381
29	32/370	44/342	37/259	48/429
30	29/399	24/366	33/292	35/464
31	23/422	32/398	42/334	54/518
32	23/445	44/442	40/374	35/553
33	32/477	39/481	37/411	30/583
34	16/493	29/510	34/445	30/613
35	16/509	44/554	49/494	16/629
36	3/512	38/592	73/567	18/647
37	--	47/639	46/613	7/654
38	--	34/673	45/658	--
39	--	40/713	45/703	33/687
40	--	20/733	5/708	9/696
41	--	12/745	26/734	--
42	--	10/755	28/762	--

451. Jim Constable, Pitcher, Washington Senators.

Jim Constable's career, and life, unraveled in 1958. He was waived by the Giants, signed by the Indians, waived again and signed by the tail-ender Senators, pitching a combined 45 unproductive innings. That winter, he went to Cuba to play with the Cienfuegos team headed by his Senators teammates Camilo Pascual and Pedro Ramos. He landed in the denouement of Fidel Castro's Cuban Revolution, which ousted the Batista regime on December 31. Constable and other players fled to Mexico, and he lost money left in a Cuban bank. Worse, he had a nervous breakdown. He later said that he, like his father, was manic-depressive and that the stresses of the season and the Cuban situation had overwhelmed him, *The Johnson City* (Tennessee) *News & Neighbor*, a hometown paper, reported. It was serious enough that Constable did not play the 1959, 1960 and 1961 seasons. He began pitching semipro ball back home, though, and was signed by the Braves. In his comeback season, he went 16–4, 2.56 with Class AAA Toronto and got a call-up to the majors. In a final note of redemption, he shut out the Pirates in a late-season start—his only complete game and one of his three victories in the big leagues.

452. Chico Fernández, Shortstop, Philadelphia Phillies.

It's a Fourth of July doubleheader at Yankee Stadium, 1961, and the Tigers are in a pennant race for the first time in more than a decade. Win and the Tigers retain their slim hold on first place, lose and the Yankees take over. It's the top of the ninth inning, two out, tie game, the Tigers have loaded the bases and the batter they want is up: Rocky Colavito. The season is not quite half over and Colavito has 20 homers and

54 RBI and is hitting .280 with a .417 on-base percentage. He has homered 118 times the previous three seasons. Dancing off third base, amid the energy of a crowd of 74,246, is Chico Fernández, while the rookie right-hander Rollie Sheldon gathers himself on the mound to confront Colavito with the game on the line. Suddenly Fernández is dashing home, the worst possible move. Colavito ducks out of the way as Fernández dives headfirst, tapping home plate ahead of John Blanchard's tag. "I said to the reporters after the game that if I had been out I would have been sent to the minors," Fernández told *The Detroit Free Press* in 2015, adding that "nobody thought I would steal under those circumstances with Colavito at the plate. I actually had to slow down because I thought Rocky might swing and hit me in the head." Perhaps the ploy should not have been a total surprise: Four years earlier, Fernández, then with the Phillies, stole home with the slugging catcher Stan Lopata, who had hit 32 homers the year before, at the plate. A week before that, Fernández had attempted to steal home against the Cardinals, but he missed the plate as he slid past and was tagged out.

453. Les Moss, Catcher, Chicago White Sox.

Les Moss was ready to be a major league manager. He had caught in the majors for 13 years, had been a coach with the White Sox, and had managed three years in the minors, including the previous two seasons with the Tigers' Class AAA team. He knew the young players coming up, essential as Ralph Houk was stepping down as manager in Detroit, which was finally coming out of a long rebuild. Moss got the job … and two months into the 1979 season, with a 27–26 record, he was fired. General manager Jim Campbell later expressed his frustration to *The Detroit Free Press* about Moss's reticent ways; Campbell was not getting the feedback and insight on players he wanted from Moss. So he acquired the opposite of buttoned-up and tight-lipped: Campbell hired Sparky Anderson. The Tigers were marginally better under Anderson (56–50), but five years later they won the World Series. At the time of Moss's firing, Detroit players were uncertain about it. But in 2015, Alan Trammell, the Tigers' young shortstop in 1979, said: "Now that I fast-forward from then until now, it was the right thing to do. It didn't mean Les wasn't going to be a good manager. I think he would have been. But he would not have been a Sparky Anderson." Moss never managed in the majors again.

454. Phil Clark, Pitcher, St. Louis Cardinals.

In his book *The Long Season*, Jim Brosnan tells about his mixed feelings when he learned that the Cardinals were demoting his friend and fellow reliever Phil Clark. Brosnan, 29, had not pitched well over the first month of the 1959 season, but Clark, 26, had pitched worse and more sporadically. By May 9, when the team had to pare its roster to 25 players, Clark was lugging an 11.57 ERA and had not pitched in 10 days. After learning his fate, Clark went to use the trainer's phone to call his wife. "He spoke in a low voice, a crushed-hope sort of tone," Brosnan wrote. Clark left the room and Brosnan, with misgivings, let him go. "At cut-down date in organized baseball it's every man for himself," he wrote. "My first reaction was relief that it wasn't I who had just lost his job. Both Clark and I had been mutually and similarly ineffective." But that didn't really matter. "What they were looking for in the front office was a head for the ax," Brosnan said. "Any young victim would do." Young Phil Clark would never pitch in the majors again.

455. Larry Doby, Outfielder, Detroit Tigers.

Larry Doby was the second Black player in the major leagues, after Jackie Robinson. He was the second Black manager in the major leagues, after Frank Robinson. But he was second to none among some of his young Black teammates as his career progressed. Al Smith, a fellow outfielder in Cleveland, said in *We Played the Game*, "The guy who helped me the most as a fielder was Larry Doby." Doby taught him how to play hitters, what to expect from his pitchers (fly balls off Early Wynn, line drives off Bob Lemon and Mike García), how to play the wind in drafty Municipal Stadium. Jim (Mudcat) Grant called Doby his "greatest hero" and said in *We Played the Game*, "The most I ever learned about the game was from him." Grant said Doby's lessons extended off the field—how to dress, how to be responsible in the community. And Doby, a quiet man, was entrée to a remarkable stable of Black celebrities, Grant said, including Count Basie, Sarah Vaughan, Miles Davis, Billie Holiday and Adam Clayton Powell, Jr. Doby had his own, unusual tutor—Tris Speaker, the superlative early twentieth-century center fielder in Cleveland who happened to have been a member of the Ku Klux Klan in Texas. Yet Speaker worked with Doby to convert him from a middle infielder to a center fielder. Joe Posnanski wrote in *The Baseball 100* that Speaker called his collaboration with Doby "one of the great thrills of his life." Speaker had earlier told Shirley Povich of *The Washington Post*, "I get a personal pleasure out of working with a kid who can do so many things so well." When Doby was elected to the Hall of Fame, he made sure to thank Tris Speaker.

456. Jerry Casale, Pitcher, Boston Red Sox.

After Jerry Casale's modest, five-year career in the major leagues ended, he went home to New York City and eventually ran an Italian restaurant, Pino's, in Midtown Manhattan. He did not have trophies to display, but Casale did have a moment of triumph he showed off there—a home run he smacked off the Yankees' Bob Turley at Fenway Park to help secure one of his 13 wins in the 1959 season. A 20-foot mural showed "a younger, lither version" of Casale, as *The New York Times* described it, about to hit the homer. He was also happy to play a tape his brother had made of the moment. "I've hit that home run 45,000 times by now," he told *The Times* in 2003. He was, sadly, about to close the restaurant. "I believe we have the best little restaurant in the whole area," he said. "But I also believe I was the best ballplayer ever."

457. Los Angeles Dodgers Team Card.

It did not take long for the Brooklyn Dodgers to become the Los Angeles Dodgers. Of the 38 Dodgers in 1959—the team's second season in Los Angeles—only 18 had played in Brooklyn. Brooklyn needed 52 years to win its first World Series. Los Angeles needed two.

458. Gordon Jones, Pitcher, San Francisco Giants.

In 1965, the last of his 14 seasons in pro ball, Gordon Jones pitched 45 games at Class AAA and one game—one inning—with the Houston Astros. He had impressed the right people in Houston, though, because he was named the pitching coach the next season. The Astros, playing their second season in the Astrodome in 1966, weren't very good, but they improved their record by seven wins and their ERA by 0.08. Houston brought in a new manager, but it kept Jones as the pitching coach. After three months, the team was in last place while allowing the most runs in the league despite playing in the 'Dome. The sacrificial lamb was Jones, who was replaced in early July by Jim Owens, whom Jim Bouton would compare favorably in *Ball Four* to Johnny Sain as a pitching coach. Houston's pitching improved. So did its record. But it's often the pitchers, not the pitching coach. Larry Dierker and Don Wilson were young pitchers who benefited from experience. The Astros acquired Denny Lemaster, who had two solid seasons. Mike Cuellar (whom Jones was credited with teaching an effective curveball) was a veteran anchor in Houston before going on to greater success in Baltimore. Owens remained with the Astros for five more seasons, but Gordon Jones's career in baseball was over.

459. Bill Tuttle, Outfielder, Kansas City Athletics.

Bill Tuttle was a center fielder for 11 years, with a reputation for a good glove and a mediocre bat (.259 in his career, although he did hit .300 once). But that's not why he became renowned in clubhouses after his retirement. Tuttle developed oral cancer, which was attributed to his using chewing tobacco for 40 years, and over time he lost part of his jaw, his cheek, some teeth and numerous taste buds, according to his *New York Times* obituary. He became the face, literally, of an effort to get chewing tobacco out of the game, visiting clubhouses to show players what chew could do. After his death, his widow, Gloria Tuttle, told *The Times*'s Richard Goldstein: "They would see my husband's face and they would just look. Bill would give his story and you could hear a pin drop. Then they would hug us. Million-dollar players would come up with tears in their eyes and cans of tobacco in their hands and they would say, 'I want you to throw this away for me.'"

Card 459: After Bill Tuttle, disfigured by years of using smokeless tobacco, spoke to players about it, some handed him cans of the stuff and said, "I want you to throw this away for me."

460. Bob Friend, Pitcher, Pittsburgh Pirates.

Bob Friend was so intense on the mound that Dick Groat said his Pirates teammates called him "Nervous-

Nervous." Another Pirate, Frank Thomas, called Friend "a nervous type" in *We Played the Game* and said he would agitate Friend "to take his mind off what he had to do on the mound. I'd get him so mad that he took it out on the opposition." Friend's unease was understandable. He came up as a 20-year-old in 1951, and the Pirates went 64–90. Then they got worse: four straight last-place finishes, followed by two next-to-last finishes. Over one three-year stretch, the Pirates lost 317 games. The year after that, Friend became the first pitcher from a last-place team to lead his league in ERA. As Groat acknowledged, "we were a bad ballclub behind him." For a decade, Friend never missed a start and never went on the disabled list. Even with their eventual successes, his 15 Pirates teams finished a combined 209 games below .500. Winning 193 games with that collection of teams was an accomplishment.

461. Mickey Mantle Hits 42nd Homer for Crown.
Mickey Mantle won his third home run title in 1958, and it looked as if he would do so easily. On September 9, he hit his 40th homer, putting him six ahead of Rocky Colavito. Mantle hit only two more homers, though, while Colavito got hot, with seven in his final 13 games. That included one in his final at-bat of the season. He was due up third in the bottom of the ninth, but Cleveland already had the game won, and Colavito lost out by one home run, 42–41. Colavito *did* win the home run crown in 1959 ... with 42.

462. Colavito's Great Catch Saves Game.
Some notable fiction has been written about baseball, and one piece of it seems to be on the back of this card. Its details of this catch are skimpy—no year, for example—but the card says it was in "the late innings" against the Yankees with Cleveland holding a one-run lead. But no box score or game account of a Yankees-Indians game in 1956, 1957 or 1958 seems to fit the details. Then again, the card also says, "He leaped high in the air, snared the ball and toppled among the fans in the lower grandstand." Rocky Colavito is snaring the ball, but he sure isn't leaping high in the air or toppling into the grandstand.

463. Kaline Becomes Youngest Bat Champ.
Al Kaline won the American League batting title in 1955 at the age of 20. It was not something he came to relish, Kaline told *Sports Illustrated* in 1964. "The worst thing that happened to me in the big leagues was the start I had," he said. "This put the pressure on me. Everybody said this guy's another Ty Cobb, another Joe DiMaggio. How much pressure can you take? What they didn't know is I'm not that good a hitter." Cobb also won a batting title at 20 ... but he was one day older than Kaline.

464. Mays' Catch Makes Series History.
In his magnificent book about this 1954 World Series game, *A Day in the Bleachers*, Arnold Hano writes that this was not even the best Willie Mays catch he ever saw. But there is no arguing that it was one amazing catch, made 420 feet or more from home plate. And an amazing throw. And in the eighth inning of a tie game in Game 1 of the World Series. Joe Posnanski relates a story from Monte Irvin in *The*

Baseball 100, in which Irvin recalled telling Mays, "That was a helluva catch, roomie. I didn't think you'd make it," to which Mays replied, "I had it all the way."

465. Sievers Sets Homer Mark.

Roy Sievers set a home run record? He was playing in an era of Ted Williams and Mickey Mantle and then Rocky Colavito, so what record could this be? Ahhh, the Senators team record. Which he set at 25—25—before nudging it up to 29 the next season! Ultimately, Sievers hit 42 home runs in 1957, when the distance down the left-field line at cavernous Griffith Stadium was reduced to 350 feet from 386 feet. (Still, quite a poke.) Sievers also led the league in RBIs that season with 114. He did that in an offense in which the second-best RBI man on his team had 64.

466. Pierce All-Star Starter.

The White Sox ace Billy Pierce was the American League starter in the All-Star Game three times—in 1953, 1955 and 1956—pitching three innings all three times. He began his All-Star efforts with eight and two-thirds scoreless innings before giving up one run. In those nine innings, he faced only 30 batters and struck out nine. But his All-Star record? 0–1.

467. Aaron Clubs World Series Homer.

The 1957 season was when Hank Aaron first made his reputation as a slugger. The year before he had led the National League in batting, total bases, hits and doubles, but it was in 1957 when his power broke out—Aaron hit a league-leading 44 homers, his career best at that point by 17. Then in the World Series he hit three more. This one, a three-run shot, came in Game 4, with the Braves trailing in the game, 1–0, and the Series, two games to one. Milwaukee went on to win the game and the Series.

468. Snider's Play Brings L.A. Victory.

Topps lets us know that in his first season playing in the Coliseum in Los Angeles, Duke Snider thrilled fans and frustrated opponents with his defensive play. This play, however, was not at the Coliseum, which did not have fans in seats right behind the wall in center field. His defensive numbers slipped while playing in the vast Coliseum outfield after his years in the cozy confines of Ebbets Field—center field, as the analyst Joe Sheehan likes to say, is a young man's game, and Snider was 31 when he started playing in Los Angeles. His days as a full-time center fielder were over—once he arrived in L.A., he never started more than 65 games in center.

469. Hustler Banks Wins M.V.P. Award.

What stands out in the list of National League Most Valuable Player Award winners in the 1950s?

1950: Jim Konstanty, Phillies (won pennant).
1951: Roy Campanella, Dodgers (lost playoff for pennant).
1952: Hank Sauer, Cubs (finished fifth).

Card 469: Hustler Banks Wins M.V.P. Award. Of the 10 MVP Awards in the National League in the '50s, Ernie Banks won two on a fifth-place team. So did another Cub.

1953: Campanella, Dodgers (won pennant).
1954: Willie Mays, Giants (won pennant).
1955: Campanella, Dodgers (won pennant).
1956: Don Newcombe, Dodgers (won pennant).
1957: Hank Aaron, Braves (won pennant).
1958: Ernie Banks, Cubs (finished fifth).
1959: Banks, Cubs (finished fifth).

The writers apparently liked Cubs, even on second-division teams—although in fairness to Banks, he was second in the NL in Wins Above Replacement in 1958 (to Willie Mays) while leading the league in homers and RBIs, and he was an overwhelming first in WAR in 1959.

470. Musial Raps Out 3,000th Hit.
When Stan Musial smacked a pinch-hit double on May 13, 1958, he became the eighth major leaguer with 3,000 hits. It came against the Cubs, who, curiously, he had the least success against (not counting the expansion Colt .45s, against whom he batted only 91 times). The Cubs "held" Musial to a .317/.400/.539 batting line. He collected his 3,000th hit at age 37, as he was proving he was not washed up. The hit made him 43 for 88 on the year, for a .489 batting average to go with a .558 on-base percentage and .789 slugging percentage.

471. Tom Sturdivant, Pitcher, New York Yankees.

Plenty of ex-ballplayers have tried to move on to political careers. Some have succeeded. Jim Bunning served in the U.S. House of Representatives and the Senate. Wilmer (Vinegar Bend) Mizell was a congressman. More than a century ago, a couple of players with brief baseball careers were U.S. senators or governors. But ballplayers have often lost, too, despite name recognition from baseball. Walter Johnson lost a race for Congress. Cap Anson was defeated for sheriff in Cook County, Illinois, and Honus Wagner lost his bid for sheriff in Allegheny County, Pennsylvania. (And both lost badly.) Bobby Richardson was beaten in his race for Congress. Tom Sturdivant had more modest political aspirations—a seat in the Oklahoma State Senate, according to his SABR Bio Project biography. He entered the race while still in baseball but said he would retire if he won. No need: He was released by the Mets in July (although he hooked on with the Class AAA Oklahoma City 89ers—nothing like keeping his name before the voters) and lost his race in November.

472. Gene Freese, Second Baseman-Third Baseman, Philadelphia Phillies.

Tim Freese related a wonderful story that he said his father, Gene, told him, according to Gene's obituary on the newspaper website nola.com. According to Tim Freese, his dad was batting in a game against Tommy Lasorda (the future Dodgers manager) and Gene's brother George, who was seven years older, was in the outfield. Lasorda threw at Gene, and, the account goes, George charged the mound from the outfield in defense of his little brother. The details are a bit off, but on May 24, 1955, Lasorda, pitching in relief against the Pirates in a game the Dodgers lost, 15–1, did hit Gene Freese with a pitch in the seventh inning. Except George Freese was his brother's teammate, not Lasorda's. And played third base, not the outfield. George no doubt came to Gene's defense, but little brother was actually his competition that season. Both played third base—Gene in 65 games, George in 50—and Gene won the spot. After the '55 season, George was taken by the Cubs in the minor league draft.

473. Mike Fornieles, Pitcher, Boston Red Sox.

Mike Fornieles set an American League record in 1960 with 70 appearances as a relief pitcher. He also averaged more than an inning and a half per outing that season, and the rest of his career he averaged about two innings per relief appearance. While pitching regularly in the majors in the 1950s and early '60s, Fornieles—who *Cuban Baseball Legends* noted was not a big man at 5 feet 10 and, at least initially, 155 pounds—also shouldered a heavy pitching load at home in the Cuban winter league. In 1952, he pitched 239⅓ innings between the minors and the majors (where he threw a one-hit shutout in his debut), then added 155 innings that winter in Cuba. (Total 394⅓.) In 1956, Fornieles pitched 126⅔ innings between the White Sox and the Orioles, then threw 142 innings in Cuba. (Total: 268⅔.) In 1957, he hurled 182⅓ innings for the Orioles and the Red Sox and went on to pitch 155 more that winter in Cuba. (Total: 337⅓.) In 1958, it was 110⅔ innings in Boston, 135 more the next winter in Cuba. (Total: 245⅔.) He was recognized as Fireman of the Year after his stellar 1960 season, but, his 70 games notwithstanding, he added 120 more innings that winter in Cuba. (Total: 229.) Contention between the United States and Cuba shut down major leaguers' participation in the Cuban league, even (or perhaps especially) for Cuban players. Fornieles' reduced workload, however, coincided with reduced effectiveness—perhaps a consequence of all those innings.

474. Moe Thacker, Catcher, Chicago Cubs.

Ballplayers come from big cities and small towns. But from 1963, when Moe Thacker played his final inning for the Cubs, and 1987, when Jack Savage threw his first pitch for the Dodgers, no ballplayer who grew up in Louisville, Kentucky, played in the major leagues. Louisville had a population of about 400,000 when Thacker finished up, about 300,000 when Savage made the majors. (And the metropolitan area was around a million.) Small Kentucky towns like Yosemite (population 660), Greensburg (about 2,000), Stanford (3,000), Paintsville (4,000) and Greenville (4,000) produced major leaguers in that quarter-century. So did Lynn, an area so small it was unincorporated, but was home to Don Gullett. A few ballplayers who were born in Louisville did arrive in the majors—Mike Greenwell with the Red Sox, Dave Anderson with the Dodgers—but they had moved away very early on. Plenty of Louisvillians have reached The Show since, but that long drought remains a mystery.

475. Jack Harshman, Pitcher, Baltimore Orioles.

As a 21-year-old first baseman in Class AAA, Jack Harshman hit 40 home runs, second in the American Association. Two years later, in 1951, he slugged 47 home runs for Class AA Nashville—18 more than anyone else in the league (and 24 more than another young slugging prospect, Frank Thomas). But after not hitting major league pitching in brief stints in 1949 and '50, Harshman was never called up in 1951 by the Giants. "He drove in 141 runs. And still I wanted to make a pitcher out of him," the Nashville owner, Larry Gilbert, later told *The Saturday Evening Post*. "Well, I was thinking about all the 108 times he fanned. And his lousy .251 batting average. Terrible!" Gilbert said that as a hitter, Harshman "would never do," citing their ballpark's short right-field porch. But the Nashville manager was having Harshman throw batting practice, and it changed his career. In 1952, Harshman was a pitcher. By 1954, he was a rotation regular for the White Sox, going 14–8, 2.95 (ERA+ of 128), and over five years, he was 60–49, 3.23 (119 ERA+). But he could still hit for power, swatting 19 home runs as a pitcher—14th on the career list—and hitting six in a season twice.

476. Cleveland Indians Team Card.

Cleveland has infamously not won a World Series since 1948—the longest current drought in the major leagues. It has won only four pennants since then, in 75 seasons. The team finished below .500 five times in the eight seasons from 1957 to 1964. And it would get much worse: From 1969 through 1993, Cleveland had only four winning seasons—and the best of them was 84–78. That is nearly three and a half decades of futility. And yet the Cleveland franchise had a winning overall record through 2023: 9,760–9,300, a .512 clip.

477. Barry Latman, Pitcher, Chicago White Sox.

Barry Latman grew up in Los Angeles in a Jewish family sufficiently observant that when he was 10, his parents had him stop playing baseball so he could study for his bar mitzvah, as he told Danny Peary for *We Played the Game*. As a professional, he would not pitch on the High Holy Days, according to his SABR Bio Project biography, although his teams did not encounter them as often as Sandy Koufax's did. (Hank Greenberg and Shawn Green also notably sat out important games on Yom Kippur.) Jews were playing in professional baseball as far back as the 1860s and have constituted about 1 percent of major league players, according to *The Forward*, a Jewish news outlet. *The Forward* reported in 2021 that over the previous decade, an average of 14 Jewish players a year were in the majors. (Although the Jewish Virtual Library's most recent list shows more Jewish owners and top front-office executives than players.) The list of recent Jewish players has included such high-profile players as Alex Bregman, Max Fried, Ryan Braun, Joc Pederson and Kevin Pillar. *The Forward*'s Peter Dreier picked an All-Jewish All-Star team, and it looks pretty good: **Catcher:** Harry Danning, 1933–41. **First base:** Hank Greenberg, 1930–47. **Second base:** Ian Kinsler, 2006–19. **Shortstop:** Alex Bregman, since 2016. **Third base:** Al Rosen, 1947–56. **Outfield:** Shawn Green, 1993–2007; Ryan Braun, 2007–20; Sid Gordon, 1941–55. **Pitcher:** Sandy Koufax, 1955–66. For decades Jewish players were subject to the casual racism that infected baseball (and society). The use of what we would now consider slurs was common for Jews and various ethnic groups and then Blacks when they reached the major leagues. It was so common that the slurs were even used toward players others merely *thought* were Jewish. For example, *The Forward* noted, Buddy Myer, whose family had converted to Christianity at least two generations earlier, was once spiked by Ben Chapman. Chapman (who later, as Phillies manager, spewed some of the worst racial invective toward Jackie Robinson) called Myer antisemitic names even as he was spiking him.

478. Roberto Clemente, Outfielder, Pittsburgh Pirates.
Roberto Clemente was a hypochondriac. Everyone said so. Myron Cope, writing in *Sports Illustrated* in 1966, captured the widely held belief that Clemente was "baseball's champion hypochondriac." Even his managers were skeptical of his injuries. But hypochondria does not necessarily mean the injuries or ailments are not real; it is a preoccupation with them. Clemente certainly did have injuries. A car wreck after the 1954 season left him with a back injury that bothered him throughout his career. A sore elbow—at one point he had to throw underhand—cost him more than a month of the 1959 season, his SABR Bio Project profile said. In 1965, he needed off-season thigh surgery. In 1972, he missed almost a month with heel injuries. But Clemente did not hide his injuries, and his stellar play made people wonder whether he really was injured. "The case history of Clemente is the worse he feels, the better he plays," *The Sporting News* quoted his manager, Bobby Bragan, as saying in 1957. He was the inverse of Mickey Mantle, who said little publicly about his injuries but played and performed. Mantle was regarded as heroic, Clemente as a whiner. Yet both were Hall of Famers (even if Mantle had the superior career), and they played almost an identical number of games and were similarly durable. Clemente played 2,433 games over 18 seasons; Mantle, 2,401 over 18 years. Mantle had 12 seasons with at least 140 games and two more with at least 120; Clemente put together 10 seasons with at least 140 games and four with at least 120. Mantle did play

65 postseason games to Clemente's 26, but Clemente spent many off-seasons playing winter ball in Puerto Rico. As for the notion that he obsessed over his injuries, Clemente said: "Hypochondriacs cannot produce. I produce!"

479. Lindy McDaniel, Pitcher, St. Louis Cardinals.

Lindy McDaniel was such a hot prospect that the Cardinals offered him $50,000 to sign in 1955. First, he had to persuade his devout mother, who, according to McDaniel's *New York Times* obituary, was skeptical of a life in baseball, to let him sign. Then he had to persuade the Cardinals to agree that he could attend church every Sunday. They said yes, McDaniel later told *The Christian Chronicle*, as did every other team he pitched for. "I knew I couldn't survive the game unless that happened," he said. McDaniel attended Abilene Christian College and Florida Christian College while playing ball, wrote a newsletter called *Pitching for the Master* and was an ordained minister for decades. His overt Christianity did not always sit well with teammates. He wrote in a 2014 edition of *Pitching for the Master*: "Earlier with the St. Louis Cardinals, I had roomed with Jim Brosnan, a relief pitcher acquired from the Cincinnati Reds who was busy writing books. He took pride in being an atheist and never really enjoyed talking to a dumb, uninformed, Bible believing and flat-earthish person like me." He also called Jim Bouton, another book-writing relief pitcher, an atheist. McDaniel said his religious principles did make him popular with teammates when he came up with the Cardinals. The team—owned by the Busch beer family—would give players free cases of beer, McDaniel wrote. "Since I didn't drink," he said, "players became very friendly wanting me to give them my cases." As an example to young people, he said, he eventually asked the Cardinals to stop sending him the free beer.

480. Red Schoendienst, Second Baseman, Milwaukee Braves.

The year 1958 was a terrifying challenge for two longtime All-Stars who were headed to the Hall of Fame. First, in January, Roy Campanella, the Dodgers' 36-year-old catcher, rolled his car on an icy Long Island road and was left a quadriplegic, just weeks before the team was to begin its first spring training as the Los Angeles Dodgers. Weeks after the season, Red Schoendienst, the Braves' 37-year-old second baseman, who had felt fatigued and unwell throughout the year, had tests done in November; doctors diagnosed tuberculosis. He spent four months in a sanitorium yet managed to recover enough to get three at-bats and a handful of innings in September. He was the lucky one, of course, able to play ball again, even if compromised. Campanella regained some use of his arms, but he spent the rest of his life in a wheelchair. Yet he remained connected to the Dodgers in various roles, even moving to Los Angeles two decades after the accident. He outlived expectations, dying at 71. Schoendienst returned to his haven with the Cardinals, as a player, a coach, and a longtime manager (with a World Series title). He also held positions in the front office. He died at 95.

481. Charlie Maxwell, Outfielder, Detroit Tigers.

Charlie Maxwell's home run history was always unusual. His first three major league homers came as a pinch-hitter—a three-run homer, a two-run shot and a grand slam. In 1960, five of his 24 homers were hit in extra innings, a major league record. And of course, he hit home runs on Sundays. Lots and lots of Sundays—40 homers in all, according to research by Herman Krabbenhoft and Jeff Kabacinski. That's 27 percent of his career total of 148. On Sunday, May 3, 1959, Maxwell homered in four consecutive at-bats in a doubleheader against the Yankees (three in the nightcap), and for the season 12 of his 31 homers came on Sundays. On Sunday, July 29, 1962, while playing for the White Sox, he homered three times in another doubleheader against the Yankees. He smacked five Sunday homers that year. "There are unusual things that happen in baseball," Maxwell told *The Detroit Free Press* in 2019, "and I guess my Sunday homers are one of them."

482. Russ Meyer, Pitcher, Kansas City Athletics.

Who was more notorious, Russ Meyer the ballplayer or Russ Meyer the filmmaker? They were of German descent, were born 19 months apart, served in World War II and wound up with careers in the public eye. The ballplayer was nicknamed "Mad Monk"; the filmmaker, "King of the Nudies." Meyer the ballplayer vexed umpires, managers and even a television network. He managed all three in one incident, as Robin Roberts related in his autobiography. Meyer was incensed by an umpire's call, was ejected, wouldn't leave the field until his manager went to the mound and then hurled the rosin bag ... which, after going 30 feet into the air, landed on his head, sending white powder all over. Once he got to the dugout, he turned and grabbed his crotch, which was caught by *Game of the Week* cameras and led to a rule, Roberts wrote, that prevented dugout shots on TV for a decade. He once took a swing at a photographer, challenged Jackie Robinson to a fight and bought a $50 "diamond" on the street in New York that predictably turned out to be fake, his SABR Bio Project biography said. Meyer the filmmaker, meanwhile, got started directing independent "sexploitation" movies in the 1950s—his first feature film was *The Immoral Mr. Teas*—and fixated on large breasts. He did land a deal with 20th Century–Fox, resulting in a movie, *Beyond the Valley of the Dolls*, with a screenplay by Roger Ebert. It was widely panned but made millions. He returned to independent filmmaking, but Meyer the ballplayer made a move to respectability after his playing career. His *New York Times* obituary said he spent 12 years with the Yankees' organization, mostly as a minor league pitching coach, but one year as Buck Showalter's bench coach—in 1992, for the Andy Stankiewicz-Mel Hall-Danny Tartabull Yankees.

Card 482: Russ Meyer the pitcher was nicknamed "Mad Monk." Russ Meyer the filmmaker was nicknamed "The King of the Nudies." Both earned their notoriety.

483. Clint Courtney, Catcher, Washington Senators.

Two of the most infamous fighters of the '50s, Clint Courtney and Earl Torgeson, wore glasses. Torgeson quickly learned to take his off before he got into it. Courtney was just as quick to fight: opposing players, teammates, umpires, minor leaguers, major leaguers, nobodies, future Hall of Famers. In 1950, an opposing general manager, Frank Lane, told Courtney's manager with the Browns, Rogers Hornsby, how much he admired the rookie catcher nicknamed Scrap Iron. "Too bad the little son of a gun wears glasses," Lane said, according to Courtney's SABR Bio Project profile, to which Hornsby replied, "Glasses or not, Courtney'll fight his way into the big leagues." And he did. Billy O'Dell, Courtney's teammate on the Orioles, said, "He and Billy Martin used to fight almost every time we'd play the Yankees." Courtney also had a well-covered fight with the Yankees' Phil Rizzuto. "There's the meanest man I ever met, but I'm glad he's on my side," Satchel Paige, a Browns teammate, said, according to Courtney's *New York Times* obituary. Bob Turley called him "a free spirit with a bad temper." In *We Played the Game*, Les Moss said, "'Scrap Iron' would fight all the time, but I don't know how many he won." And to hear teammate Joe DeMaestri tell it in *We Played the Game*, Courtney was often on his own. "We liked Courtney off the field," he said, "but to be honest, not too many guys from our side went out to help him when he started punching somebody. We felt that he started it, so he could finish it." There were other costs. Courtney made his major league debut with the Yankees in late September 1951, but he was traded to the Browns (first to worst) two months later. General manager George Weiss exiled him "because he didn't like his difficult reputation," Baseball Almanac said. Over the remaining 10 years of Courtney's career, the Yankees won eight pennants.

484. Willie Kirkland, Outfielder, San Francisco Giants.

The Giants needed an infusion of talent in 1958, their first season in San Francisco. The final New York Giants team had gone 69–85 and, aside from Willie Mays and 40-year-old Hank Sauer, the offense wasn't very good. Then the talent arrived. These were Giants rookies in '58: Orlando Cepeda, Felipe Alou, Leon Wagner and Willie Kirkland, three outfielders and a first baseman (Cepeda) who subsequently wound up playing the outfield some because the Giants brought up Willie McCovey in 1959. Those four rookies accounted for 113.5 career Wins Above Replacement (Cepeda, 50.1; Alou, 42.2; Wagner, 11.7; Kirkland, 9.5). Although Kirkland's career finished as the least productive of that very productive group, you would have expected otherwise after his first four seasons, in which he hit .260/.324/.463, with 84 home runs and an OPS+ of 112. His career then waned in the United States, but he was a star for six years in Japan, where he hit another 126 homers.

485. Ryne Duren, Pitcher, New York Yankees.

Ryne Duren was the measuring stick for heat in the major leagues in his brief prime. "We'd say [so-and-so] can throw almost as hard as Duren," Jim Kaat said in Duren's autobiography. A decade later, Steve Dalkowski was the standard for heat in pro ball in his tortured run in the minor leagues. "Fastest I ever saw," Ted Williams said after facing Dalkowski for one pitch in a spring training game, as recalled by

The Seattle Times. Duren was a big right-hander with glasses and horrible control, of his pitches and his drinking; Dalkowski was a slight left-hander with worse control, of his pitches and his drinking. Both were known to throw warm-up pitches to the backstop screen, although Duren later said that some of them were for effect, to shake up looming hitters. His wildness and poor eyesight were legendary (his good eye was 20/70), and his thick-lensed glasses—later tinted to cut down on glare—gave batters' further pause. He was six years into his minor league career before he averaged fewer than six walks per nine innings, although that made Duren a control artist compared to Dalkowski. Here's a quick comparison of some numbers.

	K/9	W/9	H/9		K/9	W/9	H/9
Duren	9.6	6.0	6.8	Dalkowski	12.5	11.6	6.3

The key difference, besides those walks: Duren's numbers are for his 10 years in the majors, Dalkowski's for his nine years in the minors. He never threw a major league pitch. Alcohol ruined their careers. Duren was fortunate to gain sobriety after his playing days, became an addiction counselor for four decades and died at 81. Dalkowski died at 80 after developing alcohol-related dementia that plagued him for 15 years.

486. Sammy White, Catcher, Boston Red Sox.

While he was a catcher for the Red Sox, Sammy White opened a bowling alley in nearby Brighton, Massachusetts, in 1960. He was so involved with the business that when Boston traded him to Cleveland that winter, he decided to retire and focus on running the lanes. (The next year the Braves coaxed him out of retirement.) The lanes became notorious two decades later, when four employees were murdered—bludgeoned and shot—in a robbery that netted $4,800 as the business opened one Monday morning in 1980, *The Boston Globe* reported. A bloody bowling pin found at the scene was one of the murder weapons, the police said. A former employee was found guilty and sentenced to life in prison, and the case was the impetus for the return of capital punishment in Massachusetts in 1982. Sammy White's Brighton Bowl closed three years later. But the episode lingered in memory: a 2002 horror film, *Cabin Fever*, featured an account of it.

487. Hal Brown, Pitcher, Baltimore Orioles.

For years I played softball with a guy called Tiny who was about 6 foot 2 and 250 pounds or more. Hal Brown was called Skinny because, the North Carolina Sports Hall of Fame related, he said, "I was fat as a baby, and being in a Southern town and one of eight children, you know, everybody had to have a nickname." So there you have some Southern irony: a fatty named Skinny. To compound it, when he grew up, Skinny wasn't fat—he was 6 foot 2 and 180. So maybe that's irony layered on irony. This is straightforward: Despite regularly throwing a knuckleball, he led the American League in fewest walks per nine innings in 1959 and '60, at 1.8 and 1.2 That was the middle of a four-year stretch in which he walked only 107 batters in 586⅓ innings—1.6 per nine. The AL average? More than twice that, 3.5 walks per nine innings.

488. Walt Moryn, Outfielder, Chicago Cubs.

Walt Moryn was a slugger, not a defensive marvel. *The Chicago Tribune* called him "slow-footed." A former teammate said he was "just ordinary in the field." One of his Cubs managers, Bob Scheffing, wouldn't exactly agree. "He told me he could play first base and he couldn't," Scheffing said during spring training in 1957, according to Moryn's SABR Bio Project biography. "Then he told me he could play left field and he couldn't. Frankly, I'm not even impressed with his work in right field." Yet Moryn became celebrated in Chicago for a defensive play—a game-ending catch that saved Don Cardwell's 1960 no-hitter. The 6-foot-2, 220-pound Moryn—they called him Moose—caught Joe Cunningham's sinking line drive at his shoe tops in shallow left-center field, making Cardwell, who had been acquired from the Phillies two days earlier, the first player to pitch a no-hitter in his first appearance after being traded. "He made me famous," Cardwell told *The Tribune* after Moryn's death in 1996.

489. John Powers, First Baseman-Outfielder, Cincinnati Redlegs.

This was baseball in the '50s: John Powers, a slugger in the minors, was inserted into major league lineups as a pinch-hitter 113 times—75 percent of his career games—despite a lifetime slash line of .195/.281/.330. It's not as if he was any standout as a pinch-hitter, going 19 for 98, with 29 strikeouts and nine walks. In the one season when he was remotely successful off the bench, he was merely three for nine (with a home run). Powers played for seven managers in seven major league seasons, and they all kept sending him up there to pinch-hit, presumably hoping he would run into a home run. One further oddity: Baseball Reference shows that Powers, a left-handed hitter, had only three plate appearances, out of 242, against left-handers. He flied out to center, walked and was hit by a pitch.

490. Frank Thomas, Third Baseman-Outfielder, Cincinnati Redlegs.

No ballplayer could have enjoyed negotiating a contract with Branch Rickey. He was a general manager or its equivalent for four decades, with the Browns, the Cardinals (where he created the farm system, ensuring a supply of cheap, young players), the Dodgers (where he integrated the major leagues, ensuring a supply of cheap, Black players) and the Pirates (where he brought in young talent that paid off in a 1960 pennant, but he also paid out huge bonuses to numerous amateurs who never panned out). The New York sportswriter Dick Young called him "El Cheapo." Dizzy Dean called him "a cheap bastard." *The Deadball Era* quotes two fan favorites who loathed Rickey. Enos Slaughter said Rickey "would go to the vault to get change for a nickel," *The Deadball Era* related. And Eddie Stanky said of a negotiation with Rickey, "I got a million dollars' worth of advice and a very small increase." George Shuba, a Dodgers outfielder, recalled being shamed into taking a smaller contract because Rickey had left a bogus inflated contract of a teammate where Shuba would see it and change his expectations. All of which Frank Thomas would believe. Thomas was a capable slugger with the Pirates as they struggled mightily in the mid-'50s, averaging 27 homers over six full seasons. He was also adept enough defensively to play center field as a young Pirate and also play extensively at third and first base. But Thomas had no such success negotiating with Rickey, the Pirates' GM through

1955. Thomas said in *We Played the Game* that Rickey told him that if he accepted what Thomas thought was a lowball contract, he would make it up to him the next season if Thomas had another good year. "I didn't know any better," Thomas said, "so I believed him." He did have a good year and got another lowball offer. That led to a contract dispute in which Thomas said Rickey told him: "Go ahead and hold out. I'll keep you out of baseball for five years." Rickey said he would never reveal a player's salary, but the papers had a figure for Thomas's contract—double what he had actually made. "He treated me like I was dirt on his feet," Thomas said at a SABR panel in 2018. After leaving the Pirates, Rickey maneuvered back into the baseball spotlight by joining a high-profile effort to create an eight-team competitor, the Continental League. The plan eventually failed when Major League Baseball offered some of the new league's proposed owners teams

Card 490: Slugger Frank Thomas had a long history of unhappy contract negotiations with Branch Rickey. "He treated me like I was dirt on his feet."

in expanded American and National leagues. Which ultimately affected Frank Thomas: He became an Original Met, the only power source on a 120-loss team.

491. Don Blasingame, Second Baseman, St. Louis Cardinals.

Don Blasingame was the Reds' second baseman until he lost the job in 1963 to a rookie his teammates called Charlie Hustle. But Blasingame—known as Blazer—had some hustle of his own. After his 12-year major league career ended, he held the record for hitting into the fewest double plays per at-bat—one per 123 ABs. That's 43 double plays in 5,296 at-bats. He was supplanted by Don Buford, who hit into only 34 double plays in 4,553 at-bats—a ratio of 1:134. Blazer and Buford had remarkable parallels. Both were named Don—not Donald. Both played second base, although Buford transitioned to the outfield with the Orioles. Both won a World Series championship. And both played three seasons in Japan after their major league careers ended.

492. Gene Conley, Pitcher, Philadelphia Phillies.

Gene Conley played six seasons in the NBA while also pitching professionally—11 years in the majors. His rookie year with the Celtics, the 6-foot-8 Conley was a teammate of 6-foot-8 Ed Macauley, which apparently sparked some confusion that led Conley to sign autographs "Ed Macauley." "When I played basketball with the Boston Celtics, I was always confused with Macauley by autograph hunters," Conley told the *Washington Star* columnist Francis Stann in 1957. "I got tired of explaining that I was Gene Conley, so I just wrote Ed's name." Conley had the unique distinction of winning championships in the NBA (three) and Major League Baseball (one, with the Braves). His baseball career ended in 1963, hastened by basketball injuries, and his basketball career the next spring.

493. Jim Landis, Outfielder, Chicago White Sox.

The Go-Go Sox of 1959 won the pennant while compiling more stolen bases than home runs. But "I thought that was overrated," Jim Landis once told *The San Francisco Chronicle*. "We didn't steal that many bases. Aparicio did." By the standards of later decades, the White Sox did *not* steal that many bases—113—but it was 45 more than the No. 2 team in the American League. And Landis undersold his own contribution; he stole 20 bases, third in a league in which Luis Aparicio led everyone with 56. But there is no question that the White Sox's more steals-than-homers approach was unusual for a pennant winner. No AL champion had done it since the 1945 Tigers, playing at the end of World War II with baseballs that were not designed for power. And only six AL teams have done it since—the most recent being the 2014 Royals. (Although when they won the World Series the next year, the Royals had far more homers than steals.) The other five teams include some you would not automatically associate with more speed than power: the 1974 Athletics, the 1976 Yankees, the 1980 Royals, the 1989 Athletics and the 1993 Blue Jays. Those 2005 World Series champion White Sox, with the reputation for playing Ozzie Guillén "small ball"? Not a chance: They had 200 homers and 137 steals.

494. Don Pavletich, Catcher, Cincinnati Redlegs.

Don Pavletich learned a lot about good catchers, because so many good catchers kept him on the bench. First was Johnny Edwards, who won two Gold Gloves and made the All-Star team three consecutive years with the Reds. Then, just as Edwards began to fade, along came Johnny Bench. Before long Pavletich was traded, eventually to the Red Sox, and the next season Boston called up Carlton Fisk. "That's it for me," Pavletich told *The Milwaukee Journal Sentinel*. "Just my luck." It really was it for him: As Fisk was hitting .313 in 14 games in September 1971, Pavletich got off the bench once—to pinch-hit, a groundout to third on September 1, that was the last at-bat of his career.

495. Johnny Podres, Pitcher, Los Angeles Dodgers.

Sports Illustrated named Roger Bannister its Sportsman of the Year for 1954. Bannister had, after all, become the first runner to break four minutes in the mile. In 1955, its Sportsman of the Year was Johnny Podres, a 23-year-old left-hander whose fabulous changeup would break no speed records. The 1955 season was actually nothing special for Podres; he was 9–10 with a 3.94 ERA, and he missed chunks of midseason with shoulder and rib injuries. He pitched into the eighth inning only twice in the final three and a half months of the regular season, during which he went 2–6, 4.96. But Podres *was* special in the World Series. With the Dodgers trailing the Yankees, two games to none, he pitched a complete game and won, 8–3, in

Ebbets Field. Manager Walt Alston told him that if there was a Game 7, he would be the starter, and that was how it played out. Podres pitched an eight-hit shutout—aided by Sandy Amoros's famed catch of Yogi Berra's slicing fly ball in the sixth inning—to deliver the Dodgers their only World Series title in Brooklyn. The Dodgers had lost the World Series to the Yankees in 1941, 1947, 1949, 1952 and 1953, but riding Podres's left arm, "next year" became "this year" for Brooklyn in 1955.

496. Wayne Terwilliger, Second Baseman, Kansas City Athletics.

Satchel Paige famously had his "Six Rules for Staying Young": "1. Avoid fried meats, which angry up the blood. 2. If your stomach disputes you, lie down and pacify it with cool thoughts. 3. Keep the juices flowing by jangling around gently as you move. 4. Go very light on the vices, such as carrying on in society. The social ramble ain't restful. 5. Avoid running at all times. 6. Don't look back. Something might be gaining on you." Wayne Terwilliger had his own six rules for a long life, but he was Wayne Terwilliger, not Satchel Paige, so who knew? *His* rules: "1. Associate with young people. 2. Get up early. 3. Move with some bounce in your step (even if you have to force it). 4. Diet: Plenty of distilled water, veggies, chicken. 5. Find some time each day to be by yourself. 6. Ignore the aches and pains and varicose veins." These two gentlemen just may be worth listening to. Paige pitched until he was ... well, no one is quite certain how old he was, but he pitched 100 innings in a season twice in Class AAA when he was at least in his 50s. And Twig? He also stayed in the game forever. He was a minor and major league player, a minor league coach and manager, a major league coach and an independent league coach and manager until he was 85. He drew a paycheck from baseball for 62 years (he sat out one year to run a bar—then returned to baseball for 36 years). He finally stepped aside in 2010. "I didn't move quite as fast and you need to when you're coaching first base and a line drive comes at you," he said, according to RIP Baseball. "I said something to my wife and doctor, and they were like, 'It's about time.'"

497. Hal R. Smith, Catcher, St. Louis Cardinals.

Hal Smith—not to be confused with the other '50s catcher named Hal Smith (he was a W.)—grew up to be an All-Star catcher by hurling baseballs at a Dr Pepper sign on his family's store in Barling, Arkansas, according to his SABR Bio Project biography. It's one of a long line of stories of youngsters throwing balls (or rocks or whatever they had) at unusual targets (often barns or other kids) and building up their arms, as Joe Posnanski notes in *The Baseball 100*. But unusual throwing doesn't always end in childhood. In 1936, the Hall of Famer Walter Johnson, then 48 years old and retired for nine years, accepted the challenge of duplicating the folkloric tale of George Washington's throwing a silver dollar across the Rappahannock River near Fredericksburg, Virginia. (Never mind that silver dollars did not exist in Washington's childhood.) Most accounts list the river's width at 372 feet, although the front-page article in *The New York Times* says it was 272 feet; *Washington Baseball History* says that shorter distance is probably inaccurate. Johnson's attempt was arranged for February 22—Washington's birthday—and coincided with the planting of 200 cherry trees, a nod to another Washington myth. Johnson owned a farm in Maryland and spent weeks practicing, even coyly telling Fredericksburg officials at one point: "I am practicing with a dollar against my barn door. Arm getting stronger, barn door weaker." Snow covered the ground on the appointed day, as can be clearly seen in photos in *The Times*, and Johnson, wearing a shirt and tie—he did take off his suit coat—threw the first of three silver dollars as a practice throw. It fell short, "to a disappointing shout and simultaneous splash near the opposite bank," *The Times* reported. The second practice throw cleared the river, as did the next throw, which counted and which most observers measured at 386 feet (*The Times* said 286 feet, 6 inches). A stone mason came up with the coin, and, as is often the case with sports memorabilia today, he turned down the first offers for the coin—$100, then $150. *The Times* said he was holding out for a higher bid.

498. Dick Hyde, Pitcher, Washington Senators.

Relievers were burned out in the '50s, too. Dick Hyde, a submarine artist, was the best reliever in the American League in 1958, compiling a 10–3 record with a 1.75 ERA and a league-leading 19 saves for a moribund Senators team that finished 61–93. He pitched 103 innings in 53 games (and gave up a single home run), a year after appearing in 52 games and throwing 109 innings. He was 12th in the Most Valuable Player voting. "The Senators had me up throwing in the bullpen almost every day," he said, according to Baseball Reference's Bullpen page. "My arm was never the same after that year, and I was just hanging on the next couple of years before retiring." Indeed: He pitched only 84 more major league innings, with a 5.04 ERA.

499. Johnny O'Brien, Second Baseman, Milwaukee Braves.

Johnny O'Brien and his twin, Eddie, were famous basketball players and bonus baby baseball players. But they are also part of a short list of twins who have both played in the major leagues. *Baseball Almanac* counts 10 pairs of twins who both reached the majors, and it is safe to say that being a twin is not something that would help on a scouting report. Among them only José Canseco has had a robust career. Here's a look at the twins and their career Wins Above Replacement.

Player, Positions	WAR	Years	Player, Positions	WAR	Years
George Hunter, OF, P	0.3	1909–10	Bill Hunter, OF	-0.3	1912
Joe Shannon, OF, 2B	-0.1	1915	Red Shannon, 2B, SS, 3B	3.0	1915–26
Roy Grimes, 1B	10.5	1920–26	Ray Grimes, 2B	-0.4	1920
Bubber Jonnard, C	-1.8	1920–37	Claude Jonnard, P	1.5	1921–29
Johnny O'Brien, 2B, SS, P	0.0	1953–59	Eddie O'Brien, SS, 3B, OF	-1.9	1953–58
Mike Edwards, 2B, SS	-1.7	1977–80	Marshall Edwards, OF	-0.2	1981–83
Stan Cliburn, C	-0.2	1980	Stew Cliburn, P	3.1	1984–88
José Canseco, OF	42.4	1985–2001	Ozzie Canseco, OF	-0.6	1990–93
Ryan Minor, 3B, 1B	-2.5	1998–2001	Damon Minor, 1B	0.1	2000–04
Taylor Rogers, P	6.2	2016–23	Tyler Rogers, P	6.1	2019–23

The O'Briens, the Cansecos and the Shannons were all teammates in the majors. The Rogers boys became teammates on the Giants for the 2023 season, but on April 11, 2022, they were opponents: in Padres versus Giants, Taylor got a save, Tyler the loss.

500. Vic Wertz, First Baseman, Boston Red Sox.

When Vic Wertz died, a headline in his hometown paper in York, Pennsylvania, read: "The man who hit the ball Mays caught." Despite a productive 17-year career as a hitter, despite overcoming polio in midcareer, that's how Wertz is remembered. He hit a sharp fly ball to deep center field in the eighth inning of Game 1 of the 1954 World Series, with runners on first and second and the score tied. But Willie Mays tracked it down—maybe 425 feet from home plate—to turn it into an out. "It would have been a home run in any other park—including Yellowstone," one newspaperman wrote. Had it fallen for a hit, Wertz would have become the first player to have five hits in a World Series game. Here's what he did when Mays *couldn't* make a play that day: two-run triple to deep right field; single to left; single to right; double to left-center. Wertz was eight for 16 in the Series with a .500/.556/.938 slash line. He just had the misfortune to hit a ball where Mays could get to it.

501. Bobby Tiefenauer, Pitcher, Cleveland Indians.

Bobby Tiefenauer's knuckleball was so good that he pitched 1,836 innings in the minor leagues with a 144–86 record and a 2.70 ERA. In one Class AAA season, he went 17–5 with a 1.89 ERA. Unfortunately for Tiefenauer, his knuckleball was so erratic that he pitched only 316 innings in the major leagues, all in relief, with a 9–25 record and a 3.84 ERA. His SABR Bio Project biography reports that when he was asked what happened when his knuckler did not knuckle, Tiefenauer said, "I usually back up third and take a shower." Teams were more willing to take a chance on a knuckleballer then—Hoyt Wilhelm became a standout in the '50s, and subsequently there were knuckleball stars like Phil Niekro, Joe Niekro and R.A. Dickey and very good pitchers like Charlie Hough, Tom Candiotti and Tim Wakefield. By 2021, *The Los Angeles Times* said, citing Fangraphs, the only pitchers who were recorded throwing knucklers in a game were position players. In that *L.A. Times* article, Andrew Friedman, a Dodgers executive, said that when he was with the Tampa Bay Rays, the team tried a special camp to try to create knuckleball pitchers, with Hough working with the pitchers. "There are so few people on Planet Earth that could actually do it—way fewer than guys who could throw 100," Friedman said. "The feel required for it, I think, is almost a more difficult skill." The Ringer reported that six players—in the majors and minors—had thrown a knuckler in 2019, according to data from TrackMan. None of them threw a professional pitch in 2022. A knuckleballer did surface in 2021—Mickey Jannis, a 33-year-old rookie who got into his first game that June for the Orioles. First and last: He yielded seven runs, eight hits and four walks in three and a third innings and spent 2022 pitching in independent ball. Another knuckleballer, Matt Waldron, put up an 8.44 ERA in Class AAA in 2022 but reached the majors for 41⅓ innings in 2023.

502. Al Dark, Third Baseman, Chicago Cubs.

Al Dark was a complex man who complicated his career more than once. As a Giants teammate, Willie Mays said, Dark helped him adjust to the major leagues. As the Padres' manager, Ozzie Smith said, Dark helped him gain the confidence to succeed. But when he managed the Giants, one of the most diverse teams baseball has had, Stan Isaacs of *Newsday* quoted Dark as saying in 1964: "We have trouble because we have so many Negro and Spanish-speaking players on this team. They are just not able to perform up to the white players when it comes to mental alertness." Dark insisted he was misquoted, his comments taken out of context. Several Black and Hispanic Giants, including Mays, rallied to his defense. But some Hispanic players on that team, including Orlando Cepeda and Felipe Alou, said that Dark asked them not to speak Spanish "because other players feared what they might be saying," Dark's *New York Times* obituary said, and that he banned Latin music from being played in the clubhouse. Reggie Jackson, who played for Dark in Oakland, said the manager had explained his handling of players coming back from injury by saying, "The one thing you've got to understand is that Black boys heal quicker than white boys," *The San Francisco Chronicle* said. Dark was quite open about being a born-again Christian and avoiding vices—"I never drank, never smoked, never chewed, never anything like that," he told *The Chronicle* in 2012—but his *Times* obituary noted that he had a long-running affair while married (although he eventually married the

Card 502: Al Dark had a checkered history with Black and Latino players both as a teammate and as a manager, plus resentments throughout the roster. Willie Mays praised him; Sal Bando said, "You couldn't manage a meat market."

other woman). His players in Oakland were sometimes openly contemptuous. Sal Bando said, "You couldn't manage a meat market" as Dark was on his way to managing the A's to their third consecutive World Series championship. Dark was a very good player (he was Rookie of the Year and accumulated 2,089 hits plus MVP votes in six seasons) who was traded six times and a capable manager who was fired five times—six if you count the time Charlie Finley fired him, rehired him and fired him again within 24 hours.

503. Jim Owens, Pitcher, Philadelphia Phillies.

In June 1960, *Sports Illustrated* wrote about "a group of wild-living, fun-loving, hell-raising players" known as the Dalton Gang who happened to make up a considerable portion of the Phillies' pitching staff: Jim Owens, Dick (Turk) Farrell, Jack Meyer and a newcomer to the gang, Seth Morehead. The article detailed heavy drinking, unruly behavior, fines from the team—it was quite a list. A month later, Farrell and Owens sued *Sports Illustrated*'s owner, Time Inc., seeking $100,000 and a retraction, according to an Associated Press report. They eventually reached a settlement, but Jim Bouton quoted Owens in *Ball Four* as saying that "we'd have gotten a helluva lot more money if one of the guys hadn't attacked a maid a week before the trial." Whatever the accuracy of the descriptions in *SI*, the Dalton Gang did enough to earn its notoriety. Si Burick, longtime columnist for *The Dayton Daily News*, which covered the Reds extensively, wrote that Owens was "known as an athlete of questionable off the field habits, one who has been especially indiscreet in the drinking league." Phillies manager Gene Mauch told Burick, "There are people in baseball who drink as much as he does, maybe more, but they don't get into trouble like him." What kind of trouble? One year in spring training, he got into a barroom brawl. One winter in Venezuela, he sustained a leg wound, apparently in another barroom brawl. In 1961, Mark Tomasik wrote on a Cardinals history site, Owens became upset with Mauch and threatened to quit. That prompted Larry Merchant of *The Philadelphia Daily News* to describe him as "a magnificent pitcher from the eyebrows down." Merchant also said the reason for Owens's sulking was "as clear as a head full of vodka stingers." His problems began early; while pitching for Class AAA Miami, he missed a start because, as *The Miami News* euphemistically put it, he was "in no condition to go on." In 1961, he left the Phillies in March, RIP Baseball said, after he was disciplined for "a hotel incident" and did not return until July. Owens and Farrell were reunited on the Houston expansion team, and their antics were a little more subdued. But not over. The Astros historian Bob Hulsey wrote that in 1964, the two slipped an alligator into the clubhouse whirlpool in spring training. As RIP Baseball noted, "That was how they discovered teammate Walt Bond *really* did not like reptiles." Yet Owens was respected enough that when the Astros released him in 1967, they made him a pitching coach.

504. Ossie Álvarez, Infielder, Detroit Tigers.

Ossie Álvarez was one in a long line of Cuban players signed by the Senators—in fact, one of numerous Cuban shortstops signed by the Senators. The American League integrated more slowly than the National League, but it did introduce Hispanic players a bit more quickly. Four Blacks and six Latinos were in the Opening Day lineups for American League teams in 1959, as recorded by Baseball Reference; the National League lineups included 13 African Americans and four Latinos. Overall, AL teams used 13 African American and 15 Hispanic players in 1959, while the NL included 31 African Americans and 15 Latinos. Hispanic players were concentrated in the middle infield and on the mound in the AL; Minnie Miñoso was the only full-time Hispanic outfielder in the league, although Héctor López played some outfield, too.

505. Tony Kubek, Shortstop, New York Yankees.

Yogi Berra, Mickey Mantle and Whitey Ford had long careers in New York, and Roger Maris, Bill Skowron, Clete Boyer and even Héctor López played well into their 30s, although finishing elsewhere. But it was not the same for the sound defensive infields for the successful Yankee teams of the late '50s. and early '60s. Shortstop Tony Kubek, super-utilityman Gil McDougald, second baseman Bobby Richardson and third baseman Andy Carey all retired relatively early, despite their prowess. Kubek retired at 29 because of a chronic neck injury. McDougald stepped aside at 32 because he did not want to be drafted by an expansion team, which would have required moving. Richardson was induced to hang on an extra season, but he still retired at 30, for family reasons. And Carey left the game, also a year later than he anticipated, at 31. An earlier third baseman, Bobby Brown, retired at 29 to go into medicine. And second baseman Jerry Coleman, wary that he might be traded and have to uproot his family, quit at 33.

506. Bob Purkey, Pitcher, Cincinnati Redlegs.

Bob Purkey learned the knuckleball from Pirates general manager Branch Rickey after coming down with a sore arm in 1955, according to *The Neyer/James Guide to Pitching*. In his final *Historical Baseball Abstract*, James estimated that Purkey threw his knuckler 20 to 40 percent of the time. Purkey insisted he was more than a knuckleball pitcher, but, according to his SABR Bio Project Biography, he needed it as a strikeout pitch against big swingers. His career peaked in 1962, when Purkey went 23–5 with a 2.81 ERA (and a 143 ERA+; he was pitching half the time in the tight confines of Crosley Field for the third-place Reds). Purkey received a single vote for the Cy Young Award, won by Don Drysdale, who had comparable numbers (25–9, 2.83) while playing for a pennant winner in the pitchers' haven at Dodger Stadium (his ERA+ was 128). James theorized that Purkey's identification as a knuckleballer cost him in the voting. "Why didn't he win it?" James wrote. "Well, you've got a big, strong handsome pitcher with a knockout fastball, pitching in Los Angeles, against an average-sized, average-looking slop pitcher pitching in Cincinnati."

507. Bob Hale, First Baseman, Baltimore Orioles.

When teams routinely had pitching staffs of nine or 10—and room for 15 or 16 position players—there were roles for specialty players that really no longer exist. Like the professional pinch-hitter. Bob Hale was one of them—not at the level of Smoky Burgess or Dave Philley or Elmer Valo but relied on often enough that over his seven seasons he had 278 plate appearances as a pinch-hitter and only 392 as a position player. His role surfaced as a 21-year-old rookie with the Orioles in 1955, when he pinch-hit 27 times in 190 plate appearances while hitting .357/.376/.407. When he was 22, that role was more pronounced. He played 51 games at first and pinch-hit 44 times—a less successful season, though, as is often the case with pinch-hitters, with a .237/.274/.309 line. He kept a job, but he never came close to playing in the field again with any regularity. Hale played 224 major league games over the next five seasons but only 25 in the field. The rest of the time he was a pinch-hitter. His final numbers as a pinch-hitter—.247/.273/.299, with no home runs—help explain why he was out of the game at age 28.

508. Art Fowler, Pitcher, Los Angeles Dodgers.

When Billy Martin became a manager, he needed a pitching coach. And a drinking buddy. With Art Fowler, he got both. They first met in 1950 as young minor leaguers at a spring training game, according to Fowler's SABR Bio Project profile, and they formed a friendship that lasted until Martin's death in an alcohol-related car wreck in 1989. When Martin first became a manager, at Class AAA Denver in 1968, he reached out to Fowler. (Fowler improbably returned to the active roster two years later, at age 48, and went 9–5, 2.91.) He then followed Martin to Minnesota, Detroit, New York, New York, again, Oakland, New York, again, and again, and again: Whenever Martin was fired, so was Fowler. His staffs often improved, but that was far from his only role. "He was one of Billy's boys," Willie Randolph told *The Hartford Courant*. "They knew each other for a long time, drinking buddies and hang-out buddies and stuff like that. Billy had a lot of faith in him." Fowler had a simple philosophy—"Throw strikes"—but he and Martin were not wedded to one approach to a pitching staff. In 1978, for example, their Yankees employed both Rich Gossage and Sparky Lyle in a standout bullpen; two years later, their Athletics staff had 94 complete games, 52 more than any other American League team. Their loyalty to each other had few bounds and certainly meshed when it came to the Yankees owner George Steinbrenner. Martin famously said of Reggie Jackson and Steinbrenner, "One's a born liar, the other's convicted." Hours later he was fired. After Fowler was let go in 1983—for once without Martin—he had his own comments: "I won't ever badmouth George Steinbrenner. He's all right. But he doesn't know anything about baseball, and he listens to the wrong advice."

509. Norm Cash, First Baseman-Outfielder, Chicago White Sox.

In 1961, Stormin' Norman Cash had a season that no other hitter in the '60s would duplicate. He batted .361 (highest in the major leagues between 1957 and 1971), swatted 41 home runs and drove in 132 runs for the Tigers. Even Cash couldn't come close to duplicating it; the batting average was his career best by 75 points, the RBIs his best by 39 and the homers a best as well. The fun-loving Cash couldn't help but hint at how that season might have happened. "I owe my success to expansion pitching, a short right-field fence, and my hollow bats," he told a sportswriter. In retirement, he showed *Sports Illustrated* how he had corked his bats in '61—drilling a hole in the barrel and filling it with a mixture of sawdust, cork and glue. There is doubt that corking a bat is a real boon for a hitter. *Smithsonian Magazine* reported that two university researchers, Alan Nathan and Lloyd Smith, performed a study that showed that a baseball came off a corked bat—in the lab, at least— slower than off a normal bat, although they said "it may well allow a batter to hit the ball solidly more often." Smith's conclusion: "If your goal is to hit more home runs, you should have a heavy bat. If your goal is to have a higher batting average, you should have a lighter bat." Whatever the science is, players have used corked bats … and they have also been caught. Notable corkers have included Sammy Sosa, Albert Belle, Graig Nettles (he had SuperBalls fly out of his bat), Amos Otis ("I had enough cork and SuperBalls in there to blow away anything," he said, according to ESPN), Chris Sabo, Billy Hatcher and Wilton Guerrero (Vladimir Sr.'s light-hitting older brother). Belle's bat was infamously confiscated by the umpires and swiped back during the game by a teammate who crawled through duct work to get it. One thing almost all the corkers had in common was denial. Nettles said he used a bat a fan gave him; Hatcher said he used a pitcher's bat; Sosa said it was a bat he reserved for batting practice and mistakenly used in a game. To his credit, Guerrero 'fessed up: He said he had had the bat for two or three months but used it only on the day it split apart on a groundout.

510. New York Yankees Team Card.
The Yankees won 10 World Series championships between 1947 and 1962, part of their record haul of 27 titles. Only one other team has won as many as 10 overall—the Cardinals, with 11. The Yankees also won five Series in a row, from 1949 to '53; six of the 16 teams competing for the first Series in 1903 have fewer than that overall—the Braves, the Tigers, the White Sox, the Twins/Senators, the Orioles/Browns and the Cubs.

511. George Susce, Pitcher, Detroit Tigers.
George Susce's father—also named George, but not a Senior—was a catcher who couldn't hit, a longtime coach, a renowned bench jockey and a pugnacious if not successful baseball fighter (his SABR Bio Project biography, quoting a *Cleveland News* writer, said he waged 37 fights and lost 36 of them). He also was, apparently, a nettlesome negotiator. When George the Younger was a high school phenom, Dad was a coach with Cleveland, which ardently pursued the youngster. He signed instead with the Red Sox. Soon thereafter, the Indians released Susce the Elder, his SABR bio says. This scenario was replayed six years later when a younger Susce, Paul, was an All-American pitcher at Auburn and Dad was a coach with the Kansas City Athletics. The A's badly wanted Paul Susce, but Dad insisted he get a three-year contract. The A's said no, Paul Susce signed with the Pirates and Dad was quickly let go by Kansas City. Dad may not have been the best talent scout: Young George pitched only 409⅔ major league innings, going 22–17, 4.42; Paul Susce washed out after one minor league season.

512. George Altman, Outfielder, Chicago Cubs.
When George Altman's life zigged, he found a way to zag. He went to college at Tennessee A&I (now Tennessee State University) on a basketball scholarship, but when a baseball program started up, he joined it, too. Upon graduation he had a chance to become the basketball coach at LeMoyne College. Instead, he took an athletic department official's advice and played a summer with the Kansas City Monarchs in the dying-gasp Negro American League, where his manager was Buck O'Neil. O'Neil soon connected him with the Cubs, making Altman one of the last players to jump from the Negro leagues to organized ball. A year in the military set back his development, but he made the Cubs as a 26-year-old rookie in 1959. In four seasons in Chicago, he batted .287/.351/.485 with a 122 OPS+ and 74 homers. Then he was traded to the Cardinals, to the Mets and back to the Cubs, his performance and opportunity dwindling. But Altman transitioned to Japan and became a star. In eight seasons, he averaged .310/.378/.561 with 205 homers. He overcame colon cancer and, as detailed in Robert Whiting's *The Chrysanthemum and the Bat*, efforts by his ex-manager to effectively blackball him. Because of Altman's popularity and insistence on fitting in so well, Whiting said, other Americans were urged to "be like

Altman." His career in baseball was finally over in his 40s, but he began a new one that also lasted: He was a commodities trader for 13 years and bought a seat on the Chicago Board of Trade, which he said "was no easy task." "They have a saying—bulls and bears make money, but hogs get slaughtered," Altman said in an interview for College Black Nines. "A lot of that also is for baseball. It's the same thing at the plate. You can't be swinging at everything."

513. Tom Carroll, Shortstop, Kansas City Athletics.

The bonus baby rule impeded Tom Carroll's career. Forced onto the major league roster for his first two seasons, he got six and 18 plate appearances with the Yankees. He pinch-ran 34 times, too, but otherwise he sat. A lot. That was the return on the Yankees' $35,000 investment. After a season in the minors and a couple of trades, he went to bat seven more times in the majors, with the Athletics. In 1960, at the age of 23, he wrapped up his baseball career. But he earned a degree from Notre Dame in 1961, and his life quickly became more interesting. Carroll joined the CIA after graduation and worked there for 27 years before becoming a corporate consultant on Latin America for another 18 years, according to an obituary posted by his family.

514. Bob Gibson, Pitcher, St. Louis Cardinals.

When Bob Gibson led the majors with a 1.12 earned run average in 1968, it was the lowest ERA since 1914, when Dutch Leonard posted a 0.96 for the Red Sox. The only lower ERA in the 20th century was 1.04 by Three Finger Brown of the Cubs in 1906. No one has come close to Gibson's ERA since (Luis Tiant compiled a 1.60 in the American League in '68). Here are the 10 lowest ERAs since 1968, not counting Shane Bieber's 1.63 and Trevor Bauer's 1.73 in the pandemic-shortened, 60-game 2020 season:

ERA	Player	Year	ERA	Player	Year
1.53	Dwight Gooden	1985	1.74	Ron Guidry	1978
1.56	Greg Maddux	1994	1.74	Pedro Martínez	2000
1.63	Greg Maddux	1995	1.75	Justin Verlander	2022
1.69	Nolan Ryan	1981	1.76	Tom Seaver	1971
1.70	Jacob deGrom	2018	1.77	Clayton Kershaw	2014

Yes, 1968 was the Year of the Pitcher, but it's not as if 1906 and 1914 were anything like the 1930s. If you make the adjustments for time period and leagues and ballparks that go into ERA+, Gibson's season still looks awfully good. The top 10 ERA+ seasons:

ERA+	Player (ERA)	Year	ERA+	Player (ERA)	Year
291	Pedro Martínez (1.74)	2000	258	Bob Gibson (1.12)	1968
279	Dutch Leonard (0.96)	1914	253	Three Finger Brown (1.04)	1906
271	Greg Maddux (1.56)	1994	243	Walter Johnson (1.39)	1912
260	Greg Maddux (1.63)	1995	243	Pedro Martínez (2.07)	1999
259	Walter Johnson (1.14)	1913	233	Christy Mathewson (1.28)	1905

Gibson's season ranks sixth in ERA+ versus third in ERA. The only ones better? Martínez, Maddux and a couple of deadballers. Pretty select company no matter how you rank them. Gibson did lose nine games in 1968, but by these scores: 5–1, 3–2, 1–0, 2–0, 3–1, 6–4, 3–2, 1–0, 3–2. Gibson gave up 27 runs in those games—only 19 of them earned—but the Cardinals scored only 12.

Card 514: Bob Gibson's ERA of 1.12 in 1968 has no competitors in any full season since; the next best is Dwight Gooden's 1.53 in 1985.

515. Harmon Killebrew, Third Baseman, Washington Senators.

Read about '50s baseball and you'll read how big and strong Ted Kluszewski was. A college football teammate of Klu was reported to have said that "if you ran around him, you were out of bounds." He had massive biceps that he showed off by wearing a jersey with no sleeves. Harmon Killebrew was nowhere near as big (who was back then?), but he was darned strong, too. Like Kluszewski, he couldn't run and had little range afield (although Killebrew did play several years at third and in the outfield before shifting to first, while Kluszewski was always a first baseman, as the DH did not exist). Kluszewski had a seven-year stretch in which he was one of the most feared hitters in the National League. You did not hear quite the same story about Killebrew in the American League, but here's the thing—his first seven years as a star were better than Kluszewski's, and then he added seven more, in the Deadball II era, that were basically as good. Klu was a superstar slugger (average, power) for a good stretch and then he was ordinary; Killebrew was a superstar slugger (on-base skills, power) for twice as long. Here's a look on a per-162-game basis:

	PA	R	H	2B–3B–HR	RBI	BB–SO	BA/OBP/SLG	OPS+
Kluszewski, 1950–56	616	89	171	27–2–32	105	52–33	.306/.366/.535	135
Killebrew, 1959–65	606	89	134	18–2–41	102	87–112	.263/.373/.546	147
Killebrew, 1966–72	622	83	132	20–1–36	106	115–90	.265/.401/.528	158

Kluszewski is in the Reds Hall of Fame, and he earned it. Killebrew is in the National Baseball Hall of Fame, and *he* earned it.

516. Mike García, Pitcher, Cleveland Indians.

From 1949 through 1956, the Cleveland Indians had a formidable rotation, about as good as any team has had: Bob Feller (before he began to fade into part-time use),

Early Wynn, Bob Lemon and Mike García. The first three pitchers are in the Hall of Fame, but García had a four-year stretch that was the equal of any put together by Wynn or Lemon, if not on the level of Feller's best four-year span. García's success simply was not as enduring as his rotation mates'. García's last good season came at age 33. Wynn was a 20-game winner at 40; Lemon won 20 games at 35. Feller, perhaps surprisingly, had his last excellent season at 32, but his greatness and workload in his early years were unsurpassed by his fellow Indians, and he had some success as an aging pitcher in a reduced, hybrid role. Here's a look at the rotation members' best four-year stretches:

Player	*W-L*	*Pct.*	*ERA*	*ERA+*	*IP*	*WHIP*
Bob Feller, 1938–41	93–44	.679	3.15	136	1237.2	1.328
Early Wynn, 1953–56	77–43	.604	3.04	129	1030.0	1.223
Bob Lemon, 1951–54	83–47	.638	3.01	121	1118.0	1.272
Mike García, 1951–54	79–41	.658	2.84	128	1076.2	1.230

The others had longevity *and* success, as these career totals attest: Feller was 266–162 in 3,827 innings; Wynn, 300–244, 4,564 innings; Lemon, 207–128, 2,850 innings; García, 142–97, 2,174⅔ innings.

517. Joe Koppe, Shortstop, Philadelphia Phillies.

Sports Illustrated was detailing in a 1963 preview of the Los Angeles Angels why the 1962 team had led the league in errors and unearned runs. "Joe Koppe and Felix Torres have a tendency to wave at ground balls on the left side of the infield," *SI* wrote in part. This may have been somewhat unfair; *Baseball Players of the 1950s: A Biographical Dictionary* said that as a minor leaguer Koppe "showed great range but was charged with an incredibly high number of errors." That last part was not unfair. Koppe's error totals by year across seven minor leagues to start his career: 40, 85, 71, 57, 63, 56, 51. His fielding percentage was below .900 those first four seasons. He calmed his erratic ways, but even in the majors, where he accumulated 400 at-bats only once, he was in the top 10 shortstops in errors twice. Perhaps this explains why Koppe was willing to wear a glove on the wrong hand on his 1964 Topps card.

518. Mike Cuellar, Pitcher, Cincinnati Redlegs.

Cleveland wasn't the only organization with a formidable rotation. The Baltimore Orioles, for a season, had a rotation to challenge Cleveland's early '50s starters for success. In 1971, the Orioles' four starters—Jim Palmer, Dave McNally, Mike Cuellar and Pat Dobson—each won at least 20 games, only the second time a team had done that. (The only other one: the 1920 Chicago White Sox, in the year after the rigged World Series.) McNally was 21–5, 2.89; Palmer was 20–9, 2.68; Cuellar was 20–9, 3.08; and Dobson was 20–8, 2.90. They started all but seven of the Orioles' games that season, and Baltimore won its third consecutive pennant plus the World Series. Dobson was the anomaly—the '71 Orioles were his third team in three years—but Cuellar, Palmer and McNally were every bit as dominant a group as those earlier Indians. They combined to go 178–72 (.712) with a 2.94 ERA over 2,419⅓ innings in the three pennant-winning years. Unlike McNally and Palmer, who had received large bonuses to sign with the Orioles as amateurs ($80,000 and $50,000, respectively), Cuellar was an unlikely part of a powerhouse triumvirate. He had played ball in his native Cuba before signing with the Reds and making the majors at 22, but he quickly returned to the minors and stayed there, on merit, until he was 27. He did not have a meaningful big-league season until he was 29 and with the Astros. He had been encouraged in winter ball to throw a screwball by Rubén Gómez in 1964, according to Cuellar's SABR Bio Project biography. And the Astros pitching coach Gordon Jones revamped his curve in 1966, the season he finally broke through: 12–10, 2.22 (155 ERA+). Two years later, however, his 8–11 record masked his effectiveness and Houston traded him for outfielder Curt Blefary. Blefary hit .234/.334/.370 over four years and was finished; Cuellar shared the American League Cy Young Award in 1969 and went 143–88, 3.18 for the Orioles. He wound up being part of a line of outstanding left-handed screwball pitchers, from Carl Hubbell to Warren Spahn to Juan Marichal to Cuellar to Fernando Valenzuela to Tom Browning (throw in lefty relievers Tug McGraw and Willie Hernandez as well). "Miguel was a magician out there," his teammate Boog Powell said in Cuellar's *Baltimore Sun* obituary. "He made hitters look comical, like they could have swung three times before the ball got there. A couple of times, I almost had to call timeout because I was laughing my head off." Billy Martin, then the Tigers' manager, had a more serious observation: "His fastball couldn't black my eye, but he owns my hitters' minds." Now, however, the screwball is all but gone (and some players, according to a 2014 *New York Times* article, believe the pitch is a myth anyway). "Pitchers have given it up," Don Baylor told *The Times* in 2014. "Coaches don't even talk about it. It's not in the equation."

519. Infield Power: Dick Gernert-Frank Malzone-Pete Runnels.

These Red Sox infielders were fairly productive in 1958—Pete Runnels was second in the league in average at .322 and had an OPS+ of 130, while Dick Gernert and Frank Malzone each had an OPS+ of 102. But power? That's all Gernert had to offer, but his 20 home runs were only the second time he cracked 20 in his career. He wasn't even in the top 10 in the league. Malzone hit 15 homers (and surpassed that only twice in his career). Runnels hit as many as 10 homers once. And it wasn't in 1958.

520. Don Elston, Pitcher, Chicago Cubs.

Don Elston and Bill Henry, Cubs relievers, were the inspiration for the creation of the save, Jerome Holtzman acknowledged. As Holtzman, the longtime Chicago sportswriter, said in an appreciation of Elston after his death in 1995, he was miffed that Roy Face was widely considered to be the top reliever in baseball, especially after his 18–1 season in 1959. Face, Holtzman wrote, earned nine or 10 of those wins after giving up the tying run. (*Sports Illustrated* wrote in 2019 that the number was actually five, but it was the principle, not the number, that mattered.) Elston and Henry were better closers, Holtzman believed, and he looked for a way to prove it. He came up with an idea for the save, proselytized for a decade and saw it become an official statistic in 1969. It was the first new official statistic in Major League Baseball since the RBI was adopted in 1920. Holtzman said that when he told Elston the save was created with him in mind, Elston smiled and replied: "I'm glad to hear that. It's helped relief pitchers make a lot of money." How much money? Tyler Kepner of *The New York Times* wrote, upon Holtzman's death in 2008, that he interviewed Holtzman in 1999 for an article on José Mesa, the Mariners' closer. "Holtzman remembered how Mesa, upon learning he was in Holtzman's presence, ran across the clubhouse and wrapped him in a bear hug," Kepner wrote. "Holtzman, Mesa explained, had helped him make millions of dollars." And the millions keep coming: The Mets re-signed closer Edwin Diaz in late 2022 for $102 million. Elston actually had only 64 saves, and he was too early to get rich off them: His top salary, Holtzman wrote, was probably $30,000—about $300,000 in 2023 dollars.

521. Gary Geiger, Outfielder, Boston Red Sox.

Read Joe Posnanski's *The Baseball 100* and you'll see story after story of a father helping his son become a ballplayer. In Gary Geiger's case, it was his sister who made him a hitter. Geiger, his brother William and his sister Linda played hours of baseball together while growing up in the tiny Illinois community of Sand Ridge. Linda was the pitcher. Always, she told *The Southern Illinoisan* in Carbondale after Geiger's death in 2006. "That's the thing I remember most, they made me pitch to them because one of them would bat and the other would field," she said. "I really didn't want to do it because they hit line drives back at me and that part wasn't much fun. I wasn't a real good pitcher, but I could get the ball up there where they could hit it, and that's all they cared about." Geiger learned well enough that he had a 12-year career, but he was frequently injured, hated flying, drank to deal with the flights (his sister said), and became an alcoholic who died of cirrhosis of the liver at the age of 59.

522. Gene Snyder, Pitcher, Los Angeles Dodgers.

The Dodgers became synonymous with excellent pitching, but that was after 1959. That year, four of the team's top six pitchers had earned run averages of 3.97 or higher. (And yet the team captured the World Series.) Two Dodgers, Gene Snyder and Fred Kipp, pitched their only major league games in 1959, and another, Bill Harris, pitched the final inning and two-thirds of a career that lasted only eight and two-thirds. Snyder had been pitching professionally since 1950, never finding the strike zone. He averaged 7.2 walks per nine innings in the minors, and he was marginally better in his 26⅓ innings as a Dodger: 6.8 walks per nine. He walked 20 of the 128 batters he faced and threw seven wild pitches. He had only four chances as a fielder and made one error. A throwing error, of course.

523. Harry Bright, Infielder, Pittsburgh Pirates.

Harry Bright was early evidence that the Yankee dynasty that began in the late 1940s might be coming to an end. Bright had cycled through the organizations of the Yankees, the Cubs, the White Sox, the Tigers, the expansion Senators and the Reds before the Yankees purchased the 33-year-old infielder's contract at the start of the 1963 season. He had labored through 16 seasons, mostly in the minors—a first baseman without enough power, a second baseman-third baseman-shortstop without enough defensive chops—but the Yankees, coming off back-to-back World Series championship seasons, acquired him to fortify their lean bench. Mickey Mantle broke his foot, Yogi Berra was aging, the Yankees had four regulars with an OPS+ well below 100, so players like Bright, Phil Linz and Jack Reed were called on. The Yankees did not bring in role players like Johnny Mize or Enos Slaughter or Héctor López or Bob Cerv, who had bolstered the Yankees through all those glory years. Yes, the part-time play of Mantle and Berra; the stellar play of the other stars; excellent defense; and solid pitching propelled the Yankees past the rest of a lackluster American League in '63. But when it came to Game 7 of the World Series, with the Yankees trailing the Dodgers, 3–2, with two out in the ninth, the Yankees had to tap Harry Bright to try to save their season. Predictably, he could not; he was Sandy Koufax's Series-record 15th strikeout of the game. Bright was back to start the 1964 season, when the bench was stretched, again, to aid an infield whose highest OPS+ would be 90. The stars were enough for another Yankee pennant but not enough to stave off another World Series loss. And by the Series, Bright was long gone, having accumulated only six plate appearances in New York and playing a half-season in Class AAA before he was released that September. In 1965, Bright and the Yankees were both saying their goodbyes. Although he hung around the minors for several more years, Bright faded out of the majors that season. At the same time, the Yankees—their stars gone or shedding productivity, their farm system failing to produce adequate replacements—nosedived and began a 12-year drought between pennants.

524. Larry Osborne, First Baseman, Detroit Tigers.

Seven years before he won the Triple Crown in the American League, Carl Yastrzemski did his best to play spoiler in a Triple Crown bid in the American Association. Yaz was a 20-year-old outfielder in 1960 who was proving he could hit, but with only doubles power, for the Minneapolis Millers. Also in the league was Larry (Bobo) Osborne, a beefy 24-year-old first baseman for the Denver Bears who was trying to capture that Triple Crown. Osborne went five for seven in Denver's final two games to wrest the batting title from Yastrzemski, .342 to .339, while also leading the league in homers (34) and RBIs (119). Osborne hit 175 home runs in the minor leagues—one of them, a towering blast pulled down the right-field line, was the longest home run I ever saw hit at the Class AAA ballpark in Indianapolis—but he could not duplicate that in the major leagues. Osborne finished 435 home runs and 3,262 hits behind Yazstremski in the majors.

525. Jim Coates, Pitcher, New York Yankees.

"I have never thrown at anyone to hit them," Jim Coates said following a 1966 brawl that began after he hit a batter on the shoulder while pitching for Class AAA Seattle. (It was so ugly the batter sought Coates out at a hotel the next day and punched him in the face.) Many of Coates's contemporaries, however, believed otherwise. Consider these assessments told to Danny Peary: "Coates was one of the few pitchers who would deliberately throw at a batter's head," Johnny Klippstein said.

"Jim Coates was a bad guy. He used to throw at me all the time," Vic Power said. "I don't want to name the pitchers who threw at me on purpose ... but if you guessed Jim Coates, I wouldn't say you were wrong," Minnie Miñoso said. "Bob Turley would throw inside but not out of meanness. But Jim Coates was a bugger," Jim Landis said. Even his teammates questioned Coates's motives, Jim Bouton wrote in *Ball Four*. "Coates was famous for throwing at people and then not getting into the fights that resulted," Bouton said. "There'd be a big pile of guys fighting about a Coates duster and you'd see him crawling out of the pile and making for the nearest exit. So we decided that if there was a fight while Coates was pitching, instead of heading for the mound, where he was not likely to be, we'd block the exits."

526. Bob Speake, Outfielder, San Francisco Giants.

Often, ballplayers are at a loss for what to do when their playing careers end. Bob Speake figured it out. His baseball career concluded in 1959, when he had just turned 29. He went home to Springfield, Missouri, and got into the business of bowling, but by the mid-'60s he decided to found the American Family Life insurance company, in Topeka, Kansas. That turned out more successfully than baseball; Speake ran the company for 31 years before retiring. "He ended up staying with that company and he became very wealthy," his nephew Mark Harrell told Baseball History Comes Alive in 2017. "Not bad for a guy who used to milk cows and raise chickens when he was a kid!"

527. Solly Hemus, Infielder-Manager, St. Louis Cardinals.

Player-managers were, for decades, a constant in baseball. *And the Skipper Bats Cleanup* notes that there have been 23 player-managers of more than 500 games and dozens more with shorter tenures. That persisted even through the 1950s. In 1955, five of the 16 teams had player-managers; the next year, four did. Some held the dual jobs for years; for others, it was a short-term proposition. Over baseball's long history, a few were very successful (Lou Boudreau, Mickey Cochrane, Joe Cronin, Frankie Frisch, Bucky Harris and Bill Terry, among others, won pennants). But only 14 players have simultaneously managed since baseball integrated in 1947 (and two of them, Cronin and Mel Ott, already held the roles in '47 and would not last much

Card 527: Solly Hemus was one of the last player-managers. He tried to ease out Stan Musial and antagonized budding stars Bob Gibson and Curt Flood. They all outlasted him.

longer). Solly Hemus was one of the last player-managers, ingratiating himself sufficiently with the Cardinals' owner, Gussie Busch, that he was hired in 1959. That the Cardinals hired a player-manager may not have been a surprise—Hemus was their third of the decade—but Hemus himself was. And he was not a success. Hemus aggravated his aging superstar, Stan Musial. Thinking Musial was all but finished (he wasn't), Hemus benched him for lengthy periods. Musial felt that left him rusty and unable to get in a hitting groove, as both *Stan Musial: An American Life* and *Musial: From Stash to Stan the Man* make abundantly clear. Hemus also alienated his budding Black stars: Bob Gibson and Curt Flood, who Hemus thought would both fail to make it in the majors, considered him racist, according to Musial's biographers. Both were offended when Hemus, who had been grazed by a pitch from a Black pitcher for the Pirates, Bennie Daniels, yelled, "You Black bastard," as he ran to first base. Daniels threw close to Hemus later in the game; Hemus responded by throwing his bat at Daniels and a brawl began. Gibson was also upset that Hemus confused him for a while with Julio Gotay, a Black Puerto Rican. Gibson wrote in his autobiography that he was ready to quit baseball because of Hemus but that a coach, Harry Walker, interceded, saying, "He'll be gone long before you will." Walker was correct. Hemus had a surprise winning season in his second year, but after a 33–41 start in 1961, he was fired. Since then, only two men—Pete Rose and Frank Robinson—have been player-managers for more than a partial season. Robinson did both jobs for two years, Rose for two-plus. Below is a list of the player-managers since integration and their records. You may not see another one.

Player-Manager, Team, Years	*Record*	*Pct.*
Pete Rose, Reds, 1984–86	194–170	.533
Don Kessinger, White Sox, 1979	46–60	.434
Frank Robinson, Indians, 1975–76	160–158	.503
Hank Bauer, Athletics, 1961	35–67	.343
Solly Hemus, Cardinals, 1959–61	190–192	.497
Harry Walker, Cardinals, 1955	51–67	.432
Eddie Joost, Athletics, 1954	51–103	.331
Eddie Stanky, Cardinals, 1952–53	171–137	.555
Marty Marion, Browns, 1952–53	96–161	.374
Fred Hutchinson, Tigers, 1952–53	87–149	.369
Phil Cavaretta, Cubs, 1951–53	169–213	.442
Lou Boudreau, Indians/Cubs, 1942–50, 1952	1,162–1,224	.487
Mel Ott, Giants, 1942–48	427–492	.466
Joe Cronin, Senators/Red Sox, 1934–47	1,236–1,055	.540

528. Pittsburgh Pirates Team Card.

The Pirates staggered through the '50s, but in 1958 they earned their first winning record in a decade, at 84–70. They regressed a bit the next year, to 78–76, but shortstop Dick Groat said he thought it was a year when the team "found the last pieces to our championship puzzle" and eventually took a big step forward. "It would take us a year to learn to play together," Groat said in *We Played the Game*, "but in

1960 we would be ready for a title run." The Pirates would win their first pennant since 1927 and their first World Series championship since 1925.

529. George Bamberger, Pitcher, Baltimore Orioles.
Mike Cuellar once said of his Orioles manager, Earl Weaver, "All Earl knows about pitching is he couldn't hit it," as related in *Nine Innings*. But Weaver knew enough to hire George Bamberger as his pitching coach. Bamberger pitched 18 seasons in the minors and 14⅓ innings in the majors. He started coaching while still pitching in the minors and developed a philosophy. "The most important pitch is a strike," he told Dave Anderson of *The New York Times* in 1979. "But the trick is to change speeds. Trying to pinpoint a pitch is crazy. Throw the ball down the middle, but don't throw the same pitch twice. Change the speed." It worked: In his 10 seasons in Baltimore, Bamberger's pitchers won 20 games 18 times. Bamberger made the rare move from pitching coach to manager, taking over the Brewers in 1978, and the irony was that his team became known as "Bambi's Bombers." Milwaukee, which was 11th in the league in runs scored in 1977, led the league in runs and homers in '78, buoyed by the acquisitions of Gorman Thomas and Larry Hisle. The Brewers won 93 games. Their pitching also improved markedly under Bamberger, from 11th in the league in ERA to eighth. In 1979, the Brewers were fourth in ERA and won 96 games. Bamberger missed half of the next season because of heart bypass surgery, but the team won 86 games and was third in ERA. He was an astute baseball man. After managing the Mets to a 65–97 record in 1982 and a 16–30 start in '83, he resigned. "I don't want to suffer anymore," he said.

530. Wally Moon, Outfielder, Los Angeles Dodgers.
In thoroughbred racing, they talk about "horses for courses"—racehorses that have a knack for success on certain tracks. Baseball is like that, too. Think of all the left-handed batters who have thrived at Yankee Stadium. Or Wade Boggs banging doubles off the Green Monster at Fenway Park. Or Bobby Thomson dumping his "Shot Heard 'Round the World" onto the short porch at the Polo Grounds. Or any Colorado Rockies hitter ever in Denver. Or Wally Moon. He came up in St. Louis, a left-handed hitter able to take advantage of Sportsman's Park's cozy right-field dimensions—310 down the line, although with an 11½-foot wall and a 25-foot screen. In five seasons as a Cardinal, Moon, pulling the ball, hit 50 home runs at home and 28 away. Then he was traded to the Dodgers and the Los Angeles Memorial Coliseum. It was a short poke down the right-field line, but the fence quickly fanned out to 390 feet in right-center—a death valley for lefty pull hitters. But left field ... the fence was 251 feet away, with a 42-foot screen. Johnny Klippstein called it "a pitcher's nightmare" and said, "The fence seemed to be right behind the infield." Moon noticed. He conferred with his ex-teammate Stan Musial, according to Moon's *Los Angeles Times* obituary, and learned an inside-out swing that allowed him to loft the ball over the left-field screen. "Moon shots," they called them. And once again, Moon was taking advantage of the peculiarities of his home ballpark. In his three seasons at the Coliseum, he hit 37 homers there and only 12 on the road. (He also hit 44 doubles at home and 28 on the road.) At this point in his career, Moon had hit 115

homers at home (the equivalent of Rob Deer or Dick Stuart) and 40 away from home (the equivalent of Delino DeShields). But when the team moved into Dodger Stadium in 1962, the Moon shots ended: Over four seasons, Moon hit only five homers in Chavez Ravine, where it was 330 feet down the lines and 380 to the power alleys, and 17 on the road.

531. Ray Webster, Infielder, Cleveland Indians.

Ray Webster grew up in little Grass Valley, California, but he had big ambitions. When he was a 21-year-old Cleveland rookie, according to his obituary at RIP Baseball, he said: "Ted Williams was always everything I ever wanted to be as a ballplayer. I know I have a long way to go, but I'm sure going to keep trying." He never came close, of course. Webster played only 47 major league games—almost half as a pinch-hitter or pinch-runner—and batted .195/.250/.325 with an OPS+ of 59. He was a shaky fielder, too. Reflecting on the start of his career in Cleveland in a 2017 interview with Bill Nowlin, he said: "I was hitting the ball pretty good. At that age, though, you're a little cocky. You never know." And, he said, when he was traded to Boston, "I got to see the man I liked the most, Mr. Williams." Not only that, but Webster also once replaced Williams in the lineup, after Williams pinch-hit. "I consider myself very lucky," he said.

532. Mark Freeman, Pitcher, Kansas City Athletics.

Mark Freeman had a forgettable major league career. He pitched 87⅓ innings over two seasons, compiling a 3–3 record and a 5.56 ERA. But for one day late in the 1959 season, Freeman had it going. He was pitching for the Yankees against the Orioles in the next-to-last game of the season. This was the worst Yankees team since 1925, but still, they were the Yankees, and there was Freeman with a four-hit shutout and a 2–0 lead through six innings, nine outs away from his first major league win. Then it unraveled in the seventh: a walk, a double, a sacrifice fly and a single and it was a 2–2 game. Marv Throneberry hit for him in the bottom of the inning (he struck out, of course), and the Yankees lost in the 11th. The next spring, Freeman was traded to the Cubs for Art Ceccarelli; neither one pitched in the majors again after that season.

533. Darrell Johnson, Catcher, New York Yankees.

Darrell Johnson managed the Red Sox to an unexpected pennant in 1975, then lost an epic World Series to the Reds (Ed Armbrister, Bernie Carbo, Luis Tiant, Carlton Fisk, Bill Lee, Tony Pérez, Joe Morgan, Pete Rose). His managing in Game 7 was widely criticized; the taciturn Johnson had not made many friends in the press box even while winning a pennant. Years later, he told *The Hartford Courant* that general manager Dick O'Connell had done his best to tutor him on press relations. "He taught me that there is no such thing as a stupid question and told me: 'Stop having the veins pop in your neck when somebody, in your opinion, asks you a stupid question. It might not be stupid to them, and learn to deal with that. Quit getting angry and help these people do their job the best you can do,'" he said. Johnson never stopped reliving aspects of that World Series loss, including his decision to have Cecil Cooper pinch-hit for reliever Jim Willoughby in a tie game in the bottom of the eighth in Game 7. Cooper fouled out, and the rookie reliever Jim Burton lost the game in the ninth. "I wouldn't change a thing," Johnson told *The New York Times* in 1985, "except that I'd probably have Cecil hit a home run."

534. Faye Throneberry, Outfielder, Washington Senators.

Strike 1: His name was Faye. Not just Faye, but Maynard Faye. Strike 2: His intellect did not match his eye-hand coordination; he was held back twice in grade school and quit high school two years before he was scheduled to graduate, according to his SABR Bio Project biography. A *Washington Post* columnist wrote that Throneberry was "the Calvin Coolidge of baseball ... a reticent young man who feels cheated if he can't answer every question with 'yes' or 'no.'" Throneberry became the Red Sox's starting left fielder when Ted Williams feigned retirement for the first two months of 1955, but even he knew he could not replace the Splendid Splinter. "Fill the shoes of Ted Williams?" he said. "Not me." And Strike 3: He was Marv Throneberry's older brother, with an even more futile baseball career: Faye, .236/.307/.358, with 29 homers in 1,453 plate appearances; Marv, .237/.311/.416, with 53 homers in 1,331 plate appearances. Marv was renowned for his defensive lapses, and so was Faye. One sportswriter noted that grounders "went through him like sand escaping an enlarged sieve," his SABR profile said. It was Marv's fate to play for the Mets, Faye's to play for the Senators. In his four years in Washington, the Senators were 252–364 (an average of 63–91), with three last-place finishes. While Marv made his name after baseball hawking beer, Faye made his by becoming an award-winning bird dog trainer.

Card 535: Rubén Gómez was called "El Divino Loco"—the "Divine Crazy One"— because "he could not be intimidated on the mound." Although he was occasionally chased off it.

535. Rubén Gómez, Pitcher, Philadelphia Phillies.

Rubén Gómez was a legend in his native Puerto Rico, where he pitched for 29 seasons, until he was 49. His nickname was "El Divino Loco"—"The Divine Crazy One"—because "he could not be intimidated on the mound," *The Puerto Rico Herald* wrote after his death in 2004. Luis Rodríguez Olmo, a former major leaguer who managed Gómez on the island, said Gómez once swatted the former Negro leagues star Terris McDuffie on the leg with a bat in a winter league game, *The Herald* said. "McDuffie said something that Ruben didn't like," Olmo said. "Ruben picked up a bat and whacked him in the knee. He didn't ask questions." Major leaguers would have believed the story, as Gómez developed a reputation for throwing at batters. As a rookie in 1953, Gómez —egged on by his manager, Leo Durocher—hit the Dodgers' Carl Furillo with a pitch, breaking his hand. (Furillo went into the Giants' dugout and put Durocher in a headlock.) Three years later, Gómez hit the Braves' Joe Adcock on the wrist. The players exchanged words as Adcock, who had been hit numerous times—including on the head— went to first base. Gómez threw the ball at Adcock, who chased him into the dugout. Bob Buhl said Gómez locked himself in the clubhouse and grabbed an icepick, but Adcock never made it that far. Thomas Van Hyning wrote in Gómez's SABR Bio Project biography, "He insisted in 1958 that he was no headhunter, though (this after a bench-clearing episode with the Pittsburgh Pirates)." He *was* in the National League's top 10 in hit batters in four of his 10 seasons. All this overshadows how good Gómez was as a young major leaguer (30–20, 3.13 ERA, 134 ERA+ in his first two seasons) and especially in Puerto Rico. There, he was 174–119 over three decades (sometimes pitching in the neighborhood of 200 winter innings), almost all of them with the Santurce Crabbers. "He was the guy in Puerto Rico, he was everybody's idol," Orlando Cepeda told *The New York Times*.

536. Danny Kravitz, Catcher, Pittsburgh Pirates.

The 1959 season was Danny Kravitz's best as a player, but it may have been the worst for his career. He managed what was then a career high in plate appearances, 169, and batted .253/.274/.377. But the Pirates had acquired Smoky Burgess before that season, and it became clear that they did not need two overweight, left-handed-hitting catchers who were defensively challenged. Especially one who really didn't hit that well and especially couldn't pinch-hit that well. Kravitz batted .189/.295/.245 without a single home run in 61 career trips to the plate as a pinch-hitter, while Burgess was the pinch-hit king: .285/.376/.434 with 16 homers in 590 plate appearances. After playing in only eight games—seven as a pinch-hitter— in the first seven weeks of the 1960 season, Kravitz was traded to Kansas City for an overweight, right-handed-hitting catcher who *could* play defense, Hank Foiles. The Pirates, of course, won the World Series; the Athletics, of course, finished last. Kravitz's only reward: a $250 World Series share from his ex-teammates.

537. Rudy Árias, Pitcher, Chicago White Sox.

Rudy Árias, a little Cuban left-hander (he weighed about 155), pitched only one season in the major leagues, but he wound up telling a couple of good stories about pitching to Mickey Mantle. The first came from spring training. As Árias recalled to Don Zminda for *Go-Go to Glory: The 1959 White Sox*, Mantle was one of the two batters Árias feared most (Ted Williams was the other). Árias got a 2-2 count on Mantle when his catcher called for a changeup. Mantle crushed it. "That ball almost hit the sun," Árias said, laughing as he told Zminda. The second story comes from Baseball Happenings. In Árias's words: "Jim Rivera told me, 'Rudy, when Mickey Mantle comes up, if you throw him a knuckleball, I will give you a six-pack of beer.' I throw it, Mantle waited and waited, and man, he got a pop-up to second base." Árias may have embellished the story, as box score play-by-play does not reveal him ever getting Mantle to pop out to second. Mantle faced Árias twice and flied out to center both times—in the fourth inning of a June 17 game with the Yankees leading, 6–2, and in the ninth inning of a tie game on May 16. Would Árias have thrown a knuckler to Mantle in the ninth inning of a tie game to win a bet?

538. Chick King, Outfielder, Chicago Cubs.

Baseball Reference lists two dozen players who were universally called Chick, and another dozen who were sometimes called Chick. Fourteen of them were actually named Charles, and two more were Chesters. Charles Gilbert King was the most recent of the Chicks, and his major league career ended after the 1959 season with a mere 85 plate appearances over five years. Chick Hafey was an outfielder whose best years with the Cardinals in the 1920s and '30s (and friends on a Veterans Committee) got him into the Hall of Fame. But other Chicks had more unsettling lives. Chick Stahl had been the player-manager for the last 40 games of the 1906 season in which the Boston Red Sox finished 49–105. He decided to quit as manager in spring training but, as captain, he kept leading the team while Boston sought a successor. But he drank carbolic acid, a medication he had for a foot infection, in his hotel room and died almost instantly. A newspaper account at the time said the Boston players believed it was an accident, but his death was ruled suicide. Then there was Chick Gandil, one of the Black Sox accused of throwing the 1919 World Series and barred from baseball. Gandil always insisted he had no role in a fix. At age 81, he said, "I'm going to my grave with a clear conscience." Sixteen months later he did.

539. Gary Blaylock, Pitcher, St. Louis Cardinals.

The most exciting thing about Malden, Missouri, where Gary Blaylock lived for many years, is something you really can't see: the New Madrid Fault, which spawned some of the largest earthquakes in U.S. history in the winter of 1811–12 (one caused bells to ring in Richmond, Virginia, 900 miles away). But the little town, now about 4,000 residents, has produced some talented people—including Gary Blaylock. He pitched 125⅔ innings in his one season in the majors, but he was the pitching coach for the 1985 World Series champion Kansas City Royals after tutoring Bret Saberhagen, among others, in the minors. Malden's other notables include Hub Pruett, a major league pitcher for a decade who struck out Babe Ruth more than he did any other batter (13 times in 31 match-ups); Derland Moore, a defensive lineman who played 14 seasons in the NFL; and George Richey, Tammy Wynette's manager—and fifth husband. Stand by your man ... again ... and again ... and again....

540. Willy Miranda, Shortstop, Baltimore Orioles.

If only Willy Miranda could have batted solely with runners on second and third. In that situation, he was a .323/.429/.484 hitter. That's a .913 OPS. Of course, that's impossible. Miranda batted only 42 times with runners on second and third over a nine-year career, and pretty much the rest of the time he did not hit at all: He had a career .222/.282/.271 slash line. But he defined "good field, no hit." "He was the best defensive shortstop I've ever seen, and I've seen plenty," Tommy Lasorda, a teammate of Miranda's in Cuba, said in his *New York Times* obituary. Brooks Robinson, who played alongside Miranda with the Orioles, told Danny Peary that Miranda was "a terrific shortstop with a lot of range and a great arm. He could go in the hole and throw guys out better than anyone I ever saw, including Luis Aparicio." And Miranda did it, Robinson said, with a decrepit glove reinforced with tongue depressors. Curiously, his first major league appearance was at first base—a ninth-inning defensive replacement for Mickey Vernon. He never played first again.

541. Bob Thurman, Outfielder, Cincinnati Redlegs.

The Reds were slow to integrate; they were the next-to-last team in the National League to employ a Black player, in 1954. Cincinnati borders Kentucky and was not always hospitable to Black or Latino players. "The worst fans were in Cincinnati," Hank Thompson, one of the early Black players in the game, said, according to *Baseball's Great Experiment*. But in 1955, the Reds added Bob Thurman; in 1956, Frank Robinson, Brooks Lawrence, George Crowe and Curt Flood; in 1957, Joe Taylor; in 1958, Vada Pinson and Don Newcombe and two Latino players, Danny Morejón and Orlando Peña. Thurman was far older than all of them, although, in the way of many ballplayers, he had fudged his age—by six years. He was actually 38 when he joined the Reds after cycling through the systems of the Yankees (in 1949; they did not integrate in the majors until 1955) and the Cubs. He became the "traveling secretary" for the Reds' Black players, *Baseball's Great Experiment* says, making housing arrangements in an era when Black players were generally on their own to find places to stay. Thurman also could play, despite his age. In five years of part-time play with the Reds, he went to the plate 735 times—just over a full season's worth—and batted .246/.314/.465 with 35 home runs, 11 triples, 106 runs and 106 RBIs. At 39, he batted .295/.340/.532 and hit three consecutive home runs and a double in one game; at 40, he hit 16 homers in 206 plate appearances. He was a good enough right fielder that his presence forced Roberto Clemente to play left field in the 1954–55 Puerto Rican Winter League (they teamed with Willie Mays in the outfield). Thurman also pitched some in the Negro leagues and with some frequency in winter ball. He became a scout whose first signee was Rudy May, who won 152 games, and he was said to be instrumental in the Reds' signing Johnny Bench, Hal McRae, Gary Nolan and Wayne Simpson. Even though his own chance came so late, his widow, Dorothy Thurman, said, according to his SABR Bio Project biography, "He never seemed to regret not getting a chance earlier."

542. Jim Perry, Pitcher, Cleveland Indians.

When the Tigers acquired Jim Perry in 1972, the Detroit manager, Billy Martin, said, "We got the non-cheating Perry." This was true; Jim Perry was not known for throwing a spitter, as his brother, Gaylord, was. Gaylord used his wet one to win 314 games and a spot in the Baseball Hall of Fame; Jim used his conventional pitches to win 215 games and a spot in the Twins Hall of Fame. "You know what, mine is as important as his," Jim told *The Twin Cities Pioneer Press* in 2011, the year he was honored by the Twins. Jim led his league in wins twice; Gaylord did so three times. Jim won a Cy Young Award; Gaylord picked up two. But Jim won a World Series, something Gaylord never managed. Their 529 combined wins are second among major league brothers only to Phil and Joe Niekro's 539.

543. Corsair Outfield Trio: Roberto Clemente-Bob Skinner-Bill Virdon.

From early in the 1956 season until the middle of the 1963 season, Roberto Clemente in right, Bill Virdon in center and Bob Skinner in left often made up the Pirates' outfield. According to the statistical site High Heat Stats, they rank third in games started together by outfielders in the same positions, with 542. (Coincidentally, almost the same as their Topps card number.) They came in behind only the 556 games by the St. Louis Browns' Ken Williams, Jack Tobin and Baby Doll Jacobson from 1920 to 1925 and the 552 games by the Toronto Blue Jays' George Bell, Lloyd Moseby and Jesse Barfield from 1981 to 1989. Curiously, three other Pirates outfields are among the 28 outfields that have started more than 300 games together: No. 9, Woody Jensen, Lloyd Waner and Paul Waner, 386, 1931 to 1938; 11. Willie Stargell, Matty Alou and Clemente, 365, 1966 to 1970; and 15. Adam Comorosky, Lloyd Waner and Paul Waner, 344, 1927 to 1933.

544. Lee Tate, Shortstop, St. Louis Cardinals.

Lee Tate had been a shortstop with a consistently decent batting line for six straight seasons in the minors when, at age 26, he earned American Association All-Star honors with the Cardinals' Class AAA Omaha team in 1958, batting .292/.356/.353. The competition to be the St. Louis shortstop was hardly fierce. That season, Eddie Kasko, the regular, and the reserves Dick Schofield and Rubén Amaro managed OPS+ totals of 46, 66 and 43. Abysmal. But in a September call-up, Tate was no better: .200/.282/.257 with an OPS+ of 42. The next year, he made the Opening Day roster and again, the competition was not daunting. The newly acquired Alex Grammas would hit .269/.337/.348 for a 78 OPS+, and the backup Wally Shannon showed no on-base skills with a .284/.292/.337 line and a 63 OPS+. Tate, however, played his way back to AAA, hitting .140/.232/.260 with an OPS+ of 28. 28! He never returned to the majors.

545. Tom Morgan, Pitcher, Detroit Tigers.

Nolan Ryan and Randy Jones were pitchers with almost nothing in common. Ryan was a right-hander who threw harder than just about anyone else in the game, although often not in the strike zone. He took a while to ascend to stardom, but then stayed there for two decades. Jones, meanwhile, was a left-hander who threw softer than just about any other established pitcher in the game, invariably with command of the strike zone. His star rocketed up in his third season but quickly faded, his career trickling away in a decade. But these two opposites had one important thing in common: Tom Morgan as their pitching coach. Ryan hooked up with Morgan with the Angels in 1972 after five seasons as an enigmatically erratic strikeout artist with the Mets. Later, Ryan told *The Los Angeles Times* that he was at a crossroads then, but "fortunately, Tom was there to help, the first pitching coach who really taught me anything about mechanics." Ryan's walk rate dropped by almost 40 percent that first season, and his already excellent strikeout rate mushroomed by more than 25 percent. "I remained pretty erratic, but that was still the turning point of my career," Ryan told *The L.A. Times* after Morgan's death in 1987. "Those mechanics gave me the basis on which to build. If it wasn't for the interest Tom took in me and all that time he spent with me, I don't know where I'd be." Jones's transformation was also dramatic if not as long-lasting. He led the National League in losses in 1974 with the Padres. The next year, Morgan became his pitching coach and Jones led the league in ERA (2.24) and ERA+ (156) while posting a 20–12 record. The next year, he won the Cy Young Award after going 22–14. Jones told Friars on Base, a Padres news and opinion site, in 2010: "I went into '75 and Tom Morgan wanted to make some changes to my mechanics and I bought into what he wanted to do." For all the accolades about mechanics, Morgan was widely known as a player for the ungainly way he walked. The Yankees announcer Mel Allen nicknamed him Plowboy

Card 545: Tom Morgan never had more than 11 wins or 11 saves in a season, but Nolan Ryan and Randy Jones swore by him as a pitching coach who excelled at tweaking mechanics.

because, *The Los Angeles Times* said, of his "shuffling and bent gait that made it appear as if he was pulling a plow." Morgan credited his own pitching coach, Jim Turner of the Yankees, with helping make the adjustments to learn a sidearm curve and a changeup that propelled him to success in the majors.

546. Al Schroll, Pitcher, Philadelphia Phillies.

Al Schroll won only six games in the majors, but one was mighty memorable. In the final week of the 1961 season, Schroll, pitching for the Twins, took a no-hitter into the ninth inning against the Indians. It was far from a perfect game—he had walked two batters and hit one—but he had a 10–0 lead and would be facing two pinch-hitters and Ty Cline, who was batting .148. But Don Dillard, who was in the midst of a remarkable season as a pinch-hitter (15 for 39 with a .429/.487/.657 line), spoiled Schroll's bid for fame with a leadoff single to center. Gone was the no-hitter. Schroll walked the next two batters and then yielded a triple to Tito Francona. Gone was what would have been his first major league shutout. A groundout made it 10–4 before Schroll retired John Romano and Vic Power to secure the victory. The heady moment was fleeting: Four days later, starting the next-to-last game of the season, Schroll gave up five runs in two-thirds of an inning. Those were his last major league pitches.

547. Jim Baxes, Third Baseman, Los Angeles Dodgers.

Jim Baxes spent 12 years trying to make the major leagues with the Dodgers, and when he finally did, he was the Opening Day third baseman in 1959. Baxes was a nondescript fielder, but he was a slugger—he hit 30 or more homers in the minors three times and 20 or more in four other seasons—and Los Angeles needed some pop in a lineup populated by fading Dodgers from Brooklyn and a cast of youngsters. And he hit as he never really had; he started the first eight games and batted .280/.379/.560. His playing time was slashed over the next two and a half weeks as Jim Gilliam was moved to third base, but Baxes was hitting .303/.395/.515 after playing in 11 of the Dodgers' 26 games, in which they were 14–12. Then Baxes was traded to Cleveland for the aging infielder Fred Hatfield, who never played an inning for Los Angeles. Baxes hit with power in Cleveland—15 homers in 270 plate appearances—but it wasn't enough to keep him in the big leagues. Two years later, he retired with 219 minor league home runs.

548. Elmer Singleton, Pitcher, Chicago Cubs.

When Elmer Singleton made his professional debut in 1940 with the Wenatchee Chiefs of the Western International League, Lou Gehrig was only a year into retirement. Ted Williams was in his second season in the majors. Stan Musial hadn't yet made it to the majors. The United States was on the sidelines in World War II. When Singleton retired from professional baseball in 1963 (at 45, he was four years older than his manager with the Seattle Rainiers), Pete Rose, Willie Stargell, Gaylord Perry, Dave McNally and Mickey Lolich were all making their major league debuts. The United States was becoming seriously embroiled in fighting in Vietnam. The country had gone through four presidents in that time; Singleton had gone through 10 major league organizations and 23 seasons (14 in the Pacific Coast League).

549. Howie Nunn, Pitcher, St. Louis Cardinals.

Pitching coaches have pitchers run before games to stay in shape. Pitchers tend not to enjoy this. (This is one reason pitchers liked Johnny Sain as their pitching coach. He would say, "You don't run the ball over the damn plate.") Jim Brosnan noted in his book *Pennant Race* that he suggested that, as the 1961 season—and the pennant race—chugged into September, the pitchers should not run as much so as to save themselves for the stretch. One Reds pitcher asked Brosnan's roommate, Howie Nunn, how many miles he had run that season. Nunn had been plagued by a sore arm and at that point had thrown only 36 innings. Brosnan noted Nunn's lament: "Nunn claimed that he counted every one of his steps from spring training till October. 'I've got more miles than innings pitched, I know that,' he said." And it stayed that way. Nunn pitched in only eight more major league games … and his team lost every one of them.

550. Symbol of Courage: Roy Campanella.

Through the first half of the '50s, two catchers mattered most: Roy Campanella and Yogi Berra. They were both short and had unusual builds and distinctive approaches at bat (Campanella pulled just about everything, Berra hit the ball everywhere). But each won three Most Valuable Player Awards—Campy in 1951, '53 and '55, Yogi in 1951, '54 and '55. No other catcher has won more than two MVPs. Here's how they compared for 1950 through 1955:

Player	G	PA	H	HR	RBI	BB	SO	BA/OBP/SLG	OPS+
Campanella	775	3,147	799	178	594	330	309	.288/.367/.536	134
Berra	869	3,679	974	161	651	331	137	.295/.362/.497	133

In that six-year stretch, Campanella threw out 59.9 percent of would-be base stealers to Berra's 53.0 percent, while allowing 40 percent fewer steals. Berra had the edge in overall WAR in that stretch, 29.2–27.8, because Campy had one season, 1954, in which he was badly hampered by injuries. Injuries cost Campanella in 1952 as well, and recurring hand injuries compromised his 1956 and '57 seasons, while Berra played with unprecedented frequency, averaging 143 games at catcher from 1950 to 1955. When the Dodgers plotted their move to Los Angeles for the 1958 season, it was hoped that the aging Campanella, who had been playing professionally since he was 15, would get healthy enough to take advantage of the short left-field fence at the Los Angeles Coliseum. But in January 1958, Campanella was paralyzed in a car accident. As Ed Roebuck and Art Fowler described in *We Played the Game*, 16 months later at an exhibition game against the Yankees at the Coliseum, Pee Wee Reese took Campanella onto the field in his wheelchair, the lights were turned out and the crowd of 93,000 lit matches in his honor. "It was unbelievable," Roebuck said.

551. Fred Haney, All-Star Manager.
Like Casey Stengel, Fred Haney had a laughable managerial record before he landed a dream job. From 1939 to 1941, he managed the Browns for two-plus seasons and then was demoted to the minors. Branch Rickey hired Haney to manage the Pirates in 1953 and fired him after three seasons. In his five full seasons as a major league manager, Haney had lost 497 games. He secured a job for 1956 as a coach with the Braves, who had finished second in the league the year before. Mired in fifth place at 24–22, Milwaukee fired its manager, Charlie Grimm, and tapped Haney. The Braves flourished, finishing the season with a 68–40 run that left them one tantalizing game behind the first-place Dodgers. "Fred was a smarter manager and figured out more ways to win," Bob Buhl told Danny Peary. Stacked with good hitters and a robust rotation, Milwaukee won the next two pennants and the 1957 World Series and then dropped the 1959 pennant in a playoff with the Dodgers after losing second baseman Red Schoendienst for the year with tuberculosis. For that, Haney was fired, never to manage again. "We didn't understand why Fred Haney was fired because nobody could have done more with a team than he did with us," Buhl said. Interestingly, on teams with the sluggers Hank Aaron, Eddie Mathews and Joe Adcock, Haney's Braves were well above average in their rate of sacrifice bunts. (Haney's Pirates teams had been as well, but they were last in homers every year. Runs, too.) Haney was well *below* average in pitchers used, as befits a team with Warren Spahn, Lew Burdette and Buhl. Apropos of nothing: Haney managed the Pacific Coast League Hollywood Stars beginning in 1950, the first of four years that the Stars players wore shorts, not baseball pants, for day games and

warm night games, his SABR Bio Project biography said. The newspapers called them "scanties." Somehow, shorts resurfaced with the White Sox for three games in 1976. The owner, Bill Veeck, called them "Hollywood shorts." Infielder Jack Brohamer expressed reservations: "I'm not going to wear short pants unless they let me wear a halter top, too."

552. Casey Stengel, All-Star Manager.

In the early 1970s, the Kansas City Royals created a Baseball Academy at which good young athletes who did not necessarily have a background in baseball were instructed in the ways of the game, an effort to develop ballplayers basically out of nowhere. Several of the instructors were ex–Yankees, including Tommy Henrich, who knew a little something about instruction on the diamond. A few months after his retirement at the end of the 1950 season, Henrich became a key instructor in Casey Stengel's prize innovation: a preseason instructional school two or three weeks before the Yankees' spring training began. As Robert Creamer wrote in *Stengel: His Life and Times,* Stengel badly wanted the instructional school—a precursor, in a small way, of the future instructional leagues. Creamer wrote that at Stengel's school "the Yankees assembled about forty of their brightest young minor-league players and exposed them to the wisdom and knowledge of Stengel, his coaches and several other instructors, including Henrich." Mickey Mantle, Creamer wrote, "was the prize of the school, the nugget," but other excellent young Yankees—Gil McDougald, Bill Skowron, Bob Cerv—went through the school. The flood of young, well-schooled talent fueled the Yankees' dynasty through the 1950s, and Stengel won pennants in nine of his first 10 seasons with the team.

553. Orlando Cepeda, All-Star First Baseman.

The Giants were blessed with two young slugging first basemen whom they developed in the 1950s and who would go on to the Hall of Fame, but the problem became which one doesn't play first base? Orlando Cepeda was Rookie of the Year in 1958 and an All-Star in '59 by the time Willie McCovey, who was four months younger, was called up. To get both bats in the lineup, the Giants tried Cepeda at third base, an experiment that ended after horrifying results in four games. He then became a left fielder—he was faster, and McCovey, being left-handed, was a more natural fit at first; McCovey became Rookie of the Year. Cepeda suffered through two more seasons playing about half the time in the outfield. His days at first kept McCovey, who had great power and very good on-base skills, on the bench. Then in 1962 they swapped—Cepeda owned first base, and it was McCovey who was lumbering around the outfield. A solution came, unhappily, when Cepeda was hurt in 1965 and missed almost the entire season and then was traded. His reward: an MVP season and a World Series title in 1967 with the Cardinals. And no more games in the outfield.

554. Bill Skowron, All-Star First Baseman.

In 1959, Bill Skowron was having his best season. By July 25, two and a half weeks after he played in the year's first of two All-Star Games, he was batting

.298/.349/.539 with 15 home runs in 309 plate appearances with a 145 OPS+. His Yankees, however, were not doing so well, stumbling along at a .500 pace. Then Skowron got hurt—he fractured his wrist when a base runner collided with him as he reached for an errant throw (the sort of play that badly hurt Cliff Floyd a quarter-century later)—and the Yankees' chances of catching up were doomed. Elston Howard shifted to first base, but that could not paper over the team's other flaws, and the Yankees lost the pennant for only the second time since 1948. "We really missed Bill Skowron," Ryne Duren said.

555. Bill Mazeroski, All-Star Second Baseman.

In many respects, Bill Mazeroski was the Ozzie Smith of second basemen. Both left their peers (and fans) in awe of their defense and were nominal threats at bat, although each hit a famous postseason home run. Smith won 13 Gold Gloves, Mazeroski eight. Smith hit with less power, but he could run and would take more walks; Mazeroski hit 138 homers. Their batting lines are similar. Mazeroski was .260/.299/.367 with an OPS of .666 and an OPS+ of 84 (playing most of his career in expansive Forbes Field), while Smith hit .262/.337/.328 with an OPS of .665 and an OPS+ of 87. Yet Mazeroski's teammate Frank Thomas thought that Maz could have been a much better hitter and that George Sisler, a Hall of Famer who was a Pirates hitting coach, messed him up after the 1958 season, in which Mazeroski hit .275 with 19 homers at age 21. Thomas said in *We Played the Game* that Sisler "would change him into a Punch-and-Judy hitter" and added "Sisler made Maz hit the ball to all fields and he would never hit that many homers again or have that high an average." Thomas was correct on both counts.

556. Nellie Fox, All-Star Second Baseman.

In his *New Historical Baseball Abstract*, Bill James lists Nellie Fox as fifth on his list of the five worst rookies who went on to the Hall of Fame. Two are pitchers—Bob Gibson and Red Ruffing—so we'll compare only the hitters.

Player, Year	PA	H	2B-3B-HR	BA/OBP/SLG	OPS+
1. Mike Schmidt, 1973	443	72	11-0-18	.196/.324/.373	92
2. Ty Cobb, 1905	165	36	6-0-1	.236/.288/.298	85
3. Nellie Fox, 1949	296	63	6-2-0	.255/.354/.296	75

Schmidt became one of the game's premier power hitters, of course, and Cobb one of the game's very best hitters. Fox was never a consistently great batter, but he did lead the league in hits four times and in singles eight times, rarely struck out and accumulated 2,661 hits and, perhaps surprisingly, 502 extra-base hits. He was on base often enough that he scored 100 runs four times, something his speedy keystone mate, Luis Aparicio, never did once.

557. Ken Boyer, All-Star Third Baseman.

The Baseball Hall of Fame lists only 15 third basemen among its ranks, not including three Negro league stars who are in. Fewer third basemen are in the Hall than any other position, unless you count newer specialties like relievers (eight) or

DHs (maybe four: Edgar Martínez, Frank Thomas, Harold Baines, David Ortiz). Six of the third basemen in the Hall were voted in by a veterans committee, which leaves only nine third basemen voted in by the writers since balloting began in 1936. That's nine in eight and a half decades. Either third basemen haven't been very good or they have been overlooked. Ken Boyer is sometimes mentioned as a possibility. In *The Politics of Glory*, Bill James wrote, "Ken Boyer probably should be in the Hall of Fame," and that was in 1994, when memories of Boyer were still reasonably fresh. If you look at Wins Above Replacement, Boyer is below eight of the nine third basemen voted in by the writers (he ranks well above No. 9, Pie Traynor) but behind only one of the veterans committee selections (Ron Santo). Comparing the players by OPS+ (and thus stripping out defense), Boyer, who won five Gold Gloves, is ahead of five Hall of Famers.

Card 557: Ken Boyer, All-Star, has Hall of Fame credentials that surpass those of almost every third baseman voted in by a veterans committee.

Player	BA/OBP/SLG	WAR	OPS+	Player	BA/OBP/SLG	WAR	OPS+
Mike Schmidt	.267/.384/.527	106.8	148	Scott Rolen	.284/.361/.490	70.1	122
Eddie Mathews	.271/.378/.509	96.1	143	Home Run Baker	.307/.363/.448	62.8	135
Wade Boggs	.328/.415/.443	91.4	131	Jimmy Collins	.294/.344/.409	53.3	113
George Brett	.305/.373/.487	88.6	135	Deacon White	.300/.341/.379	45.5	127
Chipper Jones	.303/.401/.529	85.3	141	Pie Traynor	.320/.362/.435	38.5	107
Brooks Robinson	.267/.325/.401	78.5	105	George Kell	.306/.368/.414	37.6	112
Paul Molitor	.306/.369/.448	75.6	122	Freddie Lindstrom	.311/.351/.449	28.3	110
Ron Santo	.277/.362/.464	70.5	125	Ken Boyer	.287/.349/.462	62.8	116

558. Frank Malzone, All-Star Third Baseman.

Twenty-one American Leaguers have won at least one Gold Glove at third base in the first 66 years of the award, but only one earned it while playing for the Red Sox: Frank Malzone, from 1957 to 1959. That is three of the 66 awards. Boston infielders just haven't won many Gold Gloves—one at shortstop (Rick Burleson, 1979); four at second base (Doug Griffin, 1972; Dustin Pedroia, 2008, '13 and '14); and four more at first (Kevin Youkilis, 2007; George Scott, 1967, '68 and '71). At least Malzone was voted the Gold Glove winner. He said he felt cheated out of the 1957 Rookie of the Year Award. The Baseball Writers Association of America, *The Christian Science*

Monitor wrote, was pressured that year by a New York writer, Dan Daniel, to create a definition for "rookie" well into that September. None had existed before, but suddenly Malzone had had too many at-bats before 1957 to qualify as a rookie. And Yankees shortstop Tony Kubek, who had a season inferior to Malzone's, was selected Rookie of the Year.

559. Ernie Banks, All-Star Shortstop.

Ernie Banks and Alex Rodriguez were outlier slugging shortstops who both played the position for eight full seasons before moving defensively. They were from different eras, but their numbers were not so different. (Banks's seasons were 5 percent shorter in those pre-expansion days.)

Player	PA	H	2B-3B-HR	RBI	BB	SO	XBH	TB	BA/OBP/SLG	OPS+
Banks	5,167	1,344	209-58-296	852	448	572	563	2,557	.290/.353/.552	138
Rodriguez	5,479	1,491	279-20-340	969	550	933	639	2,830	.311/.387/.590	148

Both were generally durable (Banks led the league in games played in six of those eight seasons; Rodriguez played at least 161 games in four of them). Banks won two MVP awards and one Gold Glove (which was not awarded in his first three seasons); Rodriguez had an MVP and two Gold Gloves while playing shortstop. Rodriguez led the league in homers three times and RBIs and extra-base hits once each; Banks led in homers and RBIs twice each and extra-base hits four times. Each led the league in slugging once while at short. As young shortstops, they were the bright faces of their franchises, but at the end of their careers their teams unsubtly tried to push them out the door at age 40. While both were clearly fading, Banks was beloved by fans but unloved by his manager; Rodriguez was reviled by fans and disgraced by steroids.

560. Luis Aparicio, All-Star Shortstop.

Of all the players voted into the Hall of Fame as position players, Luis Aparicio has the lowest OPS—on-base percentage plus slugging percentage. His .653—.311 on-base percentage, .343 slugging percentage—is at the bottom of the abyss below Joe Tinker (.661), Rabbit Maranville (.657) and Ray Schalk (.656), whose careers ended in 1916, 1935 and 1929. Obviously, it was not his bat that got Aparicio into the Hall (or earned him All-Star selections in 10 seasons). Fangraphs calculated Aparicio as fifth in defensive runs above average since World War II, behind only Ozzie Smith, Brooks Robinson, Mark Belanger and Cal Ripken. Interestingly, four of the top five played for the Orioles, although Aparicio was in Baltimore for only five years.

561. Hank Aaron, All-Star Outfielder.

No one made the All-Star team in more seasons than Hank Aaron did (21), and no one played in more All-Star Games (he, Willie Mays and Stan Musial all played in 24). The only years Aaron did not make his All-Star team were as a rookie in 1954 (he really had no claim despite 11 homers at the All-Star break) and in his final season in 1976. The All-Star Game was no home run derby for Aaron, who hit only two homers in 72 Midsummer Classic plate appearances. In fact, Aaron did not hit well at all in All-Star Games, posting a .194/.222/.284 line. Musial and Mays far outhit him in the games. Musial batted .317/.394/.635 with a record six homers in All-Star Games, while Mays hit .307/.366/.533 with three homers.

562. Al Kaline, All-Star Outfielder.

For two decades, Al Kaline and Roberto Clemente had overlapping careers as the best right fielders in their leagues. They were very different but very potent hitters, and both were superlative in right field. Kaline won 10 Gold Gloves, Clemente 12. Kaline was selected to the All-Star team 15 times, Clemente a dozen. Clemente famously just reached an offensive milestone (3,000 hits); Kaline agonizingly just missed two (399 homers, .297 batting average). All while playing for a single team.

Player	PA	H	2B-3B-HR	RBI	BB	SO	BA/OBP/SLG	OPS+
Kaline	11,597	3,007	498–75–399	1,582	1,277	1,020	.297/.376/.480	134
Clemente	10,212	3,000	440–166–240	1,305	621	1,230	.317/.359/.475	130

563. Willie Mays, All-Star Outfielder.

The notion that Willie Mays's offense was diminished by playing in Candlestick Park has been floated here and there pretty much since that wind-blown ballpark opened in 1960. As if 660 home runs, 3,293 hits, a .301 batting average and an OPS+ of 155 didn't suggest he could hit anywhere. Bill James, using the far less complete statistics available at the time, wrote in the 1985 version of his *Historical Baseball Abstract* that he didn't think it was so. Nearly four decades later, the rich statistical data available indicate that playing at Candlestick had a minimal effect on Mays's numbers. Let's look at his statistics from his three home ballparks as a Giant and skip his 151 plate appearances as an aging Met.

Ballpark	BA/OBP/SLG	PA	HR	PA/HR
Polo Grounds	.318/.387/.601	1,690	98	17.2
Seals Stadium	.307/389/.560	661	32	20.7
Candlestick Park	.298/.387/.563	3,524	203	17.4

It didn't really matter where Mays played; his home/road splits are unbelievably similar. (Mays hit a few homers at the Polo Grounds as a visitor against the early Mets.)

	PA	R	H	2B	HR	RBI	BB	TB	BA/OBP/SLG
Home	6,027	1,017	1,583	258	335	929	721	2,968	.302/.387/.567
Road	6,469	1,043	1,700	265	325	974	746	3,098	.301/.382/.549

Heck, he was even hit by pitches almost exactly as many times at home as on the road: 23–21.

564. Mickey Mantle, All-Star Outfielder.

Much myth-making has gone into the story of Mickey Mantle, plenty of it because of his tape-measure home runs. (And that's a term that came into vogue because of Mantle.) The gold standard for stories about his titanic blasts is usually the 565-foot (perhaps) blow he hit off Chuck Stobbs. But a website devoted to Mantle—Mickey Mantle: The American Dream—puts that as seventh longest on Mantle's long-hit parade. Here's how the website measured his longest homers. (Myths may apply.)

	Distance	Date	Pitcher	Ballpark	HR Side
1.	734 feet	May 22, 1963	Bill Fischer, Athletics	Yankee Stadium	Left
2.	656 feet	March 26, 1951	Tom Lovrich, USC	Bovard Field	Left
3.	650 feet	June 11, 1953	Art Houtteman, Tigers	Briggs Stadium	Left
4.	643 feet	Sept. 10, 1960	Paul Foytack, Tigers	Tiger Stadium	Left
5.	630 feet	Sept. 12, 1953	Billy Hoeft, Tigers	Yankee Stadium	Left
6.	620 feet	May 30, 1956	Pedro Ramos, Senators	Yankee Stadium	Left
7.	565 feet	April 17, 1953	Chuck Stobbs, Senators	Griffith Stadium	Right
8.	550 feet	June 5, 1955	Billy Pierce, White Sox	Comiskey Park	Right
9.	535 feet	July 6, 1953	Frank Fanovich, A's	Connie Mack Stadium	Right
10.	530 feet	April 28, 1953	Bob Cain, Browns	Busch Stadium	Right

That 734 feet is not an actual distance, but the website's estimate of the potential distance of a ball that barely missed clearing the façade on top of Yankee Stadium. Don't buy 734 feet? A physicist named James McDonald estimated the blast at 650 to 700 feet had the façade not been in the way, *The Los Angeles Times* reported. Mantle did call it "the hardest ball I ever hit." The second-longest homer on the list was in a spring training game against the University of Southern California, so perhaps it needs an asterisk. Five of these long shots came in 1953, when the 21-year-old Mantle hit only 21 homers.

565. Wes Covington, All-Star Outfielder.

This is a curious card because Wes Covington was never an official All-Star. He hit like one in 1958, as a platoon player—.330/.380/.622 with 24 home runs in only 324 plate appearances. Against right-handed pitchers he hit like Lou Gehrig: a .366/.413/.715 line, with 23 homers in a mere 259 plate appearances. (Against left-handers he hit like José Uribe.) For the first half of 1959, Covington hit well again, although with doubles power, not home

Card 564: Did Mickey Mantle, All-Star, really hit a 734-foot home run? Maybe. And he may have hit five other homers more than 600 feet.

run power. Then he began to slump and eventually tore ligaments in an ankle, ending his season on August 20. Losing his bat probably did not cost the Braves the pennant; they finished 22–12 without him to force a tie with the Dodgers before losing in a playoff series. "He'd have to hit .400 to help a club," Bob Buhl said in *We Played the Game*, "because he wasn't that good in left field."

566. Roy Sievers, All-Star Outfielder.

The St. Louis Browns, perpetual losers who were founded in 1902, played their final game in 1953 before moving to Baltimore. By 1965, vestiges of the Browns in the major leagues were hard to find. Slugging Roy Sievers, 38, was trying to hold on to a job with the Senators. Don Larsen, 35, was hanging on with the Astros, who, bad as they were, traded him to Baltimore two weeks into the season for a light-hitting outfielder whom they never employed in Houston. Sievers's bat and power were done, and in mid–May the Senators released him. Larsen, though, clung to a spot in the Orioles' bullpen, the only remaining Brown in the majors … until the Athletics signed the 59-year-old (or so) Satchel Paige to start a game on September 25 in a promotional effort to drum up attendance. (It worked, sort of; Paige drew a crowd of 9,289 for a team that averaged fewer than 7,000 fans a game at home.) Paige threw three shutout innings, which would have made him the last Brown to play in the majors, except Larsen returned in 1967 for three games, and four innings, with the Cubs. And with that, the last chapter of the Browns, who never won a World Series, was finally written.

567. Del Crandall, All-Star Catcher.

It was hard to get noticed as a defensive catcher in the National League for most of the 1950s with Roy Campanella behind the plate in Brooklyn. But Del Crandall managed. He led NL catchers in assists six times, in runners caught stealing five times, and in fielding percentage four times. He also led, six times, in Total Zone Runs, whose numbers go back only to 1953 (thus missing a big chunk of Campanella's prime). Crandall also won four Gold Gloves, which were not awarded until 1957. John Roseboro, Campanella's successor with the Dodgers, called Crandall "the most complete catcher during my time in the league." In *Glory Days with the Dodgers*, Roseboro said: "He could catch the bad pitch and block the plate. He didn't have a strong arm, but he made up for it with a quick release and accuracy." Braves manager Charlie Grimm referred to Crandall as his "assistant manager"—the same praise Casey Stengel heaped on Yogi Berra.

568. Gus Triandos, All-Star Catcher.

When Gus Triandos was sent to the Orioles by the Yankees in the famed 17-player trade in late 1954, he was considered a "fine prospect," according to newspaper accounts, but not always a catcher. When he was talked about as a catcher, he ranked behind Hal Smith in the players traded to Baltimore. And when the 1955 season began, it was Smith behind the plate for the Orioles, with Triandos at first base. But Triandos wound up being one of the most valuable players in the trade. He was the Orioles' full-time catcher for six seasons and hit 142 homers for Baltimore, while Smith lasted only a season and a half in Baltimore. Only two other players, Gene Woodling (33.3) and Don Larsen (18.4), had higher career totals of Wins Above Replacement than Triandos (14.1). (Surprisingly, the key player in the trade, Bob Turley, had only 13.2 WAR; his peak was high but not long. And Smith, who would become known for a big homer in the 1960 World Series, had only 4.2 WAR and caught as many as 100 games only twice.) There was considerable filler in the big trade; nine of the players had sub-zero career WAR and another player never made it to the majors. Triandos might have been even more valuable had he been deployed differently. Bill James wrote in his *New Historical Baseball Abstract* that Triandos, "had he not been a catcher and had he reached the majors earlier, could very probably have hit 400 or even 500 major league homers."

569. Bob Friend, Right-Handed All-Star Pitcher.
Bob Friend was the Pirates' ace from 1955 to 1963, one reason they rose from a last-place team in 1955 to a winning team in four of the last five seasons in that stretch. His won-lost record was not exceptional at 142–138 for a .507 percentage, but it was better than his team's (.490). Curiously, he fared little better against the ordinary teams of that era than against the Dodgers and the Braves, perennial contenders who won six of those nine pennants. Friend was 39–40 with a 3.43 ERA against the Braves and 20–20 with a 3.48 ERA against the Dodgers, while going 103–98, 3.22 against the rest of the National League. Another curiosity: Friend was 24–41, 3.93, in his career against the Phillies, who played .462 ball from 1951, when Friend broke in, through 1961, just before expansion.

570. Bob Turley, Right-Handed All-Star Pitcher.
Bob Turley pitched only one season in Baltimore, but he continued to live in the Baltimore area. He even joined with a group of local businessmen to open a bowling alley, Bob Turley's Bowl, in the Baltimore suburb of Bel Air in 1960, although by then he had been pitching for the Yankees for five years. One of the co-founders recalled to *The Baltimore Sun* that Turley's star presence helped attract Baltimore Colts players, including Johnny Unitas. Turley and Unitas once met for a bowling match (Turley won, three games to two), but a sports columnist noted that they hardly threatened the game's immortals. (Turley apparently threw more strikes on the diamond.) Bowling and baseball had enduring ties. Cap Anson opened lanes in Chicago in 1898 when the game was getting its footing. John McGraw and Wilbert Robinson owned lanes in Baltimore when they played for the 19th-century Orioles. Everett Scott, a former captain of the Yankees and the Red Sox, opened a bowling alley in Fort Wayne, Indiana, early in the 20th century. Ballplayer ownership of lanes mushroomed in the 1950s; Gil Hodges (Brooklyn), Pee Wee Reese (Louisville, Kentucky), Nellie Fox (Chambersburg, Pennsylvania) and Bobby Shantz (Chalfont, Pennsylvania) all owned lanes, for example. And Yogi Berra and Phil Rizzuto shared ownership of a bowling alley in Clifton, New Jersey. These ballplayers were mostly owners, not bowlers, but there have been some excellent ballplayer-bowlers: Pitcher John Burkett, who won 166 games, earned prize money in several professional tournaments and had rolled 32 perfect games as of 2022. Mookie Betts once rolled a perfect

game, too. Occasionally it worked the other way: Earl Anthony, named the Greatest Bowler Ever by the American Bowling Congress, was offered a $35,000 bonus in 1960 to sign with the Orioles, Baseball Reference said, but the deal fell through when he tore his rotator cuff the next day. He went to work as a forklift operator and joined the company bowling team.

571. Warren Spahn, Left-Handed All-Star Pitcher.

Only five pitchers have won more games than Warren Spahn, who had 363 victories, and none of them threw a pitch after 1930. And no pitcher has earned an All-Star berth in as many years as Spahn, who was honored in 14 years from 1947 to 1963. Tom Seaver was named an All-Star in 12 years, Roger Clemens in 11, and Steve Carlton, Tom Glavine and Randy Johnson in 10 each. Greg Maddux, the closest modern pitcher to Spahn in wins with 355, was an All-Star only eight times, as was Nolan Ryan (324 wins). Only one pitcher, Cy Young, had more seasons with at least 20 victories; he had 15, while Spahn and Christy Mathewson had 13 each. Spahn won 23 games at age 42. And he led his league in wins a record eight times, and in the '40s, '50s and '60s. How did he do all this? "You have to be able to throw strikes," Spahn said, according to his *New York Times* obituary. "But you try not to whenever possible." One oddity: He had 363 wins on the mound and 363 hits at bat.

572. Billy Pierce, Left-Handed All-Star Pitcher.

Billy Pierce earned more victories than any other White Sox left-hander, with 186, but in 1954 it was not clear he would get there. He developed a sore arm, missed three weeks in June and had his worst season since 1949. His record was 9–10, and his ERA soared by three-quarters of a run to 3.48. That fall, the Yankees, seeking pitching help after losing the pennant for the first time since 1948 and sitting on a wealth of infield and catching talent, took interest in Pierce. *The New York Times* reported that the White Sox wanted "a lot" for Pierce—"a lot" being 23-year-old third baseman Andy Carey. Carey had just hit .302/.373/.423 with a 121 OPS+ while playing above-average defense. Yankees general manager George Weiss was not interested in giving up that much for Pierce, though, especially as the team had just pulled off its huge trade for Bob Turley and Don Larsen. That turned out best for the White Sox: They had undervalued Pierce, and the Yankees had overvalued Carey. Carey was a pedestrian hitter the rest of his career and played as many as 130 games only twice. Pierce, meanwhile, was used judiciously the first month of the 1955 season and then regained his form. He led the American League that year with a 1.97 ERA—the runner-up, Whitey Ford, was far behind at 2.63, and Pierce was the only qualifying pitcher in the '50s to post a sub–2.00 ERA. Over his final seven seasons in Chicago, he compiled a 110–73 record (.601) with a 3.17 ERA and 122 ERA+. Pierce was small, even for his era—about 5 feet 10 and 160 pounds—but he was definitely a power pitcher. "That little so-and-so is a marvel," Joe DiMaggio said once after batting against Pierce, according to Pierce's *Detroit Free Press* obituary. "So little—and all that speed. And I mean speed. He got me out of there on a fastball in the ninth that I'd have needed a telescope to see."

Extra Innings

Ted Williams, Outfielder, Boston Red Sox.
Ted Williams did not have a 1959 Topps card, but no story of '50s baseball (or baseball cards) is complete without him. According to a history of his trading cards at Dean's Cards, Williams savvily played companies against one another and wound up in the sets of four companies during his career: Play Ball (1939–41), Bowman (1950–51, '54), Topps (1954–58) and Fleer (1959–60). He was in both the Bowman and Topps sets in 1954, after he ended his exclusivity with Bowman for a better deal, and he appeared on the first and last cards of the Topps set. But for 1959, he left Topps to sign with Fleer, which agreed to put out an 80-card Williams-only set. His baseball numbers for the 1950s are eye-popping, even though Williams missed most of two seasons while serving in the Korean War: .336/.476/.622, with 227 home runs, in 995 games. And that decade *lowered* his career numbers.

Bibliography

Aaron, Hank, with Lonnie Wheeler. *I Had a Hammer: The Hank Aaron Story.* New York: HarperCollins, 1991.

Allen, Maury. *Yankees: Where Have You Gone?* Champaign, IL: Sports Publishing, 2004.

Barra, Allan. *Yogi Berra: Eternal Yankee.* New York: W.W. Norton, 2009.

Bjarkman, Peter C., and Bill Nowlin. *Cuban Baseball Legends: An Alternative Universe.* Phoenix: Society for American Baseball Research, 2016.

Bouton, Jim. *Ball Four.* New York: Dell, 1970.

Boyd, Brendan C., and Fred C. Harris. *The Great American Baseball Card Flipping, Trading and Bubble Gum Book.* New York: Ticknor & Fields, 1991.

Breslin, Jimmy. *Can't Anybody Here Play This Game?* New York: Viking Press, 1963.

Brosnan, Jim. *The Long Season.* Ann Arbor: University of Michigan Press, 1960.

_____. *Pennant Race.* New York: Harper & Brothers, 1962.

Chieger, Bob. *The Cubbies: Quotations on the Chicago Cubs.* New York: Atheneum, 1987.

Clavin, Tom, and Danny Peary. *Roger Maris: Baseball's "Reluctant Hero."* New York: Simon & Schuster, 2010.

Cohen, Robert W. *The 50 Greatest Players in Philadelphia Phillies History.* Guilford, CT: Lyons Press, 2022.

Creamer, Robert W. *Stengel: His Life and Times.* New York: Simon & Schuster, 1984.

Dickson, Paul. *Leo Durocher: Baseball's Prodigal Son.* New York: Bloomsbury, 2017.

Duren, Ryne, with Tom Sabellico. *I Can See Clearly Now.* Chula Vista, CA: Aventine Press, 2003.

Durocher, Leo, with Ed Linn. *Nice Guys Finish Last.* New York: Simon & Schuster, 1975.

Eisenberg, John. *From 33rd Street to Camden Yards: An Oral History of the Baltimore Orioles.* New York: McGraw-Hill, 2001.

Fallon, Michael. *Dodgerland: Decadent Los Angeles and the 1977–78 Dodgers.* Lincoln: University of Nebraska Press, 2016.

Fitts, Robert K. *Wally Yonamine: The Man Who Changed Japanese Baseball.* Lincoln: University of Nebraska Press, 2008.

Freedman, Lew. *Early Wynn, the Go-Go Sox and the 1959 World Series.* Jefferson, NC: McFarland, 2009.

_____. *Hard-Luck Harvey Haddix and the Greatest Game Ever Lost.* Jefferson, NC: McFarland, 2009.

Frommer, Harvey. *New York City Baseball: The Last Golden Age: 1947–1957.* New York: Macmillan, 1987.

Giglio, James. *Musial: From Stash to Stan the Man.* Columbia: University of Missouri Press, 2001.

Gutlon, Jerry M. *It Was Never About the Babe: The Red Sox, Racism, Mismanagement, and the Curse of the Bambino.* New York: Skyhorse, 2015.

Hano, Arnold. *A Day in the Bleachers.* Cambridge, MA: Da Capo Press, 1995.

Hiner, Jason. *Mac's Boys: Branch McCracken and the Legendary 1953 Hurryin' Hoosiers.* Bloomington: Indiana University Press, 2006.

Jackson, Ransom. *Handsome Ransom Jackson: Accidental Big Leaguer.* Lanham, MD: Rowman & Littlefield, 2016.

James, Bill. *The Bill James Historical Baseball Abstract.* New York: Villard, 1986.

_____. *The New Bill James Historical Baseball Abstract.* New York: Free Press, 2001.

_____. *The Politics of Glory.* New York: Macmillan, 1994.

Kahn, Roger. *The Boys of Summer.* New York: Harper & Row, 1972.

_____. *A Season in the Sun.* New York: Berkley, 1978.

Kelley, Brent. *Baseball's Bonus Babies.* Jefferson, NC: McFarland, 2006.

Kepner, Tyler. *K: A History of Baseball in Ten Pitches.* New York: Anchor Books, 2019.

Krell, David. *1962: Baseball and America in the Time of JFK.* Lincoln: University of Nebraska Press, 2021.

Leavy, Jane. *Sandy Koufax: A Lefty's Legacy.* New York: HarperCollins, 2002.

Lewers, Bill. *Six Decades of Baseball: A Personal Narrative.* Bloomington, IN: Xlibris, 2009.

Marazzi, Rich, and Len Fiorito. *Baseball Players of the 1950s.* Jefferson, NC: McFarland, 2009.

Moffi, Roger, and Jonathan Kronstadt. *Crossing the Line: Black Major Leaguers, 1947–1959.* Iowa City: University of Iowa Press, 1994.

Neyer, Rob, and Bill James. *The Neyer/James Guide to Pitching.* New York: Fireside, 2004.

O'Keeffe, Michael, and Teri Thompson. *The Card: Collectors, Con Men, and the True Story of History's Most Desired Baseball Card.* New York: Harper, 2007.
Okrent, Daniel. *Nine Innings.* New York: Ticknor & Fields, 1985.
Peary, Danny. *We Played the Game: 65 Players Remember Baseball's Greatest Era, 1947–65.* New York: Hyperion, 1994.
Perry, Gaylord, and Bob Sudyk. *Me and the Spitter.* New York: E.P. Dutton, 1974.
Pluto, Terry. *The Curse of Rocky Colavito.* New York: Simon & Schuster, 1994.
Posnanski, Joe. *The Baseball 100.* New York: Avid Reader Press, 2021.
Rapoport, Ron. *Let's Play Two: The Legend of Mr. Cub, the Life of Ernie Banks.* New York: Hachette, 2019.
Roberts, Robin, and Paul C. Rogers III. *The Whiz Kids and the 1950 Pennant.* Philadelphia: Temple University Press, 1996.
Robinson, Frank, with Dave Anderson. *Frank: The First.* New York: Holt, Rinehart & Winston, 1976.
Roseboro, John, with Bill Libby. *Glory Days with the Dodgers and Other Days with Others.* New York: Atheneum Books, 1978.
Scimonelli, Paul. *Joe Cambria: International Super Scout of the Washington Senators.* Jefferson, NC: McFarland, 2023.
Shropshire, Mike. *Seasons in Hell.* Lincoln: University of Nebraska Press, 2005.
Stein, Fred. *And the Skipper Bats Cleanup.* Jefferson, NC: McFarland, 2002.
Sullivan, Frank. *Life Is More Than Nine Innings.* Honolulu: Editions Limited, 2008.
Turbow, Jason, with Michael Duca. *The Baseball Codes: Beanballs, Sign-Stealing, and Bench-Clearing Brawls.* New York: Anchor, 2011.
Tygiel, Jules. *Baseball's Great Experiment: Jackie Robinson and His Legacy.* New York: Oxford University Press, 1983.
Vecsey, George. *Stan Musial: An American Life.* New York: Ballantine, 2011.
White, Gaylon. *The Bilko Athletic Club.* Lanham, MD: Rowman & Littlefield, 2014.
Whiting, Robert. *The Chrysanthemum and the Bat.* New York: Dodd, Mead, 1977.
Zminda, Don, ed. *Go-Go to Glory: The 1959 Chicago White Sox.* Skokie, IL: ACTA, 2009.
Zumsteg, Derek. *The Cheater's Guide to Baseball.* Boston: Mariner Books, 2007.

Publications

Akron Beacon-Journal, Atlanta Journal-Constitution, Baltimore Business Journal, Baltimore Sun, Baseball Digest, Boston Globe, Chicago Sun-Times, Chicago Tribune, Christian Science Monitor, Cleveland Plain Dealer, Dalton (Georgia) *Daily Citizen News, Detroit Free Press, Detroit News, Greenwich* (Connecticut) *Time, Hartford Courant, Houston Chronicle, Jamestown* (New York) *Post-Herald, Lakeland* (Florida) *Ledger, Lansing* (Michigan) *State Journal, Los Angeles Sentinel, Los Angeles Times, Maysville* (Kentucky) *Ledger Independent, Middletown* (Connecticut) *Press, Milwaukee Journal Sentinel, Moultrie* (Georgia) *Observer, Nanticoke* (Pennsylvania) *Times Leader, Newsday, New York Times, New York World-Telegram, Virginian-Pilot* (Norfolk, Virginia), *Utica* (New York) *Observer-Dispatch, Palm Beach* (Florida) *Post, Philadelphia Daily News, Pittsburgh Post-Gazette, Puerto Rico Herald, SABR Research Journal, San Francisco Chronicle, San Jose Mercury News, Saturday Evening Post, Smithsonian Magazine, Southern Illinoisan, Spokane Spokesman-Review, Sporting News, Sports Illustrated, Twin Cities Pioneer Press, Washington Post*

Websites

Ballparks.com, Baseball Almanac, Baseball Happenings, Baseball History Comes Alive, Baseball in Wartime, Baseball Reference, Bleacher Report, Bowl.com, Chicago Baseball Museum, College Black Nines, Deadball Era, DeansCards, Encyclopedia of Baseball Catchers, ESPN.com, Fangraphs, Friars on Base, Hardball Times, Jewish Virtual Library, Mickey Mantle: The American Dream, MiLB.com, MLB.com, (Mostly) Complete List of Knuckleball Pitchers, Moultrie Ram Roundup, Pinstripe Alley, Radical Baseball, RetroSimba, Ringer, RIPBaseball, SABR Bio Project, Shepherd Express, Sports Collectors Digest, This Date in Astros History, This Great Game, Washington Baseball History

Index

Numbers in ***bold italics*** indicate pages with illustrations

Aaron, Hank 7, 12, 42, 58, 62, 70, 77, 95, 110, 135–136, 139–140, 143, 156, 164–165, 170, 171, 207, 211–212
Abad, Fernando 67
Abernathy, Ted 56–57
Abilene Christian College 175
Abrams, Cal 103
Acker, Tom 66, 105
Ackerman, Michael B. 125
Adams, Babe 50
Adams, Bobby 82, 83
Adcock, Joe 77, 110, 201, 207
Agee, Tommie 44
Agganis, Harry 53
Aguirre, Hank 15–16
The Akron Beacon Journal 65
All-Star teams 10, 11, 12, 13, 14, 19, 24, 34, 35, 36, 38, 39, 52, 65, 69, 84, 89, 95, 97, 107, 109, 124, 129, 132, 134, 137, 143, 154, 160, 170, 175, 208, 211, 212, 216
Allen, Dick 112, 127
Allen, Mel 205
Allison, Bob 40, 41, 142
Almada, Mel 128
Almonte, Danny 55
Alomar, Robbie 156
Alou, Felipe 36, 48, 66, 112, 177, 184
Alou, Jesus 36
Alou, Matty 36, 204
Alou, Moisés 36
Alston, Walt 105, 149, 151, 162, 182
Altman, George 189–190
Alvarado, Frank 98
Álvarez, Ozzie 186
Amaro, Rubén 59, 204
Amateur draft 1, 120
American Association 112, 114, 126, 204
American Basketball Association (ABA) 10
American Bowling Congress 216

American League 11, 153, 158
Amoros, Sandy 182
Anadarko, Oklahoma 162
And the Skipper Bats Cleanup 196
Anderson, Bob 64, 163
Anderson, Dave (ballplayer) 173
Anderson, Dave (journalist) 154, 198
Anderson, Harry 31
Anderson, Sparky (George) 7, 118–119, 166
The Andy Griffith Show 144
Anson, Cap 172, 215
Anthony, Earl 216
Antonelli, Johnny 134, 154
Aparicio, Luis 2, 14, 89, 90, 108, 146, 147, 181, 203, 209, 211
Appier, Kevin 122
Ardmore Cardinals 70
Árias, Rudy 201, 202
Arizona Instructional League 83
Arizona-Texas League 136
Arkansas Travelers 22
Armbrister, Ed 199
Arroyo, Luis 99, 127
Ashburn, Richie 33, 103, 110–111
Ashcraft, Jennifer 124
Aspromonte, Ken 153–***154***
Associated Press 24, 122, 125
Astrodome 163, 167–168
The Athletic 44
Atlanta Braves 95, 162, 164, 189; *see also* Boston Braves; Milwaukee Braves
Atlanta Crackers 39, 71
The Atlanta Journal-Constitution 95
Attanasio, Ed 115
Auburn University 127, 189
Auerbach, Red 53, 113
Auker, Eldon 57
Austin, Jimmy 69

Autry, Gene 65
Averill, Earl (father) 103–104
Averill, Earl (son) 103–104
Ávila, Bobby 30, 90, 128

Bagwell, Jeff 77
Bahamas 72, 77
Bahnsen, Stan 127, 153
Bailey, Ed 38, 70
Baines, Harold 210
Baker, Del 37
Baker, Dusty 156
Baker, Gene ***78***-79
Baker, Home Run 210
Ball, Neal 162
Ball Four 46, 55, 64, 127, 143, 147, 158, 168, 186, 196
Ballparks.com 13
Baltimore Business Journal 8
Baltimore Colts 215
Baltimore Orioles 7, 11, 19, 20, 25, 30, 32, 34, 35, 41, 48, 57, 61, 63, 68, 70, 73, 83, 89, 92, 95, 102, 107, 115, 117, 122, 128, 134, 140, 148, 153, 158, 159, 161, 168, 172, 173, 177, 178, 180, 184, 187, 189, 192, 193, 198, 199, 202, 211, 214, 215, 216; *see also* St. Louis Browns
The Baltimore Sun 32, 83, 102, 115, 146, 157, 193, 215
Bamberger, George 198
Bando, Sal 185
Banks, Ernie 24, 33, 49, 64, 75, 83, 91, 123, 130, 158, 170–***171***, 211
Bannister, Roger 181
Barber, Steve 48
Barclay, Curt 105–106
Barfield, Jesse 204
Barra, Allen 142
Barragan, Cuno 14
Bartkowicz, Peaches 35
Baseball Almanac 17, 35, 126, 130, 177
Baseball America 8, 39

Index

Baseball and America in the Time of JFK 38
baseball cards 54, 71, 160
Baseball Digest 35
Baseball History Comes Alive 196
Baseball in Wartime 60
The Baseball 100 136, 145, 160, 167, 169–170, 182, 194
Baseball Players of the 1950s: A Biographical Dictionary 37, 192
Baseball Reference ix, 3, 16, 25, 72, 75, 83, 122, 126, 128, 129, 163, 179, 183, 186, 216
Baseball's Bonus Babies 31, 109, 119
Baseball's Great Experiment 52, 70, 108, 203
Batavia Pirates 79
Bates, Del 37
Battey, Earl 29, 39–40, 160
batting helmets 8, 91
Bauer, Hank 79, 102, 197
Bauer, Trevor 190
Bauman, Joe 126
Baumann, Frank 14, 54
Baumholtz, Frank 46, 156
Baxes, Jim 206
Baxes, Mike 136
Baylor, Don 193
Beamer, Frank 144
Beamon, Charlie 63
Bécquer, Julio 33
Bedingfield, Gary 60
Belanger, Mark 146, 211
Bell, Buddy 112, 129
Bell, David 112
Bell, Gary 114
Bell, George 204
Bell, Gus 41, 129, 143
Bella, Zeke 85
Belle, Albert 188
Beltré, Adrián 69, 156
Bench, Johnny 29, 203
Berberet, Lou 34
Berg, Moe 25
Bernier, Carlos 73, 78
Berra, Dale 104
Berra, Yogi 16, 34, 41, 50, 60, 85, 97, 99, 104, 108, 137, 142, 156, 182, 187, 195, 206, 207, 214, 215
Berres, Ray 54
Bertoia, Reno 30–31
Bessent, Don 26
The Best We've Got: The Carl Erskine Story 72
Betts, Mookie 215
Beyond the Valley of the Dolls 176
Biasatti, Hank 46
Bieber, Shane 190
Big Ten 32
Biggio, Cavan 104

Biggio, Craig 104
Bilko, Steve 17–**18**, 65, 162–163
The Bilko Athletic Club 18
The Bill James Historical Baseball Abstract 17, 34, 40, 104, 108, 115, 124, 143, 145, 158, 187, 212; *see also The New Bill James Historical Baseball Abstract*
The Bingo Long Traveling All-Stars and Motor Kings 86
The Black Aces: Baseball's Only African-American Twenty-Game Winners 62
Black Sox (Chicago) 2, 22, 129, 202
Blackburn, Ron 144
Blackwell, Ewell 144
Blanchard, Johnny 16, 40, 166
Blasingame, Don 180
Blaylock, Bob 70
Blaylock, Gary 202
Blefary, Curt 108, 193
Blue, Vida 140
Blyleven, Bert 140, 149
Boggs, Wade 198, 210
Bolger, Jim 14
Bolling, Frank 95
Bond, Walt 186
Bonds, Barry 92, 126, 164, 165
Bonus babies 1, 14, 21, 31, 35, 39, 48, 82, 84, 110, 116, 119, 122, 134, 159, 183, 190
Boone, Aaron 85, 112
Boone, Bob 85, 112
Boone, Bret 85
Boone, Ray 85
Boozer, Bob 10
Boros, Steve 116
Boston Braves 17, 21, 55, 82, 95, 98, 112, 134, 162; *see also* Atlanta Braves; Milwaukee Braves
Boston Bruins 82
Boston Celtics 82, 112, 180
Boston College 82
Boston Globe 15, 159, 178
Boston Red Sox 8, 12, 14, 17, 21, 26, 30, 32, 36, 39, 42, 47, 49, 52, 53, 54, 56, 58, 61, 66, 73, 76, 77, 78, 82, 88, 90, 91, 93, 97, 98, 100, 102, 104, 107, 108, 111, 114, 122, 127, 131, 132, 136, 143, 151, 159, 162, 167, 172, 173, 178, 181, 184, 189, 193, 194, 199, 200, 202, 210, 215, 217
Boswell, Tom 105
Bouchee, Ed 16–17
Boudreau, Lou 39, 132, 196, 197
Bouton, Jim 46, 55, 64, 66, 99, 127, 143, 147, 158, 168, 175, 186, 196
Bovard Field 213
Bowman, Bob 73

Bowman baseball cards 141, 217
Bowsfield, Ted 78
Boyd, Bob 30, 31
Boyd, Dennis (Oil Can) 77
Boyer, Cletis **84**–85, 92, 160, 187
Boyer, Cloyd 84
Boyer, Ken 84, 113–114, 120, 156, 209–**210**
Boyer, Len 85
Boyer, Lynn 84
Boyer, Mabel 84
Boyer, Ron 84
Boyer, Wayne 84
The Boys of Summer 10–11, 72
Bragan, Bobby 174
Branca, Ralph 145
Brandt, Jackie 102
Braun, Ryan 174
Brecheen, Harry 66
Bregman, Alex 174
Breslin, Jimmy 155
Bressoud, Eddie 10, 90, 153
Brett, George 50, 111, 152, 210
Brewer, Tom 21, 22, 121
Bridges, Rocky **111**
Briggs, John 59
Briggs, Johnny 59
Briggs, Walter 67
Briggs Stadium (also Tiger Stadium) 67, 77, 213
Bright, Harry 194–195
Brinkman, Eddie 97
Brock, Lou 44, 74, 101–102, 117
Brodowski, Dick 131, 132
Broglio, Ernie 63, 101–102, 117
Brohamer, Jack 208
Brooklyn Dodgers 1, 10, 11, 14, 22, 42, 52, 54, 55, 58, 81, 85, 103, 105, 106, 108, 109, 112, 118, 129, 136, 144, 145, 162, 167, 170, 172, 179, 181, 182, 201, 206, 207, 214, 215; *see also* Los Angeles Dodgers
Brosius, Scott 17
Brosnan, Jim 9, 37, **64**, 94, 147, 166–167, 175, 206
Brown, Bill 33
Brown, Bobby 187
Brown, Buster 82
Brown, Dick 23, 24
Brown, Ed 33
Brown, Hal 178
Brown, Joe L. 75, 79
Brown, Three Finger 190
Brown, Walter 33
Brown, William 33
Browning, Tom 193
Bruntlett, Eric 161
Bruton, Bill 55, 77
Buddin, Don 10, 14
Buford, Don 180
Bugscuffle, Oklahoma 82
Buhl, Bob 32, 62, 122, 154, 156, 201, 207, 214

Index

Bunning, Jim 172
Burdette, Lew 57, 62, 117, 160, 207
Burgess, Smoky 20, 35, 156–157, 187, 201
Burick, Si 186
Burkett, John 215
Burks, Ellis 77
Burleson, Rick 151, 210
Burns, George 162
Burns, Tom 88
Burnside, Pete 82, 125
Burton, Ellis 76
Busch Stadium 213
Busch, August 50, 197
Bush Stadium 152
Buzhardt, John 40–*41*
Byrd, Harry 68
Byrne, Tommy 98

Cabin Fever 178
Cabrera, Asdrúbal 162
Caesar, Julius 162
Cain, Bob 213
Cairo, Illinois 82
California League 63, 90
The (California) Valley Times 111
Callison, Johnny 39, 41
Cambria, Joe 33
Campanella, Roy 23, 108, 160, 170, 171, 175, 206–207, 214
Campbell, Jim 166
Canadian Football League (CFL) 7
Candiotti, Tom 184
Candlestick Park 10, 212
Canseco, José 134, 183
Canseco, Ozzie 183
Can't Anybody Here Play This Game? 155
Caray, Chip 95
Caray, Harry 95
Caray, Skip 95
Carbo, Bernie 199
Card: Collectors, Con Men, and the True Story of History's Most Desired Card 54
Cardwell, Don 109, 179
Carew, Rod 131, 163
Carey, Andy 18–19, 187–188, 216
Caribbean Series 80
Carlton, Steve 17, 80, 216
Carmel, Duke 56
Carnaroli, Hank 32
Carolina League 85
Carpenter, Bob 31
Carrasquel, Alex 89
Carrasquel, Chico 89
Carroll, Tom 190
Carty, Rico 40
Casale, Jerry 167
Cash, Norm 39, 188–189
Castro, Fidel 165

Causey, Wayne 157
Cavaretta, Phil 197
CBS Sports 159
Ceccarelli, Art 75, 199
Cedeño, César 163
Cepeda, Orlando 26, 33, 66, 127, 139–140, 177, 184, 201, 208
Cerv, Bob 35, 195, 208
Cey, Ron 81
Chadwick, Henry 121
Chalmers Award 159
Chandler, Happy 66
cheating 13, 188
The Chicago Sun-Times 109
The Chicago Tribune 9, 33, 51, 76, 83, 89, 179, 214
Chicago White Sox 2, 6, 11, 13, 14, 15, 18, 19, 21, 22, 26, 31, 33, 36, 39, 40, 41, 47, 48, 51, 52, 53, 54, 59, 62, 71, 82, 87, 89, 94, 96, 97, 100, 105, 108, 114, 119, 123, 129, 130, 134, 137, 147, 148, 150, 154, 159, 160, 166, 170, 173, 176, 181, 188, 189, 192, 194, 201, 216
Chicago White Stockings 88
Chiti, Harry **29**, 149
Chrisley, Neil 62–63
The Christian Chronicle 175
The Christian Science Monitor 210–211
The Chrysanthemum and the Bat 161, 189
Chuck, Bill 146
CIA 190
Cicotte, Al 22
Cicotte, Eddie 129
The Cincinnati Enquirer 119
Cincinnati Reds (or Redlegs) 7, 12, 15, 22, 25, 30, 34, 38, 39, 41, 53, 57, 61, 62, 66, 70, 74, 75, 76, 85, 86, 91, 97, 101, 111, 112, 117, 118, 125, 129, 129, 139, 143, 145, 147, 152, 156, 157, 160, 163, 175, 179, 180, 181, 187, 193, 194, 199, 203
Cincinnati Reds Hall of Fame 191
The Cincinnati Times-Star 143
Clabaugh, Moose 126
Clancy, Max 25
Clark, Phil 166–167
Clarkson, Bus 80
Clemens, Roger 77
Clemente, Roberto 45, 50, 73, 78, 80, 135, 174–175, 203–204, 212
Clendenon, Don 14
Cleveland Indians 6, 8, 11, 16, 22, 23, 24, 29, 30, 32, 33, 37, 42, 48, 56, 59, 62, 65, 67, 69, 76, 77, 80, 81, 82, 86, 89, 90, 91, 93, 94, 96, 98, 100, 101, 102, 104, 112, 114, 120, 121, 125, 128, 131, 132, 134, 137, 141, 152, 153, 154, 157, 161, 162, 167, 169, 173, 184, 189, 191, 192, 203, 205, 206; *see also* Cleveland Naps
Cleveland Naps 162; *see also* Cleveland Indians
The Cleveland News 189
The Cleveland Plain Dealer 62, 90, 125, 132, 154
Clevenger, Tex 76, 102
Cliburn, Stan 183
Cliburn, Stew 183
Cline, Ty 205
Clooney, George 97
Clooney, Rosemary 97
Coates, Jim 99, 195–196
Cobb, Ty 22, 169, 209
Cochrane, Mickey 29, 196
Colavito, Rocky 26, 56, 66–67, 76, 134, 152, 165–166, 169, 170
Coleman, Gordy 15
Coleman, Jerry 187
Coleman, Rip 20
Coleman, Vince 113
Coles, Chuck 41
College Black Nines 190
College of Coaches 51, 63, 82–83
College World Series 93
Collins, Eddie 79, 104
Collins, Eddie, Jr. 104
Collins, Jimmy 69, 210
Colón, Bartolo 55
Colorado Rockies 162, 198
Comiskey, Charles 151
Comiskey Park 25, 53, 137, 213
Como, Perry 75
Comorosky, Adam 204
Concepción, Dave 89
Cone, David 143
Conley, Bob 42
Conley, Gene 46, 112–113, 180, 181
Connie Mack Stadium 213
Connors, Chuck 46
Consolo, Billy 14, 19
Constable, Jim 165
Continental League 1, 180
Coolidge, Calvin 60, 162, 200
Cooney, Jimmy 162
Cooper, Cal 62
Cooper, Cecil 146, 200
Cooper, Walker 47, 149
Cope, Myron 174
Corbett, Brad 8
Cotton States League 80
Counsell, Craig 163
Count Basie 167
Courtney, Clint 96, 177
Covington, Wes 99, 213–214
Craddock, Walt 95
Craft, Harry 83
Crandall, Del 36, 38, 70, 108, 154, 214

Index

Creamer, Robert 133, 136–137, 208
Crispus Attucks High School (Indianapolis) 118
Cronin, Joe 196, 197
Crosby, Bing 15
Crosley Field 13, 163, 187
Crossing the Line: Black Major Leaguers, 1947–59 11, 25, 30, 55, 70
Crowe, Brad 118
Crowe, George 22, 77, 80, 124, 203
Crowe, Ray 118
Crues, Bob 126, 136
Cuba 24, 33, 165, 172, 186, 193, 201, 203
Cuban Baseball Legends 172
The Cubbies, Quotations on the Chicago Cubs 16
Cuellar, Mike 168, 192–193, 198
Cullen, Blake 123
Cunningham, Joe 74, 96–97, 108, 127, 179
The Curse of Rocky Colavito 152
Cy Young Award 6, 54, 145, 148, 193, 203, 205

Daley, Arthur 22, 61
Daley, Bud 89, 93–94
Daley, Pete 93–94
Daley, Richard J. 33
Dalkowski, Steve 177–178
Dalrymple, Clay 34
Dalton Gang 58, 185–186
Dalton, Georgia 116
The Dalton (Georgia) Daily Citizen News 116–117
Damn Yankees 119
Damon, Johnny 88
Daniel, Dan 15, 211
Daniels, Bennie 197
Danning, Harry 174
Danville, Illinois 109
Dark, Al 36, 51, 64, 147, 158, 184–*185*
Dascoli, Leo 91
Davenport, Jim 65–66
Davie, Jerry 86
Davis, Captain Alfonza 10
Davis, Miles 167
Davis, Tommy 144
A Day in the Bleachers 80, 169
The Dayton (Ohio) Daily News 186
D.C. Stadium 42
The Deadball Era 179
Dean, Dizzy 179
Dean's Cards 217
Debusschere, Dave 46
Deer, Rob 199
deGrom, Jacob 54, 190
Delmore, Vic 64
Delock, Ike 159

Delsing, Jim 137–138
DeMaestri, Joe 24, 177
Demeter, Don 60
Denver Bears 101, 114, 132, 188, 195
The Denver Post 132
Depken, Craig 124
DeShields, Delino 199
The Detroit Free Press 104, 166, 176, 216
The Detroit News 104
Detroit Red Wings 86
Detroit Tigers 5, 7, 12, 15, 20, 26, 30, 34, 39, 40, 45, 50, 55, 56, 62, 67, 76, 77, 80, 86, 89, 90, 91, 95, 101, 104, 109, 110, 111, 114, 115, 120, 122, 125, 127, 135, 137, 141, 147, 151, 160, 161, 162, 166, 167, 175, 181, 186, 188, 189, 193, 194, 195, 203, 204
Detroit Wolverines 88
Devine, Bing 73–74, 117
Diaz, Aledmys 117
Diaz, Edwin 194
Dickey, Bill 142
Dickey, R.A. 184
Dickson, Murry 12
Didier, Mel 116
Dierker, Larry 19, 168
Dillard, Don 42, 205
DiMaggio, Dom 36, 125
DiMaggio, Joe 100, 147, 148, 169, 216
Distefano, Benny 150
Ditmar, Art 132–*133*
Diunte, Nick 63, 120
Dobbek, Don 42
Dobson, Pat 192
Doby, Larry 29, 56, 87, 154, 167
Dodger Stadium 18, 54, 138, 149, 187, 199
Dodgerland 138
Dolgan, Bob 132
Dominican Republic 35, 67, 79
Donovan, Dick 6
Doolittle, Sean 30
Dotterer, Dutch 97–98
Douglas, Whammy 126, 156
Downing, Al 127
Downing, Brian 163
Drabowsky, Moe 146–147
Drake, Sammy 146
Drake, Solly 146
Drebinger, John 29, 133
Dreier, Peter 174
Driesell, Lefty 53
Dropo, Walt 8, 36, 53
Drott, Dick 9, 97
Drysdale, Don 17, 81, 88–89, *138*, 140, 187
Drysdale, Ginger 138
Dudley, Clise 82
Duffy, Frank 25
Duke University 53

Dungannon, Virginia 111
Dunston, Shawon 72
Duquesne University 46–47
Duren, Ryne 177–178, 209
Durocher, Leo 24, 80, 83, 97, 123, 148–149, 201
Duvall, Adam 44
Dykstra, Lenny 111

Early Wynn, the Go-Go Sox and the 1959 World Series 94
East Texas League 126
Easter, Luke 29
Eastern League 103
Eau Claire Bears 112
Ebbets Field 42, 54, 129, 170, 182
Ebert, Roger 176
Eckersley, Dennis 116
The Ed Sullivan Show 75
Edes, Gordon 144
Edmonds, Jim 134
Edwards, Johnny 181
Edwards, Marshall 183
Edwards, Mike 183
Eichhorn, Mark 57
Eisenberg, John 147
Eisenhower, Dwight 66, 159
Elia, Lee 104
Elliot, Jim 146
Ellis, Sammy 96
Elston, Don 193, 194
Encyclopedia of Baseball Catcher's Equipment 29
Ennis, Del 86, 114
Erasmus High School (Brooklyn) 139
Erskine, Carl 72, 144
ESPN 144, 188
Esposito, Sam 159
Essegian, Chuck 94
Estrada, Chuck 48
Evangeline League 24
Evans, Dwight 76

Face, Roy 74, 119, 155, 193
Fairfax (Los Angeles) High School 94
Fairly, Ron 21, 42–*43*
Fallon, Michael 138
Fan Letters to a Stripper 60
Fangraphs 3, 184, 211
Fanovich, Frank 213
Fargo, Donna 144
Farrell, Kerby 157
Farrell, Turk 58, 185
Fear Strikes Out 125
Federal League 1
Feller, Bob 32, 132, 140, 191–192
Fenway Park 10, 92, 167, 198
Fernández, Chico 166
Ferrarese, Don 82
Ferrick, Tom 98

The 50 Greatest Players in Philadelphia Phillies History 86
Finigan, Jim 19
Finley, Charlie 63, 67, 113, 185
Fischer, Bill 76, 213
Fisher, Eddie 94
Fisher, Jack 48
Fisk, Carlton 76, 151, 181, 199
Fitz Gerald, Ed 15
Fleer baseball cards 217
Flood, Curt 48, 74, 114, **124**, 125, 138–139, 197, 203
Florida Christian College 175
Florida Marlins 51
Floyd, Cliff 209
Foiles, Hank 34, 100–101, 201
Forbes 80
Forbes Field 150
Ford, Gerald 159
Ford, Whitey 11, 21, 98, 127, 133, 156, 187, 216
Fornieles, Mike 172–173
Forsch, Bob 122
The Fort Wayne (Indiana) News-Sentinel 71
Fort Wayne Pistons 53
Fort Worth, Texas 109
Fort Worth Cats 71
The Forward 174
Foundation for Economic Freedom 67
Fowler, Art 187–188, 207
Fox, Nellie 14, 111, 130, 147, 209, 215
Foytack, Paul 77, 213
Fraley, Oscar 145
franchise moves 1, 35
Francona, Terry 93
Francona, Tito 90, 91, 152, 205
Frank: The First 154
Franklin High School (Indiana) 118
Fredericksburg, Virginia 182–183
Freedman, Lew 94
Freehan, Bill 149
Freeman, Mark 199
Freese, Gene 172
Freese, George 172
Freese, Tim 172
Frey, Jim 97
Frick, Ford 1, 16, 66, 130, 143
Fridley, Jim 156
Fried, Max 174
Friedman, Andrew 184
Friedman, Harold (Boomie) 129–130
Friend, Bob 31, 155, 168, 169, 215
Frisch, Frankie 131, 196
From 33rd Street to Camden Yards: An Oral History of the Baltimore Orioles 147
Fryman, Travis 8

Fuld, Sam 44
Furcal, Rafael 55, 162
Furillo, Carl **68**–69, 94, 201

Gaedel, Eddie 137–138
Gainer, Del 25
Game of the Week 6, 176
Gandil, Chick 202
García, Mike 30, 132, 167, 191–192
Gardner, Billy 32
Garr, Ralph 44
Garver, Ned 81
Garvey, Steve 68–69
Gasparino, Dan 85
Gehrig, Lou 70, 206, 213
Geiger, Gary 60, 194
Geiger, Linda 194
Gentry, Gary 109
George Washington University 96
Georgia-Alabama League 84
Georgia Tech 65
Gernert, Dick 8, 53, 193
Giallombardo, Bob 60, 112
Gibson, Bob 10, 21, 37, 47, 74, 80, 82, 88, 117, 190–**191**, 197
Gibson, Kirk 116
Giel, Paul 7
Giglio, James 50, 51
Gilbert, Larry 173
Giles, Warren 13, 66
Gilliam, Jim 81, 105, 155, 206
Ginsberg, Joe 25, 149
Ginsburg, Ruth Bader 50
Glavine, Tom 17, 216
Gleason, Bill 148
Glory Days with the Dodgers 214
Glynn, Bill 81
Go-Go to Glory: The 1959 Chicago White Sox 100, 201
Gold Glove Award 39, 59, 63, 73, 84, 106, 114, 124, 127, 135, 137, 145, 147, 159, 160, 163, 210, 211, 212, 214
Goldberg, Joe 100
Goldstein, Richard 168
Gómez, Chile 128
Gomez, Lefty 140
Gómez, Rubén 80, 130, 190, **200**–201
Gonder, Jesse 155
Gonzalez, Juan 134
Gooden, Dwight 140, 143, 190
Goodman, Billy 36, 131
Gordon, Joe 90
Gordon, Sid 174
Gorman, Tom (born 1919) 164
Gorman, Tom (born 1925) 163
Gorman, Tom (born 1957) 163–164
Goryl, John 28, 51
Goslin, Goose 2
Gossage, Rich 188

Gotay, Julio 197
Graff, Milt 60, 61
Grambling State University 44
Grammas, Alex **6**–7, 204
Grant, Jim (Mudcat) 62, 127, 167
Grass Valley, California 199
Gray, Dick 81
Gray, Dolly 82
The Great American Baseball Card Flipping, Trading and Bubble Gum Book 56, 104, 157
This Great Game 115
Green, Gene 16
Green, Lenny 70
Green, Pumpsie 82
Green, Shawn 174
Green, Ted 72
Greenberg, Hank 13, 174
Greensburg, Kentucky 173
Greenville, Kentucky 173
Greenwell, Mike 77, 173
Greenwich, Connecticut 85
The Greenwich Time 85
Greinke, Zack 163
Griffin, Doug 210
Griffin, Punk 33
Griffith, Andy 144
Griffith, Clark 33, 151
Griffith Stadium 5, 12, 26, 42, 71, 170, 213
Griggs, Hal 157
Grim, Bob 98–99, 153
Grimes, Ray 183
Grimes, Roy 183
Grimm, Charlie 214
Grissom, Marv 80–81, 102
Groat, Dick 46, 53, 161, 168, 197
Gromek, Steve 22, 88
Gross, Don 75–76
Groth, Johnny 55
Grove, Lefty 17
Guerrero, Vladimir, Jr. 103–104
Guerrero, Vladimir, Sr. 104, 188
Guerrero, Wilton 188–189
Guettler, Ken 126
Guidry, Ron 190
Guillén, Ozzie 89, 146, 181
Gullett, Don 173
Gwynn, Tony, Jr. 104
Gwynn, Tony, Sr. 104, 134

Haas, Eddie 43
Haddix, Harvey 48, 61, 66
Hadley, Kent 43, 47
Hafey, Chick 202
Hale, Bob 187
Hall, Bill 20
Hall, Mel 176
Hamner, Granny 158–159
Hamtramck, Michigan 35
Handsome Ransom Jackson: Accidental Big Leaguer 141

Index

Hanebrink, Harry 112
Haney, Fred 8, 38, 207–208
Hankyu Braves 157
Hanlon, Ned 151
Hano, Arthur 80, 169
Hansen, Ron 90, 161–162
Hansen, Snipe 82
Hanshin Tigers 104
Hardball Times 58, 60, 86–87
Hard-Luck Harvey Haddix and the Greatest Game Ever Lost 74
Harder, Mel 140
Hardwick, Patricia 60
Hardy, Carroll 56
Harlem Globetrotters 157
Harrell, Billy 157
Harrell, Mark 196
Harris, Bill 194
Harris, Bucky 88, 196
Harris, Gail 135
Harris, Lum 30
Harrist, Earl 88
Harshman, Jack 173
The Hartford 188, 199
Hartman, Bob 43–44
Hatcher, Billy 188
Hatfield, Fred 206
Hauser, Joe 126
Healy, Egyptian 82
Hearn, Jim 24
Hegan, Jim 80, 132
Hegan, Mike 7
Held, Woodie 67, 90
Helena Seaporters 80
Heman, Russ 96
Hemus, Solly 51, 74, **196**–197
Hendrick, George 153
Henrich, Tommy 134, 208
Henry, Bill 19, 193
Herbert, Ray 51, 52
Hernandez, Keith 140
Hernandez, Willie 193
Herrera, Pancho 44
Herrmann, Ed 116
Hershberger, Mike 113
Herzog, Whitey 100, 140–141
Higgins, Mike (Pinky) 15, 73
High, Andy 131
High Heat Stats 204
Higuera, Teddy 128
Hillman, Dave 111
Hiner, Jason 159
Hisle, Larry 198
History of the Trowbridge Family in America 79
Hoak, Don 12
Hobbie, Glen 117
Hodges, Gil 19, 42, 59, 91, 215
Hoeft, Billy 109, 120, 213
Hoffman, Ben 105
Hoffman, Trevor 30
Holland, Michigan 73
Holliday, Billie 167

Holliday, Matt 134
Hollywood Stars 20, 207
Holmes, Tommy 130
Holtzman, Jerome 193–194
Holtzman, Ken 140
Home Run Derby 18
Horlen, Joel 54
Hornsby, Rogers 177
Houdini, Harry 87
Hough, Charlie 184
Houk, Ralph 34, 99, 156, 166
House, Frank 109, 149
Houston Astros 116, 151, 167–168, 186, 193, 214; *see also* Houston Colt .45s
Houston Buffaloes 126
The Houston Chronicle 38
Houston Colt .45s 6, 8, 10, 19, 22, 37, 45, 58, 63, 73, 74, 76, 111, 153, 171; *see also* Houston Astros
Houtteman, Art 213
Howard, Arlene 142
Howard, Elston 16, 34, 40, 141–142, 160, 209
Howard, Frank 32, 40
Howard, Ryan 86
Howsam, Bob 118–119
Howser, Dick 90
Hoyt, Waite 139–140
Hubbell, Carl 193
Hughson, Tex 102
Hulsey, Bob 186
Hundley, Randy 29
Hunter, Bill 183
Hunter, Billy 8, 68
Hunter, George 183
Hunter, Jim (Catfish) 140
Hunter, Tab 119
Hutchinson, Fred 113, 197
Hyde, Dick 76, 183

Idaho Falls Russets 14, 101
If I Had a Hammer: The Hank Aaron Story 62
Ilitch, Mike 86
The Immoral Mr. Teas 176
Indiana University 159
Indianapolis Indians 27, 47, 56, 84, 89, 157
The Indianapolis Star 118
integration of baseball 1, 30, 67, 78–79, 82, 83, 167, 186, 203
International League 163
Irvin, Monte 80, 107, 169, 170
Isaacs, Stan 185
It Was Never About the Babe 14

Jablonski, Ray 65, 120
Jackson, Larry 143
Jackson, Lou 44
Jackson, Randy **141**
Jackson, Reggie 149, 185, 188
Jackson, Ron 27
Jacobson, Baby Doll 204

Jacobson, Beany 82
James, Bill 3, 17, 24, 34, 40, 66, 108, 115, 124, 143, 145, 158, 161, 163, 187, 209–210, 212, 215
James, Johnny 38
Jamestown Falcons 86
The (Jamestown, New York) Post-Herald 22, 23
Jannis, Mickey 184
Jansen, Kenley 30
Japanese baseball 43, 51, 84, 90, 104, 157, 161, 177, 180, 189
Jay, Joey 62, **92**–93
Jeffcoat, Hal 30, 48
Jenkins, Ferguson 123
Jensen, Jackie 143–144
Jensen, Woody 204
Jeter, Derek 7, 153
Jethroe, Sam 78
Jewish Virtual Library 174
John, Tommy 48, 53
Johnson, Connie 11
Johnson, Darrell 199–200
Johnson, Deron 44–45
Johnson, Ernie 95
Johnson, Ernie, Jr. 95
Johnson, Randy 17, 21, 141, 216
Johnson, Walter 172, 182–183, 190
The Johnson City (Tennessee) News & Neighbor 165
Jones, Chipper 210
Jones, Cleon 44
Jones, Gordon 167–168, 193
Jones, Randy 204–205
Jones, Sam **27**–28, 80
Jones, Willie 69
Joost, Eddie 197
Joplin Miners 7, 8
Judge, Aaron 126, 153
Jurges, Billy 145

K: A History of Baseball in Ten Pitches 149
Kaat, Jim 127, 134, 140, 159, 163, 177
Kabacinski, Jeff 176
Kahn, Roger 10–11, 72, 87
Kaline, Al 15, 31, 50, 127, 141, 169, 212
Kansas City Athletics 7, 10, 12, 17, 19, 20, 24, 26, 28, 35, 43, 47, 51, 57, 58, 59, 60, 66, 67, 71, 75, 76, 81, 84, 85, 89, 95, 98, 100, 101, 106, 109, 113, 116, 126, 133, 136, 140, 144, 147, 151, 152, 153, 163, 164, 168, 176, 182, 189, 190, 199, 201, 214; *see also* Philadelphia Athletics; Oakland Athletics
Kansas City Blues 132
Kansas City Monarchs 11, 189
Kansas City Royals 57, 140, 181, 202, 208

Index

Kansas City Royals Baseball Academy 96, 208
Kasko, Eddie 76, 113, 204
Kazanski, Ted 35
Keaton, Buster 87
Keegan, Bob 31
Kell, George 36, 147, 210
Kelley, Brent 119
Kellner, Alex 31, 35–36
Kelly, Zack 62
Kemmerer, Russ 63, 76, 142
Kennedy, Bob 83
Kennedy, Forrest (Frosty) 126
Kennedy, Pres. John F. 42, 71
Keough, Marty 14, 104
Keough, Matt 104
Kepner, Tyler 149, 194
Kershaw, Clayton 17, 190
Kessinger, Don 197
Killebrew, Harmon 42, 76, 92, 109, 142, 191
Kindall, Jerry 51, 93
King, Chick 202
The Kingsport (Tennessee) Times News
Kinsler, Ian 174
Kipp, Fred 87, 194
Kirkland, Willie 65, 75, 177
Kitty League 42, 87
Klaus, Billy 102–103
Klein, Lou 83
Kline, Ron 74, 89–90
Klippstein, Johnny 51, 195–196
Kluszewski, Ted 10, 15, 191
KMOX 70
Knorr, Fred 67
Knuckleball 29, 46, 122–123, 178, 184, 187, 201–202
Kolstad, Hal 52
Konstanty, Jim 98, 170
Koosman, Jerry 109
Koppe, Joe 160, 192
Korcheck, Steve 96
Korean War 136, 142, 217
Koufax, Sandy 17, 37, 38, 53, 54–55, 112, 120, 138, 149, 173–174, 195
Krabbenhoft, Herman 176
Kravitz, Danny 201
Krell, David 38
Ku Klux Klan 118, 167
Kubek, Tony 28, 90, 92, 153, 187, 188, 211
Kucks, Johnny 98–99
Kuenn, Harvy 15, 26, 67, 91, 152
Kurowski, Whitey 65
Kuzava, Bob 22

Labine, Clem 88, 144–145
labor relations 26, 49, 123, 124–125, 139
Lafayette High School (Brooklyn) 112

The (Lakeland, Florida) Ledger 19
Landis, Jim 52, 181, 196
Landrith, Hobie 102, 149, 153
Lane, Frank (Trader) 50, 56, 65, 67, 71, 112, 152, 177
The Lansing (Michigan) State Journal 20
Larker, Norm 37, 38, 42
Larkin, Barry 156
Larsen, Don 19, 23, 68, 80, 136–137, 145, 214–215, 216
Lary, Frank 12, 141
Lasorda, Tommy 172, 202
Latinos and baseball 44, 55, 78–79, 186
Latman, Barry 173–174
Lau, Charley 76, 86
Lavagetto, Cookie 27, 110
Law, Vern 8, 146, 155
Lawrence, Brooks 25, 203
Lazzeri, Tony 126
Leavy, Jane 138
Lebovitz, Hal 62
Lee, Bill 76, 199
Lee, Don 45
Lee, Thornton 45
Lehman, Ken 14
Lemaster, Denny 168
LeMaster, Johnnie 25
Lemke, Bob 57
Lemon, Bob 22, 30, 32, 81, 167, 192
Lemon, Jim 27, 71
LeMoyne College 189
Lennon, Bob 126
Leo Durocher: Baseball's Prodigal Son 83
Leonard, Dutch 190
Leonard, Elmore 128
Lepcio, Ted 14, 122
Leppert, Don 49
Leroux, Buddy 151
Let's Play Two 83, 123
Lewers, Bill 66
Liddle, Don 80–81
Life Is More Than Nine Innings 113
Lilliquist, Derek 128
Lillis, Bob 45
Lindstrom, Charlie 104
Lindstrom, Freddie 104, 210
Linfield College 17
Linz, Phil 41, 195
Little Caesar's 86
Little League 92, 128
Little Rock Travelers 47
Lockman, Whitey 148–149
Loes, Billy 117, 118
Logan, Johnny 37, 57, 74–**75**
Lolich, Mickey 206
Lollar, Sherm 34, 137
Lombardi, Ernie 115
Long, Dale 49, 150, **150**

The Long Beach (California) Press-Telegram 39
The Long Season 64, 166
Longhorn League 126
Lopat, Eddie 68
Lopata, Stan 166
López, Al 13, 19, 22, 47, 81, 94, 132, 137, 148
López, Héctor 24, 144, 186, 195
Los Angeles Angels 1, 5, 6, 18, 38, 47, 65, 77, 79, 86, 89, 153, 192, 204
Los Angeles Coliseum 54, 106, 148, 170, 198, 207
Los Angeles Dodgers 1, 2, 6, 9, 10, 11, 13, 17, 26, 37, 42, 45, 51, 54, 55, 68, 69, 72, 74, 81, 87, 88, 89, 91, 94, 97, 105, 112, 113, 116, 128, 135, 138, 144, 146, 149, 151, 152, 155, 160, 167, 170, 171, 173, 175, 181, 187, 194, 195, 198, 206, 207, 214, 215; *see also* Brooklyn Dodgers
Los Angeles Red Devils 22–23
The Los Angeles Sentinel 146
The Los Angeles Times 26, 42, 56, 61, 86, 87, 94, 97, 107, 116, 119, 128, 163, 184, 198, 204, 205, 213
Louisville, Kentucky 173
Louisville Colonels 56
Lovrich, Tom 213
Lown, Turk 54, 94
Lukas, Paul 158
Lumenti, Ralph 110
Lumpe, Jerry 92
Lynch, Jerry **34**–35, 41
Lynn, Fred 151
Lynn, Kentucky 173

Maas, Duke 56, 99
Mabe, Bob 125–126
MacArthur, Douglas 66
Macauley, Ed 180–181
Mack, Connie 104, 151
Mack, Earle 104
MacPhail, Lee 102
Mac's Boys: Branch McCracken and the Legendary 1953 Hurryin' Hoosiers 159
Madden, Bill 118
Maddux, Greg 140, 159, 163, 190, 216
Maglie, Sal 80, 88
Mahaffey, Art 97
Major League Baseball 121
major league expansion and expansion draft 1, 5–6, 8, 10, 19, 37, 45, 47, 63, 73–74, 91, 102, 114, 143, 152–153, 155, 180
Maldeen, Missouri 202
Malkmus, Bobby 51
Malzone, Frank 73, 159–160, 193, 210

Index

Manager of the Year 63
Manatee (Florida) Community College 96
Mantilla, Félix 52–53
Mantle, Mickey 7, 11, 12, 20, 28, 50, 77, 87, 106, 127, 138, 169, 170, 174, 187, 195, 201–202, 208, 212–*213*
Maranville, Rabbit 211
Marcell, Everett (Zigg) 23
Marichal, Juan 26, 193
Marion, Marty 197
Marion Red Sox 131
Maris, Roger 5, 24, 28, 43, 56, 59, 66–67, 77, 82, 89, 106–107, 126, 152, 187
Markusen, Bruce 8
Marquez, Luis 73, 78
Marshall, Jim 51
Martin, Billy 63, *101*, 116, 177, 187–188, 193, 203
Martin, Morrie 16
Martinez, Edgar 210
Martinez, J.D. 134
Martinez, Pedro 21, 190
Martyn, Bob 17
Mathews, Eddie 31, 69, 70, 110, *164*–165, 207, 210
Mathewson, Christy 22, 151, 190, 216
Matinale, Kenneth 70
Mauch, Gene 99, 112, 186
Maule, Tex 61
Maxwell, Charlie 15, 175–176
May, Lee 156
May, Rudy 203
Mayberry Days Festival 144
Mayfield Clothiers 87
Mays, Carl 56, 57
Mays, Willie 11, 12, 20, 26, 33, 39, 60, 66, 70, 80–81, 103, 110–111, 139–140, 143, 164–165, 169, 170–171, 177, 184, 203, 211–212
The Maysville (Kentucky) Ledger Independent 33
Mazeroski, Bill 126, 133, 150, 209
MC Hammer 48
McAnderew, Jim 109
McAnulla, Chuck 49
McAuliffe, Dick 90, 113, 163
McCarthy, Sen. Joe 39
McCarthy, Johnny 25
McClymonds High School (Oakland, California) 48, 63
McCormick, Frank 131
McCormick, Mike 49, 116
McCovey, Willie 11, 26, 66, 70, 93, 127, 208
McCraw, Tommy 96
McDaniel, Jimmie 45
McDaniel, Lindy 74, 146, 175
McDevitt, Danny 128–129

McDonald, James 213
McDonald, Jim 98
McDougald, Gil 19, 78, 92, 121, 153, 187–188, 208
McDowell, Sam 32, 48
McDuffie, Terris 200
McGlothen, Lynn 44
McGraw, John 215
McGraw, Tug 193
McGwire, Mark 50, 126
McLish, Cal 162
McMahon, Don 5
McMillan, Roy 145–146, 147
McNally, Dave 139, 192, 206
McQuery, Max 25
Me and the Spitter 53
Mead, Doug 16
Medwick, Joe 119
Mejías, Román 72, 73
Mele, Sam 134
Memorial Stadium (Baltimore) 92
Memphis Chickasaws 18
Mendoza, Mario 26
Menke, Denis 95
Merchant, Larry 186
Mesa, José 194
Messersmith, Andy 139
Metro, Charlie 83
Metropolitan Stadium (Minneapolis) 91
Mexico and the Mexican League 71, 78, 107, 128
Meyer, Jack 91, 185
Meyer, Russ (ballplayer) *176*
Meyer, Russ (filmmaker) 176
Miami Marlins (American Association) 186
The Miami News 186
Miami University 25
Michael, Gene 25
Michigan History Magazine 67
Mickey Mantle: The American Dream 213
The Middletown (Connecticut) Press 93
Midnight Cowboy 64
Mikan, George 23
Miksis, Eddie 22
Miller, Bob 31
Miller, Bob G. 135
Miller, Bob L. 135
Miller, Marvin 50, 123–124, 125, 138
Miller, Stu 61
Milwaukee Braves 5, 6, 13, l7, 21, 23, 24, 31, 32, 36, 42, 43, 45, 52, 53, 55, 57, 58, 61, 62, 67, 70, 74, 76, 77, 79, 87, 92, 95, 99, 101, 104, 110, 122, 129, 142, 152, 152, 154, 156, 160, 164, 165, 170, 171, 175, 178, 181, 183, 201, 207, 214; *see also* Atlanta Braves; Boston Braves

Milwaukee Brewers 7, 26, 44, 198
The Milwaukee Journal Sentinel 178
Mincher, Don 92
Minneapolis Millers 195
The Minneapolis Tribune 78
Minnesota Twins 13, 28, 32, 39, 40, 48, 49, 62, 76, 91, 93, 100, 101, 114, 127, 134, 143, 149, 160, 189, 205
Minor, Damon 183
Minor, Ryan 183
Miñoso, Orestes (Minnie) 11, 29, 30, 56, 67, 76, 127, 152, 155, 186, 196
Miranda, Willy 202–203
Mitchell, Dale 80, 131
Mitchell, Garrett 44
Mizell, Wilmer (Vinegar Bend) 172
Mobile, Alabama 109
Moford, Herb 32–33
Molina, Bengie 115
Molitor, Paul 210
Monbouquette, Bob 58
Moneyball 116
Monroe, Marilyn 2, 18, 147–148
Monroe, Zach 38
Montemayor, Felipe 73, 78
Montgomery, Bob 91
Montreal Expos 43, 143
The Montreal Gazette 162
Montreal Royals 108–109, 162
Monzant, Ray 116
Moon, Wally 102, 113, 198–199
Moore, Derland 202
Moore, Ray 100
Moran, Billy 65
Morandini, Mickey 162
Morehead, Seth 85, 185
Morejón, Danny 203
Moret, Rogelio 8
Morgan, Joe (manager) 100
Morgan, Joe (player) 19, 134, 199
Morgan, Tom 98, 204–*205*
Morley, Bill 73
Morris, Jack 80
Moryn, Walt 49, 74, 179
Moseby, Lloyd 204
Moss, Les 166, 177
Mossi, Don 94, 104, 160–161
Most Valuable Player Award 9, 11, 13, 14, 30, 51, 53, 69, 80, 84, 129, 145, 152, 160, 170–171, 183, 185, 207, 208, 211
The (Mostly) Complete List of Knuckleball Pitchers 29
Mota, Manny 157
Moultrie (Georgia) High School for Negro Youth 96
The Moultrie (Georgia) Observer 20

Index

Mount Airy, North Carolina 144
Mousie, Kentucky 42
Mueller, Don 130–131
Muffett, Billy 79, 80, 102
Munson, Thurman 142, 153, 156
Murcer, Bobby 10
Murray, Jim 42, 61, 163
Murtaugh, Danny 10, 79
Musial, Stan 33, **50**–51, 64, 65, 74, 82, 97, 120, 127, 145, 171, 197, 198, 206, 211–212
Musial: From Stash to Stan the Man 50, 197
Mussina, Mike 163
Myer, Buddy 174

Nankai Hawks 104
Naragon, Hal 134
Narleski, Ray 160–161
Nash, Billy 69
Nashua Dodgers 108–109
Nashville Volunteers 173
Nathan, Alan 13, 188
National Baseball Hall of Fame 5, 15, 22, 30, 33, 52, 82, 91, 102, 103, 105, 123, 127, 130, 132, 134, 139, 141–142, 152, 167, 174, 175, 177, 183, 191, 192, 202, 203, 208, 209, 210, 211
National Basketball Association (NBA) 46, 53, 113, 157, 180, 181
National Football League (NFL) 9, 16, 32, 44, 144, 202
Naylor, Bo 160
Neal, Charlie 34, 155
Neeman, Cal 130, 150
Negro leagues 2, 23, 30, 79, 80, 83, 95, 109, 128, 141, 189, 200, 203, 209
Nelson, Rocky 162–163
Nettles, Graig 188
Neun, Johnny 162
The New Bill James Historical Baseball Abstract 158, 161, 163, 209, 215; *see also The Bill James Historical Baseball Abstract*
New England League 109
New Madrid Fault 202
New York City Baseball 105
The New York Daily News 44, 118
New York Giants 1, 7, 10, 13, 20, 24, 38, 48, 67, 77, 80, 81, 105, 106, 107, 134, 139, 148, 155, 164, 171, 177, 184; *see also* San Francisco Giants
New York Mets 6, 9, 17, 25, 29, 44, 57, 63, 109, 111, 114, 125, 135, 153, 155, 161, 172, 180, 189, 198, 200, 204, 212
The New York Times 10, 11, 16, 19, 22, 29, 35, 37, 40, 45, 50, 61, 66, 68, 77, 80, 81, 87, 93, 105, 106, 107, 113, 114, 117, 121, 122, 125, 133, 138, 139, 140, 141, 144, 151, 154, 155, 167, 168, 175, 176, 177, 182, 183, 184, 193, 194, 198, 200, 201, 203, 216
The New York World-Telegram 24
New York Yankees 2, 7, 10, 12, 16, 18, 19, 20, 22, 23, 26, 28, 32, 33, 34, 35, 36, 38, 40, 43, 44, 52, 56, 57, 59, 60, 63, 68, 70, 73, 77, 78, 79, 84, 85, 89, 92, 93, 96, 97, 98, 100, 101, 106, 110, 114, 115, 119, 121, 126, 128, 132, 133, 136, 137, 140, 141, 142, 143, 144, 150, 151, 153, 154–155, 162, 164, 165, 167, 172, 176, 177, 181, 182, 187, 188, 189, 190, 194, 195, 199, 203, 205, 207, 208, 209, 211, 214, 215, 216
Newark Eagles 11
Newberry College 62
Newcombe, Don 108–109, 171, 203
Newhouser, Hal 140
Newsday 185
The Neyer/James Guide to Pitching 187
Niarhos, Gus 137
Nice Guys Finish Last 149
Nichols, Dolan 128
Nichols, Jack 113
Niekro, Joe 184, 204
Niekro, Phil 45, 184, 204
Nieman, Bob 134
Nine Innings 198
1951 Cleveland Indians Sketch Book 116
Nixon, Russ 97, 120–**121**
Nixon, Willard 127–128, 141
Nola, Aaron 120
Nolan, Gary 203
Noren, Irv 22–**23**
The (Norfolk) Virginian-Pilot 100
North Carolina Sports Hall of Fame 178
Nowlin, Bill 199
Nunn, Howie 206
Nuxhall, Joe 139

Oakland Athletics 44, 48, 57, 63, 101, 104, 116, 162, 181, 185, 188; *see also* Kansas City Athletics; Philadelphia Athletics
Oakland Oaks 63, 101
The Oakland Tribune 82
O'Brien, Eddie 47, 183
O'Brien, Johnny 47, 183
O'Connell, Danny 31–32
O'Connell, Dick 199
O'Dell, Billy 83, 177
O'Donnell, George 87
Offerman, José 15
Ohio State University 32
Ohlendorf, Ross 137
Ohtani, Shohei 120, 127
Oklahoma City 89ers 172
Oklahoma State Senate 172
The Oklahoman 162
Oliva, Tony 92
Oliver, Gene 45, 46
Olmo, Luis Rodríguez 200–201
Omaha Cardinals 204
O'Neil, Buck 44, 189
O'Rourke, Orator Jim 104
O'Rourke, Queenie 104
Orth, Al 25
Ortiz, David 210
Osborne, Cary 74
Osborne, Larry 195
Osteen, Claude 74
Ostrowski, Joe 98
Oswalt, Roy 100
Otis, Amos 188
O'Toole, Jim 46
Ott, Mel 20, 148, 196–197
Owen, Mickey 29
Owens, Jim 168, 185–186
Ozark, Danny 79

Pacific Coast League 15, 18, 20, 126, 136, 207
Padgett, Ernie 162
Pafko, Andy 13, 77
Pagliaroni, Jim 15
Paige, Satchel 11, 30, 31, 82, 117, 125, 177, 182, 214
Paintsville, Kentucky 173
The Palm Beach (Florida) Post 82
Palmeiro, Rafael 134
Palmer, Jim 21, 140, 192
Pappas, Milt 48, 140, 143
Parker, Robert B. 116
Parnell, Mel 141
Pasadena Junior College 22
Pascual, Camilo 99, 100, 102, 142, 149, 165
Pavletich, Don 181
Peace, Warren 11
Pearson, Albie 6
Peary, Danny 16, 148, 161, 167, 173, 195, 207
Pederson, Joc 156, 174
Pedroia, Dustin 144, 210
Pelekoudas, Chris 42
Peña, Orlando 91, 203
Pendleton, Jim 58
Pennant Race 64, 206
Pérez, Eduardo 104
Pérez, Tony 104, 199
Perry, Gaylord 26, 53, 203, 206
Perry, Jim 203–204
Pesky, Johnny 12, 79

Peters, Gary 54
Peterson, Richard (Pete) 65
Petry, Dan 80
Pfeffer, Fred 88
Philadelphia Athletics 19, 31, 35, 57, 132; *see also* Kansas City Athletics; Oakland Athletics
The Philadelphia Daily News 99, 186
Philadelphia Phillies 7, 16, 22, 24, 31, 33, 34, 35, 40, 42, 44, 50, 51, 52, 54, 58, 59, 65, 69, 73, 77, 82, 85, 86, 91, 98, 99, 103, 109, 112, 117, 118, 119, 120, 123, 124, 125, 127, 129, 136, 143, 149, 152, 158, 161, 162, 165, 166, 170, 172, 180, 185, 186, 192, 200, 205, 215
Philley, Dave 33, 73, 187
Phillips, Bubba 62
Phillips, Taylor 39
Phoenix Senators 136
Piedmont League 58
Pieper, Pat 64
Pierce, Billy 21, 52, 89, 148, 170, 213, 216
Piersall, Jim 122, 125, 152
Pignatano, Joe 9, 10
Pilarcik, Al 7
Pillar, Kevin 174
pinch-hitters and pinch-hitting 14, 31, 34, 35, 56, 73, 94, 156–157, 179, 187, 201, 205
Pinson, Vada 41, 48, 163, 203
Pioneer League 90
Piqua, Kansas 87
Pitching for the Master 175
Pittsburgh Crawfords 79
Pittsburgh Pirates 8, 15, 20, 25, 30, 31, 34, 38, 45, 49, 51, 53, 57, 58, 60, 61, 63, 70, 72, 73, 75, 76, 78, 83, 87, 89, 95, 96, 100, 105, 110, 111, 119, 133, 144, 150, 155, 156, 162, 165, 168, 169, 172, 179, 187, 189, 194, 197, 198, 201, 204, 207, 215
The Pittsburgh Post-Gazette 47, 61
Pitula, Stan 131
Pizarro, Juan 54, 62
Play Ball (TV) 95
Play Ball baseball cards 217
Players Association 123, 124
Plews, Herb 132, 133
Pocatello Cardinals 90
Podres, Johnny 88, 181–182
Polish Falcons 65
The Politics of Glory 210
Polo Grounds 10, 80, 105, 198, 212
PONY League 86
Pope, Dave 80, 81
Porter, J.W. 82
Porterfield, Bob 60
Portland Beavers 47
Portocarrero, Arnie 35
Posnanski, Joe 53, 115, 136, 145, 160, 167, 169, 194
Post, Wally 73, 143
Povich, Shirley 167
Powell, Adam Clayton, Jr. 167
Powell, Boog 32, 146, 193
Powell, Ray 55
Power, Vic 67, 76, 196, 205
Powers, John 179
Presley, Elvis 128
Price, David 62
Priddy, Jerry 154–155
Princeton University 137
Prudential Insurance 146
Pruett, Hub 202
The Puerto Rican Herald 200
Puerto Rico 62, 200–201; winter league 80, 175, 203
Purdue University 32
Purkey, Bob 75–76, 187

Qualters, Tom 119–120
Quisenberry, Dan 57

race relations in baseball 29, 30, 33, 70, 87, 88, 118, 160, 167, 184, 197, 203
Radatz, Dick 58
Radical Baseball 70
Raines, Larry 157
Ramos, Pedro 28, 99–100, 142, 165, 213
Randolph, Willie 188
Random Baseball 77
Rapoport, Ron 123
Rappahannock River 182–183
Raydon, Curt 105
Reed, Jack 195
Reed, Ron 46
Reese, Pee Wee 105, 146, 155, 158, 207, 215
Reichardt, Rick 1
relief pitchers 5, 6, 19, 37, 76, 80, 93, 94, 119, 144–145, 160–161, 183, 193–194
religion and baseball 13, 146, 173, 175
Reniff, Hal 127
Renna, Bill 26
Repulski, Rip 65, 73
Reuschel, Rick 142
Reynolds, Allie 32, 68, 98
Reynolds, Jack (Hacksaw) 97
Reynolds, Will 97
Rhiel, Billy 62
Rhoden, Rick 122
Rhodes, Dusty 81
Rice, Del 36
Rice, Jim 152
Rice, Sam 131
Richards, Paul 11, 19, 48, 122, 137, 153
Richardson, Bobby 28, 78, 92–93, 172, 187–188
Richey, George 202
Richmond Virginians 33, 66
Ricketts, Dave 46
Ricketts, Dick **46**
Rickey, Branch 1, 8, 79, 96, 108, 150, 151, 179–180, 187, 207
Righetti, Dave 122, 153
Rigney, Bill 13, 77
The Ringer 184
RIP Baseball 24, 33, 42, 43, 64, 65, 77, 134, 135, 158, 182, 186, 199
Ripken, Billy 160
Ripken, Cal, Jr. 146, 211
Rivera, Jim 71, 201
Rizzuto, Phil 68, 127, 146, 177
Roach, Mel **21**
Roberts, Curt 78
Roberts, Robin 50, 52, 86, 123, 124, 138, 140, 145, 158, 176
Robinson, Brooks 69, 73, 84, 147, 159–160, 203, 210, 211
Robinson, Chuckie 160
Robinson, Frank 41, 48, 63, 82, 154, 157–**158**, 160, 167, 197, 203
Robinson, Humberto **129**–130
Robinson, Jackie 1, 2, 19, 22, 33, 52, 108–109, 118, 124, 145, 176
Robinson, Wilbert 215
The Rochester (New York) Democrat & Chronicle 135
Rock Hill Cardinals 118
Rodgers, Andre **72**, 77
Rodgers, Buck 26
Rodgers, Johnny 10
Rodriguez, Alex 20, 164–165, 211
Rodriguez, Aurelio 160
Roebuck, Ed 207
Rogers, Taylor 183
Rogers, Tyler 57, 183
Rojas, Luis 36, 112
Rojas, Mel 36
Rolaids Fireman of the Year Award 46, 159, 172
Rolen, Scott 210
Romano, John 47, 67, 205
Romonosky, John 90
Rookie of the Year Award 9, 16, 40, 44, 45, 63, 109, 140, 153, 159, 185, 208, 210, 211
Rose, Pete 5, 9, 97, 197, 206
Roseboro, Johnny 38, 160, 214
Rosen, Al 80, 174
Rudolph, Don **59**–60, 180
Runnels, Pete 53, 131, 193
Rush, Bob 57, 142
Russell, Bill 48, 112
Ruth, Babe 5, 22, 70, 126, 130, 202
Ryan, Bob 15

Index

Ryan, Nolan 80, 151, 190, 204–205
Ryder, Mitch 35
Rypien, Mark 16

Sabathia, C.C. 62
Saberhagen, Bret 202
SABR Research Journal 29
Sadecki, Ray 49, 117
Sadowski, Bob 47
Sadowski, Ed 47
Sain, Johnny 98, 126–127, 134, 168, 206
St. Henry, Ohio 143
St. Louis Browns 8, 11, 19, 34, 81, 82, 87, 98, 137, 155, 176, 179, 189, 207, 214; *see also* Baltimore Orioles
St. Louis Cardinals 6, 12, 16, 17, 24, 27, 34, 35, 42, 45, 46, 50, 51, 52, 53, 54, 65, 70, 73, 74, 76, 79, 84, 85, 89, 94, 96, 101, 102, 103, 107, 110, 113, 117, 118, 119, 120, 124, 127, 139, 140, 145, 151, 157, 162, 166, 175, 179, 180, 182, 186, 189, 190, 191, 196, 197, 198, 202, 204, 206, 208
St. Louis Sports Hall of Fame 119
St. Petersburg Cardinals 118
Salt Lake City Bees 90
Samford, Ron 80
Sammy White's Brighton Bowl 178
San Diego Padres (National League) 112, 116, 184, 205
San Diego Padres (Pacific Coast League) 96
The San Francisco Chronicle 181, 185
San Francisco 49ers 90, 96
San Francisco Giants 1, 7, 10, 13, 20, 26, 30, 31, 36, 49, 53, 57, 61, 65, 70, 72, 79, 86, 93, 102, 116, 117, 120, 127, 134, 139, 145, 152, 153, 161, 167, 177, 196, 208; *see also* New York Giants
San Jose Red Sox 108
Sand Ridge, Illinois 194
Sandberg, Ryne 16
Sandoval, Juan 126
Sandy Koufax: A Lefty's Legacy 138, 139
Sanford, Fred 98
Sanford, Jack 93
Santa Ana (California) High School 97, 98
Santo, Ron 43, 210
Santurce Crabbers 80, 201
The Saturday Evening Post 13, 36, 73, 173
Sauer, Hank 145, 170, 177
Savage, Jack 173
Sawatski, Carl 22

Sawyer, Eddie 7, 130
Schalk, Ray 211
Scheffing, Bob 179
Scherzer, Max 21
Schilling, Curt 21
Schmidt, Bob 38
Schmidt, Mike 69, 86, 209
Schmidt, Willard 57
Schoendienst, Red 31–32, 50, 97, 175, 207
Schofield, Dick 25–26, 156, 204
Schreiner, Dr. Richard 72
Schroll, Al 205
Schultz, Howie 46
Schumacher, Hal 122
Score, Herb 23, 32, 121, 131
Scott, George 53, 108, 210
Scranton Red Sox 108
Seals Stadium 10, 48, 134, 136, 212
A Season in the Sun 87
Seasons in Hell 8
Seattle Angels 195
Seattle Mariners 20, 162
Seattle Pilots 46, 114
Seattle Rainiers 206
The Seattle Times 177
Seattle University 47
Seaver, Tom 109, 190, 216
Secrest, Charlie 47
Seitz, Peter 125
Selig, Bud 127
Selleck, Tom 161
Seminick, Andy 159
Semproch, Ray 65
Sgt. Bilko 18
Seton Hall University 59
Sewell, Joe 130
Shannon, Joe 183
Shannon, Red 183
Shannon, Wally 204
Shantz, Bobby 73–74, 133, 215
Sharman, Bill 46
Shaw, Bob 37, 53
Shea Stadium 10
Shealy, Al 62
Shecter, Leonard 64
Sheehan, Joe 170
Sheldon, Roland 55, 127, 166
Sherry, Larry 94
Shipley, Joe 48
Shoken, Fred 158
Shoken, Will 158
Showalter, Buck 19, 176
Shreveport Sports 47
Shuba, George 179
Siebern, Norm **106**–107
Siena College 157
Sievers, Roy 27, 71, 119, 131, 170, 214
Siluria, Alabama 65
Simmons, Andrelton 146
Simmons, Curt 117, 136

Simpson, Harry (Suitcase) 110, 116–117
Simpson, Luther (Suitcase) 116
Simpson, Wayne 203
Singleton, Elmer 206
Singleton, Ken 134
Sioux City Soos 49
Sisler, Dave 104, 112, 121–122, 137
Sisler, Dick 104
Sisler, George 30, 112, 209
Six Decades of Baseball: A Personal Narrative 66
Skinner, Bob 45, 204
Skinner, Joel 112
Skizas, Lou 114–115
Skowron, Bill 32, 187, 208
Slaughter, Enos 12, 52, 179, 195
Smith, Al 11, 148, 167
Smith, Bob (born 1895) 30
Smith, Bob (born 1928) 30
Smith, Bob (born 1930) 30
Smith, Bobby Gene **54**
Smith, Hal 24, 75, 214, 215
Smith, Hal R. 182–183
Smith, Lloyd 188
Smith, Mississippi Mike 30
Smith, Ozzie 146, 184, 209, 211
Smith, Texas Mike 30
Smithsonian Magazine 188
Snider, Duke 10, 11, 94, 97, 103, 170
Snyder, Gene 194
Society for American Baseball Research ix, 3
Solis, Marcelino 71
Sooner State League 70
Sosa, José 35
Sosa, Sammy 126, 188
Southeastern Conference 127
Southern Association 47, 126
The Southern Illinoisan 194
Southwest League 126
Spahn, Warren 6, 17, 61, 62, 134, 150, 193, 207, 216
Spalding, Albert 151
Speake, Bob 196
Speaker, Tris 167
Special Olympics 72
Spencer, Daryl 161
Spitball 53, 203
Spoelstra, Watson 134
Spokane Indians 45
Sport 161
Sporting News 9, 10, 15, 31, 50, 74, 153, 174
Sports Broadcasting Hall of Fame 159
Sports Collectors Digest 27, 49, 160
Sports Illustrated 6, 16, 26, 28, 44, 61, 87, 110, 119, 121, 127, 143, 145, 147, 150, 169, 174, 181, 185, 188, 192, 193

Sportsman's Park 198
Spring, Jack 16
Springer, George 134
Squires, Mike 150
Stafford, Jim 127
Stahl, Chick 202
Staley, Gerry 54, 94
Stallard, Tracy 82
Stan Musial: An American Life 50, 197
Stanford, Kentucky 173
Stankiewicz, Andy 176
Stanky, Eddie 76, 113, 145, 148, 179, 197
Stann, Francis 181
Stargell, Willie 204, 206
Staub, Rusty 43
Steinbrenner, George 63, 101, 188
Stengel, Casey 23, 61, 68, 78, 79, 98–99, 115, 132–133, 136–137, 144, 153, 154, 155, 156, 207–208, 214
Stengel: His Life and Times 23, 133, 136, 208
Stephens, Gene 88
Stephenson, Jerry 116
Stevens, R.C 20, 95–96
Stewart, Dave 122
Stieb, Dave 122
Stigman, Dick 48
Stobbs, Chuck **12**–13, 28, 213
Stock, Milt 103
Stockton, Dick 159
Stockton Ports 63
Stone, Dean 97
Stone, Jesse 116
Stram, Hank 32
Strawberry, Darryl 11
Strickland, George 69
Stuart, Dick 45, 51, 126, 199
Sturdivant, Tom 98–99, 172
submarine pitchers 57–58, 183
Sudyk, Bob 53
Sullivan, Frank 112–113
Sullivan, Haywood 14, 151
Sullivan, Marc 151
Sunday, Billy 146
Sunkel, Tom 126
Susce, George (father) 189
Susce, George (son) 189
Susce, Paul 189
Sutcliffe, Rick 122
Sutton, Don 139

Tampa Bay Rays 184
Tanana, Frank 80
Tanner, Chuck 51, 77
Tappe, El 51, 82–83
Tartabull, Danny 176
Tasby, Willie 48
Tate, Lee 204
Taylor, Joe 203
Taylor, Sammy 63–64, 150

Taylor, Tony 24
Taylor, Zack 137
Tebbetts, Birdie 36, 85
Tejada, Miguel 55
Tekulve, Kent 57
Temple, Johnny 117
Tennessee A&I University 189
Terry, Bill 196
Terry, Ralph 93, 99, 126–127, 133, 150
Terry, Zeb 55
Terwilliger, Wayne 182
Texas League 22, 126
Texas Rangers 8, 101
Thacker, Moe 150, 173
This Side of Cooperstown 162
Thomas, Frank (born 1929) 10, 41, 169, 173, 179–**180**, 209
Thomas, Frank (born 1968) 160, 210
Thomas, Gorman 198
Thomas, Lee 53
Thomas, Valmy 77, 160
Thompson, Hank 203
Thomson, Bobby 49, 77, 156, 198
Three Rivers Stadium 61
Throneberry, Faye 200
Throneberry, Marv 114, 135, 153, 155, 199, 200
Thurman, Bob 80, 203
Thurman, Dorothy 203
Tiant, Luis 76, 190, 199
Tiefenauer, Bobby 184
Time 84, 85, 185
The Times Leader (Nanticoke, Pennsylvania) 18
Tinker, Joe 211
Tishimingo, Mississippi 128
Tishimingo Blues 128
Tobin, Jack 204
Tomanek, Dick 131
Tomasik, Mark 186
Tomjanovich, Rudy 35
Toonerville Folks 116
Topps baseball cards 1, 2, 54, 116, 121, 141, 160, 170, 192, 204, 217
Torgeson, Earl 123, 176
Toronto Blue Jays 49, 57, 162, 181
Toronto Maple Leafs 76, 165
Torre, Frank 23, 24–25, 110
Torres, Felix 192
Total Baseball 158
Townsend, Happy 82
Trammell, Alan 146, 166
Traynor, Pie 210
Tresh, Tom 93, 153
Triandos, Gus 34, 68, **115**–116, 214–215
Trout, Mike 20, 144, 163
Trowbridge, Bob 79
Trucks, Virgil 54, 97, 122, 151

Truman, Bess 71
Truman, Pres. Harry S 122
Tulowitzki, Troy 162
Tulsa Oilers 70
Tupelo, Mississippi 128
Turley, Bob 23, 99, 68, 78, 167, 177, 196, 215–216
Turner, Jim 99, 205
Turner, Ted 95
Tuttle, Bill 111, **168**
Tuttle, Gloria 168
The Twin Cities Pioneer Press 203
Twins Hall of Fame 203
2 Bucs at the Holiday House 75
Tygiel, Jules 52, 108

Uecker, Bob 26, 46
Uni Watch 158
Unitas, Johnny 215
United Press International 93, 130, 145
U.S. House of Representatives 50, 171–172
U.S. Senate 50, 171
University of Arizona 51, 93
University of Illinois 115
University of Kansas 40
University of Massachusetts 110
University of Michigan 116
University of Minnesota 7, 93
University of Mississippi 128
University of Notre Dame 190
University of Texas 17
University of Virginia 21
Unser, Del 103
Urban, Jack 10
Urias, Julio 126
Uribe, José 213
The Utica (New York) Observer-Dispatch 122

Valentin, John 162
Valentinetti, Vito 18
Valenzuela, Benny 102
Valenzuela, Fernando 128, 193
Valo, Elmer 187
Vancouver Mounties 96
Van Hekken, Andy 73
Van Hyning, Thomas 201
Vaughan, Sarah 167
Vaughn, Mo 77, 134
Veal, Coot 20
Vecsey, George 28, 50, 114, 144
Veeck, Bill 29, 100, 137–138, 208
Velarde, Randy 162
Venezuela 78, 89
Verlander, Justin 21, 190
Vernon, Mickey 40, 53
Versalles, Zoilo 90, 142
Vietnam War 206
Villante, Tom 118
Virdon, Bill 45, 63, 204

Index

Virgil, Ozzie 67
Virgin Islands 77, 160
Visser, Lesley 159
Vizquel, Omar 89, 146

Wagner, Honus 22, 172
Wagner, Leon 86–87, 177
Wakefield, Tim 184
Waldron, Matt 184
Walker, Harry 113, 196
Walker, Jerry 48
Walker, Brig. Gen. Kenneth 10
Wall, Murray 17
Walls, Lee 34, *37*, 49, 155
Walls, Rich 39
Wally Yonamine: The Man Who Changed Japanese Baseball 90
Walsh, Ed (father) 104
Walsh, Ed (son) 104
Walters, Bucky 30
Wambsganss, Bill 162
Waner, Lloyd 130, 204
Waner, Paul 204
Ward, John Montgomery 151
Ward, Preston 58, 59
Washington, George 182
Washington Baseball Monthly 182
The Washington Post 13, 105, 119, 125, 167, 200
Washington Senators 1, 5, 6, 9, 15, 18, 26, 30, 33, 40, 42, 51, 56, 57, 60, 63, 71, 74, 76, 80, 82, 88, 90, 96, 99, 100, 102, 108, 109, 110, 119, 122, 132, 137, 142, 143, 149, 153, 154, 155, 161, 177, 183, 186, 189, 191, 194, 200, 214
The Washington Star 181
Washington State Horseshoe Pitching Association Hall of Fame 155
We Played the Game 9, 16, 122, 144, 148, 154, 156, 157, 161, 162, 165, 167, 169, 170, 173, 177, 197, 207, 209, 214
Weaver, Earl 49, 198
Webster, Ray 199
Wehmeier, Herm 152
Wehmeier, Jeff 152
Weiss, George 68, 177, 216
Welk, Dick 88
Wenatchee Chiefs 206
Wendell, Turk 58
Wertz, Vic 53, 80, 81, 184
West Haven Yankees 122

West Texas-New Mexico League 126, 136
Western Hills (Cincinnati) High School 97
Western International League 206
Western League 49, 126, 132
Western Michigan University 27
Westlake, Wally 81
Wheat, Zack 50
Where Have You Gone? 89
Whisenant, Pete 9
White, Bill 74, 124, 127
White, Deacon 210
White, Gaylon 18
White, Sammy 113, 178
Whiting, Robert 161, 189
Whiz Kids 7, 123
The Whiz Kids and the 1950 Pennant 86, 103, 136
Wichita Braves 112
Wilber, Del 37
Wilhelm, Hoyt 94, 122–123, 184
Wilhelm, Kaiser 82
Wilks, Ted 65
Will, Bob 139
Will, George 139
Willey, Carl 33–34, 35
Williams, Andy 97
Williams, Dick 63, 100, 116
Williams, Gerald 44
Williams, Ken 204
Williams, Lefty 129
Williams, Stan 150
Williams, Ted 36, 45, 50, 56, 88, 90, 95, 131, 159, 170, 177, 199, 200, 201, 206, 217
Williamson, Ned 88
Willingham, Josh 146
Willits, Ward 125
Wills, Maury 2, 45, 105
Wilson, Don 168
Wilson, Red 12
Wine, Bobby 25, 59
winter leagues 30, 35, 78, 80, 172, 193, 203
Wise, Casey 67
Witt, George (Red) 38
Wood, Wilbur 127
Woodeshick, Hal 37, 76
Woodling, Gene 57, 66, 67, 68, 215
World Series 11, 12, 15, 18, 19, 22, 23, 26, 32, 38, 40, 44, 52, 53, 56, 57, 61, 62, 63, 80, 81, 85, 91, 93, 94, 98, 102, 106, 107, 115, 116, 117, 118, 119, 124, 129, 132, 133, 134, 135, 136, 145, 147, 148, 150, 152, 154, 160, 164, 166, 170, 173, 180, 181, 182, 184, 189, 192, 195, 198, 201, 202, 208, 214, 215
World War II 16, 25, 32, 55, 58, 60, 69, 95, 107, 126, 139, 151, 176, 181, 206, 211
Worthington, Al 13, 96, 127
Wright, Frank Lloyd 125
Wright, Glenn 162
Wrigley, Phil 82
Wrigley Field (Chicago) 75, 91, 104–105
Wrigley Field (Los Angeles) 18
WSB-TV 95
WTBS-TV 95
WUST 70
Wynette, Tammy 202
Wynn, Early 11, 32, 87–**88**, 132, 148, 167, 192
Wynn, Jimmy 19

Yancey, Bill 55
Yankee Stadium 10, 28, 40, 87, 92, 100, 165, 198, 213
Yankees-Athletics trades 27, 35, 89, 106, 126
Yastrzemski, Carl 47, 56, 195
Yawkey, Jean 151
Yawkey, Tom 151
Yogi Berra: Eternal Yankee 142
Yonamine, Wally 90
York, Jim 33
York, Rudy 11
York White Roses 102–103
Yosemite, Kentucky 173
Yost, Eddie 5, 69
Youkilis, Kevin 210
Young, Chris 137
Young, Cy 216
Young, Dick 179
Young, Steve 85
Yount, Robin 20

Zabala, Aneurys 67
Zanni, Dom 49
Zauchin, Norm 8, 53, 108
Zernial, Gus *147*–148, 156
Zimmer, Don 80, 83, 97
Zimmerman, Jeff 35
Zimmerman, Jerry 14, 49
Zimmerman, Ryan 156
Zminda, Don 201
Zuverink, George 73

www.ingramcontent.com/pod-product-compliance
Lightning Source LLC
Chambersburg PA
CBHW060341010526
44117CB00017B/2912